India's Development Scenario

India's Development Scenario

Challenges and Prospects

Edited by
Yatindra Singh Sisodia

RAWAT PUBLICATIONS
Jaipur • New Delhi • Bangalore • Mumbai • Hyderabad • Guwahati

ISBN 81-316-0208-7

Published by
Prem Rawat for **Rawat Publications**
Satyam Apts, Sector 3, Jawahar Nagar, Jaipur 302 004 (India)
Phone: 0141 265 1748 / 7006 Fax: 0141 265 1748
E-mail: info@rawatbooks.com
Website: www.rawatbooks.com

New Delhi Office
4858/24, Ansari Road, Daryaganj, New Delhi 110 002
Phone: 011 2326 3290

Also at Bangalore, Mumbai, Hyderabad and Guwahati

Typeset by Rawat Computers, Jaipur
Printed at Chaman Enterprises, New Delhi

Contents

Preface

Development is a multidimensional phenomenon. Some of its major dimensions include the level of economic growth, level of education, level of health services, degree of modernization, status of women, level of nutrition, quality of housing, distribution of goods and services, and access to communication. In India, the pace and pattern of development has not been uniform. The factors which are found to be more important for the overall development process relate to basic needs like education, availability of food, minimum purchasing power and facilities like safe drinking water, health care, infrastructure, etc. Since independence in 1947, India has made enormous strides towards the progress of the nation. The concerted and coordinated efforts of the national governments through Five-Year Plans, starting from 1951, have changed the economic scenario of the country considerably. Agricultural production has risen steadily and progress of industrialization has increasingly played a role in India's development. During 1950–51, agriculture contributed about 50 per cent of country's Gross Domestic Product (GDP) but in 1992–93 its share reduced to 26 per cent. There are, indeed, many areas of economic and social development in which India's performance has been credible. However, overall success in reducing poverty, ignorance and inequality has been quite limited. Various factors, such as the level of literacy, female education, nutritional standards, infant mortality, morbidity, employment, income distribution, public distribution system, political commitments, etc., and their corresponding interactions, contribute to striking variations among the states in the livelihood of common people.

It is genuinely felt that people have to be in the forefront of the fight against corruption, communalism, casteism and criminalization of politics and life in the country. A social movement or a widespread national movement is needed to cleanse the system. Such a social movement need not be merely negative but for positive purposes. Social movements are particularly required for fighting poverty, population growth and environmental degradation. All the aforementioned factors are posing grave challenges but at the same time they are also bringing in new opportunities. In the matter of interface with the citizen there is an enhanced accent on transparency and right to information. In India, development definitely and conceptually denotes progress—social, economic, political, educational, cultural, scientific, and technological. The unfortunate fact, however, is that despite considerable progress, marked disparities have emerged in income and in the poor people's access to resources and economic opportunities.

Keeping in view the significance of this topical issue, the Madhya Pradesh Institute of Social Science Research (MPISSR), Ujjain organized a National Seminar on *India's Social, Political and Economic Development: Challenges, Achievements and Ways Ahead* (May 24–26, 2006) to discuss threadbare the multifaceted issues related to development in India. The financial support for the seminar was provided by the Planning Commission, Government of India. The seminar was aimed to discuss the broad themes, viz., Review of India's Development Policy and Strategy in the Preceding Decades; Policies, Strategies and Programmes of Education, Health, Social Security, Poverty Alleviation, Employment Generation, and Infrastructural Development for Basic Amenities; and Decentralized Governance and Responsive Administration; Development and Issues of Environment, Agriculture, Industry and Trade.

This volume is an attempt to identify, document and comprehend the broad trends emanating across the states. It is important to understand and analyze the process and direction of pace and pattern of the development, which would have a significant impact and critical lessons for charting out the future course of action for effective people-centric development across the country.

First of all, I would like to acknowledge the Planning Commission, Government of India for providing financial support to organize this seminar. I would like to express my deep sense of gratitude to R.S. Gautam, President, MPISSR, Ujjain for his continuous encouragement, valuable advice with appreciation and encouragement to work purposively. I am deeply indebted to B.R. Purohit, Professor Emeritus, MPISSR, Ujjain for his special interest in the present volume. He took great pains to go through the papers and made many constructive suggestions. I would also like to express my gratefulness to Neeta Tapan, Visiting Faculty,

MPISSR, Ujjain for her valuable input on individual papers, which helped me to identify and rectify inaccuracies in the papers.

I would like to express my sincere thanks to D.C. Sah, Director, MPISSR, Ujjain for inspiring me to bring out this volume. I am thankful to my colleagues L.P. Gautam, Sandeep Joshi, Ashish Bhatt, S.S. Chandel, Manu Gautam and Tapas Dalapati for their valuable suggestions and help extended during the editing of this volume.

My sincere thanks are due to all the paper contributors, without whose cooperation this volume would not have been possible.

I would like to extend my personal thanks to my better half, Surya for her constant encouragement and support in my academic endeavours.

Finally, I would like to express my thanks to Pranit Rawat of the Rawat Publications, Jaipur for showing interest in this manuscript and bringing out the volume in time.

Yatindra Singh Sisodia

1 Introduction

Yatindra Singh Sisodia

India, after independence in 1947, chose parliamentary democracy as a form of government. The political decision-makers and planners of that time dreamt of India as a nation with self-sufficiency, based on equality and all-round development. After having treaded for six decades on the path of development, India has witnessed many achievements and simultaneously encountered many nagging problems. We can be proud of our achievements in some specific areas like self-sufficiency in foodgrains, structuring of strong industrial base, raising expectancy of life and higher percentage of literacy. First and foremost, we have succeeded in maintaining the unity of the nation and kept this vast country together. We have built up a huge infrastructure, industrial and human. We have the largest number of technically and technologically competent personnel. We have the third largest reservoir of human talent in the world.

The greatest achievement of India since independence has been the establishment of a democratic system of government and politics. Indian democracy is the product of a complexity of factors. Several strands of thought and experience have gone into it: western liberal and parliamentary ideas, socialist concepts, the deeply rooted traditions of India both Hindu and Buddhist, and the ideas and methods propagated by Mahatma Gandhi like the panchayat system and democratic decentralization. In the interplay and interpenetration of these ideas and methods, a distinctly Indian variety of democracy has been in the making that is not only important to India but also relevant to the emerging new world of pluralism. Besides, the revolutionary implications of universal adult suffrage that we adopted, are unfolding themselves today. The lower and poorer sections of society and women are being drawn into the political system as active players. Time is overdue for meeting the aspirations of these sections of society, particularly women, for their economic and political empowerment.

India is today a considerable industrial and technological power of the world, and promises to be an economic giant in the twenty-first century. The economic reforms that we launched in the 1990s with the liberalization and opening up of our economy, have reached a decisive stage. The country has moved to a high trajectory of growth with a growth rate of 7 to 8 per cent of GNP envisaged for the next few years. Two broad parameters of progress we have made—one is the revolution in the production of foodgrains making the country self-sufficient in food and the other is the rise in the average expectation of life of an Indian which more than doubled since independence.

On the negative side, we can count the perennial problems of unemployment, illiteracy and poverty accentuated by an ever-increasing population. At the same time, low per capita income, inadequate infrastructure, feudalistic mindset of the traditionalists, poor condition of rule of law and ethics in public life can also be counted on the negative side. India has no doubt marched ahead to a great distance in these sixty years, but the challenge of eradicating poverty remains unresolved. We have yet to banish hunger from our land. We have yet to eliminate illiteracy. We have yet to ensure that every Indian enjoys good health. During the last sixty years, India has had to face formidable challenges in the areas of economic, technological and social development. The massive programmes that have been launched in these fields over the years have not yielded the desired fruits. Notwithstanding all these, we have yet to provide for our people safe drinking water, basic health facilities, electricity supply and other basic necessities of daily life.

We have crossed the one billion population mark. Compare this with the total population of a country like Switzerland, which has no more than seven million people. Our annual addition of 15 million odd would match the total population of a country like Australia and many others. Rising population throws up new challenges and problems with its own peculiarities. The social pressures generated by the ever-increasing population are enormous and so also its massive burden on civic amenities and the socio-economic infrastructure.

The latest literacy levels indicate that we still have over 350 million illiterates in India. This number is larger than the total population of any other country in the world except China. Illiteracy causes many ills and also generates its own problems. Poverty and unemployment are the other two critical problems, which are interrelated. Even if we assume that the number of people living below poverty line has dropped to 27 per cent or so (as per the latest survey) or even to 25 per cent, 250 million people or a quarter of population still lives below poverty line.

Globalization is becoming a critical factor not only in trade and commerce, financial services, entertainment, electronics and in cultural exchanges but also in more serious areas of public administration. No country can remain insulated from the outside world. If we cannot fight them, we have to join them. The presence of globalization is being felt in India as never before. With the passage of time it is bound to increase. Corruption is also one of the most significant hindrances in the development. Bribery and corruption are getting social sanction, rather open acceptance. There is a plethora of instances where an individual is promoting malpractices or unfair means to protect and promote his vested interests.

All the aforementioned factors are posing grave challenges but at the same time they are also bringing in new opportunities. In the matter of interface with the citizen there is an enhanced accent on transparency and right to information. In India, development definitely and conceptually denotes progress—social, economic, political, educational, cultural, scientific and technological. The unfortunate fact, however, is that despite considerable progress, marked disparities have emerged in income and in the poor people's access to resources and economic opportunities.

In this Volume

Keeping in view the significance of such burning social, political and economic issues, the Madhya Pradesh Institute of Social Science Research, Ujjain organized a three-day National Seminar on *India's Social, Political and Economic Development: Challenges, Achievements and Ways Ahead* to discuss threadbare the multifaceted issues of development in India. For articulation of views and presentation of papers in the seminar, the themes identified were as follows: Review of India's Development Policy and Strategy in the Preceding Decades; Policies, Strategies and Programmes of Education, Health, Social Security, Poverty Alleviation, Employment Generation, and Infrastructural Development for Basic Amenities; Decentralized Governance and Responsive Administration; and Development and Issues of Environment, Agriculture, Industry and Trade.

The first part, *Review of India's Development Policy and Strategy in the Preceding Decades* has six chapters that review the development policy and strategy of India in preceding decades. This part provides adequate details of the policies and strategies along with the present scenario of development in the country as a whole. The second part, *Policies, Strategies and Programmes for Basic Amenities* has again six chapters. One chapter is related to education wherein the case of adult literacy is discussed at length while the other two chapters deal with the issue of poverty and food security. Remaining chapters deal with the aspects of nutrition deprivation, employment generation and resource degradation. The third part, *Decentralized Governance and Responsive Administration* has two chapters. Out of these, one chapter analyzes the issue of development of Panchayat Raj in India in detail while the other is based on empirical evidences gathered from the field to understand relevance, potentials and demonstrations. The fourth and last part, *Development and Issues of Environment, Agriculture, Industry and Trade* has four chapters. While the first chapter in this part provides detail on India's trade dynamics with SAARC, the second chapter elaborates the macro aspect of Indian agriculture. The third critically analyzes displacement with a case of Bokaro Steel Plant. And the last chapter discusses pattern of development and environment quality in Gujarat.

Review of India's Development Policy and Strategy in the Preceding Decades

In this part, the first paper *Governance and Development: Initiatives from Below* by G. Palanithurai makes a very pertinent and valid argument that people who are continuously being marginalized are unable to get the benefits of development and are losing hope in the system of governance and argues forcefully that the system which we have created for governance has helped only a few sections of the society. In the present scenario, we are reduced to simply voters and beneficiaries from our position of citizens of India. The old feudal institutions are spreading social malaise in the form of casteism, regionalism and cultural genocide. Irrespective of these socio-economic paradoxes evident in Indian society, our nation is facing a phase of social transformation through the process of decentralized governance. Palanithurai further argues that many have come to believe apparently that India has struck deep roots in democracy and it has become a shining model for many of the developing countries. However, those who have studied carefully the functioning of the democratic structures in terms of delivery of services and justice to the deprived have come to the conclusion that the whole democratic structure has been co-opted to the design of the elites. The imposed democracy has not percolated into the roots of Indian society and, as a result, citizens cannot participate in the process of governance, except the elections. And, therefore, India will really shine, if our masses have a real signature over each and every development initiative undertaken by government functionaries for achieving our national goals and objectives.

Madhusudan Ghosh, in his paper on *Economic Reforms, Growth and Regional Divergence in India,* examines long-run growth performance and regional convergence in per capita income across 15 major Indian states during 1960–61 to 2001–02. Contrary to the prediction of the neo-classical growth model, the study offers evidence against σ-convergence and absolute β-convergence. The results also reveal that regional divergence has increased considerably during the post-reform period relative to the pre-reform one. The presence of conditional β-convergence signifies that the states have been moving only towards their own differing steady-state income level. Eleven of the fifteen states have been driving the observed divergence in per capita income. The divergence is explained by inter-state variations in human capital, production structures, and physical, social and economic infrastructure. The results suggest that economic policy measures for improving physical, social and economic infrastructure can have significant effect on long-run growth potential as well as convergence of income across states. Targeting public investment in human capital and infrastructure for the states with lower steady-state levels could improve overall growth performance and reduce regional imbalance.

Ajit Kumar Singh's paper on *Inter-State Variations in Levels of Economic Development: A Sectoral and Temporal Study* elaborates the whole issue of the pattern and trends, which has been done on inter-state disparities in levels of development using multivariate analysis. The analysis has been carried out separately for the four major sectors of the economy, namely, agriculture, industry, economic infrastructure and social infrastructure. The analysis has been carried out at five points of time centring on the years 1960–61, 1970–71, 1980–81, 1990–91 and 2000–01. The years have been chosen to observe the decennial variations, which is a reasonable time frame for the policy to get translated into actual plans and see its consequent impact on different indicators of development. This paper is confined to 17 major states of India and excludes the special category states, which are mostly small entities with specific problems and distinct geographical and cultural identities. The composite index of development has been derived on the basis of the principal component analysis using SPSS package in two stages. In the first stage composite indices have been prepared for each selected sectors. First principal component has been used to arrange states in order of development in accordance with the level of variation if it explained more than 70 per cent of the variation. If first principal component accounted for less than 70 per cent of variation, a weighted composite index was used by aggregating factor scores of the first and second (and in a few cases the third) principal component using the percentage of variation explained as weights. In the second stage, the overall composite index was derived by adding the composite indices of development for all the sectors. States were then ranked according to the weighted factor scores.

Jyotish Prakash Basu's paper on *Impact of Foreign Aid on Social Sector: The Indian Case* attempts to examine the impact of foreign aid on social sector in India. Two indicators are taken into analysis. First, infant mortality rate (IMR) and second is the enrolment of girl students at the primary school level. The share of foreign aid in social sector is 19 per cent, followed by the energy sector—power contributes 32 per cent foreign aid. In the social sector, the share of foreign aid in health sector is found to be the highest (51.4%). The share of aid in education and rural development is 16.4 per cent and 14.4 per cent respectively. The share of aid in Gross Domestic Product (GDP) is about less than 2 per cent. The flow of foreign aid is concentrated in few states like Karnataka, Gujarat, West Bengal, Orissa and Andhra Pradesh. This paper has important policy implications. It states that although there are 48 donor countries giving aid to India, but no consequent impact is evident in case of reduction observed in IMR nor can any positive effect on girls' enrolment in primary education. There is a need to monitor the utilization of aid through proper channel. Government and non-governmental organizations (NGOs) may take active role in monitoring the utilization of aid in the specific sector.

D.C. Sah and Alok R. Chaurasia in their paper on *Growth and Development Linkages in Madhya Pradesh*, argue that economic growth appears to have contributed only marginally to human development processes. On the other hand, low levels of human development in the state appear to be a major stumbling block in spurring economy-driven development. The lopsided development puts a break on human progress and the lopsided human development inhibits rapid economic growth. The per capita domestic product of the state is lower than national average and much lower in comparison to the better performing states like Punjab, Gujarat and Maharashtra. The indifferent performance of agriculture is not only acting as constrain for the overall economic performance of the state, it is also reflected in the levels of social and economic de-linking. The authors argue that the nexus between political elites, bureaucracy and contractors disconnects the poor from development affairs of the village. The political unfreedom in the community is evident in the remote rural areas.

Basanta K. Sahu's paper on *Issues in Socio-Economic Development of Backward States with Special Reference to Orissa* highlights the fact that when some poorer states have performed better and successful in reducing poverty and regional disparities during 1990s, a resource-rich state like Orissa failed to handle issues relating to growing regional disparities and poverty. Sahu's analysis is further extended to the evolution of disparities in Orissa with respect to a larger set of socio-economic- poverty indicators. Not only overall growth rate in Orissa was poor during 1990s as compared to the 1980s, among other backward states also, regional disparity seems to have increased with respect to incidences and distribution of poverty. Sector-specific growth in the state has not been conducive for reduction in poverty and regional disparity. The typical structural problem of the state economy along with lack of social and economic infrastructure, localized and poor pace of industrialization, poor human development and recurrence of natural calamities are major problems. The development models followed in the state have failed to address the intra-state and inter-state disparity, social disparities and cumulative disadvantages of people, especially in the southern and northern regions, where poverty is concentrated. This has led to increasing marginalization and very high outmigration in backward and tribal areas. The paper suggests some key areas for policy intervention, such as structural issue of state economy (poor or no inter-sectoral linkages), investment in agricultural sector, provision of dependable infrastructure, resource-based development programmes, rationalized displacement of tribals, social sector development, reduction in cumulative impact of natural calamities, improvement of governance and strengthening of institutions.

Policies, Strategies and Programmes for Basic Amenities

In this part, the first paper *Universalization of Education through Adult Literacy Programmes: Some Empirical Evidences* is authored by S.K. Pant. The paper makes an argument that literacy has always remained an area of importance and also of concern for our planners, policy makers and social activists. As a result, it has always figured at the core of planning since the inception of five-year plans. After independence, the tryst with education took a far more ambitious and dynamic form and many new and innovative initiatives were taken. However, their impact is a mixed one. It could be called a stage of success and failures, triumph and disappointments and of integration and marginalization. The success, triumph and integration were achieved in the form of manifold increase in the number of schools and teachers, physical infrastructure, enrolment level of students and overall literacy rates, whereas disappointments, failure and marginalizations were seen largely in the form of high drop-out rates, both at the primary and secondary levels, deterioration in the quality of education and increasing marginalization of the disadvantaged sections.

Amita Shah's paper on *Land Degradation and Poverty in India: Evidence and Policy Implications* makes an elaboration of changing profile of use, quality and ownership of land among the major states in India. This is followed by an analysis of co-relates of land, income poverty and human development across the states. The author further discusses major coping mechanisms, presently adopted by people, especially poor, and addresses their future sustainability and policy options for promoting more sustainable and also equitable land use so as to provide livelihood support to the poor. The analysis is mainly based on secondary data pertaining to ownership, and quality of land; poverty and indicators of human capability; and other indicators influencing economic growth across major states in India.

Shilp Shikha Singh, in her paper, attempts to unravel the paradox of hunger. She brings to light the collective nature of hunger where social images are constructed to justify the denial of societal space to a chosen group of people. Rights approach provides the legitimate space to react and also a platform to start the process of bargaining on equal footing. Nevertheless, one has to be cautious while using such an approach for a socially and economically marginalized group since mobilization generated around the issue of rights has the potential to damage the existing ties within the society. Here, the sustainability of intervention in the form of alternative support group outside the immediate society becomes very crucial. It is here that voluntary organizations functioning within the framework of rights approach tend to miscalculate their influence and potential. Unless the community is sensitized and awakened by the interventionists (in this case the voluntary organizations) to the need of managing political power, the entire endeavour will turn futile within no time.

Rudra Narayan Mishra's paper on *Nutrition Deprivation at Household Level: Evidence from a National Survey* looks at the characteristics and composition of the undernourished household itself. For the purpose, a national level survey has been used. The analysis is based upon fifteen major states of India. The paper clearly shows that household characteristics like occupation and social background are important factors associated with the nutritional deprivation of the household. In urban set-up it was found that the households involved in casual labour are in disadvantageous position across the social groups. Whereas in case of a rural set-up it was found that the incidence of calorie deprivation is higher among Scheduled Caste (SC) and Scheduled Tribe (ST) households in any given occupation. More importantly, the paper also found that households with girl child and more dependent population (like old and minor) than the given male members are more likely to be undernourished. The implication is straight; it is this dependent population for whom the nutritional deprivation would be higher. For any targeting, which aims to fight undernourishment, we must focus on the characteristics and the composition of the households, rather than on any single characteristic.

Seema Joshi, in her paper on *Employment Generation Potential in the Organized Retail Sector in Urban Areas,* analyzes the structure of employment in urban areas. She argues that in 1999–2000, only miniscule 7.08 per cent of the total labour force was engaged in the organized sector while remaining major chunk of labour force (92%) was absorbed in the unorganized sector. Within the organized sector, the employment growth potential in public sector is limited because of the problems of excess staff, severe financial constraints and declining employment elasticity. The paper has brought to forefront the need for development of organized private services sector, especially retail services, for generation of employment in the organized sector.

William Joe's paper on *The Strategy of Zoning amidst Resource Degradation* discusses the intensification of income deprivation and filth among the traditional fishing community of Kerala in 1970s and early 1980s because of stagnating fish catch. The stagnation was caused due to the alarming increase in the size of the fishing vessels, gear, engine power and destructive fishing practices like mini trawling along the inshore waters. The adversely affected traditional fishermen firmly agitated against this and demanded state action. Consequently, the policy of zoning was adopted which provided specific zones of territorial sea for traditional fishermen and trawlers along with banning of trawling during monsoon season. Zoning is a redistributive strategy and enquiry into the long-run impact of such natural resource management policies on welfare of the people becomes inevitable. This paper explains the theoretical rationale for zoning in the sea and examines its effectiveness on the fisheries sector, especially upon resource conservation and income generation. It also finds that because of certain institutional difficulties this welfare enhancing policy cannot avoid the re-emergence of the open access crisis.

Decentralized Governance and Responsive Administration

This part contains two papers. Yatindra Singh Sisodia, in his paper on *Evolution of Panchayat Raj in India: An Analysis of Development from Independence to Post-73rd Amendment Scenario*, makes an attempt to document the development process of Panchayat Raj in India. The Constitution of India promulgated in January 1950 for setting up a democratic and semi-federal political system, included Article 40 relating to the panchayats. The lead in establishment of the Panchayat Raj was taken in 1959. During the next two decades, however, Panchayat Raj began to stagnate in the first few years (1965–70) and then started even declining in efficacy of its role in promotion and management of development processes in the rural areas. This trend continued till 1985. It was widely recognized by the government, public leaders and intelligentsia that the Panchayat Raj Institutions (PRIs) were not able to "acquire the status and dignity of viable and responsive people's bodies". For this purpose, the 73rd Constitution Amendment Act, 1992 was passed by the Union Parliament. The 73rd amendment to the Constitution of India not only gives a constitutional status to the panchayats, it also provides uniformity and formal structure to these traditional institutions of self-governance for the sake of their effective functioning. The 73rd amendment initiates a fundamental restructuring of governance and administrative system of the country, based on the philosophy of decentralization and power to the people. A decade of Panchayat Raj in India has been a matter of debate and speculation about its performance and impact. The responses of state governments to the implementation of Panchayat Raj varied significantly. Nevertheless, it is hoped that these little republics will work for greater equality for all to create a society of the equals in India.

G. Palanithurai's paper entitled *Panchayats: Relevance, Potentials and Demonstrations* is based on empirical evidences and makes an attempt to answer the questions like: To what extent the objectives of decentralization of powers have been realized? If not, why? Whether obstacles and barriers have been identified? If they have been, why they are not removed? Given the background and the powers and the resources devolved, what changes have been created in governance and in the process of development? For the past one decade discussions have been held in different forums on the powers devolved, functionaries transferred and finances given to the grassroots institutions to achieve what decentralized governance has to know in terms of development. Institutions have been created, frameworks for local governance have been evolved through legislation, elections have been conducted, elected representatives are in power and activities are being carried out through these institutions.

Development and Issues of Trade, Agriculture, Industry and Environment

In the first paper of the fourth and last part, *India's Development and its Trade Dynamics with SAARC*, Ganesh Kawadia and Gunjan Malhotra assert that India is the fastest growing country of the world. It is growing at an average rate of 7 to 8 per cent per annum. The economic reforms undertaken since 1991 have influenced both India's industrial policy and external economic relations, which include the trade, foreign investment and financial relations. Import quotas were removed (fully only in July 2001), tariffs came down slowly, currency was devalued, the foreign investment policy was liberalized and various external financial transactions were eased out. As a result, India's share of foreign trade in GDP has increased from 15.6 per cent in 1991–92 to 25 per cent in 2004–05. This expansion of trade is expected to develop better trade linkages with the members of SAARC countries. Though SAARC was formed to accelerate the process of social and cultural cooperation but in view of globalization, the member countries are working towards economic cooperation. India is not only a big economy in the SAARC but is also a fast growing economy. Its trade dynamics is thus important in the SAARC region for overall development of the region. This paper is an attempt to understate the trade dynamics of India with its poor partners, particularly after the policies of liberalization.

Yogesh Bandhu Arya's paper is on *Indian Agriculture at the Crossroads: Challenges and Prospects.* In this paper it has been argued that in the recent past, Indian agriculture is facing several new challenges on internal and external fronts due to stagnation in cultivable area, production and productivity with surfacing of new frontage. The new economic policy of globalization and liberalization and emergence of WTO are likely to have greatest impact on the rural poor through their influence on the agricultural sector. Simultaneously, corporatization of agriculture and new private investment in agribusiness sector are the major challenges for the existing farming system as well as farming community. India recently faced the problems of abundance with respect to foodgrains. However, large number of poor agricultural households and their income vulnerability along with the slowdown in agriculture growth in the 1990s are major concerns for policy makers. Therefore, there is need to monitor progress in two key policy areas for sustainable agricultural and reliable source of income for millions of people. First, reorientation of government expenditures towards more productivity enhancing public investment and second, to make Indian agriculture globally competitive.

Binod Narayan's paper *The Problem of Industrial Displacement in Jharkhand: A Case Study of Bokaro Steel Plant* demonstrates a very pertinent issue, which in recent years, has caused intense debate among academics, social activists and planners: the involuntary displacement of people from their productive assets, particularly land and homes, due to industrial and infrastructure projects. In Jharkhand, about 15 lakh persons comprising of about 6.2 lakh (41.28%) STs, 2.1 lakh (14.16%) SCs and 6.7 lakhs (45.01%) of other categories were displaced up till 1995, for various development projects like water resource, industrial, mining, defence establishments, wildlife sanctuaries, etc. The author argues that it is high time for the people as well as the government in Jharkhand to reformulate a proper resettlement and rehabilitation (R&R) policy, as there are so many industrial and development mega projects in the pipeline. The Jharkhand government has drawn serious criticism from the opposition camp as well as the tribal groups ever since it started signing MoUs for setting up industrial units in the mineral-abundant state. The paper interprets the nature of development-induced displacement and its consequences with special reference to Bokaro Steel Plant so that an effective R&R policy for Jharkhand may be formulated for speedy industrial development of the state in future.

Hansa Jain, in her paper on *Patterns of Development and Environment Quality in Gujarat* attempts to study the pattern of development in Gujarat. Gujarat stands at the first position in terms of per capita income (Economic Survey, 2003–04) in India. However, in terms of quality of environment, it is the worst. She elaborates a district level analysis in which the pattern of development is determined in terms of income, education, health, basic services, infrastructure, urbanization and economic participation. Further, an attempt is made to analyze the quality of environment in the various districts of Gujarat and to find the factors that are responsible for the deteriorating quality of environment. The quality of life is further linked with the development index to determine how the environment is linked with development during the early and later stages of development.

Looking Ahead

Now, if we have to move into the 21st century, we should avoid competitive populism and identify the areas where state should intervene. The state should not intervene in all areas. It should intervene in critical areas only, which are specifically identified. In this regard, there should be a broad consensus on our policy matters. It is now argued by the intelligentsia that the policy functions of the state shall remain with it but in a large number of areas like education, health, transport and communications, human resource development, etc., the operational aspect should pass on to the civil society. In fact, one can visualize a greater interface between the civil society and the government in the years to come. The citizen should influence decision-making because therein lies the essence of genuine democracy. Another corollary of the downsizing of the government will be the simultaneous decentralization of authority and devolution of powers and the removal of the present ambivalence of the state governments in empowering the urban local bodies and the PRIs. After the adoption of the 73rd and 74th amendments to the Constitution, the states have enacted follow-up legislations for the setting up and functioning of these bodies. Although almost a decade has passed since this transfer of power began, it has not gathered full momentum. The state governments generally have been half-hearted in granting financial and functional powers to these local bodies. And, therefore, it is urgently required to provide funds, functions and functionaries to local bodies.

It is genuinely felt that people have to be in the forefront of the fight against corruption, communalism, casteism and criminalization of politics and life in the country. A social movement or a widespread national movement is needed to cleanse the system. Social movements are particularly required for fighting poverty, population growth and environmental degradation. Illiteracy, for example, has become a disgrace and the greatest obstacle in the progress of the country. In the area of globalization, development strategy should comply with the international demand. In this context, importance should be given to agro-processing and market-oriented production. For this purpose, multinational companies can be involved. In the present era of globalization, information and communication technology is very much necessary for development. In this context internet can be an important tool to bridge the gap between market, state and the people. More importance should be given to research and development in indigenous techniques for evolving self-sustaining technology.

The new century is a century of the youth. India, too, with a cultural heritage of thousands of years, has now become a young nation. Nearly 70 per cent of its population is less than the age of 35. These young men and women are more ambitious, more aware, and more active than their predecessors. They not only think big, but they also work hard to realize their dreams. And, therefore, need is to trap these human resources in nation-building. The need of the hour is to organize people, educate them and empower them. In this context, state can play the role of a facilitator and rest should be transferred to the people for their own development.

The present pattern of governance suggests that our quasi-federal structure is very likely to become more and more federal in character implying that the states and the constituent units of the Union may acquire stronger socio-economic muscles. The demand for autonomy may not be acceded to in the way it is understood. But it is realistically believed that of the three concepts, viz., 'autonomy', 'devolution' and 'decentralization', the latter two will become more pronounced. One major achievement of the last sixty years is a better integration of the constituent units of India and this process of integration is likely to become more mature and even more effective. With greater maturity in the political governance of the country, with a more visionary administration, vigilant and forward-looking judiciary and an effective civil society, Indian polity is expected to move in a positive direction.

Part I

Review of India's Development Policy and Strategy in the Preceding Decades

2 Governance and Development

Initiatives from Below

G. Palanithurai

People who are getting benefits from the government directly and indirectly through the policies, decisions and resource allocations, options are not branded as beneficiaries by the government but they are the real beneficiaries and they are complacent and give a positive picture about the achievements made by the state and central governments over a period of time through the five-year plans and schemes. People who are continuously marginalized and are unable to get the benefits of development are losing hope in the system of governance and argue forcefully that the system which we have created for governance has helped only a few sections of the society. The social malaise which the founding fathers of our nation identified as aberrations of our social system continue to dominate and as a result, the marginalized and neglected have started working against the present established order.

At present India is considered one of the few nations emerging as economic giants. But in the Human Development Index, India is in the 127th position; in the Gender Development Index it is in the 98th position; in corruption, India stands in the 88th position. It is in India, that the largest number of children are affected by malnutrition in the whole of the world; the largest number of women (54%) in the age group 18–46 are affected by anaemia. On the one side India is shining and on the other it is stinking. On seeing the functioning of our democracy, many have come to the conclusion that India has struck deep roots in democracy and it is a shining model for many of the developing countries. Those who have studied carefully the functioning of the democratic structures in terms of delivery of services and justice to the deprived have come to the conclusion that the whole democratic structure has been co-opted to the design of the elites. The imposed democracy has not percolated into the roots of Indian society and as a result, citizens cannot participate in the process of governance, barring in the elections. Constitutional provisions, development schemes and programmes have not created any impact as they had to. Till 1990, the Indian state and political system had to follow the democratic socialistic pattern of governance and planning for development. After 1990, there was a marked departure in the development process. The poor could not get their due share and needed justice in the process of development in the market era as everything is determined on the basis of the market scenario. While looking at the institutional development, infrastructure facilities, scientific advancement, technological innovation and upgradation, India can certainly be placed on the advanced side. But their impact on the life of the poor, marginalized, vulnerable women, tribals, and children is poor. Indian farmers have created a record in producing food between 1950 and 2000. But the same farmers are committing suicide in thousands. The Sensex points have reached a record peak in the Mumbai stock market. But very near to the stock market malnourished children, women affected due to anaemia and HIV/AIDS affected individuals are struggling to live. And 45 per cent of the people in India are still living in subhuman living conditions. In the name of industrialization and modernization we have polluted our air, water and soil and, as a result, we have invited the same industry to provide water to our people. They have come, started their industry and are providing water as a marketable commodity.

Water is an entitlement of the community but it has been made a commodity. One litre of water costs Rs 12 and the production cost lies between Rs 2 and Rs 3. Poor women have taken loans from the bank and are toiling and moiling to earn their livelihood through milch animals. The price of milk is regulated at Rs 10 per litre. How is our system rational in fixing prices for water and milk? The government is not able to provide basic services and they have been given to agencies and they are doing it in the 'pay and use' mode. But the government takes the responsibility of liquor distribution in the name of better revenue mobilization. The saddest part is fixing the target for liquor sale. In a popular democracy, the citizens are powerful forces to reckon with. But in India, citizens have been reduced to voters, beneficiaries and petitioners and are not participants in governance and development. Old feudal institutions have taken new avatars in the Indian administrative system, which ultimately keep the people away from governance and administration. Corruption cases have been registered against central and state ministers, chief secretaries, home secretaries and higher police officials have been arrested on criminal and corruption charges. In the name of development, in their own country, people are made repatriates and they are on the streets to fight for resettlement.

In the name of religion and culture, genocide is carried out in a democratic society. How civilized are we? How cultured are we? How tolerant are we? By all rational evaluation and assessment we can come to the conclusion that we have credible achievements in development but these achievements are at whose cost? Have the achievements made the people comfortable who are yearning for minimum needs? Are they leading a decent human life with minimum facilities? While looking at this scenario, a sensitive citizen has to think of measures to solve all these problems. When we think of solutions, they cannot be from the above, namely Delhi or from the state capital or the district headquarters or the block headquarters. It must be from the hamlet or the village or the community. When we think of solutions from below, one assumption has to be kept underlined. The assumption is that people, however poor they are, have skill, knowledge, capacity, development aspirations, vision and self-dignity. One should not look at them with pity. They have to be looked at with dignity. All development efforts should be made from the base value of their thinking, their skill, their capacity, their knowledge and their system of management.

This new possibility is emerging from the historic amendments to the Constitution of India. The 73rd Amendment has provided a unique opportunity full of potential for the transformation of the economy, the polity and the society. But the saddest part is the lack of awareness on the part of the people and the civil society and even the intellectuals about the potential of the new amendment. It is a well-known fact that many of the fine provisions of the Constitution are not operationalized as they are not claimed by the beneficiaries. Those who are entitled to get benefits out of these provisions are not aware of these provisions. In the same way the 73rd Amendment to the Constitution of India provides an opportunity for the poorest of the poor, women and Dalits to decide their destiny on their own. They can participate in governance, they can allocate resources, they can plan for their development, they can supervise development activities, and they can evaluate all these activities. By doing so, the poor, Dalits, women and children can claim and get their rights. By participating in the Gram Sabha activities, the character of our democracy can be changed from representative democracy to participatory democracy. By involving women in one-third of all positions in the Panchayat Raj System, the issues of women have been mainstreamed by which society is sensitized on the issues of women and children. Provision of reservation of seats at all the levels for Dalits enables the Dalits to mainstream the issues of exclusion. To give shape to the vision of the people and the leaders, the planning initiative has to be taken from below. The felt needs of the community can be met through this planning exercise at the micro level.

Public institutions act like the backbone of the poor. Failure of public institutions will create more problems for the poor. If water is polluted, the rich will purchase water from the market. Where will the poor go for water? If the primary health centre is not working, the rich will go to a corporate hospital. Where will the poor go? If children are affected due to malnutrition, the rich can supplement through medicine but the poor cannot do the same as the rich do. If a primary school run by the government is not functioning well, the rich can admit their wards in private schools, but where do the poor go for money to admit their wards in private schools. The poverty reduction exercise is getting derailed because of the improper functioning of public institutions. If primary health centre, sub-centre, public distribution shop, water supply, primary schools, cooperative banks are well managed, the poor will get rich benefits. If common properties are well maintained and properly used, the poor can get substantial advantage. For all the above activities, panchayat institutions have to take the responsibility.

There is yet another problem in the New Panchayat Raj System. In the process of power devolution, one finds that one segment of the society is gaining power and another is losing power. Collectivities that are going to gain power were powerless till date and they are not aware of the full implications of power devolution. Those who are going to lose power are aware of the full implications and, as a result, steps are taken to recapture the power through other means.

Planning from below is yet another milestone in the constitutional amendment. A planning committee is created at the district level constitutionally with the objective of preparing a perspective development plan from the grass roots with the active participation of the people. By doing so people's felt needs will be attended and the vision of the people will be realized. Natural resources and the commons will be effectively managed by the Panchayats and by doing so the livelihood of the poor will be ensured. Various schemes of the central and state governments will be dovetailed with the needs of the community, prioritized by the people through the Gram Sabha. By monitoring the public distribution system, essential commodities will reach the needy and in the same way, by monitoring the government departments, scheme benefits will reach the needy for whom the schemes are prepared/implemented.

The Gram Sabha is yet another breakthrough in governance. In an unequal society and caste ridden community, a Dalit woman is presiding over the Gram Sabha and all the voters, irrespective of their caste, whether high or low, have to accept her leadership. Her signature has got validity. A rich man or a man from the dominant community, after completing his construction, has to get a certificate from the Panchayat President for getting electricity connection. Necessarily the person has to visit the Panchayat President. As the locomotive has brought about equality, the Gram Sabha also brings about equality. All have to sit together and share ideas. A citizen from the Dalit community will raise questions on Panchayat administration and Panchayat expenditure. The Panchayat President has to listen and give a reply to the question. But this process is not going to be so smooth. It has to cross several barriers and conflicts but ultimately equality can be achieved.

Having this much of potential, why are the Panchayats not strengthened? The answer lies in the question itself. When this much of potential is in the amendment for social transformation, people who are at the helm of affairs, and those who are enjoying the fruits of the existing arrangement, have decided to work against this process of devolution. They are acting powerfully, at the same time indirectly, to resist devolution. If the transformation has to take place, either the political leadership at the Centre and the state should have political will and determination to give a push to devolution by taking a great risk as Rajiv Gandhi, Jyoti Basu, Ramakrishna Hegde, E.K. Nayanar, courageously did, or built up a mass movement from below. There is yet another way to render devolution more meaningful and constructive. It is to deepen democracy at every level through civil society organizations, opinion makers and media joining together and spreading awareness among the people about the implications of the devolution of powers. By building up the skill and capability of the local body leaders, Panchayats can be made instruments for governance at the grassroots for delivery of services. After bringing about success at the grassroots, people can join together with the Panchayat to demand proper devolution of powers.

Such exercises are silently going on in this country. However, capturing these successes and failures and analysing the same are not happening in the research institutions. At the grass-roots, 30 lakh representatives are working and their impact is not studied to the level of expectation. Our research institutions have analyzed higher level institutions like the national parliament, state legislatures, policies and programmes of governments, political systems and sub-systems but grass-roots governance is a neglected area. An array of issues can be researched on grass-roots governance. Funding agencies are financing such kind of studies by western universities and institutions. Only a few institutions in India are getting such grants from donor agencies for research in grass-roots governance. To do research on grass-roots issues, the so-called conventional scientific methods, tools and techniques will not suffice. Research institutions have to equip themselves and capture the transformations occurring in the Indian society as Indian democracy, governance, administration and development have moved towards a new horizon.

It is very difficult to affect a synergy by integrating micro movements and macro movements. But micro development can be easily achieved. Civil society organizations, academic institutions and training institutions can work together to support panchayat institutions to deliver services, administer development and social justice. A village unit can be freed from hunger, malnutrition, child labour, atrocities against women and HIV/AIDS. A village can be declared cent per cent literate and all individuals can be provided with conditions to lead a decent human life. But unfortunately everyone is looking from above, not from below. Thinking can be global but action need to be local. I am reminded of a poem of a great saint.

The Paradox of our Times

Is that we have taller buildings, but shorter tempers
Wider freeways, but narrower viewpoints
We spend more, but we have less.
We have bigger houses, but smaller families
more conveniences, but less time.
We have more degrees, but less sense
more knowledge, but less judgement
more experts, but more problems
more medicines, but less wellness.
We have multiplied our possessions, but reduced our values
We have too much, love too seldom, and hate too often.
We have learnt how to make a living, but not a life.
We have added years to life, but not life to years.
We've been all the way to the moon and back
but have trouble crossing the street to meet the new neighbour.
We have conquered outer space, but not inner space.
We've cleaned up the air, but polluted our soul.
We've split the atom, but not our prejudice.

We've higher incomes, but lower morals.
We've become long on quantity but short on quality.
These are the times of tall men, and short character;
steep profits and shallow relationships.
These are the times of world peace, but domestic warfare,
more leisure, but less fun; more kinds of food, but less nutrition.
These are the days of two incomes, but more divorces;
of fancier houses, but broken homes.
It is a time when there is much in the show window, and nothing in the stockroom.
A time when technology can bring this letter to you,
and a time when you can choose,
either to make a difference ... or just hit, delete.

—His Holiness The Dalai Lama

3 Economic Reforms, Growth and Regional Divergence in India

Madhusudan Ghosh

The issues of regional economic growth and disparity have attracted considerable attention among researchers, planners and policy makers. Since independence, the Indian government has been concerned about how to strengthen national unity and promote economic growth with regional equality. Balanced growth of all regions of the country has been considered essential for national integration, political stability and economic viability. Naturally, the issue of regional balance has been given sharp focus in all the plans, and various policies and programmes have been adopted with the pivotal need for fostering regional balance as an instrument of all-round development in the economy.

The Indian Constitution provides considerable power to the central government for allocating financial resources among the states in order to achieve balanced regional development. The Constitution has the provision for setting up Finance Commission every five years with the responsibility of recommending principles governing the centre-state financial relation for correcting the imbalances in resources and expenditures between the centre and the states, with the primary objective of reducing the regional disparity in income levels and development. The Planning Commission has also been an important institution for the transfer of resources to promote balanced regional development. As far as the distribution of plan funds among the states is concerned, the government seems to have performed its duty in fostering balanced regional development. The disbursement of plan funds has been made in such a manner that the poorer states have received proportionately larger amount of funds for development purpose relative to the richer ones (Ghosh et al., 1998). In this context, it seems pertinent to examine whether a considerable degree of regional inequality is persisting despite the Indian government's concern for its reduction.

There are other good academic reasons for learning about regional economic growth and disparity in India. Confronted with severe economic crisis with double-digit inflation and a large current account and balance of payment deficit in 1991, the Indian government adopted large-scale economic liberalization and structural adjustment programmes. The critics of India's economic reforms often argue that the reforms are responsible for the greater disparity in income among states (see, Das and Barua, 1996). Some others argue that implementation of these programmes has led to substantial growth in India after 1992, and both the rich and poor states have experienced the benefits of economic reforms (Ahluwalia et al., 1996; Ahluwalia, 2000). Against this background, it is useful to examine whether regional economic disparity has increased or decreased in India after the economic reforms.

Objective and Database

The main concern of this paper is to evaluate economic performance of 15 major states (see Table 1, for name of the states) in India over the period 1960–61 to 2001–02. It specifically examines whether there has been convergence or divergence in real per capita net State Domestic Product (SDP) across the states over the period in general and during the post-liberalization period in particular. Since the economic reforms involving large-scale structural adjustment and liberalization programmes have been adopted since 1991, we have considered this year as the cut-off point, and accordingly considered 1960–61 to 1990–91 as the pre-reform period and 1991–92 to 2001–02 as the post-reform period. Using the methodology suggested by Barro and Sala-i-Martin (1992, 1995) and Sala-i-Martin (1996), we examine whether initially disparate states in India display any tendency in real per capita net SDP to converge to or diverge from a common steady-state path during the periods. We also account for the convergence or divergence in real per capita net SDP across the states. Moreover, applying the univariate non-stationary time-series method suggested by Phillips (1987) and Phillips and Perron (1988), we have identified the states, which are diverging from the national average income.

The data used in this study were compiled from Chandhok and the Policy Group (1990) and Government of India (1995, 2003). The paper proceeds as follows: Section 3 critically reviews the existing literature; Section 4 explains the measures of convergence; and Section 5 evaluates relative economic performance of the states in terms of the level and

Table 1
Growth Performance of States

State	*Per Capita Real SDP (Rupees)*			*Annual Compound Growth Rate (%)*		
	1960–61	*1990–91*	*2001–02*	*Period 1 (Pre-reform)*	*Period 2 (Post-reform)*	*Period 3 (Entire Period)*
Andhra Pradesh	1,120	2,060	3,069	1.75	3.99	2.46
Assam	—	1,544	1,670	1.58	0.52	1.33
Bihar	832	1,197	1,225	1.18	1.81	1.01
Gujarat	1,498	2,641	4,257	1.77	4.72	2.58
Haryana	1,690	3,509	4,485	2.13	2.79	2.42
Karnataka	1,113	2,039	3,590	1.90	5.20	2.68
Kerala	1,135	1,815	2,778	1.29	3.93	2.06
Madhya Pradesh	1,163	1,693	2,084	1.32	3.07	1.86
Maharashtra	1,747	3,483	5,283	2.31	3.91	3.08
Orissa	580	1,383	1,917	2.41	2.30	2.10
Punjab	1,516	3,730	4,897	3.11	2.51	2.97
Rajasthan	1,184	1,942	2,412	1.08	3.0	1.83
Tamil Nadu	1,265	2,237	3,643	1.79	4.78	2.74
Uttar Pradesh	1,110	1,652	1,852	1.31	1.37	1.50
West Bangal	1,519	2,145	3,745	1.15	5.20	2.07
India	1,350	2,223	3,374	1.49	4.48	2.18
CV (%)	25.81	36.0	40.38	32.67	43.48	27.71

Notes: Period 1 (1960–61 to 1990–91); Period 2 (1991–92 to 2001–02); Period 3 (1960–61 to 2001–02). For Haryana and Punjab, Period 1 refers to 1965–66 to 1990–91, and Period 3 refers to 1965–66 to 2001–02. For Assam, Period 1 refers to 1970–71 to 1990–91 and Period 3 refers to 1970–71 to 2001–02.

Sources: Chandhok and the Policy Group (1990), and Government of India (1995, 2003).

growth rate of real per capita net SDP. Estimating convergence-style regression with cross-section and panel data, it also examines whether real per capita net SDP had any tendency to converge to a common steady-state path. Section 6 applies the univariate non-stationary time series technique to identify the states, which are converging to or diverging from the national average per capita income. Section 7 summarizes the main findings and draws policy conclusions.

Existing Literature

We make a critical review of the existing literature to get an idea about the findings of the earlier studies, and to compare the findings with those of the present exercise. Analysing the economic performance of 20 states over the period 1960–61 to 1989–90, Dholakia (1994) has found marked tendencies of convergence of long-term economic growth rates for the states. He identifies 1980–81 mmmas the year of break in the trend of real income after which many of the lagging states started growing, while the richer ones began to stagnate. Cashin and Sahay (1996a, 1996b) find that the dispersion in real per capita income has increased but there has been absolute convergence across 20 states over the period 1961–91. Surprisingly, their claim regarding absolute convergence is simply not borne out by the statistics they have provided. Moreover, the impact of the economic reforms adopted in the early-1990s on regional convergence has not been examined, the period of analysis being extended up to 1991. This criticism is equally applicable to Dholakia (1994). Ahluwalia (2000) reports evidence favourable to the convergence hypothesis. Analysing the economic performance of Indian states during the post-reform vis-à-vis the pre-reform period, he concludes that not all the rich states got richer relative to the poor ones, and not all the poor states got poorer. Contrary to the findings of the above studies, Marjit and Mitra (1996) and Ghosh et al. (1998) find evidence of divergence in per capita income across Indian states over the period 1960–61 to 1994–95. Ghosh and De (1998) argue that regional imbalance in physical infrastructure has been responsible for increasing income disparity across states. Nagaraj et al. (1998) find some evidence against unconditional convergence, but strong evidence in favour of conditional convergence among 17 Indian states during 1960–94. They argue that various indices of physical, economic and social infrastructure had significant effects on growth trends, and these indices explain inter-state variations in steady states. Rao et al. (1999) observe that per capita incomes across 14 major states have diverged, and inter-state disparities have accentuated during 1965–66 to 1994–95. The increases in divergence and dispersion have been much sharper since 1991. The divergence in growth rates has been largely due to the skewed distribution of public expenditures causing larger flows of investments to more affluent regions in the country. Analysing the economic performance of 21 Indian states over the period 1960–61 to 1995–96, Dasgupta et al. (2000) observe a clear tendency of divergence in per capita income across the states during the period. However, in terms of the shares of different sectors in SDP, the states appear to have converged towards the national average, implying that there has been convergence of structural parameters. It may be mentioned that the estimates of cross-state convergence regressions reported by them (in Table 6, p. 2418) are not significant enough to allow any definite conclusion regarding absolute convergence. The coefficients on initial level of per capita income having t-statistics ranging from 0.98 to 1.12 cannot be considered as statistically significant at 5 per cent level. More recently, Sachs et al. (2002) observe overall divergence in real per capita gross SDP across 14 major states during 1980–98. Divergence is particularly notable within the poorer states. Similarly, Trivedi (2002) finds that absolute convergence of per capita income has not occurred in the case of Indian states during 1960–92, although there is evidence of conditional convergence.

The review of the earlier studies clearly reveals that the results reported by the researchers are far from uniform, and a consensus is yet to emerge on the issue of convergence of income across Indian states. Moreover, the impact of the economic reforms initiated in the early-1990s on regional disparities of income was not investigated comprehensively in most of the studies. The latest year for which data were used in those studies is 1995–96, which seems to be too early to expect any major change in regional inequality. Again, while examining the regional convergence of per capita income, no attempt was made to identify the states that have been converging to or diverging from the national average income. The present exercise uses the data covering the period 1960–61 to 2001–02, and rigorously examines the impact of the economic reforms initiated in the early-1990s on the regional convergence or divergence of per capita income among the major states. We have also extended the earlier analysis by undertaking unit-root test to identify the states that have been converging to or diverging from the national average income.

Measures of Convergence

An important result that follows from the standard neoclassical growth model (Solow, 1956; Swan, 1956) is the convergence of per capita output across countries with a similar population growth rate, educational attainment, saving, investment and depreciation rates, and productivity growth. Based fundamentally on the assumption of diminishing returns to capital, the convergence hypothesis says that the growth rate in the country with lower per capita output should be higher than in the country with higher per capita output. When this happens, then inter-country differences in per capita output will disappear over time. Three concepts of convergence are distinguished in growth literature: (a) σ-convergence, (b) absolute or unconditional β-convergence, and (c) conditional β-convergence (see, Barro and Sala-i-Martin, 1992, 1995 and Sala-i-Martin, 1996).

The concept of σ-convergence concerns with cross-sectional dispersion of per capita income. σ-convergence is said to exist if the dispersion of per capita incomes across regions decreases over time. It focuses on the evolution of cross-sectional distribution of income over time. The existence of σ-convergence implies a tendency of per capita income to be equal across regions over time.

Whether the presence of σ-convergence in per capita income is due to higher growth rates of the poorer regions than the richer ones can be examined by looking into the presence of β-convergence. Absolute β-convergence is said to exist if the poorer regions tend to grow faster than the richer ones. The existence of absolute β-convergence is examined by estimating cross-sectional regression of annual average growth rate of per capita income on its initial level. Thus, testing for absolute β-convergence involves estimation of the following regression equation.

$$G_{i,t,t-\tau} = [\ln(Y_{i,t}) - \ln(Y_{i,t-\tau})]/T = \alpha + \beta \ln(Y_{i,t-\tau}) + \varepsilon_{i,t} \qquad \dots (1)$$

where $G_{i,t,t-\tau} = [ln\ (Y_{i,t}) - ln\ (Y_{i,t-\tau})]/T$ is the *ith* region's annual average growth rate of per capita income between the period t and $t-\tau$, and $ln(Y_{i,t})$ *and* $ln(Y_{i,t-\tau})$ are the natural logarithms of the *ith* region's per capita income at time t and $t-\tau$ respectively. T is the length of the period. If the coefficient on initial level of per capita income bears a statistically significant negative sign, i.e., if $\beta < 0$, then we say that there exists absolute β-convergence. The negative coefficient on initial level of per capita income signifies that the regions with lower initial level of per capita income grow faster than the regions with higher initial per capita income. The existence of β-convergence is a necessary condition for the existence of σ-convergence. It is natural that when an initially poor region grows faster than a rich one, then the levels of per capita income of the two regions will tend to be equal over time. Thus, β-convergence will tend to generate σ-convergence. It may, however, be noted that the existence of β-convergence is a necessary but not a sufficient condition for the existence of σ-convergence. For, whereas σ-convergence concerns with the question of whether or not the dispersion of cross-sectional distribution of income decreases over time, β-convergence concerns with the question of mobility of different regions within the given distribution of income (Sala-i-Martin, 1996).

Absolute β-convergence and the prediction that initially poor regions will grow faster than initially rich ones depend on the key assumption that the regions differ in their levels of capital only. In reality, however, regions may differ in many other respects such as level of technology, rate of investment, propensity to save, rate of capital depreciation, population growth rate, etc. These differences will generate different steady states for different regions. Absolute β-convergence, in such condition, holds if all regions converge to the same steady state. However, with different steady states for different regions, one has to test conditional β-convergence, holding the steady state of each region constant. Conditional β-convergence is perceptible only after other factors, which may cause variation in steady states across regions are accounted for. One way to do this is to include in regression equation (1) those variables that account for variation in steady states across regions. Thus, testing for the hypothesis of conditional β-convergence involves estimation of the following equation

$$G_{i,t,t-\tau} = [\ln(Y_{i,t}) - \ln(Y_{i,t-\tau})]/T = \alpha_i + \beta \ln(Y_{i,t-\tau}) + \sum_{j=1}^{k} \theta_j \ln(X^j_{i,t-\tau}) + \varepsilon_{i,t} \quad \text{... (2)}$$

The equation allows us to control the variables, which might influence the steady-state level of income. The choice of the control variables X^j depends on economic theory, *a priori* beliefs about growth process, and availability of data. Conditional β-convergence holds if β is significantly negative.

Growth and Regional Convergence

This section examines growth performance of the states and inter-state variation in real per capita net SDP during 1960–61 to 2001–02, with special emphasis on the nature of economic performance of the states in the post-reform period (1991–92 to 2001–02) vis-à-vis the pre-reform period (1960–61 to 1990–91). The real per capita income is measured in terms of per capita net SDP at 1980–81 prices (henceforth per capita income). The growth rate of per capita income was estimated by a log linear trend. The analysis is confined to 15 major states, which together account for around 97 per cent of the total population. The differential economic performance of the states is examined by comparing the levels and growth rates of per capita income among the states during different periods.

The levels of per capita income at different time points and their growth rates during different periods are reported in Table 1. The data reveal that there has been a wide variation in per capita income across the states, as some of the states have performed better than the others. In 1960–61, per capita income in Maharashtra (Rs 1,747), the richest state, was three times greater than that in Orissa (Rs 580), the poorest state. The variation in economic performance among the states has increased as the difference in per capita income between the richest and the poorest state has increased considerably over time. In 2001–02, per capita income of the richest state (Rs 5,283 in Maharashtra) was 4.3 times higher than that of the poorest state (Rs 1,225 in Bihar). Inter-state disparity in per capita income measured by cross-sectional Coefficient of Variation (CV) has increased from 25.81 per cent in 1960–61 to 36.0 per cent in 1990–91 and further to 40.38 per cent in 2001–02.

The estimated growth rates of per capita income presented in Table 1 reveal that growth performance of the economy during the entire period (Period 3) has been modest, the annual compound growth rate being 2.18 per cent only. This modesty is particularly observed during the pre-reform period: India's per capita income grew at the annual rate of only 1.49 per cent during 1960–61 to 1990–91. The growth performance improved in the post-reform periods as the economy achieved an annual growth rate of 4.48 per cent during 1991–92 to 2001–02. The improved growth performance of the economy is generally believed to be due to implementation of the economic reforms involving structural adjustment and liberalization programmes since 1991. These results are consistent with those of Ahluwalia et al. (1996) who argue that implementation of these programmes has led to substantial growth in India after 1992.

What, however, appears to be a matter of great concern is that there has been a wide variation in growth performance of the states. While some states growing faster than the economy have achieved rapid economic growth, others have languished with growth rate slower than the national average. The variations in growth performance of the states during the entire period and different sub-periods have been quite large. During the entire period, the annual growth rate of per capita income varies from 1.01 per cent in Bihar to 3.08 per cent in Maharashtra. The estimated growth rates in the pre-reform and post-reform periods further reveal that regional disparity has increased over time signifying that the poorer states with growth rates lower than the national average have been unable to catch up with the richer ones. A comparative study of growth performance of the states between the pre- and post-reform periods reveals that the surge in growth rate during the post-reform period has been due to remarkable improvement in growth rates of the states like Andhra Pradesh (A.P.),

Gujarat, Karnataka, Kerala, Madhya Pradesh (M.P.), Maharashtra, Rajasthan, Tamil Nadu (T.N.), and West Bengal (W.B.). Growth rates in these states in the post-reform period were significantly higher than the rates in the pre-reform period. Thus, the improved growth performance of the economy during the post-reform period has been associated with increasing regional disparity. The estimated cross-sectional CV of growth rates of per capita income has increased remarkably from 32.67 per cent during 1960–61 to 1990–91 to 43.48 per cent during 1991–92 to 2001–02 (the next section examines this in detail).

The growth performance of some of the states deserves special mention. Among the BIMARU states (Bihar, M.P., Rajasthan and U.P.), although Bihar and U.P. performed poorly, the other two states, viz., M.P. and Rajasthan performed reasonably well. Kerala, which has been praised for its achievement in human development but often criticized for under-performance in economic growth, showed marked improvement in growth rate in the post-reform periods. The deceleration in growth rate in the post-reform period in two agriculturally advanced states (viz., Haryana and Punjab) deserves closer investigation to understand the factors responsible for the loss of momentum of growth (Ahluwalia, 2000).

Divergence in Per Capita Income

This section considers different measures of convergence and examines the validity of the convergence hypothesis based on growth experience of the states. Applying the method suggested by Barro and Sala-i-Martin (1992, 1995) and Sala-i-Martin (1996), it examines whether there has been any tendency of convergence in per capita income across the states during the periods under consideration.

σ-convergence

The simplest way to test for σ-convergence is to estimate time trend of some measure of dispersion of per capita income across regions. We have computed the standard deviation (SD) of per capita income across the states for each year during the period. The estimated SDs of the logarithms of per capita income plotted against time in Figure 1 display an increasing trend, suggesting a discernible increase in per capita income disparity among the states. This trend has persisted throughout, with the exception of some fluctuations in some of the years.

A clear picture about overall time trend (t) and structural breaks in the trend functions of SD of per capita income during the period can be obtained from the estimated results of the following equations.

$$SD = 0.219 + 0.0047\,t; \qquad R^2 = 0.819. \qquad \ldots(a)$$
$$(25.61)^{*}\ (13.48)^{*}$$

$$SD = 0.244 + 0.0028\,t - 0.117D_1 + 0.0049\,D_2\,;\ R^2 = 0.913;\ T_B = 1990\text{–}91. \qquad \ldots(b)$$
$$(34.17)\ (7.12)^{*}\ (-1.701)^{**}\ (2.627)^{*}$$

Notes: D_1 = 1 for t > 1990–91, 0 otherwise; D_2 = t for t > 1990–91, 0 otherwise. T_B is the year at the end of which the break occurs in the trend functions. t = 1, 2, ..., 42. Figures in parenthesis are t-statistics. * and ** indicate significant at 1 per cent and 5 per cent levels respectively.

Figure 1

Trend in SD of per Capita SDP

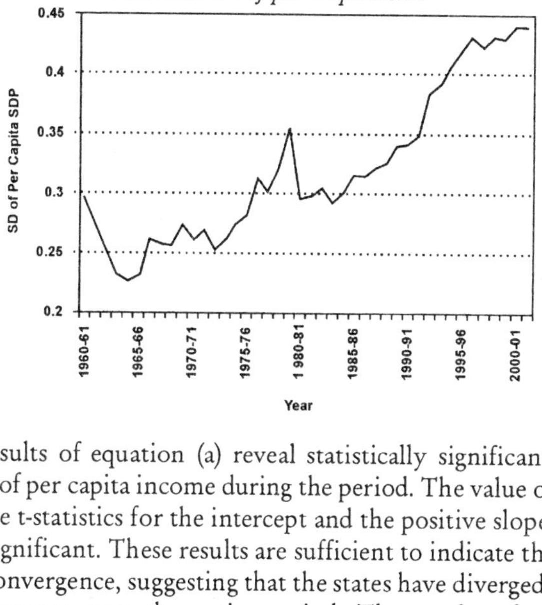

The results of equation (a) reveal statistically significant increasing trend in SD of per capita income during the period. The value of R^2 is quite high, and the t-statistics for the intercept and the positive slope coefficient are highly significant. These results are sufficient to indicate that there has been no σ-convergence, suggesting that the states have diverged in terms of per capita income over the entire period. The results of equation (b) further reveal that the rate of divergence has increased after the economic reforms. When we allow for changes in the intercept and slope of the trend function at the end of 1990–91 incorporating two dummy variables (D_1 and D_2), we find that the slope of the trend has increased significantly after a fall in the intercept. This suggests that the rate of divergence in per capita income has increased significantly after the implementation of the economic reforms.

Absolute β-convergence

The test for absolute or unconditional β-convergence hypothesis is performed by estimating equation (1) by the Ordinary Least Squares (OLS) method for the whole period as well as for different sub-periods. We have estimated the equation for two measures of growth rate of per capita income: (i) annual average growth rate; (ii) annual compound growth rate computed by estimating a log-linear trend ($ln\ Y_t = a + bt + \varepsilon_t$). In the first case, the test for absolute β-convergence is performed by regressing the annual average growth rate of per capita income on its initial level. In the second case, the log-linear trend in per capita income is first estimated for each state and then the test for absolute β-convergence is performed by regressing the estimated values of *b* on the initial level of per capita income. In both the cases, the hypothesis of absolute β-convergence holds if the coefficient on initial per capita income turns out to be significantly negative.

The results of the estimated convergence regressions are reported in Table 2. It can be seen that in the case of annual average growth rate (Panel A), the coefficient on initial level of income turns out to be positive in all the regressions. However, while the positive coefficient is not statistically significant in the pre-reform period, it turns out to be significant in the post-reform period. Similarly, when the annual compound growth rate of per capita income is regressed on its initial level, the regression coefficient is found to be positive in all the cases. However, while the positive coefficient is not statistically significant in the pre-reform period, it is significant in the post-reform period. And this yielded a positive and significant coefficient for the entire period (Panel B). Overall, the regression estimates provide strong evidence that while there has been no significant divergence in the pre-reform period there has been significant divergence of per capita income across the states in the post-reform period.

A comparative study of the rates of divergence between the pre- and post-reform periods further reveals that the rate of divergence has increased considerably during the latter period. It can be seen from Panel A of Table 2 that the rate of divergence has increased from 0.075 per cent during the pre-reform period to 1.97 per cent during the post-reform period. Panel-B of the table shows that the rate has increased from 0.29 per cent to 1.62 per cent. This suggests that the on-going economic reforms since 1991 have aggravated the inter-state disparities in income. These results are consistent with the evidence of increasing σ-divergence reported above. Thus, contrary to the prediction of the neoclassical growth model, we find strong evidence of absolute divergence in per capita income across the Indian states. The states with higher initial levels of incomes grew faster than those with lower initial levels of incomes did.

Table 2

Estimates of Absolute b-convergence in Real Per Capita Income

Period	*Constant*	*Coefficient on initial Per Capita Income in* (Y_{t-t})	*R2*
Panel A: Dependent Variable: Annual Average Growth Rate			
1960–61 to 1990–91	0.018 (0.439)	0.0008 (0.013)	0.0014
1991–92 to 2001–02	–0.118 (–1.347)	0.0197** (1.755)	0.192
1960–61 to 2001–02	–0.008 (–0.194)	0.004 (0.699)	0.039
Panel B: Dependent Variable: Annual Compound Growth Rate			
1960–61 to 1990–91	–0.0032 (–0.08)	0.0029 (0.508)	0.021
1991–92 to 2001–02	–0.0911 (–1.144)	0.0162*** (1.556)	0.157
1960–61 to 2001–02	–0.054 (–1.608)	0.011** (2.27)	0.301

Notes: Figures in parenthesis are t-statistics. ** and *** respectively denote significant at 1 per cent, 5 per cent and 10 per cent levels. Number of observations (N) = 15. However, for the periods beginning with 1960–61, N = 14.

Conditional β-convergence and Factors behind Divergence

The observed divergence in per capita income across the states may be explained by evaluating conditional β-convergence. Testing for conditional β-convergence involves estimation of equation (2), which includes as regressors not only initial level of per capita income but also some other variables which might account for the differences in steady-state income levels across states.

Following Trivedi (2002), the equation has been specified here with (in addition to the lagged per capita income, PCI) the lagged infant mortality rate (IMR) and high school enrollment rate (HSER) as proxies for non-educational and educational human capital respectively, and physical infrastructure (PHI) as a proxy for physical capital to control for steady-state per capita income of the states. The principal components technique was used to measure physical infrastructure based on two series on energy production (viz., installed capacity and generation), one series on energy consumption (high voltage electricity consumption by industry), and one series on the length of state highways. An average of the values of the variables over the previous 5 years was computed and used as a regressor. The equation was estimated by the OLS method with and without fixed effects (α_i) with the panel data for 15 major states over the period 1960–92. The OLS estimates of the equation are reported in Table 3. It shows that the initial income level has a statistically significant negative sign in both the equations, suggesting that conditional β-convergence has occurred among the states. The estimates also reveal that the conditioning variables viz., the infant morality rate has a statistically significant negative effect and physical infrastructure has a statistically significant positive effect on the steady-state level and hence on transitional growth in both the equations. The other control variable, high school enrolment rate, has a statistically insignificant negative coefficient in the equation without fixed effects, but has a statistically significant positive coefficient in the equation with fixed effects. Overall, the estimates provide strong and consistent evidence of convergence once the factors that affect steady-state levels of income are controlled for. The results thus suggest that the poorer states have been growing faster than the richer ones in their transition phase, but they are growing towards their own differing steady-states only. Therefore, the observed divergence in per capita incomes has been due to persistent differences in initial conditions resulting in differences in steady-state levels across the states.

Table 3

Results of Conditional β-convergence
Dependent variable: Growth Rate of Per Capita Real Income

Independent Variables	*Without Fixed Effects*	*With Fixed Effects*
(PCI) t–5	-0.0532*	-0.1433*
	(-3.07)	(-5.77)
(IMR) t–5	-0.0001**	-0.0001**
	(-2.14)	(-1.81)
(HSER) t–5	-0.0001	0.0015*
	(-0.29)	(2.78)
(PHI) t–5	0.0138*	0.98*
	(3.82)	(3.62)
Constant	0.41	0.98
	(3.34)	(5.73)
RMSE	0.029	0.027

Notes: Figures in parenthesis are t-statistics. * and ** respectively denote significant at 1 per cent and 5 per cent levels. RMSE = Root Mean Square Error. The estimation period is 1960–92. Number. of observations (N) = 88

Source: Trivedi (2002).

The evidence on conditional β-convergence receives strong empirical support from the results of a study (Nagaraj et al., 1998) based on a larger number of observations and a bigger set of conditioning variables accounting for differences in the steady-state per capita income levels of the states. The results of the study indicated the existence of conditional β-convergence. The evidence also suggests that differences in physical, social and economic infrastructure as well as in production structure have been responsible for the observed regional economic disparity in India (see, Nagaraj et al., 1998).

The Converging and Diverging States

The results reported above suggest that the observed divergence in per capita income across the states (indicated by the evidence against of σ-convergence and absolute β-convergence) has been due to variations in their steady-state levels. The results derived from cross-sectional convergence regressions, however, do not provide any scope for identifying the states, which are driving the divergence in per capita income. It is, however, important to identify the states, which are diverging from the national average per capita income and thus driving inter-state disparity. We have performed unit-root test for convergence under the time-series framework to identify the states that are driving the divergence in per capita income.

Under the time-series framework, convergence requires cross-state per capita income differentials to be stationary, implying that the levels of per capita income are not diverging over time. We examine the convergence hypothesis by evaluating the univariate time series properties of the differentials of per capita income of each of the 15 states relative to the national average one (henceforth, income differential). Convergence of a state's per capita income to the national average level requires that its income differential is stationary. In this case, the test for convergence of per capita income is translated to a test for the stationarity of income differential. A test of the null hypothesis of no convergence (non-stationarity) against the alternative of convergence (stationarity) is undertaken. The null hypothesis of no convergence is:

$$H_0: X_{i,t} = [ln(Y_{i,t}) - ln(Y_{*,t})] \sim I(1), \text{ for all } i = 1, 2, \qquad \ldots (15)$$

The alternative hypothesis of convergence is:

$$H_1: X_{i,t} = [ln(Y_{i,t}) - ln(Y_{*,t})] \sim I(0), \text{ for all } i = 1, 2, \qquad \ldots (15)$$

where, $X_{i,t}$ is the logarithm of per capita income of the *ith* state relative to the national average per capita income; $ln(Y_{i,t})$ and $ln(Y_{*,t})$ respectively denote the logarithms of the *ith* state's and the national average per capita incomes. *I(1)* and *I(0)* are respectively integrated of order one (non-stationary) and zero (stationary) processes. The Augmented Dickey-Fuller (ADF) (Dickey and Fuller, 1979, 1981) and Phillips-Perron (PP) (Phillips, 1987; and Phillips and Perron, 1988) methods are usually used to test for stationarity of a time series. It is, however, argued that while the ADF method yields a liberal test and depends on the choice of augmenting lags, the PP method is both conservative and more powerful, and not influenced by the choice of truncation lag parameters, particularly in a small sample (see Perron, 1988). In view of that and since our sample size is small covering only 42 years, we have used the PP test for a unit root, which is based on the OLS estimates of the following regression equation:

$$X_{i,t} = u + b\,(t - T/2) + pX_{i,t-1} + u_t \qquad \text{... (3)}$$

The test statistic $z(\hat{\rho})$ is used here to test for the null hypothesis of a unit root, H_0: ñ = 1 (see, Phillips, 1987 and Phillips and Perron, 1988, for details).

The results obtained from applying the PP test for evaluating the unit root property of income differentials are reported in Table 4. It can be seen that the null hypothesis of a unit root can be rejected for four states only (viz., Gujarat, Karnataka, M.P. and Rajasthan), implying that the income differentials of these states are stationary. This suggests that these states share a common steady-state level of per capita income with the national average. For the remaining eleven states (viz., A.P., Assam, Bihar, Haryana, Kerala, Maharashtra, Orissa, Punjab, Tamil Nadu, U.P., and W.B.), we fail to reject the null hypothesis of a unit root in income differentials, implying that income differentials of these states are non-stationary. This indicates that these states have been following the steady-state growth paths, which are different from the national average. Overall, these results indicate considerable divergence in per capita income across the states and the divergence has been due to variations in the steady-state levels among the states. The eleven states have been driving the observed regional divergence in per capita income in India.

Summary and Policy Conclusion

We have evaluated the long-run growth performance and convergence in per capita income across 15 major Indian states during 1960–61 to 2001–02.

Table 4
Unit-Root Test for Convergence

State	*Phillips-Perron Test Statistics* [$z(\hat{\rho})$]	*P-value*
Andhra Pradesh	–14.323	0.210
Assam	–1.924	0.972
Bihar	–4.380	0.863
Gujarat	–40.918*	0.0007
Haryana	–14.231	0.213
Karnataka	–23.459**	0.034
Kerala	–18.126	0.102
Madhya Pradesh	–25.545*	0.022
Maharashtra	–10.057	0.432
Orissa	–8.377	0.554
Punjab	–1.651	0.978
Rajasthan	–32.285*	0.005
Tamil Nadu	–17.964	0.105
Uttar Pradesh	–5.713	0.767
West Bengal	–10.746	0.387

Notes: * and ** respectively denote significant at 1 per cent and 5 per cent levels. The critical values tabulated in Fuller (1976, Table 8.5.1, p. 371) are used for testing the level of significance. Number of observations (N) = 42. For Haryana and Punjab, N = 37. For Assam, N = 32.

Contrary to the prediction of the neoclassical growth model, we have found strong evidence against σ-convergence and absolute β-convergence, suggesting that the Indian states had strong tendencies to diverge in per capita income over the period. An important finding is that while there has been no significant divergence in the pre-reform period, there has been significant and higher rate of divergence in the post-reform period. This indicates that the ongoing economic reforms since 1991 have led to an increase in the regional disparities in income. The evidence of conditional β-convergence indicates that the states have been moving only towards their differing steady-state income levels. Thus, the divergence in per capita incomes has been due to dispersion in the steady-state levels among the states, which is due to differences in human capital, production structures, and physical, social and economic infrastructure among them. The results of the unit-root test for convergence reveal that while only four states share the common steady-state, the remaining eleven states have followed the steady-state paths that are different from the national average. These states are thus driving the divergence in per capita income across Indian states.

These results have important implications for policy. The results suggest that economic policy measures for improving human capital, physical, social and economic infrastructure can have significant effect on long-run growth potential as well as on convergence across states. Since the divergence in per capita income across the states have been due to variations in their steady-states, targeting public investment in human capital and infrastructure for the states with lower steady-state levels could improve overall growth performance and reduce regional imbalance. Unless appropriate steps are taken to correct disparities in the spread of infrastructure through regional policies and inter-governmental transfers, divergence in per capita incomes across states will continue to widen. The existing policy of transferring proportionately larger amount of funds to relatively poorer states appears to be in the right direction. Efficient utilization of these funds by the states for infrastructural and human development could help in a great way to improve their overall growth performance and reduce regional disparities in development. The ongoing economic reforms that have led to an increase in regional disparities in income need appropriate modification if the policy makers are interested in reducing regional disparities in development indices of the country.

References

Ahluwalia, M.S. (2000), Economic Performance of States in Post-Reform Period, *Economic and Political Weekly,* Vol. 35, No. 19, May 6, 1637–1648.

Ahluwalia, I.J., Mohan, R. and Goswami, O. (1996), *Policy Reform in India,* OECD Development Centre, Paris.

Barro, R.J. and Sala-i-Martin, X. (1992), Convergence, *Journal of Political Economy,* Vol. 100, No. 2, 223–251.

Barro, R.J. and Sala-i-Martin, X. (1995), *Economic Growth,* McGraw Hill, New York.

Cashin, P. and Sahay, R. (1996a), Internal Migration, Centre-State Grants, and Economic Growth in the States of India, *IMF Staff Papers,* Vol. 43, No. 1, 123–171.

Cashin, P. and Sahay, R. (1996b), Regional Economic Growth and Convergence in India, *Finance and Development,* Vol. 33, No. 1, 49–52.

Chandhok, H.L. and The Policy Group (1990), *India Database: The Economy,* Vol. 1, Living Media India Ltd., New Delhi.

Das, S.K. and Barua, A. (1996), "Regional Inequalities, Economic Growth and Liberalisation: A Study of the Indian Economy", *Journal of Development Studies,* Vol. 32, No. 3, 364–390.

Dasgupta, D., Maiti, P., Mukherjee, R., Sarkar, S. and Chakrabarti, S. (2000), Growth and Interstate Disparities in India, *Economic and Political Weekly,* Vol. 35, No. 27, July 1, 2413–2422.

Dholakia, R.H. (1994), Spatial Dimensions of Accelerations of Economic Growth in India, *Economic and Political Weekly,* Vol. 29, No. 35, August 27, 2303–2309.

Dickey, D.A. and Fuller, W.A. (1979), Distribution of the Estimators for Autoregressive Time Series with a Unit Root, *Journal of American Statistical Association,* Vol. 74, 427–431.

Dickey, D.A. and Fuller, W.A. (1981), Likelihood Ratio Statistics for Autoregressive Time Series with a Unit Root, *Econometrica,* Vol. 49, 1057–1072.

Fuller, W.A. (1976), *Introduction to Statistical Time Series,* John Wiley and Sons, New York.

Ghosh, B. and De, P. (1998), Role of Infrastructure in Regional Development: A Study of India over the Plan Period, *Economic and Political Weekly,* Vol. 33, Nos. 47–48, November 21, 3039–3048.

Ghosh, B., Marjit, S. and Neogi, C. (1998), Economic Growth and Regional Divergence in India, 1960 to 1995, *Economic and Political Weekly,* Vol. 33, No. 26, June 27, 1623–1630.

Government of India (2003), *National Accounts Statistics,* Central Statistical Organisation, Department of Statistics, Ministry of Planning. Download from Website: http://www.mospi.nic.in.

Government of India (1995), *Economic Survey 1994–95,* Economic Division, Ministry of Finance, New Delhi.

Marjit, S. and Mitra, S. (1996), Convergence in Regional Growth Rates: Indian Research Agenda, *Economic and Political Weekly,* Vol. 31, No. 33, August 17.

Nagaraj, R., Varoudakis, A. and Veganzones, M.A. (1998), *Long-run Growth Trends and Convergence across Indian States,* Technical Papers No. 131, OECD Development Centre, January.

Perron, P. (1988), Trends and Random Walks in Macroeconomic Time Series: Further Evidence from a New Approach, *Journal of Economic Dynamics and Control,* Vol. 12, No. 2–3, 297–332.

Phillips, P.C.B. (1987), Time Series Regression with Unit Roots, *Econometrica,* Vol. 55, No. 2, 277–302.

Phillips, P.C.B. and Perron, P. (1988), Testing for a Unit Root in Time Series Regression, *Biometrika,* Vol. 75, 335–346.

Rao, M.G., Shand, R.T. and Kalirajan, K.P. (1999), Convergence of Incomes across Indian States: A Divergent View, *Economic and Political Weekly,* Vol. 34, No. 13, March 27, 769–778.

Sachs, J.D., Bajpai, N. and Ramiah, A. (2002), *Understanding Regional Economic Growth in India,* CID Working Paper No. 88, Centre for International Development, Harvard University, March.

Sala-i-Martin, X. (1996), The Classical Approach to Convergence Analysis, *The Economic Journal,* Vol. 106, No. 437, 1019–36.

Solow, R. (1956), A Contribution to the Theory of Economic Growth, *Quarterly Journal of Economics,* Vol. 70, No. 1, 65–94.

Swan, T.W. (1956), Economic Growth and Capital Accumulation, *Economic Record,* Vol. 32, No. 63, 334–361.

Trivedi, K. (2002), *Regional Convergence and Catch-up in India between 1960 and 1992,* Working Paper, Nuffield College, University of Oxford, Oxford, December.

4 Inter-State Variations in Levels of Economic Development

A Sectoral and Temporal Study

Ajit Kumar Singh

Most of the studies carried out by regional economists have used single variable approach to study inter-regional disparity mostly using per capita income as the indicator of development. The analysis of regional disparity and its trends based on a single variable started with the contributions made by Kuznets (1957) and Williamson (1965). In India also a number of studies have come out in recent years analyzing trends in inter-state disparities in terms of per capita income (Dholakia 1994; Rao et al., 1999; Singh A.K. 1999; Dasgupta et al., 2000; Shaban, 2000; Singh et al., 2003; Bhattacharya and Shaktivel, 2004).

It should be, however, realised that per capita income gives, at best, only a rough indication of relative level of the development or welfare of various regions as has been pointed out by many development economists. McGranahan, for example, disagreed with the routine practice of identifying development through per capita G.N.P. (McGrahan, 1972). Drewnowski in a similar tone stressed that "... it is generally recognized that traditional economic accounting variables cannot legitimately be used for measuring improvement in social conditions ..." (Drewnowski, 1972). As Kundu points out "univariate statistics for describing complex social process provide a partial picture and are consequently found to be inadequate both as a tool of analysis and as an input in policy making process" (Kundu, 1980). According to Sarkar "Per capita income fails to reflect the inherent process of structural transformation of socio-economic development that has taken place in a country" (Sarkar, 1999). Hence, many scholars engaged in delineating the theoretical as well as empirical problems of regionalization rely heavily on quantitative tools using multivariate data.

In this paper, it is proposed to analyze the pattern and trends in inter-state disparities in levels of development using multivariate analysis. Besides the normally used indicators of development at the sectoral level, indicators of various aspects of quality of life have also been taken up for purposes of analysis. This will help us in identifying the specific dimensions of socio-economic development in which particular states are lagging behind.

The paper is divided into eight sections including the introduction. Methodology of analysis has been discussed in section II. Sections III and IV deal with levels of agricultural and industrial development respectively, while sections V and VI deal with levels of economic and social infrastructure respectively. Section VII presents the overall development rankings. The results are summarized in the concluding section.

Methodology

The analysis has been carried out separately for the four major sectors of the economy, namely, agriculture, industry, economic infrastructure and social infrastructure. The analysis has been carried out at five points of time centring on the years 1960–61, 1970–71, 1980–81, 1990–91 and 2000–01. The years have been chosen to observe the decennial variations, which is a reasonable time frame for the policy to get translated into actual plans and see its consequent impact on different indicators of development. It was not possible to take back the exercise to 1950–51, i.e., the beginning of the planning period as sufficient data on all the selected variables for the study were not available. Where data for the particular years chosen for the study were not available, available information for the nearest year has been used. For 1960–61 information for certain newly created states was not available for which certain adjustments had to be made. In case of the year 2000–01 up-to-date data on some of the selected variables are not available. Hence, information for late nineties has been used in many cases depending upon availability. This study is confined to 17 major states of India and excludes the special category states, which are mostly small entities with specific problems and distinct geographical and cultural identities.

For purposes of meaningful analysis disaggregated data on a large number of variables need to be combined into a composite index at sectoral or overall level. Three approaches have generally been used for the purpose, namely, the index method, the ranking method and factor analysis. The first two are relatively simple exercises using the index or rank for each variable and aggregating them to arrive at a composite index. The major limitation of these two approaches is that each variable is assigned equal weight, even though all of them are not of equal significance. Sometimes arbitrary weights are given to the indicators, which reflect the subjective assessment of the scholar. There can, however, be no unanimity as to the exact weights to be assigned to each variable. Factor analysis, which assigns these weights according to objective statistical analysis, is often used to overcome this problem. Principal Component analysis is the most widely used statistical tool for this analysis. This puts, however, a heavy demand on statistical calculations, which cannot be carried out without the use of computers. Though not without its limitations Principal Component analysis has been widely used to rank regions according to levels of development.

The main objective of the Principal Component analysis is to reduce the dimensions of a complex multivariate problem. It is not uncommon that the variations in a variable can only be satisfactorily explained in terms of a large set of explanatory variables most of which are closely correlated with one another. In this situation the multiple regression analysis often fails to provide clear and meaningful answers. The coefficients of independent variable become unreliable in this situation and sometimes carry wrong signs, since these become distorted by the inclusion of other independent variables with which these show a high degree of association. The Principal Component analysis, on the other hand, takes the correlation matrix into account to produce components that are uncorrelated with one another and so enables the researcher to bypass the problem of multi co-linearity.

In Principal Component analysis we describe the total variance of a set of n points in p dimensional space by introducing a new set of p orthogonal and uncorrelated variates. The new set is formed by taking normalized linear combination of the original set, so that the rth variate generated has the largest variance. Principal Component analysis involves expressing the correlated indicators, P_1, ..., P_n as uncorrelated linear functions called Principal Components. The coordinates of each observation or variable are measured to obtain what are called factor loadings or the elements of the eigen vectors which are used to compute the scores of observations. The eigen values represent the proportion of the total variance accounted for by eigen vector.

The computation for factor loadings are done with the formula:

$$Z_j = a_j, 1P_1 + aj, 2P_2 + \ldots + a_j, nP_n$$

where $Z_j = X_j - X/\$x_j$; or standardized variable

After getting the component loadings the factor scores Y_{ij} are calculated:

$$Y_{ji} = a_{ij} \cdot z_{ij}$$

The first Principal Component is that combination which accounts for the largest amount of variation in the sample. The second Principal Component accounts for the next largest amount of variance and so on. For each factor, the factor scores can be obtained by multiplying the standardized values by the corresponding factor score coefficients using the above equation. The units of analysis, i.e., states in our case, are then arranged in a hierarchical order on the basis of factor scores thus obtained.

The composite index of development has been derived on the basis of the Principal Component analysis using SPSS package in two stages. In the first stage composite indices have been prepared for each selected sectors. First Principal Component has been used to arrange states in order of development in accordance with the level of variation if it explained more than 70 per cent of the variation. If first Principal Component accounted for less than 70 per cent of variation, a weighted composite index was used by aggregating factor scores of the first and second (and in a few cases the third) Principal Component using the percentage of variation explained as weights. In the second stage, the overall composite index was derived by adding the composite indices of development for all the sectors. States were then ranked according to the weighted factor scores. The results of the Principal Component analysis have been discussed in the following sections.

Levels of Agricultural Development

Nine indicators relating to development of agriculture have been selected to gauge the disparities amongst the selected 17 states. The indicators selected relate to different aspects of agricultural development reflecting agricultural productivity, degree of commercialization, irrigation infrastructure, use of modern technology and degree of mechanization. The selected indicators are as follows:

AGR1 : Value of Output Per Hectare (Rs)

AGR2 : Value of Output Per Male Worker (Rs)

AGR3 : Per cent Area under Non-Foodgrain Crops

AGR4 : Per cent of Gross Irrigated Area to GSA

AGR5 : Fertilizer Consumption Per Hectare of GSA

AGR6 : No. of Tractors Per 1000 Hectares of GSA

AGR7 : No. of Pump Sets Per 1000 Hectares of GSA

AGR8 : Per cent Area Irrigated by Tube wells

AGR9 : Per Capita Milk Production (Kg)

Table 1 shows the trend in Inter-state disparities, as measured by the coefficient of variation (CV). The values of CV were very high in 1960–61 and continue to be so even now in respect of almost all the indicators of agricultural development. In general, disparities were higher in case of irrigation facilities and input use as compared to productivity levels. Disparities in the indicators of productivity per worker or per hectare do not show much change over the entire period under study. This is so because agricultural disparities are largely related to the disparities in the proportion of irrigated area, which have remained more or less unchanged over the period. However, indicators of input use like fertilizer consumption show a significant decline in the extent of disparities. Similarly, the values of CV in number of pump sets per 1000 hectares and per cent area irrigated by tube wells have reduced sharply. However, these disparities still continue to be fairly high.

Table 1

Trends in Indicators of Inter-State Disparities in Agricultural Development

Indicators	*AGR 1*	*AGR 2*	*AGR 3*	*AGR 4*	*AGR 5*	*AGR 6*	*AGR 7*	*AGR 8*	*AGR 9*
1960									
MEAN	4363.4	7101.1	22.74	22.32	3.84	0.38	2.40	2.42	71.27
SD	2187.1	3173.8	15.55	13.79	3.76	0.54	3.57	4.90	87.03
CV	50.12	44.70	68.38	61.78	97.92	142.11	148.75	202.48	122.11
1970									
MEAN	5089.4	7627	25.34	26.4	15.52	1.08	20.25	8.38	50.44
SD	2554.6	3690.4	15.13	17.25	12.47	1.84	30.85	14.21	46.26
CV	50.2	48.4	59.71	65.34	80.35	170.37	152.35	169.57	91.71
1980									
MEAN	5937.7	8493	23.64	30.86	33.36	3.44	39.98	10.06	67.73
SD	2550.0	4546.6	14.58	20.34	27.31	5.42	43.29	13.35	72.37
CV	42.95	53.54	61.68	65.91	81.86	157.56	108.28	132.70	106.85
1990									
MEAN	8231.9	10509.05	30.28	34.76	69.14	7.04	62.40	17.44	82.84
SD	3516.4	6116.9	17.02	22.92	41.70	9.28	46.75	14.11	66.01
CV	42.72	58.21	56.21	65.94	60.31	131.82	74.92	80.91	79.68
2000									
MEAN	20060.65	21429.82	35.06	38.33	90.69	7.04	62.40	21.55	88.02
SD	8773.01	11968.31	17.45	22.89	46.38	9.28	46.75	16.54	71.33
CV	43.73	55.85	49.77	59.72	51.14	131.80	74.92	76.79	81.04

Table 2 shows the factor loading of selected indicators. The first principal component alone explained about 50 per cent and the second principal component about 20 per cent of the total variation. It is also observed that with the passage of time the factor loadings of various indicators have undergone significant changes. Value of factor loadings has declined markedly in case of output indicators but gone up significantly in case of indicators of input use, showing the gradual modernization of agriculture over the period. The first factor loads positively on input indicators like per cent irrigated area and use of modern technology represented by number of tractors and tube wells per 1000 ha. The second factor mainly loads on the productivity indicators and cropping pattern.

Table 2

Principal Component Loadings for Indicators of Agricultural Development

Variables	*1960*		*1970*		*1980*		*1990*		*2000*	
	First	*Second*	*First*	*Second*	*First*	*Second*	*First*	*Second*	*First*	*Second*
AGR 1	0.257	–0.023	–0.064	0.369	–0.054	0.382	–0.050	0.343	–0.041	0.263
AGR 2	0.232	0.077	0.149	0.373	0.071	0.232	0.275	0.076	–0.012	0.494
AGR 3	0.267	–0.100	–0.088	0.451	–0.183	0.455	–0.055	0.343	–0.330	0.431
AGR 4	0.001	–0.248	0.172	–0.102	0.236	–0.097	0.199	–0.055	0.238	–0.107
AGR 5	0.268	–0.013	–0.028	–0.005	0.138	0.119	0.029	0.234	–0.027	–0.057
AGR 6	0.008	0.313	0.270	0.019	0.222	–0.046	0.300	–0.103	0.280	0.117
AGR 7	0.185	–0.013	–0.174	–0.144	0.065	0.152	–0.171	0.317	–0.143	–0.113
AGR 8	–0.050	0.261	0.284	–0.054	0.204	–0.124	–0.136	0.041	0.286	–0.168
AGR 9	–0.043	0.305	0.328	–0.029	0.215	–0.056	0.371	–0.129	0.243	0.206
% of variation explained	40.8	30.3	53.3	23.9	56.9	20.7	52.8	21.5	50.9	17.9

Statewise factor scores of agricultural development are shown in Table 3, while Table 4 shows the ranks of different states in terms of factor scores. Due to considerations of space the ranking pattern of the states has been discussed on the basis of the weighted ranks only. The ranking of states in terms of agricultural development have undergone important changes over the study period. This reflects the uneven development of the agricultural sector during the study period. It is well known that the green revolution technology have primarily benefitted the northern states which are better endowed with irrigation facilities. The states of H.P., Jammu &

Kashmir, U.P., M.P., Bihar and Assam have improved their ranks over time, while West Bengal, Gujarat, A.P., Tamil Nadu, Kerala have slipped down. The ranks for 2000 show particularly large shifts as compared to the ranks in 1990. H.P., J & K and Kerala show a sharp decline in their ranks in 2000, while Assam, Bihar, West Bengal and U.P. show sharp improvement. These shifts reflect the impact of the weather conditions, which have affected the productivity of crops in some states more adversely.

Table 3

Statewise Principal Component Scores for Agriculture

State	*1960*		*1970*		*1980*		*1990*		*2000*	
	1st	*2nd*	*1st*	*2nd*	*1st*	*2nd*	*1st*	*2nd*	*1st*	*2nd*
Haryana	−0.232	1.543	2.016	0.280	1.607	−0.212	1.858	0.135	1.438	0.754
Himachal Pradesh	−0.988	−0.475	−0.022	−0.800	−0.272	−1.060	0.129	−1.350	0.080	−0.263
J&K	−0.945	−0.103	−0.035	−0.869	−0.231	−0.672	0.064	−1.170	−0.003	0.093
Punjab	0.444	3.161	2.813	0.639	2.986	0.921	3.064	0.530	2.757	1.718
Uttar Pradesh	−0.542	0.789	0.664	−0.662	0.870	−0.708	−0.177	0.077	0.872	−1.148
Assam	−0.284	−0.461	−0.572	0.219	−0.803	0.151	−0.732	−0.564	0.288	−0.602
Bihar	−0.678	−0.288	−0.126	−0.967	0.036	−1.100	−0.627	−0.726	0.404	−1.574
Orissa	−0.648	−0.412	−0.475	−0.478	−0.693	−0.487	−0.549	−0.830	−0.426	−0.558
West Bengal	−0.222	−0.346	−0.452	−0.279	−0.381	−0.190	−1.000	0.788	−0.708	−0.116
Gujarat	0.721	−0.602	−0.302	0.611	−0.394	0.890	0.026	0.161	−0.396	0.421
Madhya Pradesh	−0.679	−0.617	−0.474	−0.445	−0.507	−0.830	−0.161	−0.802	−0.108	−0.686
Maharashtra	−0.015	−0.670	−0.695	−0.343	−0.616	−0.098	−0.363	−0.409	−0.721	−0.182
Rajasthan	−0.802	0.068	0.354	−0.557	−0.076	−0.850	0.068	−0.855	0.026	−0.293
Andhra Pradesh	0.458	−0.417	−0.575	−0.017	−0.258	0.221	−0.332	0.834	−0.602	−0.141
Karnataka	−0.033	−0.648	−0.573	0.222	−0.570	0.105	−0.240	0.161	−0.619	0.165
Kerala	2.878	−0.618	−0.653	3.370	−1.025	2.840	−0.417	2.030	−1.684	2.653
Tamil Nadu	1.568	0.098	−0.893	0.081	0.324	1.080	−0.610	1.980	−0.601	−0.241

Punjab and Haryana have remained agriculturally the most developed states of the country throughout. Uttar Pradesh and Assam occupied third and fourth position in 2000. The states of Bihar, Orissa, Gujarat, M.P. and Rajasthan occupy the middle ranks. The bottom five ranks in 2000 are occupied by the states of A.P., Kerala, Tamil Nadu,

Maharashtra and West Bengal. Broadly the northern and eastern states show relatively higher agricultural development as compared to the states of western and southern states, which are less well endowed in terms of irrigation facilities.

Table 4

Ranking of States According to Composite Index of Agricultural Development

States	*1960*		*1970*		*1980*		*1990*		*2000*	
	FAC1	*RWT*	*FAC1*	*RWT*	*FAC1*	*RWT*	*FAC1*	*RWT*	*FAC1*	*RWT*
Haryana	9	4	2	2	2	2	2	2	2	2
Himachal Pradesh	17	17	5	7	9	14	3	11	6	6
J&K	16	15	6	8	7	11	5	10	8	5
Punjab	5	1	1	1	1	1	1	1	1	1
Uttar Pradesh	11	7	3	4	3	4	8	7	3	3
Assam	10	11	12	10	16	15	16	17	5	4
Bihar	13	13	7	11	5	8	15	16	4	8
Orissa	12	14	11	15	15	174	13	15	11	12
West Bengal	8	8	9	12	10	10	17	14	15	15
Gujarat	3	5	8	6	11	6	6	5	10	9
Madhya Pradesh	14	16	10	14	12	16	7	12	9	10
Maharashtra	6	9	16	16	14	13	11	13	16	17
Rajasthan	15	12	4	5	6	9	4	9	7	7
Andhra Pradesh	4	6	14	13	8	7	10	6	13	13
Karnataka	7	10	13	9	13	12	9	8	14	11
Kerala	1	2	15	3	17	5	12	3	17	16
Tamil Nadu	2	3	17	17	4	3	14	4	12	14

Notes: FAC1: Rank According to Factor 1; RWT: Rank Weighted.

Levels of Industrial Development

Industrialization is regarded as the sine qua non of economic development. The following ten indicators have been used to prepare the composite index of industrial development:

IND1 : Per cent of Manufacturing Workers to Total Workers

IND2 : Per cent of Workers in Non-Household Industry to Total Industrial Workers

IND3 : No. of Registered Factories per Lakh of Population
IND4 : Workers in Registered Factories per Lakh of Population
IND5 : Electricity Consumption per Manufacturing Worker
IND6 : Per cent Contribution of Industrial Sector to SDP
IND7 : Per cent Share of Registered Factories in Industrial SDP
IND8 : Value Added per Worker in Registered Factories
IND9 : Fixed Capital per Industrial Worker
IND10 : Per Capita SDP from Industrial Sector

The selected indicators reflect different aspects of industrial development, i.e., its relative contribution to state income and employment, the structure of industrial sector, capital intensity, productivity per workers, etc.

Table 5 shows the trends in inter-state disparity in indicators of industrial development. The values of CV show a mixed trend over time. In case

Table 5

Trends in Indicators of Inter-State Disparity in Industrial Development

Indicators	*IND 1*	*IND 2*	*IND 3*	*IND 4*	*IND 5*	*IND 6*	*IND 7*	*IND 8*	*IND 9*	*IND 10*
1960										
MEAN	9.32	77.10	2.20	650.79	757.59	11.65	47.92	3395.23	8667.06	37.92
SD	3.64	6.66	1.49	545.78	705.16	5.37	17.74	1631.49	4747.89	22.84
CV	39.06	8.64	67.73	83.86	93.08	46.09	37.02	48.05	54.78	60.23
1970										
MEAN	9.13	58.49	11.88	728.04	1868.29	11.42	54.51	7404.29	25551.65	75.79
SD	3.66	14.62	8.12	457.65	865.71	5.76	15.86	2644.82	1190.43	46.76
CV	40.09	25.00	68.35	62.86	46.34	50.44	29.10	35.72	46.60	61.70
1980										
MEAN	10.88	66.56	14.25	842.84	2159.71	14.44	60.69	19990.59	60868.23	233.22
SD	3.95	10.83	9.70	450.77	836.22	6.50	15.55	7912.26	31146.87	144.88
CV	36.31	16.27	68.07	53.48	38.72	45.01	25.62	39.58	51.17	62.12
1990										
MEAN	9.84	73.56	13.76	908.71	3077.88	16.72	64.47	80790.12	191136.47	800.39
SD	3.95	12.37	10.55	527.93	1361.86	6.77	10.40	29400.23	94558.26	465.61
CV	40.14	16.82	76.67	58.10	44.25	40.49	16.13	36.39	49.47	58.17
2000										
MEAN	9.85	73.55	13.48	840.65	3077.88	16.72	64.47	231997.35	620350.53	800.39
SD	3.95	12.37	9.67	524.28	1321.86	6.56	10.40	88518.19	334980.62	464.61
CV	40.1	16.8	71.7	62.4	44.2	40.5	16.1	38.2	54.0	58.0

of two indicators, i.e., IND2 and IND3, showing proportion of workers in non-household sector and number of registered factories per lakh of population respectively, the inter-state disparity has increased moderately over time indicating increasing concentration of industrial activity. In case of IND1, IND9 and IND10, representing per cent of workers in manufacturing, capital per worker and per capita SDP from industrial sector, CV has remained more or less constant. On the other hand, in case of four indicators, i.e., IND4, IND5, IND6, IND7 and IND8, pertaining to the factory sector segment of the industrial sector, disparities have diminished considerably over the years. Table 5 also suggests that the relative importance of the industrial sector within the state economy has increased in all the states. This may be taken as an index of the success of the policy measures to promote industrialization in all states, especially in the backward states. However, it needs to be noted that still the extent of disparities in the industrial sector are fairly sharp, especially in case of the registered sector. Another striking feature of inter-state disparities in India, which deserves notice, is that disparities in the agricultural sector are sharper as compared to those in the industrial sector.

Factor loading for indicators of industrial development are given in Table 6. The first factor explained 50 per cent to 65 per cent of total variance, while second factor explained 15 per cent to 35 per cent of total variation in different years. The explanatory power of both the factors has

Table 6

Principal Component Loadings for Indicators of Industrial Development

Variables	*1960*		*1970*		*1980*		*1990*		*2000*	
	1st	*2nd*	*1st*	*2nd*	*1st*	*2nd*	*1st*	*2nd*	*1st*	*2nd*
IND 1	0.063	-0.242	0.182	-0.249	0.162	-0.137	0.236	-0.050	0.237	-0.069
IND 2	0.137	-0.087	0.172	-0.109	0.142	0.102	0.144	-0.011	0.153	0.029
IND 3	0.159	-0.054	0.154	-0.145	0.155	0.083	0.209	0.146	0.227	0.059
IND 4	0.174	-0.006	0.165	0.017	0.186	0.018	0.232	0.049	0.225	0.033
IND 5	-0.052	0.091	0.031	-0.007	0.038	0.350	0.040	0.424	0.027	0.435
IND 6	0.198	0.046	0.139	0.117	0.174	-0.057	0.148	-0.131	0.130	-0.151
IND 7	0.191	0.161	0.068	0.335	0.097	0.175	-0.099	-1.000	-0.085	-0.086
IND 8	0.105	0.512	-0.091	0.717	0.007	0.412	-0.006	0.229	-0.021	0.332
IND 9	0.018	0.464	-0.121	-0.104	-0.124	0.385	-0.013	0.422	-0.033	0.352
IND 10	0.211	0.117	0.147	0.096	0.176	0.062	0.200	0.019	0.183	0.011
% of Variation Explained	54.8	16.7	58.9	15.6	52.1	19.4	46.7	23.8	65.2	34.8

increased over time. IND1, IND2, IND3, IND4, IND6 and IND10 load more heavily on the first factor, while IND5, IND8 and IND 9 had higher factor loadings on the second factor. The first factor reflects the relative size of the industrial sector in state economy, while the second factor reflects the technology and productivity levels of the sector in terms of use of electricity, capital intensity and productivity per worker.

Table 7 shows the factor scores of indicators for industrial development and Table 8 shows the ranks of states according to composite index of industrial development. In terms of weighted ranks, Maharashtra, West Bengal, Gujarat and Assam were industrially the most developed states in 1960. But in 2000, Gujarat occupied the first rank followed by Punjab, Maharashtra and Haryana. Tamil Nadu occupied the fifth rank in both the years.

Table 7

Statewise Principal Component Scores for Industrial Sector

State	*1960*		*1970*		*1980*		*1990*		*2000*	
	1st	*2nd*	*1st*	*2nd*	*1st*	*2nd*	*1st*	*2nd*	*1st*	*2nd*
Haryana	-0.131	-0.139	0.174	0.448	0.257	0.523	0.995	-0.315	0.893	0.419
Himachal Pradesh	-0.713	2.050	-1.281	2.200	-1.497	1.520	-0.862	1.690	-0.819	1.899
J&K	-1.240	-1.230	-1.051	-2.110	-1.015	-2.050	-0.932	-0.778	-0.919	-1.122
Punjab	0.028	-0.049	0.649	-9.660	0.693	1.110	1.398	2.040	1.229	0.794
Uttar Pradesh	-0.945	-0.211	-0.659	-0.243	-0.691	-1.140	-0.695	-0.450	-0.766	-0.049
Assam	0.760	0.659	-0.366	-0.041	-0.305	-0.523	-1.060	-1.020	-0.980	-0.901
Bihar	-0.192	1.060	-0.737	0.973	-1.031	0.905	-1.065	-0.510	-1.207	-0.846
Orissa	-0.917	1.890	-1.300	0.115	-0.917	0.864	-1.163	1.610	-1.189	0.945
West Bengal	1.940	-0.300	1.406	-0.142	0.979	-0.736	0.600	-1.520	0.498	-1.557
Gujarat	1.360	0.029	1.432	0.138	1.629	0.599	1.516	0.254	1.622	0.746
Madhya Pradesh	-0.609	-0.370	-0.760	0.036	-0.791	0.753	-0.736	0.648	-0.751	0.739
Maharashtra	1.910	0.508	1.796	1.420	1.788	0.863	1.403	0.036	1.187	0.708
Rajasthan	-0.975	-0.602	-0.874	-0.084	-0.857	0.142	-0.751	0.304	-0.753	1.079
Andhra Pradesh	-0.773	-0.863	-0.217	-0.859	-0.117	-1.210	-0.135	-0.264	-0.108	-0.860
Karnataka	-0.310	-0.264	0.182	0.545	0.356	-0.106	-0.020	-0.403	0.112	-0.084
Kerala	0.378	-1.820	0.680	-1.160	0.410	-0.802	0.270	-0.942	0.531	-1.209
Tamil Nadu	0.426	-0.340	0.929	-0.272	1.109	-0.710	1.235	-0.388	1.421	-0.700

Table 8

Ranking of States According to Composite Index of Industrial Sector

States	*1960*		*1970*		*1980*		*1990*		*2000*	
	FAC 1	*RWT*	*FAC 1*	*RWT*	*FAC 1*	*RWT*	*FAC 1*	*RWT*	*FAC 1*	*RWT*
Haryana	8	9	8	8	8	6	5	5	5	4
Himachal Pradesh	12	8	16	12	16	11	13	6	13	6
J&K	17	17	15	17	15	17	14	16	14	16
Punjab	7	7	6	5	6	7	3	1	3	2
Uttar Pradesh	15	14	11	13	11	14	10	14	12	14
Assam	4	4	10	9	10	10	15	17	15	15
Bihar	9	6	12	11	12	9	16	15	17	17
Orissa	14	11	17	16	17	16	17	11	16	13
West Bengal	1	2	3	3	3	3	6	7	7	10
Gujarat	3	3	2	2	2	2	1	2	1	1
Madhya Pradesh	11	13	13	14	13	13	11	12	10	11
Maharashtra	2	1	1	1	1	1	2	3	4	3
Rajasthan	16	16	14	15	14	15	12	13	11	9
Andhra Pradesh	13	15	9	10	9	12	9	10	9	12
Karnataka	10	12	7	7	7	5	8	9	8	7
Kerala	6	10	5	6	5	8	7	8	6	8
Tamil Nadu	5	5	4	4	4	4	4	4	2	5

Notes: FAC1: Rank According to Factor 1; RWT: Rank Weighted.

The process of industrial growth across the country has been quite uneven. The states of Assam, Bihar and West Bengal, which were relatively more industrialized states to begin with, have lost their ranks by several points. On the other hand, the states of Haryana, Punjab, Rajasthan, Karnataka and Andhra Pradesh have improved their ranks substantially. Gujarat, Maharashtra and Tamil Nadu have more or less retained their higher status. These states together with Punjab and Haryana now constitute industrially the most developed group of states in the country. The states of H.P., Karnataka, Kerala, Rajasthan, West Bengal, M.P. and

A.P. are in the middle category in terms of industrial development, while the states of Orissa, U.P., Assam, Bihar, and Jammu & Kashmir are industrially the most backward states. Broadly, the states in central and eastern India are industrially less developed as compared to the states in western and southern India.

Levels of Economic Infrastructure

Infrastructure facilities are a prerequisite of economic development. To prepare composite index of economic infrastructure we have used the following 11 indicators covering various aspects, such as, transport, electricity, communication and credit facilities:

ECOINF1 : Road Length per 100 sq km
ECOINF2 : Road Length per Lakh Population
ECOINF3 : Railway Length per 100 sq km
ECOINF4 : Electricity Consumption per capita (KWH)
ECOINF5 : Per cent of Villages Electrified
ECOINF6 : No. of Telephones per Lakh of Population
ECOINF7 : No. of Post Offices per Lakh of Population
ECOINF8 : No. of Bank Branches per Lakh of Population
ECOINF9 : Credit/Deposit Ratio
ECOINF10 : Loans by Agricultural Credit Societies per ha. of N.S.A.
ECOINF11 : No. of Registered Motor Vehicles per Lakh of Population

Table 9 reveals a mixed picture regarding the trends in disparities in indicators of infrastructure development. Inter-state disparities have gone down in case of indicators of power availability or consumption. In case of railway length, telephone connections and post offices, disparity index has remained almost at the same level throughout the period. However, in case of financial infrastructure we find that disparities have gone up over the planning period. It should be added that these indicators are affected by the demand variables depending upon the level of the economic activity in a region. Still the extent of inter-state disparities in indicators of economic infrastructure remain quite sharp as reflected by high values of CV.

The factor loadings for indicators of economic infrastructure have been given in Table 10. The first principal component explained between 33.1 and 39.2 per cent of total variance, while the second principal component explained between 14.5 and 23.4 per cent of total variance in different years. The first factor loads more heavily on indicators of electricity consumption and telephone facility, while the second factor loads more on road length, number of post offices and bank branches.

Table 9

Trends in Disparities in Indicators of Economic Infrastructure

Indicators	*INFECO 1*	*INFECO 2*	*INFECO 3*	*INFECO 4*	*INFECO 5*	*INFECO 6*	*INFECO 7*	*INFECO 8*	*INFECO 9*	*INFECO 10*	*INFECO 11*
						1960					
MEAN	29.75	207.31	2.07	32.80	14.37	72..00	12.84	1.03	47.94	15.14	206.31
SD	20.74	111.82	1.08	22.09	17.44	35.67	5.55	0.71	6.04	11.38	96.86
CV	69.71	53.94	52.17	67.35	121.36	49.54	43.22	68.93	12.60	75.17	46.95
						1970					
MEAN	53.19	255.59	2.22	83.76	29.62	169.12	15.94	2.37	60.68	73.04	338.48
SD	69.26	132.98	1.18	42.36	28.20	85.37	7.11	1.19	34.36	52.56	157.85
CV	130.21	52.03	53.15	50.57	95.21	50.48	44.60	50.21	56.62	71.96	46.63
						1980					
MEAN	68.88	257.27	2.27	135.58	62.27	259.06	24.78	5.45	56.79	236.54	956.71
SD	59.48	111.60	1.20	74.73	26.21	149.53	10.42	2.09	17.39	326.43	586.95
CV	90.29	43.38	52.86	55.12	42.09	57.72	42.05	38.35	30.62	130.00	60.78
						1990					
MEAN	86.54	285.54	2.33	269.09	91.65	717.65	20.20	7.90	61.56	665.16	2424.44
SD	77.11	157.74	1.21	136.51	11.85	360.57	8.54	2.22	17.62	996.75	1520.65
CV	89.10	55.24	51.93	50.73	12.93	50.28	42.28	28.10	28.62	149.85	62.72
						2000					
MEAN	93.17	292.68	2.33	338.35	91.81	1169.41	19.31	7.75	52.78	1512.69	4165.83
SD	85.51	163.44	1.19	178.14	11.08	875.11	8.51	2.25	19.57	2356.46	2373.16
CV	91.78	55.84	51.07	52.65	12.07	74.83	44.07	29.03	37.08	155.78	56.97

Table 10

Principal Component Loadings for Indicators of Economic Infrastructure

Variables	*1960*		*1970*		*1980*		*1990*		*2000*	
	1st	*2nd*	*1st*	*2nd*	*1st*	*2nd*	*1st*	*2nd*	*1st*	*2nd*
INFECO 1	-0.131	0.317	-0.130	0.371	-0.070	-0.140	-0.057	-0.063	-0.031	-0.139
INFECO 2	0.031	-0.114	-0.139	0.325	-0.008	0.255	-0.067	0.231	-0.166	0.239
INFECO 3	-0.094	0.418	0.073	0.046	0.021	-0.332	0.084	-0.340	0.105	-0.385
INFECO 4	0.134	0.136	0.264	-0.053	0.239	-0.075	0.293	-0.047	0.310	-0.075
INFECO 5	-0.203	0.402	0.033	0.238	0.192	0.023	0.209	0.094	0.392	-0.001
INFECO 6	0.413	-0.202	0.304	-0.092	0.229	-0.057	0.252	0.012	0.318	-0.132
INFECO 7	-0.008	0.011	0.062	-0.039	0.079	0.410	0.016	0.359	-0.037	0.373
INFECO 8	0.266	-0.025	0.186	0.082	0.222	0.184	0.128	0.261	0.150	0.205
INFECO 9	0.006	0.209	0.160	-0.019	0.012	-0.172	0.036	0.008	-0.919	0.992
INFECO 10	0.211	-0.005	0.051	0.211	-0.072	-0.021	-0.032	-0.038	-0.190	-0.101
INFECO 11	0.373	-0.060	0.245	-0.053	0.276	0.037	0.297	-0.118	-0.086	0.033
% of Variation Explained	38.8	14.5	39.2	22.6	38.1	23.4	33.8	22.6	30.7	19.9

Table 11 shows factor scores of different states and Table 12 shows the ranks of states according to composite index of infrastructure development. In terms of weighted ranks Maharashtra occupied the first rank followed by Punjab, while states of Himachal Pradesh, Orissa and Bihar occupied the lowest three ranks in infrastructure in 1960. By 1990, Himachal Pradesh had improved its position from 15th to 1st, while Punjab retained its 2nd position. Bihar continued to occupy the lowest rank. Uttar Pradesh slipped to 16th rank from 13th rank. The states of H.P., J&K, Gujarat, M.P., A.P., Karnataka and Kerala show better performance in economic infrastructure and have improved their positions over the study period. On the other hand, U.P., Assam, Bihar, Orissa, West Bengal, Maharashtra, Rajasthan and Tamil Nadu have slipped down from their earlier positions.

Presently the states of H.P., Maharashtra, Punjab, Gujarat and Jammu and Kashmir constitute the most developed group of states in terms of economic infrastructure. The group of middle ranking states includes Tamil Nadu, A.P., Karnataka, Kerala, Haryana and M.P. The states of Assam, Rajasthan, Orissa, Bihar, U.P. and West Bengal are the least developed states in terms of economic infrastructure. It may be recalled that these states are also lagging behind in industrial development.

Table 11

Statewise Principal Component Scores for Economic Infrastructure

State	1960		1970		1980		1990		2000	
	1st	2nd	1st	2nd	1st	2nd	1st	2nd	1st	2nd
Haryana	0.189	0.387	0.199	0.032	0.618	-0.719	0.765	-0.721	0.708	0.722
Himachal Pradesh	-0.968	-1.080	-0.660	0.269	0.129	3.090	0.079	2.970	0.374	2.768
Jammu & Kashmir	0.013	-1.940	-0.750	-0.685	-0.060	1.090	-0.444	1.010	-0.075	0.991
Punjab	1.523	0.137	0.950	0.441	2.262	-0.241	2.299	-0.683	1.611	-0.719
Uttar Pradesh	-0.974	0.396	-0.743	-0.378	-0.977	-0.727	-1.043	-0.906	-1.233	-0.789
Assam	-0.284	-0.924	-0.965	-0.495	-1.298	-0.287	-0.925	-0.435	-0.357	-0.384
Bihar	-1.636	1.090	-1.190	-0.227	-1.274	-0.841	-1.366	-1.050	-1.080	-0.781
Orissa	-1.161	-0.234	-1.04	-0.256	-1.239	0.676	-1.219	0.839	-1.722	1.171
West Bengal	0.626	1.850	0.999	-0.760	-0.357	-1.470	-0.705	-1.360	-1.382	-1.602
Gujarat	0.300	0.747	1.471	-0.406	1.213	-0.220	1.595	-0.277	1.162	-0.239
Madhya Pradesh	-0.571	-0.721	-0.970	-0.369	-0.761	0.048	-0.320	-0.075	-0.203	0.245
Maharashtra	2.232	-0.915	1.990	-0.448	1.294	-0.353	0.664	-0.168	1.437	-0.400
Rajasthan	-0.061	-0.827	-0.550	-0.532	-0.448	0.200	-0.571	0.180	-0.835	0.266
Andhra Pradesh	-0.584	0.103	-0.017	-0.551	-0.249	0.236	0.018	0.241	0.292	0.221
Karnataka	0.504	-0.298	0.435	0.259	0.386	0.332	0.622	0.511	0.030	0.619
Kerala	-0.245	1.280	-0.341	3.570	0.128	-0.215	-0.025	0.055	0.562	-0.391
Tamil Nadu	1.098	0.951	1.185	0.537	0.632	-0.593	0.578	-0.131	0.712	-0.252

Levels of Social Infrastructure

Social Infrastructure covers availability of educational, medical and health facilities, which play an important role in human resource development, thereby contributing to the process of economic development. Following nine indicators have been selected to prepare the composite index of social infrastructure:

SOCINF1 : No. of Primary Schools per Lakh of Population
SOCINF2 : No. of Secondary Schools per Lakh of Population
SOCINF3 : No. of Teachers per Lakh Students in Class I–IX

SOCINF4 : No. of Technical Training Institutes per Lakh of Population
SOCINF5 : Primary Health Centres per Lakh of Population
SOCINF6 : No. of Hospitals per Lakh of Population
SOCINF7 : No. of Hospital Beds per lakh of Population
SOCINF8 : No. of Doctors per Lakh of Population
SOCINF9 : No. of Nursing Personnel per Lakh of Population

Table 12

Ranking of States According to Composite Index of Economic Infrastructure

States	*1960*		*1970*		*1980*		*1990*		*2000*	
	FAC1	*RWT*	*FAC1*	*RWT*	*FAC1*	*RWT*	*FAC1*	*RWT*	*FAC1*	*RWT*
Haryana	7	7	7	8	5	8	3	7	5	10
Himachal Pradesh	14	17	11	10	7	2	7	1	7	1
Jammu & Kashmir	8	12	13	13	9	5	11	8	10	5
Punjab	2	2	5	5	1	1	1	2	1	3
Uttar Pradesh	15	13	12	12	14	15	15	16	15	16
Assam	11	11	14	16	17	16	14	14	12	12
Bihar	17	15	17	17	16	17	17	17	14	15
Orissa	16	16	16	15	15	13	16	13	17	14
West Bengal	4	4	4	7	11	14	13	15	16	17
Gujarat	6	5	2	4	3	3	2	3	3	4
Madhya Pradesh	12	14	15	14	13	12	10	11	11	11
Maharashtra	1	1	1	1	2	4	4	5	2	2
Rajasthan	9	9	10	11	12	11	12	12	13	13
Andhra Pradesh	13	10	8	9	10	10	8	9	8	7
Karnataka	5	6	6	6	6	6	5	4	9	8
Kerala	10	8	9	2	8	9	9	10	6	9
Tamil Nadu	3	3	3	3	4	7	6	6	4	6

Notes: FAC1: Rank According to Factor 1; RWT: Rank Weighted.

Table 13 shows trends in inter-state disparities in indicators of social infrastructure. For most of the variables, we find that the value of CV has increased indicating widening of disparities in the social infrastructure. The widening trend was particularly marked during the eighties and the nineties. The provision of social services largely falls in the domain of the states. The poorer states are unable to invest in the social sector as compared to the richer states. This also reflects the differences in the priorities given by different states to the social sector. The extent of inter-state disparities is, moreover, sharper in case of health facilities as compared to educational facilities.

Table 13

Trends in Disparities in Indicators of Social Infrastructure

Indicators	*INF-SOC 1*	*INF-SOC 2*	*INF-SOC 3*	*INF-SOC 4*	*INF-SOC 5*	*INF-SOC 6*	*INF-SOC 7*	*INF-SOC 8*	*INF-SOC 9*
1960									
MEAN	90.52	21.94	3849.76	0.13	0.87	3.84	53.16	63.68	72.81
SD	30.85	10.53	1062.23	0.07	0.31	1.76	20.22	44.21	29.16
CV	34.08	47.99	27.59	53.85	35.63	45.83	38.04	69.43	40.05
1970									
MEAN	77.08	7.62	3250.53	0.15	0.87	3.39	72.05	85.80	71.41
SD	27.69	3.85	453.89	0.09	0.31	2.88	23.74	39.86	25.75
CV	35.92	50.52	13.96	60.00	35.63	84.96	32.95	46.45	36.06
1980									
MEAN	78.10	8.48	2974.94	0.17	0.87	4.10	87.06	91.88	86.08
SD	34.83	3.47	549.91	0.13	0.31	2.84	41.70	28.15	25.14
CV	44.60	40.92	18.48	76.47	35.63	69.27	47.90	30.63	29.21
1990									
MEAN	73.67	11.23	2769.18	0.26	2.89	5.28	82.10	52.03	62.87
SD	36.63	4.16	505.12	0.23	1.93	5.41	56.38	28.80	37.76
CV	49.72	37.04	18.24	88.46	66.78	102.46	68.67	55.35	60.06
2000									
MEAN	79.17	19.68	2693.53	0.26	2.60	4.31	99.76	60.53	124.83
SD	34.08	11.11	783.00	0.23	0.86	4.72	55.02	31.55	73.15
CV	43.05	56.45	29.07	87.74	33.28	109.49	55.15	52.12	58.60

Table 14 shows the factor loadings for indicators of social infrastructure. The first principle component explained between 31.7 per cent and 42.9 per cent of total variance in different years, while second principal component explained between 19.9 per cent and 27.6 per cent of total variance. The first principal component is more closely related to the development of medical and health facilities, while the second is related with the educational facilities.

Table 14

Principal Component Loadings for Indicators of Social Infrastructure

Variables	*1960*		*1970*		*1980*		*1990*		*2000*	
	1st	*2nd*	*1st*	*2nd*	*1st*	*2nd*	*1st*	*2nd*	*1st*	*2nd*
INFSOC 1	0.076	−0.106	0.258	−0.219	−0.094	0.359	−0.004	−0.239	−0.041	0.347
INFSOC 2	0.293	0.077	0.109	0.232	0.248	0.135	−0.064	0.078	−0.007	0.100
INFSOC 3	0.068	0.388	0.272	−0.038	0.041	0.250	−0.047	0.180	0.037	0.224
INFSOC 4	0.369	0.013	−0.068	0.281	0.391	−0.032	−0.038	0.028	0.119	−0.566
INFSOC 5	0.059	0.388	0.292	−0.026	−0.041	0.339	0.415	−0.165	−0.020	−0.382
INFSOC 6	0.306	0.253	0.236	0.020	0.141	0.083	−0.071	0.442	0.266	0.509
INFSOC 7	0.175	0.013	0.058	0.252	−0.003	−0.153	−0.070	0.439	0.339	0.043
INFSOC 8	0.224	−0.188	−0.124	0.274	−0.355	−0.130	0.380	−0.020	0.303	−0.068
INFSOC 9	0.111	−0.153	0.130	0.164	−0.198	0.064	0.353	−0.015	0.311	−0.251
% of Variatoin explained	33.5	21.6	39.8	27.6	42.6	25.6	36.4	20.9	32.9	25.9

Table 15

Statewise Factor Scores for Social Infrastructure

State	*1960*		*1970*		*1980*		*1990*		*2000*	
	1st	*2nd*	*1st*	*2nd*	*1st*	*2nd*	*1st*	*2nd*	*1st*	*2nd*
Haryana	1.263	−0.471	−1.325	1.625	2.124	−0.884	−0.971	−0.143	−0.946	−1.372
Himachal Pradesh	−0.013	3.089	2.319	1.520	0.589	2.155	0.243	−0.423	0.836	1.821
Jammu& Kashmir	0.744	1.210	2.281	0.092	0.841	2.141	0.214	0.620	−0.807	1.938
Punjab	2.418	−0.936	−0.613	1.024	2.397	−0.155	3.471	−0.265	1.507	−0.683
Uttar Pradesh	−1.452	−0.238	−1.042	−0.961	−0.271	−0.376	−0.631	−0.827	−1.363	−0.659
Assam	0.363	0.017	0.179	−0.693	−0.134	0.148	−0.656	−0.559	−1.038	0.873
Bihar	−1.273	−0.951	−0.579	−1.358	−0.734	−0.206	−0.622	−0.783	−1.301	−0.599
Orissa	−0.901	0.738	0.882	−1.660	−1.235	1.425	−0.306	−0.687	−0.655	1.236
West Bengal	0.173	−0.582	−0.416	0.497	−0.559	−0.766	−0.081	−0.459	−0.323	−0.784
Gujarat	0.630	0.463	−0.425	0.291	−0.065	−0.797	−0.515	2.035	1.592	−0.674
Madhya Pradesh	−1.071	0.066	0.012	−1.207	−1.049	0.556	−0.135	−0.922	−0.486	0.163
Maharashtra	0.112	−0.311	−0.047	0.639	−0.054	−0.501	−0.288	1.373	1.324	−0.476

Table 15 shows the factor scores for infrastructure development and Table 16 shows the ranks of states according to composite index of social infrastructure. Over time the performance of H.P., Gujarat, M.P. and Karnataka has relatively better as they have gained several positions in relative rankings in terms of social infrastructure. On the other hand, the states of Haryana, Punjab, Assam and Orissa have slipped down. Presently, the states of H.P., Karnataka, Gujarat and Punjab occupy the top positions in terms of ranking of the states according to weighted factor scores for social infrastructure. The middle ranking states include Maharashtra, Orissa, Tamil Nadu, Kerala, Assam and M.P. The states of Rajasthan, West Bengal, A.P., Bihar, Uttar Pradesh and Haryana belong to the least developed category of states in the field of social infrastructure.

Table 16

Ranking of States According to Composite Index of Social Infrastructure

States	*1960*		*1970*		*1980*		*1990*		*2000*	
	FAC 1	*RWT*	*FAC 1*	*RWT*	*FAC 1*	*RWT*	*FAC 1*	*RWT*	*FAC 1*	*RWT*
Haryana	2	4	17	9	2	4	17	15	14	17
Himachal Pradesh	9	1	1	1	4	3	4	8	5	1
J&K	3	3	2	2	3	2	5	4	8	3
Punjab	1	2	14	4	1	1	1	1	2	5
Uttar Pradesh	17	16	16	17	10	9	15	17	17	16
Assam	6	7	4	12	8	5	16	14	15	10
Bihar	16	17	13	16	14	15	14	16	16	15
Orissa	14	11	3	11	17	7	10	12	12	7
West Bengal	7	10	11	7	13	16	7	9	9	13
Gujarat	5	5	12	10	7	10	12	3	1	4
Madhya Pradesh	15	14	6	15	16	14	8	11	11	11
Maharashtra	8	8	8	3	6	6	9	5	3	6
Rajasthan	13	13	7	14	11	8	11	10	13	12
Andhra Pradesh	12	15	9	13	12	13	13	13	10	14
Karnataka	4	6	10	8	9	11	2	6	4	2
Kerala	11	12	15	6	5	12	6	2	7	9
Tamil Nadu	10	9	5	5	15	17	3	7	6	8

Notes: FAC1: Rank According to Factor 1; RWT: Rank Weighted.

Overall Development Rankings

Composite index of overall development has been prepared by adding the factor scores of the four sub-sectors, viz., agriculture, industry, economic infrastructure and social infrastructure. Table 17 shows the ranking of the states in terms of overall index of development according to first principal component of all the four sectors as well as in terms of weighted factor scores. With a few exceptions, the two sets of ranking show very close proximity, with a correlation coefficient of above 0.9 for all the years of study (Table 18).

Table 17

Overall Development Ranking of States

States	*1960*		*1970*		*1980*		*1990*		*2000*	
	FAC1	*RWT*	*FAC*	*RWT*	*FAC1*	*RWT*	*FAC1*	*RWT*	*FAC1*	*RWT*
Haryana	7	6	6	5	2	2	2	3	5	5
Himachal Pradesh	13	10	8	8	10	5	8	7	6	2
J&K	10	11	7	10	8	7	10	10	11	8
Punjab	1	1	1	1	1	1	1	1	1	1
Uttar Pradesh	17	15	14	14	12	13	14	15	15	15
Assam	9	8	13	13	14	14	16	16	13	14
Bihar	16	16	17	17	15	17	17	17	16	17
Orissa	15	12	15	16	17	15	15	13	17	13
West Bengal	6	5	4	7	7	11	11	14	12	16
Gujarat	4	3	3	4	4	3	3	2	2	3
Madhya Pradesh	14	17	16	15	16	16	12	11	10	10
Maharashtra	2	2	2	2	3	4	5	5	3	4
Rajasthan	12	14	12	12	13	12	13	12	14	11
Andhra Pradesh	11	13	11	11	11	10	9	9	9	12
Karnataka	8	9	9	9	6	8	6	8	7	6
Kerala	5	7	10	3	9	9	7	6	8	9
Tamil Nadu	3	4	5	6	5	6	4	4	4	7

Notes: FAC1: Rank According to Factor 1; RWT: Rank Weighted.

The ranking pattern of states underwent some changes during 1960s and 1970s, but has remained more or less unchanged since then. The states of Assam, Kerala, Tamil Nadu and West Bengal, which were in the upper or middle category of development in the 1960s, have slipped several notches in their overall development rank. The slippage of West Bengal from 5th position in 1960 to 16th position in 2000 is the most dramatic feature of the development pattern observed during the study period. Similarly Assam has slipped from 8th position to 14th over this period. On the other hand, the states of H.P., M.P., J&K, Rajasthan and Karnataka have improved their relative position over time.

Development rankings of states for the different points of time selected for the study show a high degree of closeness as shown by the value of correlation coefficient between the weighted scores of states in different years (Table 18). This is especially true for the period after 1980.

Table 18

Correlation Matrix Between Ranks of States According to Composite Index of Development

Ranks	*1960*	*1970*	*1980*	*1990*	*2000*
1960	1.000	0.895	0.795	0.713	0.629
1970	0.895	1.000	0.885	0.853	0.757
1980	0.795	0.885	1.000	0.909	0.904
1990	0.713	0.853	0.909	1.000	0:927
2000	0.629	0.757	0.904	0.927	1.000

Note: All values are significant at 1 per cent level.

To check the stability in the pattern of ranking of states in different years further, we have also calculated Kendall's Index of Rank Concordance. The methodology of calculating the index is as follows. For any variable under study if all the regions had the same ranks in all the years, the variance of sum of the ranks over the years for all the states would be the maximum. The coefficient of concordance (W) can be thought of as an index of degree of actual agreement from the maximum possible or perfect agreement. The degree of actual agreement in ranks obtained by states in various years is reflected by the degree of variance among the total number of states. The Kendall's W is calculated as follows:

$$W = \frac{12\,\Sigma_{j=1}^{K} R_j^2 - 3b^2k(k+1)^2}{b^2k(k^2-1)}$$

where b is the number of sets of ranking, k is the number of individuals or states that are ranked and Rj is the sum of ranks assigned to the Jth state. W ranges between 0 and 1. Zero value occurs when there is total absence of association and value 1 result from the perfect association or agreement among the rankings.

The estimated value of the index for all the five points of study taken together comes to 0.8417. However, when we exclude 1960, the value of index rises to 0.8801. Excluding 1960 and 1970, the value of index further rises to 0.9099. The pattern of regional hierarchy in India, thus, seems to have stabilized since 1980, after going through some changes during the sixties and the seventies.

We can broadly group the states of the country in four categories according to the level of development:

(A)	Most Developed States	: Punjab, Himachal Pradesh, Gujarat, Maharashtra
(B)	Developed States	: Haryana, Karnataka, Tamil Nadu, Jammu & Kashmir
(C)	Less Developed States	: Kerala, Madhya Pradesh, Rajasthan, Andhra Pradesh
(D)	Least Developed States	: Orissa, Assam, Uttar Pradesh, West Bengal, Bihar

Table 19 shows the development ranking of states at various points of time studied.

We may here look at the correspondence of the sectoral development levels among the states. Table 20 shows the correlation matrix of weighted scores of composite sectoral indices for 1990. Economic infrastructure shows a stronger relationship with industrial development than with agricultural development. Levels of development of social and economic infrastructure are also positively correlated. Indices of industrial and agricultural development are also positively associated, though the value of coefficient of correlation is not high. However, there seems to be a disjunction between indices of social infrastructure and that of agricultural development, though it is positively but weakly correlated with industrial development. The development of social infrastructure basically depends upon the priority assigned to this sector by respective state governments rather than the level of economic development. It is well known that some states, notably Kerala, have given higher priority to social sectors even though they rank lower in terms of per capita income levels.

Conclusion

Summing up the findings of the paper we may observe that the regional structure of the Indian economy in terms of the development levels of states has remained remarkably stable for most of the planning period. Some changes in rankings took place during 1960s and 1970s, but after that

Table 19

States Ranked According to Weighted Composite Index

Ranks 1960	*1970*	*1980*	*1990*	*2000*
		(A) Most Developed States		
1 Punjab	Punjab	Punjab	Punjab	Punjab
2 Maharashtra	Maharashtra	Haryana	Gujarat	H.P.
3 Gujarat	Kerala	Gujarat	Haryana	Gujarat
4 Tamil Nadu	Gujarat	Maharashtra	Tamil Nadu	Maharashtra
		(B) Developed States		
5 West Bengal	Haryana	H.P.	Maharashtra	Haryana
6 Haryana	Tamil Nadu	Tamil Nadu	Kerala	Karnataka
7 Kerala	West Bengal	J&K	H.P.	Tamil Nadu
8 Assam	H.P.	Karnataka	Karnataka	J&K
		(C) Less Developed States		
9 Karnataka	Karnataka	Kerala	A.P.	Kerala
10 H.P.	J&K	A.P.	J&K	M.P.
11 J&K	A.P.	West Bengal	M.P.	Rajasthan
12 Orissa	Rajasthan	Rajasthan	Rajasthan	A.P.
		(D) Least Developed States		
13 A.P.	Assam	U.P.	Orissa	Orissa
14 Rajasthan	U.P.	Assam	West Bengal	Assam
15 U.P.	M.P.	Orissa	U.P.	U.P.
16 Bihar	Orissa	M.P.	Assam	West Bengal
17 M.P.	Bihar	Bihar	Bihar	Bihar

the rankings of states show a high degree of concordance. Among the more notable changes that took place over this period was the marked slipping down on the development ladder of the state of West Bengal. On the other hand, the states of Himachal Pradesh, Andhra Pradesh and Madhya Pradesh show a clear improvement in their position. The regional development policy of the central government seems to have made only a limited impact on the development of backward states.

Table 20

Correlation Matrix of Weighted Score of Composite Sectoral Indices

Sector	*Agriculture*	*Industry*	*Economic Infrastructure*	*Social Infrastructure*
Agriculture	1.000	0.381	0.191	–0.070
Industry	0.381	1.000	0.665*	0.329
Economic Infrastructure	0.191	0.665*	1.000	0.720*
Social Infrastructure	–0.070	0.329	0.720	1.000

Note: * Significant at 1 per cent level.

Geographically we find that the most developed states generally belong to the northern and western regions of the country. The states in the central and southern region fall generally in the middle category of development. The least developed set of states, consisting of U.P., Bihar, West Bengal, Assam and Orissa, falls in the north and eastern region.

We also find that there is a close correspondence in levels of agricultural development, industrial development as well as development of economic infrastructure. Social infrastructure, however, shows a disjunction with the development of the agricultural and industrial sectors. This reflects the differences in the priority given to the social sector by different states.

References

Bhattacharya, B.B. and Shaktivel, S. (2004), "Regional Growth and Disparity in India: Comparison of Pre and Post Reform Decades", *Economic and Political Weekly,* Vol. 39, No. 10.

Dasgupta, Dipankar et al. (2000), "Growth and Inter-State Disparities in India", *Economic and Political Weekly,* Vol. 35, No. 27.

Dholakia, Ravindra H. (1994), "Spatial Dimension of Acceleration of Economic Growth in India", *Economic and Political Weekly,* Vol. 29, No. 35.

Drenenowski, J. (1972), "Social Indicators and Welfare Measurement: Remarks on Methodology", *Journal of Development Studies,* Vol. 8, No. 3, April, pp. 77–90.

Kundu, A. (1980), *Measurement of Urban Processes: A Study in Regionalisation*, Popular Prakashan Pvt. Ltd., Bombay (Mumbai).

Kuznets, S. (1957), "Quantitative Aspects of Economic Growth of Nations–II", *Economic Development and Cultural Change*, Vol. V, July.

McGranahan, D. (1972), "Development Indicators and Development Models," *Journal of Development Studies*, Vol. 8, No. 3, pp. 91–102.

Rao, Govind M. et al. (1999), "Convergence of Incomes Across Indian States: A Divergent View," *Economic and Political Weekly*, Vol. 34, No. 13.

Sarkar, P.C. (1999), *Regional Disparities in India: Issues and Measurement*, Himalaya Publishing House, Mumbai.

Shaban, Abdul (2000), Growth and Disparities of Income Across Indian States", *Man and Development*, Vol. 24, No. 3.

Singh, Ajit Kumar (1999), "Inter-State Disparities in Per Capita SDP in India: Trends and Causes," *Arth Vigyan,* Vol. 51, No. 2.

Singh, Nirvikar et al. (2003), "Regional Inequality in India: A Fresh Look," *Economic and Political Weekly*, Vol. 38, No. 11.

Williamson, J.G. (1965), "Regional Inequality and the Process of National Development," *Economic Development and Cultural Change*, Vol. 13, No. 4, Part II, July.

5 Impact of Foreign Aid on Social Sector

The Indian Case

Jyotish Prakash Basu

India has made considerable progress since independence towards reducing poverty and improving social development. The incidence of poverty has declined from over 50 per cent in the 1950s to less than 30 per cent in the late 1990s. The literacy rate has increased from less than 20 per cent in 1951 to 65 per cent in 2001. According to the recent Human Development Reports of UNDP, India has moved from the category of 'low' human development to that of 'medium' human development and its present rank is 115. Nonetheless, India's performance in the social sector is far from satisfactory (Dreze and Sen, 1995). Officially foreign aid is offered in two major forms. One is capital transfer, in cash or kind, either as grants or loans. Second is technical assistance and training, usually as grants in the form of human resources and technical equipment. Mosley, Hudson, and Verschoor (2004) estimate a system of equations using data for some 46 countries in the 1990s. They find that aid is associated with higher levels of pro-poor (and health) spending and such spending is associated with lower levels of headcount poverty (or infant mortality in the case health spending). In trying to assess the effectiveness of foreign assistance, most studies focus on the impact of aid flows on GDP growth and other macro-economic variables, such as investment or public consumption, implicitly referring to the notion that aid is meant to bridge the savings-investment gap that poor countries face.

There has been much less research conducted on the impact of foreign aid on the evolution of Human Development Indicators (HDIs). This is surprising, because the objectives announced by the donor community have evolved from intensive industrialization programmes advocated in the 1950s to more recent poverty-reducing objectives such as the Millennium Developments Goals (MDGs). If the donors' objective is to reach the MDGs, then assessing their effectiveness of assistance should examine whether aid flows have a positive impact on selected HDIs. The objective of the paper is to examine the impact of foreign aid on Infant Mortality Rate (IMR) and enrolment of girl students in the primary school level of education in India. It is difficult to investigate the impact of aid on social sector over time due to the scarcity of data. Because the time series data are extremely scarce across the states.

The remainder of the paper is organized as follows—Section II presents the impact of foreign aid to economic development; Section III presents the nature and trends in foreign aid in India and its states. Section IV introduces social sector achievements of India and its states. Section V discusses the impact of aid on social sectors. Section VI describes the data set and the econometric results. Section VII concludes the paper.

Impact of Foreign Aid on Economic Development

In the 1950s and 1960s, richer countries used foreign aid to fill gaps in resource constrained economies, encouraging national investment and industrial development through central government planning (Waterston, 1965). The belief that foreign aid could help developing countries to accelerate the 'takeoff' into self-sustained growth by generating new investment permeated international assistance programmes (Rostow, 1960).

In the following decade, growing criticism of the failure of foreign aid to address issues of social equity led international aid organizations to fund projects aimed at creating physical and social infrastructure, transforming subsistence agriculture, integrating rural development, expanding small and medium-sized industries, and meeting basic human needs (Adelman and Morris, 1973; Streeten and Burki, 1978). But the focus changed in late 1980s and early 1990s as international financial organizations began to play a more influential role as channels for foreign aid and as globalization made private capital flows a stronger element in financial transfers from richer to poorer countries. The international financial organizations used structural adjustment loans to pressure governments to undertake policy reforms in which private sector development and privatization became major components of the reform package (Gwin and Nelson, 1997; Rondinelli and Montgomery, 1990). Despite the increasing emphasis on poverty reduction as an objective of foreign aid, the empirical literature seeking to evaluate the direct impact of aid on poverty and human well-being is sparse. Streeten and Burki (1978) assessed how foreign aid programme had impacted on nutrition, basic education, health, sanitation, water supply and housing and related infrastructure.

The empirical evidence that foreign aid has a direct impact on poverty is weak. There is strong evidence that foreign aid has an indirect impact on poverty and well-being through its impact on pro-poor expenditures of recipient countries (Mosley and Hudson, 2001; Verschoor 2002; Gomanee and Morrissey, 2002, and Gomanee et al., 2003). These studies have used cross-country data with the headcount index, the Human Development Index (HDI) and infant mortality as measures of poverty and well-being. The literature on the effectiveness of aid focuses almost exclusively on the macroeconomic impacts of aid, measuring the effects of aid on economic growth, savings and investment. It lacks a strong analytical framework and therefore relies heavily on empirical work. However, empirical evidence is ambiguous at best. Even though methodological issues have been refined, this literature presents rather inconclusive results.

With respect to aid's effect on development, Burnside and Dollar (1998) note that aid has no positive systematic impact on development in countries with weak incentive regimes. They evaluate the effect of aid by using infant mortality rate as a proxy for development, after observing significant decreases in infant mortality rates as countries grow economically. They found a relationship that was weaker than that between foreign aid and economic growth. Boone (1996) and Feyzioglu et al., found no significant effect of foreign aid on infant mortality rates. Svensson (1999) concluded that foreign aid has a positive long-term impact in democratic countries; but in countries with authoritarian regimes, aid is often dissipated on unproductive activities. Burnside and Dollar (1998) argued that aid does not effect policy change in recipient countries and Collier (1997) confirmed that although foreign aid disturbs the local political equilibrium, it is unlikely to bring about lasting reforms. Ultimately, the country's development path is determined by domestic political and economic factors. The market for aid continues to become diverse and complex, with more players, more options and more demands.

Foreign aid has not fulfilled its expectations for many reasons. Corruption or rent seeking is often identified as a primary cause (Krueger, 1993). If the donor-recipient relationship is modelled as a non-cooperative game, then aid has the effect of softening budget constraints, allowing governments to fund non-productive activities. Svensson (2000) argues that an increase in government revenues through foreign aid can lead to a lower provision of public goods and consequently lower welfare. He found a positive association between foreign aid and corruption in countries with divided policy processes and no systematic evidence that aid is withheld from corrupt countries. Foreign aid may also have little or no impact on economic policy reforms because of differences in the political objectives of recipients and donors. In an ideal world, the objectives of recipient governments should be to optimize social conditions and the goals of donors should be benevolence (Burnside and Dollar, 2000).

Nature and Trends in Foreign Aid in India and its States

India is home to 17 per cent of the world's total population accommodated in an area, which is 2.4 per cent of the world's total area. As against 2,820 languages in the entire world, as many as 325 languages are effectively used in India alone. The country has witnessed phenomenal educational development—both in quantitative and qualitative terms, since independence. However, the national goals of universal elementary education and total eradication of illiteracy have still remained elusive. The government is committed to achieving these national goals and has been steadily

Table 1

Population, Area, Density, Literacy and Public Expenditure in India and Some Neighbouring Countries

Particulars	*Population (millions) (2000)*	*Area (sq km)*	*Density*	*Percentage to world*		*Percentage of adult illiterate Population 2000*	*Public expr. on education as percentage of GNP (1996)*
World	6055.0 *	135604354	45	100	100	20.6	NA
Afghanistan	21.2 #	652090	33	0.48	0.35	63.7	N.A.
Bangladesh	129.2	143998	897	0.11	2.13	59.2	2.2
China	1277.6	9596961	133	7.08	21.10	15.0	2.3
India	1027 $	3287590	312	2.42	16.96	44.2	3.2
Indonesia	212.1	1904569	111	1.40	3.50	13.0	1.4
Japan	126.9	377801	336	0.28	2.10	NA	3.6
Myanmar	46.4	676578	69	0.50	0.77	15.3	1.2 &
Nepal	22.5 #	140797	160	0.10	0.37	58.6	3.2 @
Pakistan	156.5	796095	197	0.59	2.58	56.7	2.7 @
Sri Lanka	18.8 #	65610	286	0.05	0.31	8.4	3.4
Thailand	62.0 #	513115	121	0.38	1.02	4.4	4.8

Source: Statistical Yearbook, 1999 UNESCO.

* Estimated population for 2000, # Reference year 1999, $ Reference year 2001, & Reference year 1994, @ Reference year 1997

Note: The area figures of India exclude area under illegal occupation of Pakistan and China.

increasing the budgetary allocation for education. The country has also made significant strides in higher and technical education. India spent 4.02 per cent of its GDP on education during 2001–2002 but about 44 per cent of its adult population still remains to be made literate. Table 1 compares the population, area, density, literacy rates and level of public expenditure on education in India and some of its neighbouring countries. Afghanistan with 63.75 per cent adult illiterates is at the top, closely followed by Bangladesh, Nepal and Pakistan.

Table 2 reveals the number of donors' intervention in number of recipient countries, which show growing competition in the aid market. European Union, Germany, UK and Canada intervene in 48, 37 and 33 recipient countries respectively. Similarly, India, Jordan, Afghanistan and Uganda deal with 48, 30, 27 and 26 donors respectively.

Table 2

Top Scattered Donors and Recipients in 2004

Recipients	*No. of Donors*	*Donors*	*No. of Recipients*
India	48	European Union	48
Jordan	30	Germany	37
Afghanistan	27	DFID	34
Uganda	26	CIDA	33
Algeria	21	Netherlands	26
Benin	21	Japan	25
Cambodia	21	USAID	24
Vietnam	21	OECD	21
Mozambique	21	France	20
Uzbekistan	20	Sweden	19
Ethiopia	20		

Source: Complied from OECD Survey (2004).

It is important to discuss the sources of bilateral aid flow in India. India is one of the largest recipients in the world of US development and food aid. The main objective of foreign aid is to promote economic growth in poor countries and thereby lift people out of poverty.

The Government of United Kingdom (UK) has been providing bilateral development assistance to India since 1958. At present UK is the largest external development partner in terms of grants. The assistance is distributed through the Department of International Development (DFID), Government of UK.

The bilateral assistance from UK is provided in the form of grants by way of Financial Cooperation (FC) (routed through GoI budget) and Technical Cooperation (TC), which includes direct payment by DFID for consultancy services, experts, raining, etc. (which is not routed through GoI budget).

The priority areas of UK assistance are mainly in social sectors, viz., health and family welfare, rural development, environment, slum development, education and programmes relating to achieving Millennium Development Goals (MDGs).

The actual disbursements of UK assistance through GoI budget during 2003–2004 and 2004–2005 were £ 158.141 million (Rs 1,279.944 crores) and £ 180.764 million (Rs 1,506.934 crores) respectively.

The following are the fresh commitments made by DFID during 2004–2005:

(Pound in Million)

S. No.	*Name of the Project*	*Total Commitment*
1.	National AIDS Control Programmed (NACP), Phase-II	87.74
2.	Sarva Shiksha Abhiyan	190.00
3.	Orissa Public Enterprises Reform Programme, Phase-II	30.48
4.	Support for Capacity Building for Poverty Reduction (CBPR)	7.00
5.	Reproductive Child Health (RCH), Preparatory Phase	20.00

Source: Aid Accounts and Audit Division, Department of Economic Affairs, Ministry of Finance, Government of India.

IDA assistance has focused on human development and rural development sectors like agriculture, irrigation, poverty alleviation, health and family welfare education, etc.

The United States is the third largest bilateral aid donor to India, after Japan and the United Kingdom. United States bilateral development assistance to India started in 1951 and till March 2005, the total assistance extended to India has been of the order of approximately US$ 14.7 billion. The assistance mainly comprises development assistance, agricultural commodities and technical assistance. US assistance is mainly administered through the US Agency for International Development (USAID). The assistance extended by USAID at present is entirely in the form of grants. Utilization position of US assistance during the last five financial years is as under:

(Amount in US$ Million)

Year	*Grant through Budget*	*Grant as Technical Assistance*	*Grant on Account of Food Aid*	*Total Grant*
2000–01	16.634	10.320	96.600	123.554
2001–02	14.040	14.770	72.00	100.81
2002–03	12.158	12.256	57.602	82.016
2003–04	28.256	17.197	55.319	100.772
2004–05	19.230	17.569	41.700	78.449

Source: http://www.finmin.nic.in/caaa

- Food aid/agriculture commodities are given through US NGOs like: CARE—Cooperative for American Relief Everywhere and CRS—Catholic Relief Services.

Important Projects

Grant through Budget

- Innovations in Family Planning Services (IFPS)—implemented in the states of Uttar Pradesh, Jharkhand and Uttaranchal (Total grant $ 225 million)
- AIDS Prevention & Control (APAC)—implemented in the states of Tamil Nadu and Pondicherry (Total grant $ 25.25 million)
- AVERT (relating to HIV/AIDS)—implemented in the State of Maharashtra (Total grant $ 41.5 million)
- Disaster Management Support Project (DMS) (Total grant $ 16 million).

Grant as Technical Assistance

- Technical Assistance and Support Project (Total grant $ 30.22 million)
- Energy Conservation and Commercialization (ECO) (Total grant $ 55 million)
- Financial Institutions Reforms and Expansion (FIRE) (Total grant $ 72 million)
- State Fiscal Reform Management Project (REFORM) (Total grant $ 20 million).

Initially, the main thrust of US bilateral development assistance to India was on projects, which were designed to strengthen key institutions and transfer of resources for infrastructure programmes in agriculture and social forestry. Since mid-1980, however, the priority has been diversified to include science and technology dimensions focusing specifically on the commercialization of technology. Health and family welfare and disaster management have also been included in the top priority areas. USAID assistance to India is not state focused.

The four priority areas of US development assistance are:

- *Economic Growth:* Financial market reforms, state fiscal reforms, urban financial management;
- *Health:* Reduce fertility, reproductive health, healthier families, prevention of HIV/AIDS and infectious diseases, child nutrition;
- *Environment and Energy:* Better access to clean energy and water, power distribution;
- *Disaster Management:* To increase capacity in the Indian public and private sectors in all phases of the disaster cycle and thereby support the initiatives of Ministry of Home Affairs efforts to usher in a new culture of disaster prevention.

Japan has been extending financial assistance for India's development programme since 1958. Initially Japanese aid to India was channelized through the government-owned Export-Import Bank of Japan (J-Exim). During 1975–76, aid was channelized through the Overseas Economic Cooperation Fund (OECF) of Japan. From 1976–77 onwards, both project and commodity aid was being channelized through the OECF. With effect from 1st October, 1999, J-EXIM and OECF have merged and a new agency Japan Bank for International Cooperation (JBIC) is the channel for both ODA operation as well as the international economic operations function of Government of Japan.

Cumulative Japanese ODA loan to India has reached Yen 2,193.67 billion on commitment basis till 2004–2005 (i.e., about Rs 85,492 crores at current exchange rate of 100 Yen = Rs 38.96). During 2004–2005, disbursements of ODA Yen loans amounted to Yen 70.085 billion (about Rs 2,908 crores), at the exchange rate prevailing at that time.

In Financial Year 2004–2005, loan agreements for eight projects have been signed with JBIC on 31.03.2005 for an amount of Yen 134,466 million (about Rs 5,600 crores). Presently there are 31 ongoing projects with Japanese assistance. The loan amount committed for these projects is Yen 422.781 billion (i.e., about Rs 16,465 crores at current exchange rate of 100 Yen = Rs 38.9).

Trends in Foreign Aid in India and its States

The proportion of aid in Gross Domestic Product (GDP) does not exceed 2 per cent in the 1990s except in 1988-89. It is observed from Table 3 that the proportion of aid in GDP goes on falling since 2001–02.

Table 3

External Aid and Aid as a Percentage of GDP

Year	*Loans*	*Grants*	*External Aid*	*GDP at factor cost 1993–94 prices*	*Aid as % of GDP*
1980–81	3,777	76	3,853	401,128	0.960541274
1981–82	2,767	207	2,974	425,073	0.699644532
1982–83	2,549	423	2,972	438,079	0.67841645
1983–84	1,701	387	2,088	471,742	0.442614819
1984–85	4,409	471	4,880	492,077	0.991714711
1985–86	5,337	313	5,650	513,990	1.099243176
1986–87	5,730	430	6,160	536,257	1.148702954
1987–88	8,203	1,062	9,265	556,778	1.66403845
1988–89	12,856	214	13,070	615,098	2.124864656
1989–90	10,106	720	10,826	656,331	1.649472598
1990–91	7,601	522	8,123	692,871	1.172368305
1991–92	11,806	902	12,708	701,863	1.810609763
1992–93	13,082	1,012	14,094	737,792	1.9102945
1993–94	11,619	2,415	14,034	781,345	1.79613359
1994–95	12,384	1,076	13,460	838,031	1.606145835
1995–96	10,833	1,330	12,163	899,563	1.352100965
1996–97	14,209	2,933	17,142	970,082	1.767067114
1997–98	14,865	2,101	16,966	1,016,595	1.668904529
1998–99	8,321	210	8,531	1,082,747	0.787903361
1999–00	17,704	2,615	20,319	1,148,367	1.769382088
2000–01	17,184	941	18,125	1,198,592	1.512190971
2001–02	21,630	3,465	25,095	1,267,945	1.979186794
2002–03	19,915	1,230	21,145	1,318,362	1.603884214
2003–04	14,809	2,625	17,434	1,430,548	1.218693815

Source: Economic Survey 2003–2004, Government of India.

Aid as per cent of GDP

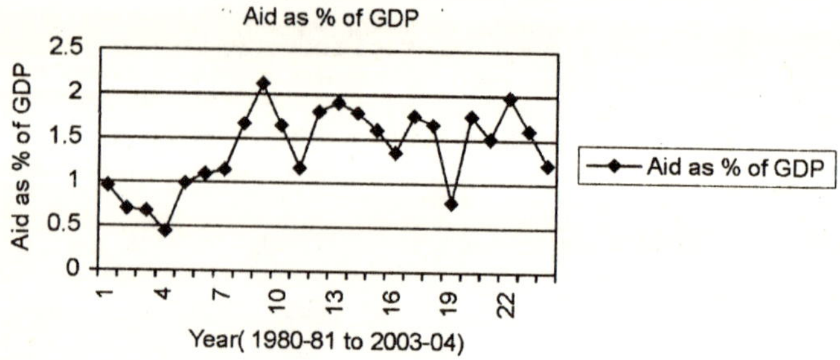

Statewise Foreign Aid in India

It has been observed from the analysis of statewise data on foreign aid that few states like Karnataka, Andhra Pradesh, Gujarat, West Bengal, Orissa, together have received about 28 per cent of total foreign aid and the central government received about 48 per cent of total aid flow in India (see Figure 1).

Sectorwise Foreign Aid in India

It has been observed that social sector contributes 19 per cent, which stands at the second position followed by the energy sector-power contributing 32 per cent foreign aid.

Trends in Social Sector in India

Literacy is an essential tool of self-defence, participation and empowerment in a modern society (Dreze and Sen, 2002). Literacy rates by states and gender in the population for 1991 and 2001 are presented in Table 4. They show that the literacy rate rose quite substantially in the last decade of the twentieth century from 52 per cent to 65 per cent, an increase of 13 percentage points. This is the highest absolute increase in any decade since the records began in 1981. From Table 2 it shows that in some states the literacy increase was particularly impressive. For example, in Rajasthan and Madhya Pradesh, literacy rates rose by 22 and 20 percentage points respectively. The increase in female literacy was especially large in these states as well as in Andhra Pradesh and Uttar Pradesh, but Bihar, starting from the lowest base among all states in 1991, made disappointing progress, as did Gujarat.

Literacy rates for the population above seven years of age as a whole are shown in Table 5. In this it is revealed that between 1992–93 to

Figure 1

Foreign Aid received by Central Government and State Governments

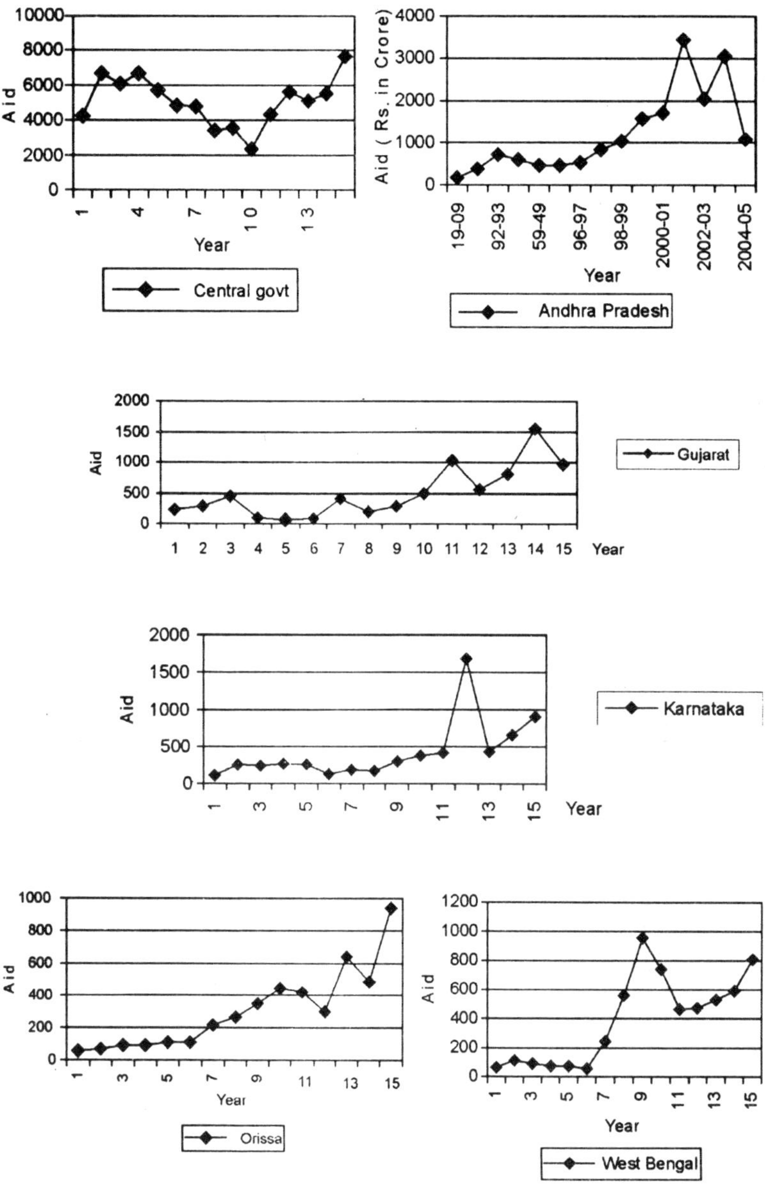

1998–99, literacy rates in the young age group rose quite rapidly for girls. For example, for rural girls aged 6–19, literacy rates rose by about 14–16 percentage points over just a six-year period. Taking rural and urban areas together, female literacy in the youngest age group 6–10 rose by nearly 14 percentage points. Overall, the national literacy rate for males and females aged 6–19 years increased by about 10 percentage points, quite substantial for a six-year period.

Table 4

Increase in Literacy Rates by States and Gender

States	*Male*			*Female*			*Persons*		
	1991	*2001*	*Increase*	*1991*	*2001*	*Increase*	*1991*	*2001*	*Increase*
Andhra Pradesh	55.1	70.9	15.8	32.7	51.2	18.5	44.1	61.1	17
Bihar	52.5	62.2	9.7	22.9	35.2	12.3	38.5	49.2	10.7
Gujarat	73.1	76.5	3.4	48.6	55.6	7	61.3	66.4	5.1
Haryana	69.1	79.3	10.2	40.5	56.3	15.8	55.9	68.6	12.7
Himachal Pradesh	75.4	84.6	9.2	52.1	67.1	15	63.9	75.9	12
Karnataka	67.3	76.3	9	44.3	57.5	13.2	56	67	11
Kerala	93.6	94.2	0.6	86.1	87.9	1.8	89.8	90.9	1.1
Madhya Pradesh	58.4	77	18.6	28.9	51	22.1	44.2	64.4	20.2
Maharashtra	76.6	86.3	9.7	52.3	67.5	15.2	64.9	77.3	12.4
Orissa	63.1	76	12.9	34.7	51	16.3	49.1	63.6	14.5
Punjab	65.7	75.6	9.9	50.4	63.6	13.2	58.5	70	11.5
Rajasthan	55	76.5	21.5	20.4	44.3	23.9	38.6	61	22.4
Tamil Nadu	73.8	82.3	8.5	51.3	64.6	13.3	62.7	73.5	10.8
Uttar Pradesh	55.7	70.9	15.2	25.3	43.9	18.6	41.6	58.1	16.5
West Bengal	67.8	77.6	9.8	46.6	60.2	13.6	57.7	69.2	11.5
India	64.1	75.6	11.5	39.3	54	14.7	52.2	65.2	13

Source: Census 1991; Census 2001.

Table 5

Increase in Age-Specific Literacy Rates, by Area and Gender

	Rural			*Urban*			*Total*		
	1993	*1999*	*Increase*	*1993*	*1999*	*Increase*	*1993*	*1999*	*Increase*
Males (Age Groups)									
6–9	59.8	70	10.2	77.5	83.8	6.3	64	73.1	9.1
10–14	79.1	85	5.9	90.5	93	2.5	82.1	87	4.9
15–19	77	83	6	89.7	91.2	1.5	80.5	85.3	4.8
Females (Age Groups)									
6–9	47.1	63.6	16.5	74.9	80.3	5.4	53.6	67.4	13.8
10–14	57.1	71.4	14.3	84.3	90.7	6.4	64.1	76.1	12
15–19	47.2	61.3	14.1	80.8	86.6	5.8	56.2	68.2	12
Total									
6–9	53.7	66.9	13.2	76.2	82.1	5.9	59	70.4	11.4
10–14	68.5	78.5	10	87.5	91.8	4.3	73.4	81.8	8.4
15–19	61.8	72.2	10.4	85.2	89	3.8	68.1	76.9	8.8

Source: Compiled from National Family Health Survey 1 and 2 (Table 3.8, and Table 2.7).

Educational Institutions

There has been considerable increase in the spread of educational institutions during the period 1950–51 and 2001–2002. This is evident from Table 6. During this period the number of Primary Schools increased by 3 times, while the upper primary schools and higher secondary schools increased by 16 and 18 times respectively. The number of colleges for general education and professional education increased by about 24 and 12 times respectively while the number of universities increased by 10 times during the period.

Growth of Enrolment

Table 7 presents the growth of sex-wise school enrolment in different stages of school education from 1950–51 to 2001–2002. The total enrolment at the primary, upper primary, secondary and senior secondary

Table 6

Growth of Recognised Educational Institutions from 1950–51 to 2001–02

Years	*Primary*	*Upper Primary*	*High/ Hr. Sec/ Inter/ Pre. Jr. Colleges*	*Colleges for General Education*	*Colleges for Professional Education (Engg., Tech., Arch., Medical and Education colleges)*	*Universities/ Deemed Univ./Instt. of National Importance*
1950–51	209,671	13,596	7,416	370	208	27
1955–56	278,135	21,730	10,838	466	218	31
1960–61	330,399	49,663	17,329	967	852	45
1965–66	391,064	75,798	27,614	1,536	770	64
1970–71	408,378	90,621	37,051	2,285	992	82
1975–76	454,270	106,571	43,054	3,667	**3,276	101
1980–81	494,503	118,555	51,573	3,421	** 3,542	110
1985–86	528,872	134,846	65,837	4,067	** 1,533	126
1990–91	560,935	151,456	79,796	4,862	886	184
1991–92	566,744	155,926	82,576	5,058	950	196
1992–93	571,248	158,498	84,608	5,334	989	207
1993–94	570,455	162,804	89,226	5,639	1,125	213
1994–95	586,810	168,772	94,946	6,089	1,230	219
1995–96	593,410	174,145	99,274	6,569	1,354	226
1996–97	603,646	180,293	103,241	6,759	1,770	228
1997–98	619,222	185,961	107,140	7,199	2,075	229
1998–99	626,737	190,166	112,438	7,494	2,113	237
1999–2000	641,695	198,004	116,820	7,782	2,124	244
2000–2001	638,738	206,269	126,047	7,929	2,223	254
2001–2002	664,041	219,626	133,492	8,737	2,409	272

Source: Selected Educational Statistics, 2002–03, Ministry of Human Resource Development

stages increased by 6, 14 and 20 times respectively since 1950–51. The girls' enrolment increased by 9, 37 and 60 times respectively during the same period in the above categories.

Table 7

Enrolment by Stages from 1950–51 to 2001–02

(in million)

Year	*Primary (I–V)*			*Middle/Upper Primary (VI–VIII)*			*High/Hr. Sec./Inter/Pre-Degree (IX–XII)*		
	Boys	*Girls*	*Total*	*Boys*	*Girls*	*Total*	*Boys*	*Girls*	*Total*
1950–51	13.8	5.4	19.2	2.6	0.5	3.1	1.3	0.2	1.5
1955–56	17.1	7.5	24.6	3.8	1.0	4.8	2.2	0.4	2.6
1960–61	23.6	11.4	35.0	5.1	1.6	6.7	2.7	0.7	3.4
1965–66	32.2	18.3	50.5	7.7	2.8	10.5	4.4	1.3	5.7
1970–71	35.7	21.3	57.0	9.4	3.9	13.3	5.7	1.9	7.6
1975–76	40.6	25.0	65.6	11.0	5.0	16.0	6.5	2.4	8.9
1980–81	45.3	28.5	73.8	13.9	6.8	20.7	7.6	3.4	11.0
1985–86	52.2	35.2	87.4	17.7	9.6	27.1	11.5	5.0	16.5
1990–91	57.0	40.4	97.4	21.5	12.5	34.0	12.8	6.3	19.1
1991–92	58.6	42.3	100.9	22.0	13.6	35.6	13.5	6.9	20.4
1992–93	57.9	41.7	99.6	21.2	12.9	34.1	13.6	6.9	20.5
1993–94	55.1	41.9	97.0	20.6	13.5	34.1	13.2	7.5	20.7
1994–95	60.0	45.1	105.1	22.1	14.3	36.4	14.2	7.9	22.1
1995–96	60.9	46.2	107.1	22.7	14.8	37.5	14.6	8.3	22.9
1996–97	61.4	46.8	108.2	22.9	15.2	38.1	15.3	8.7	24.0
1997–98	62.3	48.0	110.3	23.6	15.9	39.5	16.1	9.3	25.4
1998–99	62.7	48.2	110.9	24.0	16.3	40.3	17.3	10.5	27.8
1999–00	64.1	49.5	113.6	25.1	17.0	42.1	17.2	11.0	28.2
2000–01	64.0	49.8	113.8	25.3	17.5	42.8	16.9	10.7	27.6
2001–02	63.6	50.3	113.9	26.1	18.7	44.8	18.4	12.1	30.5

Source: Selected Educational Statistics, 2002–03, Ministry of Human Resource Development.

Enrolment of Girls

The participation of girls at all stages of education has been increasing steadily through the years as may be seen from Table 8. Since 1950–51 girl's participation has increased manifold in primary, middle, secondary/higher secondary stages and Higher Education levels from 28.1 per cent to 44.1 per cent, from 16.1 per cent to 41.8 per cent, from 13.30 per cent to 39.5 per cent, and from 10.0 per cent to 39.9 per cent respectively. However, the girl's participation is still below fifty per cent at all stages of education.

Table 8

Percentage of Girl's Enrolment to Total Enrolment by Stages

Year	*Primary I–V*	*Middle VI–VIII*	*Sec./Hr.Sec/ Intermediate (IX–XII)*	*Hr. Education (Degree & above level)*
1950–51	28.1	16.1	13.3	10.0
1955–56	30.5	20.8	15.4	14.6
1960–61	32.6	23.9	20.5	16.0
1965–66	36.2	26.7	22.0	20.4
1970–71	37.4	29.3	25.0	20.0
1975–76	38.1	31.3	26.9	23.2
1980–81	38.6	32.9	29.6	26.7
1985–86	40.3	35.6	30.3	33.0
1990–91	41.5	36.7	32.9	33.3
1991–92	41.9	38.2	33.8	32.3
1992–93	42.6	38.8	33.9	33.2
1993–94	42.7	39.1	34.3	33.5
1994–95	42.9	39.3	35.9	34.0
1995–96	43.1	39.5	36.1	36.0
1996–97	43.2	39.9	36.4	36.7
1997–98	43.5	40.3	36.6	37.5
1998–99	43.5	40.5	37.8	38.1
1999–2000	43.6	40.4	38.9	38.7
2000–2001	43.7	40.9	38.6	39.4
2001–2002	44.1	41.8	39.5	39.9

Source: Selected Educational Statistics, 2002–03, Ministry of Human Resource Development.

Scheduled Castes Enrolment

The total Scheduled Castes enrolment at the primary (I–V), upper primary (VI–VIII) and secondary/senior secondary (IX–XII) stages of school education from 1980–81 to 2001–2002 (Table 8), increased by 1.9, 3.4 and 3.7 times respectively. The Scheduled Caste girl enrolment increased by 2.5, 4.9 and 6.6 times respectively during the same period in the above stages of school education. Statewise and sex-wise details of enrolments for the year 2001–2002 are given in Table 9.

Impact of Aid on Social Sector in India

Over time, the contribution of external aid to social sector expenditure has increased. The main donors/lenders include international organizations such as World Bank several organs of the United Nations and DFID (the

Table 9

Enrolment of Scheduled Caste Students in Schools

(in '000)

Year	*Primary (I–V)*			*Middle (VI–VIII)*			*High/Hr. Secondary (IX–XII)*		
	Boys	*Girls*	*Total*	*Boys*	*Girls*	*Total*	*Boys*	*Girls*	*Total*
1	*2*	*3*	*4*	*5*	*6*	*7*	*8*	*9*	*10*
1980–81	7,213	3,768	10,981	1,621	602	2,223	906	246	1,152
1981–82	7,413	3,930	11,343	1,777	677	2,454	973	273	1,246
1982–83	7,807	4,244	12,051	1,906	741	2,647	1,091	330	1,421
1983–84	8,001	4,472	12,473	2,297	999	3,296	1,395	382	1,777
1984–85	8,040	4,651	12,691	2,543	1,123	3,666	1,524	429	1,953
1985–86	8,727	5,194	13,921	2,537	1,082	3,619	1,378	432	1,810
1986–87	7,871	4,655	12,526	2,315	1,099	3,414	1,090	376	1,466
1987–88	9,083	5,593	14,676	2,543	1,193	3,736	1,521	507	2,028
1988–89	9,431	5,771	15,202	2,584	1,257	3,841	1,546	557	2,103
1989–90	9,523	5,877	15,400	2,623	1,298	3,921	1,701	630	2,331
1990–91	9,737	6,057	15,794	2,747	1,413	4,160	1,703	635	2,338
1991–92	9,709	6,328	16,037	3,137	1,556	4,693	1,878	703	2,581
1992–93	10,317	7,034	17,351	3,478	1,933	5,411	1,822	709	2,531
1993–94	10,412	7,169	17,581	3,566	2,014	5,580	1,981	827	2,808
1994–95	10,889	7,543	18,432	3,330	1,883	5,213	1,788	803	2,591
1995–96	11,284	7,892	19,176	3,453	1,992	5,445	1,854	887	2,741
1996–97	11,754	8,368	20,122	3,621	2,176	5,797	1,952	975	2,927
1997–98	11,898	8,659	20,557	3,786	2,283	6,069	2,026	1,048	3,074
1998–99	11,123	8,377	19,500	3,748	2,388	6,136	2,068	1,149	3,217
1999–2000	11,810	8,625	20,435	3,881	2,420	6,301	2,385	1,399	3,784
2000–2001	12,059	9,136	21,195	4,066	2,628	6,694	2,418	1,394	3,812
2001–2002	12,251	9,253	21,504	4,551	2,945	7,496	2,693	1,622	4,314

Source: Human Resource Development (HRD), Ministry of Education, Government of India.

British Department for International Development). The share of external aid in sectoral spending on children in the Union budget is shown in Table 10. It is revealed that the share of external aid in sectoral spending on children in the Union budget has increased from 0.5 per cent in 1990–91 to around 29 per cent in 1997–98. On average for the 1990s, out of every Rs

100 spent on children around Rs 20 came from external aid. The share of external aid is the highest for children in the health sector. More than 50 per cent of child health expenditure came from external sources.

Table 10

Share of External Aid in Sectoral Spending on Children (Union Budget) (Per cent)

Year	*Health*	*Child Development*	*Education*	*Total*
1990–91			1.4	0.5
1991–92	32.2	16.5	2.5	13.4
1992–93	53.3	13.4	4.9	17.1
1993–94	50.6	16.7	10.3	22.7
1994–95	53.2	13.1	20.6	26.2
1995–96	40.6	12.4	19.6	21.7
1996–97	33.6	21.6	13.6	19.5
1997–98	56.3	13	26.9	28.6
1998–99	79	9.9	22.5	25.3
1999–00	63.6	15	25	25.9
Average	51.4	14.6	16.4	20.1

Source: HAQ (2001).

Figure 2

Share of External Aid in Health, Child Development and Education

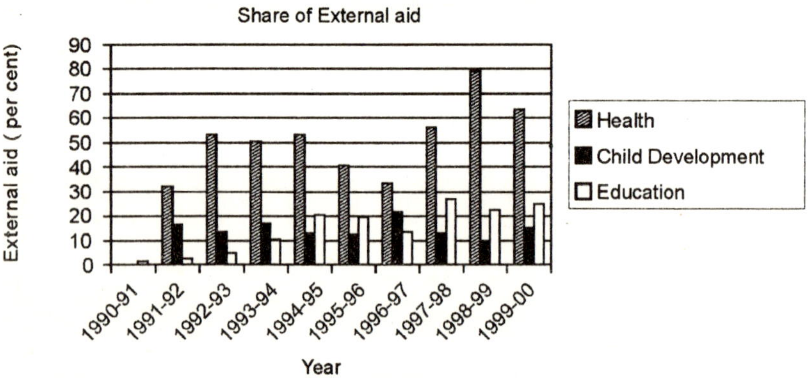

The acceleration in educational progress over the 1990s in terms of faster paced growth in literacy and school attendance is also consistent with an improvement in the supply of education over the period, both in terms of the quantity and the quality of education. There are a number of aspects to this improvement, including centrally- and externally-funded education projects, improved management via decentralization measures.

Centrally- and Externally-Funded Projects

While states per capita spending on elementary education has stagnated or even fallen in some states in the 1990s (owing to the large fiscal deficits of state governments), central government funding has risen. This has been supplemented with relatively small amounts of foreign funds for primary education from the World Bank, the UK Department for International Development (DFID), and other European bilateral aid under the District Primary Education Project (DPEP) which targets low literacy districts for educational investments. The centrally sponsored scheme included a mid-day-meal programme started in 1995; the introduction of Minimum Levels of Learning; and Total Literacy Campaigns. The DPEP has included upgrading of school facilities, provision of books, training of teachers, and the development of locally relevant curricula. The fact that the Government of India has recently brought the various schemes of external funding and centrally sponsored programmes under the banner of the Sarva Shiksha Abhiyan (Education-for-All Campaign) and reiterated its commitment to Education-for-All in its Tenth Five-Year Plan suggests that it wants to build on the momentum of educational progress generated in the past decade.

Data and the Econometric Results

The Infant Mortality Regression

In this section it has been tried to answer the following question: Does aid reduce infant mortality? We examine this question by estimating variants of the following regression:

$$\log \mathrm{HDI}_t = \beta_0 + \beta_1 \log \mathrm{Aid}_t + \beta_2 \log \mathrm{HE}_t + \beta_3 \log \mathrm{GDP}_t + \varepsilon_t \quad \ldots (1)$$

where HDI represents Infant Mortality Rate. Aid represents foreign aid, HE shows government expenditure on health sector and GDP represents gross domestic product and , is the error term. Here t = time.

Description of the data: (1) Aid: Total official development assistance Rs in crore, (2) Infant Mortality Rate (IMR) at 1,000 live births, (3) Government expenditure (Central government plus state governments) on health, Rs in crore, (4) GDP: per capita gross domestic product at 1993–94 prices, (5) EE: Government expenditure (Centre plus states) on education sector, Rs in crore.

Data from 1980–81 to 1996–97 are taken and Ordinary Least Square Method has been applied.

Results

Dependent Variable	β_0	β_1	β_2	β_3
Infant Mortality Rate	11.56 (4.58)	–0.0207 (–0.715)	–0.0010 (–0.0095)	–0.5120 (2.09)

D.W: 1.94, F= 126, R^2 =0.95
Note: Figures in the parentheses represent the t-values.

We do not find any significant impact of total bilateral aid and health expenditure on infant mortality. Our result is in line with Boone (1996) who found "no significant impact of aid on improvement in infant mortality". As expected, higher levels of development (measured by GDP) lead to lower levels of infant mortality. We have significant effect of GDP on infant mortality rate.

The Girls' Enrolment in Primary Education Regression

In this section it has been tried to answer the following question: Does aid increase the girls' enrolment in primary education? We examine this question by estimating variants of the following regression:

$$\log \text{HDI}_t = \beta_0 + \beta_1 \log \text{Aid}_t + \beta_2 \log \text{EE}_t + \beta_3 \log \text{GDP}_t + \varepsilon_t \quad \ldots (2)$$

where HDI represents girls' enrolment in primary education. Aid represents foreign aid, EE shows government expenditure on education sector and GDP represents per capita gross domestic product at 1993–94 prices and , is the error term. Here t= time. The time period ranges from 1980–81 to 1996–97.

Results

Dependent variable	β_0	β_1	β_2	β_3
Girls' enrolment in primary education	5.225 (1.245)	0.000488 (0.0133)	0.306 (1.896)	0.037 (0.088)

D.W.: 2.01, F= 236, R^2 = 0.978.

Note: Figures in the parentheses represent the t-values.

We do not find any significant impact of total bilateral aid and GDP on girls' enrolment in primary education. As expected, higher levels of expenditure on education lead to higher levels of girls' enrolment in primary education, which is significant at a lower level.

Conclusion

The following conclusions are drawn from the above analysis. First, the share of foreign aid in social sector is 19 per cent, which is followed by the energy sector: power contributes 32 per cent foreign aid. Out of the social sector, the share of foreign aid in health sector is found to be highest (51.4%). The share of aid in education and rural development is 16.4 per cent and 14.4 per cent respectively. The share of aid in Gross Domestic Product is about less than two per cent. Second, there are forty-eight donor countries giving aid to India. The priority areas of UK assistance are mainly in social sectors, viz., Health and Family Welfare, Rural Development, Environment, Slum Development, Education and programmes relating to achieving Millennium Development Goals (MDGs). Third, the flow of foreign aid is concentrated in few states like, Karnataka, Gujarat, West Bengal, Orissa, Andhra Pradesh. Fourth, from the regression analysis we do not find any significant impact of total bilateral aid and health expenditure on infant mortality rate. Our result is in line with Boone (1996) who found "no significant impact of aid on improvement in infant mortality". We have significant impact of GDP on infant mortality rate and also we do not find any significant impact of total bilateral aid and GDP on girls' enrolment in primary education. With higher level of expenditure on education, the higher is the level of girls' enrolment in primary education. This study has important policy implication. Although there are forty-eight donor countries giving aid to India, but no impact was found on infant mortality rate and girls' enrolment in primary education. There is a need to monitor the utilization of aid through proper channel. Government and Non-Governmental Organizations (NGOs) may play an active role in monitoring the utilization of aid in the specific sectors.

References

Adelman, I. and Morris, C. (1973), *Economic Growth and Social Equity in Developing Countries*, Stanford University Press, Stanford, CA.

Boone, P. (1996), "Politics and the Effectiveness of Foreign Aid", *European Economic Review*, Vol. 40 (February), pp. 289–329.

Burnside, Craig and Dollar, David (1998), "Aid, the Incentive Regime and Poverty Reduction", Policy Research Working Paper 1937, (Washington: World Bank).

– (2004), "Aid, Policies and Growth: Revisiting the Evidence", Policy Development Working Paper 3251, (Washington: World Bank).

– (2000), "Aid, Policies and Growth", *American Economic Review,* Vol. 90, September, pp. 847–67.

Clemens, Michael A., Radelet, Steven and Bhavnani, Rikhil (2004), "Counting Chickens When They Hatch: The Short-Term Effect of Aid on Growth", Centre for Global Development, Working Paper 44, Washington.

Collier, P. (1997), "The Failure of Conditionality" in C.Gwin and J. Nelson (eds.), *Perspectives on Aid and Development,* Washington, DC. ODC.

Collier, Paul, and Dollar, David (2002), "Aid Allocation and Poverty Reduction", *European Economic Review,* Vol. 46, September, pp. 1475–1500.

Collier, Paul, and Dehn, Jan (2001), "Aid Shocks and Growth", Policy Research Working Paper 2688, (Washington: World Bank).

Dalgaard, Carl-Johan and Hansen, Henrik (2001), "On Aid, Growth and Good Policies", *Journal of Development Studies,* Vol. 37, August, pp. 17–41.

Dreze, Jean and Sen, Amartya (1995), *India: Economic Development and Social Opportunity,* Oxford University Press, Oxford and New Delhi.

Dreze, Jean, and Sen, Amartya (2002), *India Development and Participation,* Oxford University Press, Oxford and New Delhi.

Easterly, William, Levine, Ross and Roodman, David (2003), "New Data, New Doubts: A Comment on Burnside and Dollar's Aid Policies and Growth 2000", *American Economic Review.*

Feyzioglu, Tarhan, Swaroop, Vinaya and Zhu, Min (1996), "Foreign Aid Fungibility: A Panel Data Analysis", *World Bank Economic Review.*

Feyzioglu, T., Swaroop, V. and Zhu, M. (1996), "Foreign Aid's Impact on Public Spending", Working Paper 1610, The World Bank, Washington, DC.

Gomanee, K., Morrissey, O., Mosley, P. and Verschoor, A. (2003), "Aid, pro-poor expenditure and poverty reduction". CREDIT Research Paper 03/03.

Gwin, C. and Nelson, J. (eds.) (1997), *Perspectives on Aid and Development,* Overseas Development Council, New York.

HAQ (2001), *India's Children and the Union Budget,* published by HAQ, Centre for Child Rights, supported by Save the Children, New Delhi.

Krueger, A.O. (1993), *Political Economy of Policy Reform in Developing Countries,* MIT Press, Cambridge, MA.

Mosley, P., Hudson, J., and Verschoor, A. (2004), "Aid, poverty reduction and the new conditionality". *The Economic Journal,* 114, F217–F243.

Mosley, P. and Hudson, J. (2001), "Aid, Poverty Reduction and the New Conditionality", mimeo. OECD, 2001, *International Development Statistics,* CD Rom (Paris, OECD).

Mosley, Paul, Hudson, John and Horrell, Sara (1992), "Aid, The Public Sector and The Market in Less Developed Countries: A Return to The Scene of Crime", *Journal of International Development,* Vol. 4 (March-April), pp. 139–50.

Murshed, S. Mansoob and Sen, Somnath (1995), "Aid Conditionality and Military Expenditure Reduction in Developing Countries: Models of Asymmetric Information", *Economic Journal,* Vol. 105 (March), pp. 498–509.

Reichel, Richard (1995), "Development Aid, Savings and Growth in the 1980s: A Cross-Section Analysis", *Savings and Development,* Vol. 19, No. 3, pp. 279–96.

Rondinelli, D.A. and Montgomery, J.D. (1990), "Managing Economic Reform: An Alternative Perspective on Structural Adjustment Policy", *Policy Sciences,* 23(1), pp. 73–93.

Rostow, W.W. (1960), *The Stages of Economic Growth,* Cambridge University Press, Cambridge, England.

Streeten, P. and Burki, S.J. (1978), "Basic Needs: Some Issues", *World Development,* Vol. 6, No. 3.

Svensson, Jakob (2000), "Foreign Aid and Rent-Seeking", *Journal of International Economics,* Vol. 51 (August), pp. 437–61.

UNDP, United Nations Development Program (2002), *Human Development Report 2002,* Oxford University Press, New York.

Verschoor, A. (2002), "Aid and the poverty-sensitivity of the public sector budget. Research Programme on Risk, Labour Markets and Pro-poor Growth" Occasional Paper 3, Department of Economics, University of Sheffield.

Waterson A. (1995), *Development Planning: Lessons of Experience,* Baltimore, M.D.: Johns Hopkins University Press.

World Bank 2001, *World Development Report 2000–2001: Attacking Poverty,* Oxford University Press, New York.

6 Growth and Development Linkages in Madhya Pradesh

D.C. Sah and Alok R. Chaurasia

Madhya Pradesh is regarded as one of the BIMARU (chronically sick) states of India. Its sickness is reflected in almost all dimensions of development, ranging from economic and social development to human development as well as in the quality of life of the people. This is so when Madhya Pradesh has probably the best potential to get rid of its chronic sickness. An attempt is made in this paper to explore the causes of chronic development sickness that prevails in Madhya Pradesh by first characterizing the patterns of economic growth, human development and then analysing the interrelationships between economic growth and human development on the basis of the empirical evidence collected between 1980 and 2000. The paper attempts to analyze how economic growth and development have influenced the human development processes and how development of human resources has contributed towards economic growth and associated social and economic development. This growth and human development interrelationship is expected to provide a better understanding of the factors that inhibit Madhya Pradesh to come out of the 'BIMARU' syndrome.

Conceptual Foundations

Economic growth has traditionally been regarded as the basis for promoting human welfare and improving the quality of life of the people. However, in recent years, the attention has been shifted to human development as an important intermediate variable in the quest towards universalization of human welfare and lasting improvements in the quality of life. The antecedents of the human development based approach of promoting human welfare and economic growth may be traced in the basic needs approach promoted by International Labour Organization and the World Bank (Streeten, et al., 1981; Fei, Ranis and Stewart, 1985). It also derives its strength from the concept of capabilities first propounded by Sen (1984). In this concept, development is seen as a process of expanding the real freedom that people enjoy; people are regarded as the real wealth of any nation or the society. The process of development, in this approach expands human capabilities by expanding the choices that people have to live full and creative lives. It is important that the development process must benefit all individuals equitably and builds upon the participation of each of them. Participation is critical in this approach of development as participation has intrinsic value for the quality of life. Being able to do something not only for oneself but also for other members of the society is one of the elementary freedoms that have been valued throughout the human history. However, the link between economic growth and human development is not obvious. It is well known that a certain characterization of economic growth can only lead to human development.

Figure 1 depicts a schematic framework linking economic development with human development. The framework identifies five critical links through which economic growth contributes to human

Figure 1

Critical Elements of the Link Between Economic Growth and Human Development

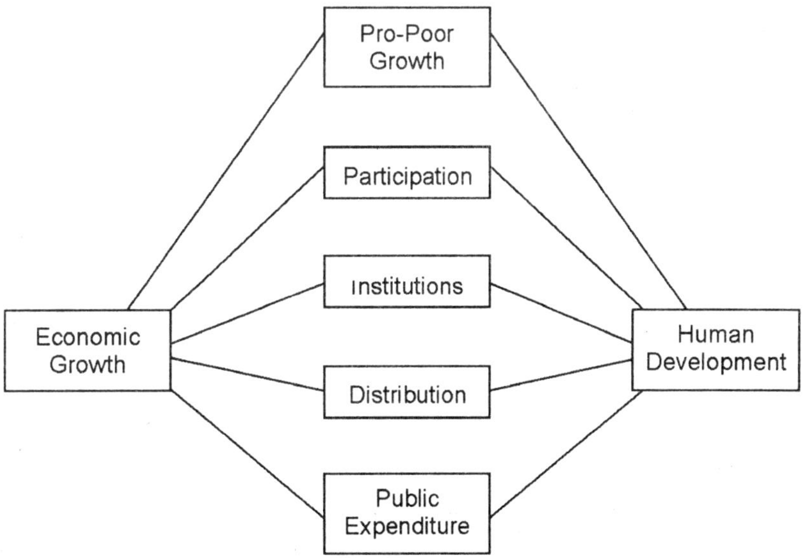

development. The first and perhaps the most important of these links is that economic growth and development processes must be pro-poor. The sector that contributes substantially to a large section of the population must be dynamic and linked with marginalized section of the society. The second important linkage is the growth must be inclusive. They must be able to provide ample opportunity of participation to all. The third important requirement for economic growth and development contributing to human development is that the economic growth and development processes must promote, support and sustain institutions at the level of the society that harness human development and contribute to improvements in the quality of life.

The fourth important requirement for economic growth and development leading to human development is that economic growth must contribute towards reducing inequality that is so pervasive in the society. The inequality that prevails in the society is not limited to the income inequality alone, although the income inequality is perhaps the most important one. The inequality that prevails in the society may also be characterized in terms of possession of knowledge and skills, in terms of health and productivity, in terms of opportunity and entitlements. Controlling inequalities during the process of economic growth and transition is, perhaps, the most challenging task in translating economic gains into human benefits. Finally, economic growth and development processes must be able to contribute to the increase in public spending on human development activities, particularly activities related to the health, education, employment and social security. In this context, it is important that all economic development activities and programmes should be viewed through a human development lens. Meeting the financial and human resources needs to meet the twin goals of *Universalization of Education* and *Health for All* must be the guiding principle for all economic growth and development activities and programmes.

An advantage of the conceptual framework described above is its policy orientation. The framework facilitates formulation of policies and programmes of economic growth and economy driven development that can facilitate and sustain human progress ultimately leading to improved quality of life and well-being of the people of the state. The framework argues that the link between economic growth and economy driven development with human development and human welfare is not automatic. This link can be strengthened if the policies and programmes adopted for economic growth take into consideration aspects of participation of the people in social and economic production, reduction in inequalities, strengthening of human development institutions, and increased public spending in social sector.

Economic Growth in Madhya Pradesh

Estimates of GDP and NDP for Madhya Pradesh are available in two series: 1980–81 series and 1993–94 series (Government of Madhya Pradesh, 1998). According to the 1980–81 series, the economy of the undivided Madhya Pradesh grew at a rate of 4.6 per cent per year during the period 1980–81 through 1997–98. On the other hand, according to the 1993–94 series, the economy of the existing Madhya Pradesh increased at a rate of 3.9 per cent per year during the period 1993–94 through 2003–04 (Table 1). These growth rates suggest that the economy of the state is yet to pick up the momentum. This growth has also been skewed; the growth of the farm sector has been the slowest. The growth of the agriculture sector in the

Table 1

Growth in the Economy of Madhya Pradesh at Factor Cost

Sector (Factors of production)	*Annual growth rate undivided Madhya Pradesh for the period 1980–81 through 1997–98 at 1980–81 prices*	*Annual growth rate existing Madhya Pradesh for the period 1993–94 through 2003–04 at 1993–94 prices*
Agriculture	3.484	-0.0285
Forestry	8.205	1.182
Fishing	14.255	7.189
Mining and Quarrying	4.741	6.292
Manufacturing	7.215	5.274
Construction	0.681	11.240
Electricity, gas, water supply	16.090	0.461
Transport	7.469	9.519
Trade, hotel and restaurants	5.066	2.692
Banking and insurance	11.018	10.106
Real estate	3.834	4.788
Public administration	6.014	5.380
Others	5.882	5.766
Total	4.578	3.881

Source: Sah and Chaurasia (2005).

undivided Madhya Pradesh was less than 3.5 per cent in between 1980–81 and 1997–98 whereas, it was negative in the existing Madhya Pradesh during the period 1993–94 through 2003–04. Growth has also been very poor in the sectors of forestry, electricity, gas and water supply in the existing Madhya Pradesh according to the 1993–94 series. By contrast, growth has been very rapid in the banking and insurance as well as in the transport sector in both the undivided and the existing Madhya Pradesh. Growth has also been very rapid in the construction sector during the nineties. In public administration also, the growth has been quite rapid in the eighties as well as in the nineties.

If the pattern of growth in different sectors of the economy of the existing Madhya Pradesh is any indication, then it is clear that economic growth in the existing Madhya Pradesh has virtually been confined to non-agriculture sector and the agriculture sector has remained grossly neglected. In the context of human development, it would be interesting to examine whether the shift in patterns of production has also resulted in a similar shift in the pattern of employment in the agriculture and non-agriculture sector.

The other feature of economic growth in Madhya Pradesh is that most of the growth in the economy has been subsumed by the rapid growth of the population. The per capita gross domestic product at 1980–81 prices increased at an average annual rate of 2.66 per cent per year in the undivided Madhya Pradesh during 1980–81 through 1997–98, whereas the per capita net domestic product increased by 2.36 per cent per year. As a result of the rapid population growth, a substantial proportion of the economic growth in the state—undivided as well as existing—has been subsumed to meet the basic needs of the growing population. There has been only a marginal increase in the average personal income of the people of the state.

But the matter of concern in the economy is the insignificant transition in its structure. Although, the share of the primary sector in the economy of the state has decreased during the 20 years under reference, yet, the economy of the state continues to depend very heavily on this sector. In the existing Madhya Pradesh, the primary sector of the economy accounted for nearly 45 per cent of the net domestic product in real terms in the year 1993–94. This proportion decreased to around 35 per cent in the year 2003–04. However, the increase in the contribution of other sectors of the economy has comparatively been much slower. For example, the contribution of the industrial sector increased by around 5 per cent while that of trade increased by around 2 per cent. Similarly, the contribution of the financial sector also increased by around 2 per cent whereas the contribution of the community services increased by only around 1 per cent. Obviously, the transition in the economy of the state during the 20 years between 1980–81 and 2003–04 has been too slow to lead to any significant restructuring of the social and economic production system, especially in the vast rural tracts of the state. The grossly unsatisfactory growth of economy reflects this lack of vibrancy.

Any discussion of economic growth and development in the context of human development must also consider growth in rural economy separately from the growth in urban economy. Unfortunately, the available data do not make such a comparison possible but some remarks can definitely be made. The very fact that the growth of the primary sector of the economy of the state has remained stagnant, if not shrinking, during the 20 years under reference makes us believe that the rural economy of the state is not in good shape. On the other hand, more than average growth in such sectors of the economy as transport, banking and insurance, real estate and even public administration indicates that more and more of the economic growth in the state is getting concentrated in the urban areas. A very rapid growth in the construction sector also supports this trend (Sah and Chaurasia, 2005). This trend and transition in the economic growth is fast resulting into the impoverishment of the rural population at the cost of concentration of employment and livelihood opportunities and accumulation of wealth in the urban areas. An implication of this trend is an increase in rural to urban migration which appears to have gained momentum in recent years, especially in those districts where opportunities and options for livelihood are shrinking. This migration trend, which has gained serious proportions in some of the districts of the state, has important implications to human development.

Any discussion on economic growth and development in Madhya Pradesh is incomplete without a discussion on within-state variations in economy driven development. In Madhya Pradesh, these variations have persisted over time. The Human Development Report for the state has been published for the years 1995, 1998 and 2002 and so indexes of economic attainment are available for these years (Government of Madhya Pradesh, 1995, 1998, 2002).

The index of economic attainment estimated in Madhya Pradesh Human Development Report 2002 is based on a minimum per capita income of Rs 4,933 (the per capita income for income-based poverty line) and targeted maximum per capita income of Rs 35,705 (the per capita income of Delhi). Using these figures, it is possible to have crude estimates of per capita income for the districts of the state. These estimates suggest that per capita income at current prices in the districts of the state was highest in district Raisen (more than Rs 17,000 per person per year) and lowest in district Jhabua, the per capita income was lowest (less than Rs 7,000 per person per year). In 18 districts of the state, the per capita income has been estimated to be less than Rs 10,000 a year whereas, in only 5 districts, the per capita income has been estimated to be at least Rs 14,000 a year. If per capita income is taken as a surrogate of the development resulting from economic growth, then, it is clear that inequality in economic growth across the districts of the state is quite substantial and there is a whopping gap of more than Rs 10,000 in the district with highest annual per capita income (district Raisen) and district with lowest annual per capita income (district Jhabua). Moreover, there appears clear regional pattern in per capita income. Majority of the districts with above average annual per capita income are located in the non-tribal region of the western and the central parts of the state. By contrast, all the districts with lowest annual per capita income are either the districts having a large concentration of tribal population or districts located in the northern part.

The income or consumption based measures of economic growth such as the domestic product or per capita domestic product are insufficient to characterize and analyze the economy driven development, especially in the context of the linkages between economic growth and human development. The key issue is that individuals and families differ in their ability to convert commodities and their associated characteristics into the achievement of functioning due to personal, family, social and environmental factors and upon public provision of key services.

Human Development in Madhya Pradesh

Human development is basically the expansion of the capabilities of an average individual. According to Sen, capability is the ability and potential to do and to be. Thus, human development may be defined as the broadening of the set of valuable beings and doings as individual can achieve and freedom to achieve valuable doings and beings. Capability gives the combinations of functioning achievable by an individual. It is a set of functioning that reflects the freedom of an individual to make choices of possible livings desired by the individual. Capabilities include endowments, individual capacity and social opportunity. The three components of capability are complementary and reinforce each other. Endowments may be at the individual, family and society level; capacity at the individual level and social opportunities at the society level.

Human Development Index

Planning Commission of India (Government of India, 2002) has provided estimates of human development index for Madhya Pradesh. According to these estimates, the human development index in Madhya Pradesh increased from 0.245 in 1981 to 0.328 in 1991 and to 0.394 in the year 2001. Madhya Pradesh is one of those states of India, which have improved their rank in terms of the human development index during the twenty years between 1981 and 2001. The rank of Madhya Pradesh improved from 14 to 12 between 1981 and 2001 among the 15 major states of the country (Government of India, 2002). The Planning Commission has also concluded that the momentum in human development in Madhya Pradesh, which started during the 1980s, could be maintained during the 1990s also. It is worth noting that in comparison to Madhya Pradesh, there has been no change in the ranking of Bihar, Orissa and Uttar Pradesh on the scale of human development index. In fact, out of the 15 major states of the country, only 3 states—Madhya Pradesh, Rajasthan and Tamil Nadu were able to improve their rank on the scale of human development index between 1981 and 2001. The record of Madhya Pradesh in the context of human development, as measured by the human development index, appears to be better than most of the other states of the country. Relatively faster improvement in the human development index in Madhya Pradesh as compared to other states of India reflects the progress made by Madhya Pradesh in human development despite slow and sluggish economic growth and associated economy driven development.

The Government of Madhya Pradesh has prepared estimates of human development index for the districts of the state for the years 1995, 1998 and 2002 (Government of Madhya Pradesh, 1995, 1998, 2002). Estimates of the human development index for the districts of the state for the year 2002 suggest that there is a wide gap in the levels of human development across the districts ranging from district Indore (0.694) as the district with best human development index to district Jhabua (0.372), the district with the poorest human development index. District Jhabua is the only district in the state with a human development index of less than 0.400. On the other hand, Bhopal is the only other district where a human development index of more than 0.650 has been estimated for the year 2002. In general, the human development index has been found to vary within a narrow range of 0.400 to 0.600 across the districts of the state around the year 2002. There are only five districts in the state in which the human development index has been estimated to be more than 0.625 but there was no district in which this index is more than 0.700. All the five districts having a human development index of 0.625 and more are located in the western part of the state and they constitute a geographical and cultural continuity. By contrast, there are five districts in the state where human development is relatively poorest, as the human development index in these districts remains less than 0.400. Barring district Jhabua, the remaining four of these districts are located in the northern part of the state. They also constitute a geographical and cultural continuity.

The human development index is the simple unweighted average of the index of economic attainment, index of educational attainment and the index of longevity. An examination of the three dimensions of the human development indices—longevity, educational attainment and economic attainment—across the districts suggests that poor human development situation in the districts of the state is particularly due to poor index of economic attainment. In terms of the index of educational attainment as well as in terms of the index of longevity, the districts of the state appear to be in a relatively better situation than in terms of the index of economic attainment. There are six districts in the state where the index of educational attainment is more than 0.800 while there are only three districts where this index is less than 0.500. Similarly, there are seven districts in the state where the index of longevity is more than 0.600 but there is no district where this index is less than 0.400. By contrast, the index of economic attainment is generally poor to very poor in most of the districts of the state. There is only one district in the state where the index of economic attainment is estimated to be more than 0.600 whereas in 9 districts, this index is less than 0.300 with district Jhabua having the lowest index of economic attainment with an index of just 0.133. The other district with an index of economic attainment less than 0.200 is Barwani, which is adjacent to district Jhabua.

Clearly, in terms of the dimension of health or longevity and the dimension of education, the record of Madhya Pradesh appears to be better than the record in terms of the dimension of income. Madhya Pradesh appears to have faired better in human development when compared with the performance in the economy and economy driven development.

Reasons for the observed marginal progress in human development in the state are not known at present. There is a pressing need to discuss and explore issues related to human development in the state as a critical development challenge as the marginal human development progress has either no or only a marginal impact on economic growth. Primary focus of human development efforts and activities in Madhya Pradesh has been on education, especially the primary education. Remaining components of human development—individual income, health, housing, etc.—have remained grossly neglected.

Health Care Delivery

The neglect of the health sector in the state can be judged from the fact that in the rural areas of the state, the death rate is highest in the country, while the infant mortality rate is second highest and this situation has remained more or less unchanged throughout the period under reference. At the level of the state government, the initiatives taken to address the health needs of the rural masses appear to have fallen short of the expectations. Most children in the state, irrespective of their social background, have a much higher risk of dying before age one, than in the country as a whole. The risk of dying is exceptionally high for children from households with low standard of living, children from Scheduled Caste and Scheduled Tribe households, rural children and for children whose mothers are illiterate. Over half of the children are underweight and stunted. Girls, in Madhya Pradesh, are more likely than boys to be underweight or stunted. Undernutrition is particularly high among children of illiterate mothers, Scheduled Tribe children and households with low standard of living. Full immunization coverage is not as high as it might be, mainly because only a third of children have received all the 3 doses of DPT and only a third have been vaccinated against measles. Drop-out rate for the series of DTP and polio vaccinations is very high (NFHS2, 1999).

On the other hand, the development and growth of the private health care delivery system is limited to largely to metropolitan towns and cities. Moreover, the private health care delivery system is literally confined to addressing the curative health needs of the people and therefore is too costly to the reach of the common people. The preventive and health promotive aspects of health care delivery remain grossly neglected in both rural and urban areas of the state, as the public health care delivery system neither has the organizational efficiency nor the administrative capacity to meet the growing health care needs of the people. The rural health care delivery system in the state is almost totally dependent upon government initiatives and government resources but the government is constrained to invest in the system because of the constrained economy. The public health care delivery infrastructure in the rural areas remains awfully weak. At the same time, there is serious shortage of skilled manpower to meet the health needs of the people. There has been some attempt to improve the availability of skilled health service providers in the rural areas through the training of 'Jan Swasthya Rakshak' and birth attendants—the tradition

'Dai'—but there is gross deficiency in terms of efficiency and effectiveness of the approach. The whole public health care delivery system continues to be highly doctor oriented, bureaucratic and vertical in the approach, management and organization with the result that masses living in rural and remote areas continue to suffer.

Madhya Pradesh also reflects serious gender inequality and negligence with respect to female health indicators. A low male-female ratio in the state is indicative of gender bias in the society. Poor women, illiterate women and women from Scheduled Tribe and Scheduled Caste have much higher fertility than most other women. There is evidence of strong son preference in the fertility performances of women in the state. Given the near exclusive emphases on sterilization, women tend to adopt family planning only after they have achieved their desired family size. Wife beating and other forms of domestic violence are fairly common in the state. Based in a weights-for-height index, more than one third of women are undernourished, and based on blood test, over half of women in the state have some degree of anaemia (NFHS2, 1999).

The only redeeming feature of human development processes in Madhya Pradesh is the progress in primary education, which has resulted in significant increase in the literacy rate during the 20 years under reference.

Elementary Education

If one tries to examine the literacy rate and the levels of school drop outs in Madhya Pradesh in 1980s and 1990s, it shall not be an exaggeration to say that education in state was a luxury afforded by a few. But of late the state of primary education in Madhya Pradesh is witnessing a noticeable change: The literacy rate in 2001 is 64 per cent, which is close to the national literacy rate 65 per cent. The improvement over the years is pleasing; a growth in literacy of 19 per cent has been achieved in last decade ending 2001. By any standard, this is a hopeful achievement. Two important interventions, initiated by state governments, changed the elementary education scenario: Rajiv Ghandi Shiksha Mission (RGSM) and the Education Guarantee School (EGS) by RGSM.

Both RGSM and EGS forced supply as well as demand-side changes in the primary education system. Universal access to primary education was the main objective of RGSM. The mission developed a model called *Padhna-Badhna Andolan* for larger societal involvement in the literacy campaign. Mission also gave expanded mandate of universalizing access to elementary education. It also tried to introduce improved textbooks at the primary level. Mission created infrastructure for training 'Jan Shiksha Kendra' at school clusters level and 'Janpad Shiksha Kendra' at Block Level for ensuring quality of education. Jan Shiksha Abhiyan was introduced as a step to create accountability for quality. The major supply push, however, came through the EGS programme of 1997. This intervention by RGSM committed a school if there is a demand for, even from a hamlet in a village. This supply push came in the wake of reforms in governance initiated by state after Panchayat Raj System became mandatory (Govinda, 2003).

The EGS programme gave right to the community to demand the Gram Panchayat to start a primary school in the locality. The Panchayat forwards the request for an EGS to Zila Panchayat. If the demand comes from the community with 25 children in tribal and 40 children in non-tribal areas and if the students have to travel more than a kilometre to attend a formal primary school, the state government commits resources for a teacher (called Guruji) and for the basic infrastructure. The community, however, has to provide space for EGS and manage the school affairs through parent-Guruji committee. By the early 2002, there were over 27 thousand EGS schools apart from 64 thousand formal primary schools in the state. These changes significantly reformed working of primary education system with positive as well as negative implications.

Despite a significant supply push, the universalization of elementary education has serious equity-based limitations. First, a relatively low literacy, is not only on account of the fact that the literacy rate of adult population is low but even among school-going-age children, the tendency of dropping out from school is high. About 20 per cent of school-going-age girls and boys in Madhya Pradesh drop out after passing class 5. The out-of-school children comprise of never enrolled and drop-out children. The analysis of reasons of children being out of school clearly reflects that it is the economic factors, as shall be discussed in length, that prevent the children from attending the school. Second, not only there are wide variations in literacy rates across districts of Madhya Pradesh but also districts with higher literacy rates tend to grow faster in literacy rates over time (Acharya, 2003). Third, the literacy rate among Scheduled Caste and Scheduled Tribe population is significantly lower than the rest. Lastly, there is a strong feeling among masses that the new education policy is creating a duality through its approach, the well-to-do have primary schools and the marginalized have to contend with EGS.

The state has pinned its hope on community pressures to change perception of the parents who do not send their children to the school

(Noronha, 2003). The village education committee (VEC) is considered to work as a catalyst for bringing the change in the perceptions of the community. It is also hoped that the community participation in the management and running of schools shall be able to solve the problem of inefficiency in primary education. Community participation and pressures could put an end to problems like absenteeism of teachers, irregular opening of schools and improving the quality of primary education. It should, however, not be forgotten that rural communities of Madhya Pradesh is not a homogenous entity; the community, though socially homogenous and vibrant, is economically stratified and politically divided (Sah and Bhatt, 2004). The three elites—political leaders, economically well-off farmers and social leaders—contest fiercely on issues of development and deprivation. Community participation, thus, would be contextual to these stratifications, mediate between them for space in development issues, political economy of primary education and the educational awareness of the parents.

The focus and attention on universalizing primary education, however, was associated with a neglect of higher education despite the fact that higher education system plays a crucial role in the processes of social and economic development by meeting the manpower needs of the social and economic production system (Mehrotra and Chaurasia, 2001). It may be argued here that although universalization of primary education is a laudable goal in itself, it is the higher education system that really contributes to the productivity of the social and economic production system. The higher education system may further be divided into professional education and non-professional education. While the professional education is more closely linked to the productivity of the economic production systems, it is the non-professional education, which contributes to the building up the society and in shaping behavioural patterns. A unique feature of the non-professional higher education system in the state is domination of the government institutions (Chaurasia, 1999). Private sector involvement or the economy driven investment in the non-professional higher education system in the state is extremely limited. One reason is that because of the dominance of the government, the non-professional higher education system in state is not adaptive to the changing needs of the social and economic production system; it is gradually getting out of context.

Economic Growth and Human Development

In view of sluggish economic growth and marginal human development progress in Madhya Pradesh during 1981 through 2001, it may be interesting to explore the relationship between economic growth and human development. This relationship can be examined at the state level as well as at the district level. The human development index estimated for each district of Madhya Pradesh for the year 1995,1998 and 2002 makes it possible to explore the empirical relationship that exists between the three dimensions of human development. Since the dimension of economic attainment used in the estimation of the human development index can also be taken as a proxy for economic growth and economic development at the district level, the relationship between the three dimensions of human development index also provides a basis for examining the relationship between economic growth and human development.

It may be pointed out that although indices of development in income, education and health have been regularly estimated for the districts of Madhya Pradesh since 1995, yet there has been little investigation of the relationship among the three dimensions of human development. This analysis may provide some very useful first hand insight into the linkages between economic growth and human development across the districts of the state.

Interestingly, the index of economic attainment has not been found to be correlated with the index of educational attainment and the index of health attainment in 1995 and in 1998 (Sah and Chaurasia, 2005). In the year 2002, the index of economic attainment has been found to be statistically significantly correlated with the index of educational attainment but not with the index health attainment (longevity). However, except the correlation between the index of economic attainment and the index of health attainment in the year 1998, all but one of the correlation coefficients (Sah and Chaurasia, 2005) are in expected direction. In other words, economic growth and associated economy development do not appear to be the main driver for human development in Madhya Pradesh, although economic growth and associated development do facilitate the human development processes, especially the progress in education. By contrast, the impact of economic growth and economy driven development on achievements in health does not appear to be very specific.

An analysis of the index of health attainment, HDI (H) on the index of income attainment HDI (I), and the index of education attainment HDI (E) after controlling the proportion of urban population (URB) proportion of Scheduled Caste population (SC) and proportion of Scheduled Tribe population (ST), on the basis of the district level data reveals interesting results (Sah and Chaurasia, 2005). The regression coefficients of HDI (H) on HDI (E) and HDI (I) respectively have not been found to be statistically significant although the sign of the regression coefficients is in expected direction. Rather, the regression coefficient of HDI (H) on the proportion of urban population in the district has been found to be statistically significant. This means that higher the urban population in a district, the higher is the index of health attainment. In other words, the health situation is likely to be better in those districts where a substantial proportion of population is urban.

Such a relationship is expected as majority of the health care facilities in the state, both public and private, are located in the urban areas. By contrast, the rural areas of the state are devoid of even the basic minimum health care services. In any case, the district level data from Madhya Pradesh suggest that there is little evidence of any statistically significant relationship between the index of health attainment and the index of economic attainment and the index of education attainment. In other words, variations in human development in terms of longevity across the districts of the state are not related to inter-district variations in economy driven development as well as variations in the levels of education as measured through the literacy rate.

Findings further suggest that the inter-district variations in the index of education attainment are statistically significantly related to the proportion of Scheduled Castes and the proportion of Scheduled Tribes population but not with the proportion of the urban population (Sah and Chaurasia, 2005). The findings also suggests that the regression of the index of education attainment on the index of income attainment is also statistically significant but only marginally. This shows that inter-district variations in economy driven development in the state influence the inter-district variations in educational development only marginally. In fact, the inter-district variations in educational development in the state are affected more by the inter-district variations in the proportion of the Scheduled Caste population.

The above analyzes confirm that the contribution of the economic development and associated economy driven development to human development processes in the state has, at best, been limited. The reason is that most of the economic growth and the economy driven development in the state has been lopsided, primarily confined to the big towns and cities only. In the vast rural and remote tracts of the state dominated by Scheduled Castes and Scheduled Tribes population as well as in small towns, there are little signs of economic progress and economy driven development of any significant magnitude that can have a telling impact on human development.

Missing Growth-Development Linkages in Madhya Pradesh

The preceding analysis suggest that whatever economic growth and economy driven development has been there in Madhya Pradesh, it has been highly unequal and confined largely to the urban areas of selected districts only. There is every evidence to suggest that the rural economy of the state, which caters most of the subsistence needs of nearly two-thirds of the population of the state, failed to grow during the period under reference. Such an economic growth is expected to have resulted in further increase in the rural-urban disparities in economy driven development and standards of living. On the basis of the available evidence, it is difficult to conclude that economic growth in the state has really resulted in any significant increase in the personal income, especially, in the rural areas. Similarly, it is also difficult to conclude that the pattern of economic growth witnessed in the state during the twenty years under reference and transition in this pattern, has really resulted in improved investment climate in the rural areas leading to the growth of rural economy.

The underlying hypothesis is that economic growth and economy driven development can have a telling impact on human development, if these changes:

1. Have a bearing on pro-poor growth.
2. Lead to increased participation of the people in the social and economic production processes.
3. Contribute to expanding and strengthening human development institutions at the level of the society and the community.
4. Result in a reduction in social and economic inequalities, particularly in the fields of education and health.
5. Encourage increased public spending in human development activities, especially health and education related activities.

In the context of human development, it may be useful to explore how the economic growth that has taken place in Madhya Pradesh has manifested in terms of these critical links. However, an exploration of the trends in these issues is still in order to understand the dynamics of economic growth and human development relationship in the state.

Pro-Poor Growth in Primary Sector

As industrial performance of Madhya Pradesh is indifferent, growth and stagnation in agricultural production is responsible for bulk of the variations in the economic performance of the state. But the agricultural sector of the state continues to be less developed and depends upon vagaries of the monsoon. With less than a fourth of its gross cropped area under irrigation, agriculture production has shown relatively high instability over the years.

Being predominantly rain fed, unirrigated paddy, jowar, soybean and pulses are its main crops during *kharif*, whereas wheat, barley and gram are its main crops grown during *rabi* season with residual moisture as well as irrigation. About 98 per cent of gross cropped area of the state is under foodgrains and oilseeds. A dramatic development in Madhya Pradesh agriculture has been introduction of soybean. Soybean created double cropping a reality in the whole of the Malwa and parts of central Madhya Pradesh in late 1970s. The region has black cotton soil, which is uncultivable during rainy season. As a result, farmers kept a large part of the land as kharif fallow and grew wheat during rabi on the fallow land. Introduction of soybean made it possible to use this current fallow during kharif under soybean and after harvesting it, used the land for growing wheat in rabi. Success of soybean—as its prices started increasing and short duration improved varieties started flooding the markets—motivated farmers to replace minor cereals by soybean. As a result, between 1980–81 and 1999–2000 area allocated to other cereals reduced from 27 per cent to less than 11 per cent. A large part of the increase in soybean area has come at the cost of minor cereals, especially jowar. The other important feature of Madhya Pradesh agriculture is substantial increase in yield of major food crops during 1980s and 1990s, especially wheat. This increase in yield was possible because of introduction of improved HYVs that are suitable for even residual moisture conditions and also because of state support for creating rural infrastructure that supports agricultural production, especially input-output markets and extension.

It can be argued that bulk of the growth in agricultural production post-1980 in the state is contributed by improvement in the yield where as pre-1980 it was expansion of area under crops that contributed most to the growth of agricultural production. Although, the impact of yield on agricultural production of Madhya Pradesh cannot be overemphasized, the production has become highly unstable owing to high risk associated with HYVs under uncertain weather and low irrigation. Moreover, the levels of yield of major crops in the state are about half of the yields attained in neighbouring western India for major foodgrains.

The growing instability in the agricultural production and productivity in Madhya Pradesh is attributed to declining capital formation in agricultural sector (Minocha, 2001). This decline in agricultural capital formation has been more constraining in post-reform period because of declining allocation to agriculture and rural development. The other reasons for relatively poor performance of agricultural sector are existence of a large number of small and marginal farmers who are unable to invest in adapting agricultural technology; poor irrigation infrastructure; relatively low yield increasing input use especially chemical fertilizers; and large scale soil erosion during early monsoon and prolonged moisture stress during latter part of the agricultural year. All these reasons are responsible for relatively low performance of agricultural sector of Madhya Pradesh in comparison to other states of the region.

With expansion of area as a source of production gains getting exhausted over the time, the need to increase productivity of land became overriding. But a responding production system requires a very different production relationship than the *zamindari* system, which had a large tilling mass with no land rights. The first agenda of Indian state, therefore, was land reforms. Madhya Pradesh economy also operated with similar concerns. After independence, Madhya Pradesh like other states enacted a series of legislation for abolition of zamindari system, securing rights of tenants and imposing ceiling on size of agricultural holdings.

As the euphoria of land reforms died down and the futility of the 'leftist agenda' became clear, the state has to bear the burden of this failed agenda; a highly unequal distribution of land in Madhya Pradesh, despite a series of land reforms, constrained the agricultural technology transfer. It can be argued that land augmenting seeds-fertilizer technology in Madhya Pradesh has benefited most to middle size farmers though the small farmers retained the traditional productivity advantage on other crops. This was mainly because of inherent advantage of small farmers with respect to higher cropping intensity, better labour absorption and superior farm management including traditional water harvesting (Rao and Storm, 1998). But on the large size of farm the productivity gains were at the cost of labour. Implications of this process of productivity gains are not encouraging for Madhya Pradesh agriculture. For, this made the base of seed-fertilizer technology too narrow to create a rapid acceleration on agricultural productivity. And more importantly, its linkages with labour absorption remained too weak.

It can be argued that despite a slow growth in yield of foodgrains, production has grown faster in Madhya Pradesh only because an improvement in the contribution of change in allocation of land to different crops. But the major beneficiaries of this development in 1990s are medium size farmers. For, this is the ideal size of farm where a farmer could experiment, adapt as well as invest sufficiently on costly inputs—seeds, weedicide and phosphatic fertilizers. The optimality of input use on medium size farms resulted in substantial yield differential across farms. Yield on medium size farms are over 1.5 to 2 times higher than other farms, including large size farms. Both the large and medium size farmers found it extremely difficult to invest on inputs at optimal rates because of the share scale of investment was high enough to take that type of risk. The medium size of farms with their characteristically low consumption elasticity had large investable surplus that found avenues of on-farm investment especially deepening and energizing their wells. This investment further improved the land productivity of these farms.

The gains of new agricultural technology, owing to investment constrains, thus, have remained confined to only a section of middle size irrigated farms. On the other hand, labour-replacing inputs did reduce labour absorption in agriculture. This development strategy, evidently, excluded a large mass from economic opportunity in the state. It can be argued that unequal economic opportunities not only constrained access to market and resources to a large section of rural masses but also resulted in depressing income, wage rate and labour absorption. The final outcome of unequal development is perpetuation of social disparity and lack of public pressures to improve social opportunities.

Participation

Perhaps the most direct link between economic growth and human development is through the participation of the people at large in the social and economic production processes. If economic growth and economy driven development lead to increased participation of the people in the social and economic production system, economic growth has a direct impact on human development.

Estimates of the work (main + marginal) participation rate and main work participation rate in Madhya Pradesh obtained from 1981, 1991 and 2001 population census are given in Table 2. The work participation rate in the state increased marginally from 42.93 per cent in 1981 to 43.70 per cent in 2001 but the main work participation rate decreased rather sharply from 38.41 per cent in 1981 to 32.22 per cent in 2001. The increase in the work participation rate in the state has been due to the increase in the number of marginal workers, particularly, female marginal workers as the average annual rate of decrease in main work participation rate between 1981 and 2001 was more or less same in males and females. If the main work, is taken as surrogate for the gainful employment, then it is clear from Table 3 that despite economic growth and associated economy driven development, opportunities of gainful employment in the state have reduced over time. The shrinking of gainful employment opportunities has been particularly severe in males in the rural areas where the proportion of male main workers decreased drastically from 55 per cent in 1981 to 45 per cent in the year 2001.

Table 2

Work Participation Rate in Madhya Pradesh (including Chhattisgarh)

Population		*All workers*				*Main workers*			
		1981	*1991*	*2001*	*Rate of change*	*1981*	*1991*	*2001*	*Rate of change*
Combined	Person	42.93	42.82	43.70	0.090	38.41	37.67	32.22	–0.806
	Male	54.48	52.26	51.83	–0.243	53.52	51.51	44.85	–0.810
	Female	30.64	32.68	35.01	0.713	22.34	22.82	18.74	–0.806
Rural	Person	46.31	46.82	47.97	0.179	40.87	40.38	33.85	–0.859
	Male	56.38	53.96	53.30	–0.273	55.30	53.07	45.20	–0.913
	Female	35.78	39.27	42.36	0.920	25.78	26.93	21.88	–0.756
Urban	Person	29.62	29.55	30.74	0.189	28.74	28.71	27.28	–0.254
	Male	47.29	46.80	47.49	0.021	46.80	46.47	43.81	–0.319
	Female	9.63	10.24	12.23	1.350	8.31	8.32	9.01	0.421

Source: Census 2001.

The foregoing discussions suggest that the growth in the economy of the state and associated economy driven development has not resulted in increased opportunities of participation of the people in the social and economic production system and the situation in the rural areas has been worse. Main work participation rate decreased in the urban areas also but the decrease was relatively slower. On the other hand, a substantial part of the increase in marginal workers may be attributed to changes in the definition of workers and non-workers in different population census. This is especially the case with female workers where the unpaid work in the family has been included in the work category for the first time in the 2001 population census.

Another important consideration in terms of participation is the transition in the structure of the labour force. It is expected that with the growth and expansion of the economy and associated transition in its structure, there will also be a transition in the structure of the labour force. However, no such transition in the labour force is visible in Madhya Pradesh and there has been very marginal shift in the structure of the labour force between 1981 and 2001. In the year 2001, more than 76 per cent of the main workers in the undivided Madhya Pradesh were either cultivators or agricultural labourers. This proportion decreased just by 3 points over the period of 20 years under reference. Even today, almost 73 per cent of the main workers in the state are either cultivators or agricultural labourers. In the rural areas of the state, this proportion is still more than 85 per cent. Even more alarming is the fact that the proportion of main workers engaged in the household level industrial activity, although an insignificant proportion of the total main workers, decreased from 3.52 per cent in 1981 to 3.47 per cent in the year 2001. This indicates that opportunities for work in the household industrial sector have definitely not improved, if not reduced. This stagnation in the work opportunities in the household industrial sector is not confined to rural areas alone. In the urban areas also, work opportunities in the household industrial sector appear to have decreased marginally despite the fact that most of the industrial and trade activities are confined to the urban areas. This stagnation in the structure of the labour force is again a reflection of a stagnant economy.

The marginal transition in the structure of the labour force in the state can also be analyzed through a different angle. The ratio of the non-agriculture output to the agriculture output in the state increased from 0.99 in 1981 to 2.01 in 2001 but the ratio of non-agriculture labour force to agriculture labour force increased from 0.31 in 1981 to 0.40 only in the year 2001. In other words, in terms of output, the ratio of non-agriculture to agriculture increased at the rate of more than 5 per cent per year but in terms of labour, this increase was less than 1.50 per cent per year. The increase in the output in the state has been confined largely in the non-agriculture sector but this increase in the output has not resulted in the similar increase in the labour force in the non-agriculture sector. This means that an increasing number of workers continue to be engaged in the ailing agriculture sector for their subsistence whereas most of the growth in the economy is confined to the non-agriculture sector. This duality in the economy of the Madhya Pradesh, obviously, obstructs an equitable distribution of the increase in the output of the economy. This duality may also impair the prospects of growth itself. In any case, the very fact that the growth of the agriculture sector in the state has remained almost stagnant but an increasing number of people of the state continue to depend upon agriculture for their subsistence has important implications to human development processes.

Institutions

The second linkage of economic growth and human development is through institutional strengthening that contributes to human capacity building. This linkage requires that the growth and expansion of the economy should result in increased investments in institutional strengthening at the level of the society as well as at the level of the government. The important question is how do institutions affect human development? One common theme across all institutions is decentralization. A shift from a highly centralized institutional structure to a decentralized institutional set-up in which local level institutions and organizations actively participate is widely regarded as essential for capabilities expansion and hence human development.

The logic of decentralized governance, in contrast to economic development, was to bring the decision-making near to the people. The aftermath of 73rd Constitutional Amendment has provided needed support to Panchayat Raj. Madhya Pradesh government has also taken significant steps to decentralise political and administrative powers and initiated the pattern of Gram Swaraj. The decentralized governance has, however, been postulated on two basic but untested propositions. First, that the society with its structural rigidity would get a legal and institutional space through decentralization to operate in accountable as well as meaningful manner. This means, decentralized governance would be able to homogenize the differences existing in the society owing to its stratification based on caste, class and gender lines. This homogenization will result in an informed decision-making at the grass-roots level. Secondly, the policy makers, at the macro level, have faith in the new system's capability to deliver, and the development process, thus, will be more responsible as well as dependable than any of the earlier tested systems of governance. Even if these hitherto untested propositions are true, the fluidity in acceptance of a macro decision to reform the governance will depend on how the micro functionaries at the grass-roots are interpreting and adapting the macro process. It is quite likely that traditional power centres still have overbearing influence in the new governance for the polity to operate democratically.

More anxious, however, will be situations where decisions in the newly created institutions succumb to pressures of traditional power centres. Past experience of working of decentralized governance would not dissipate these anxieties. The new system could also have a level of participation that renders the grass-roots institutions just a formality with no cogent decision-making role. That the informality observed in the forming of various stakeholders' committees—eight committees deal with decisions relating to agriculture, health, infrastructure, education, justice, defence, development and assets—could make them surrogate of the traditional power centres.

Decentralized governance in Madhya Pradesh is a bold step to restructuring decision-making at the grass-roots level. The politics of decentralized governance in last ten years has made its presence felt by breaking the stronghold of traditional power centres. A number of elected leaders belonging to lower social groups have emerged in the village politics. But this is not enough to bring decision-making nearer to the masses. In some guise, the structural constraints still influence functioning of the Panchayat Raj institutions. Absence of formal civil society in the region has made communities totally depend on the state for development. State's development intervention is through Panchayat Raj institutions in the form of schemes. Although execution of these schemes has shifted to grass-roots levels, the resources for them are still controlled by higher echelons. With significantly large proportion of funds allocated in the form of centrally sponsored schemes, the decentralization process has bypassed people. Local priorities do not find space in the panchayats' plans. As a result, Panchayats are reduced to identifying locations and beneficiaries for 'top-pushed' schemes. Since at eight out of ten places in the region, Gram Sabhas have not met in last one year, the decentralization process has not only resulted in mis-identification of purpose and persons but has also adversely affected people's participation. The initial enthusiasm of governance through Gram Sabha has dissipated and community's demands have remained largely unfulfilled. After the inception of Gram Swaraj, a large proportion of Gram Sabha have not met either due to lack of quorum or the traditional power structures do not want the institutions to function. Although the traditional leadership has given a way to new elected leadership—where Dalit and OBCs have challenged the upper caste hegemony—the established social hierarchy still play a dominant role in village politics. Sarpanch owing to defunct Gram Sabha has become important institution in the village. The traditional leadership strives to control the decisions of Gram Panchayat, thereby further reducing panchayat's commitments towards Gram Sabha. In a number of Gram Panchayats where Dalits or women hold the position of Sarpanch, the secretary (Panchayatkarmi) surrogates interests of traditional social structure and obstructs the decision-making process.

Available evidence (Sah, 2003) also reveals that the process to choose those whom the individuals want them to govern is free and fair. People have used their franchise in deciding who would govern them freely. But the process created fissures in an apparently homogenous community with social, political and economic interests. Once the political leaders took over their responsibility, the process of decentralized governance, instead of becoming participatory, became highly centralized. The gains of the decentralized governance have been too few and highly iniquitous. Community's expectations remained unfulfilled and participation slowly dwindled. The role of Sarpanch, and the exclusive group of his people sharing interest, has made people lose their faith on Panchayat. Political decentralization has not only fractured the apparent homogeneity of the society but has also made governance highly centralized.

The community does monitor how the governance is neglecting it. But it, however, does not get enough opportunity to register its protest about this governance. There are provisions of recall for a corrupt Sarpanch but the community by and large is unaware of these. It is only once in five years that they get the freedom to punish bad governance by rejecting those involved in the governance. More seriously, the community has no freedom in the process of planning programmes according to its needs. The blame for this 'unfreedom' to decide what and how the local development should take place falls at various levels.

The economy performs within the rules formulated by the markets. The markets govern the production and distribution of goods and services. Although in theory the markets are equal opportunity providers, in practice they also marginalize. The markets discriminate against the producers with poor technology, poor resources and poor skills. About a third of the population in the Indian rural setting are excluded from markets as producers. Sadly, they are also the individuals whom the market marginalizes as consumers. Markets marginalize the consumers that do not have purchasing power. Thus, a daily wage earner, a tribal and dry land farmer is discriminated against by the market as consumers, owing to lack of purchasing power. The irony of the decentralization process is that there are no procedures that address the issue of market failure. In fact, the economics of non-market procedures—price support, subsidy and food distribution—are so complexly intertwined that even the non-market processes marginalize the poor. The question is how to weave the economic development with the political decentralization?

In the last ten years of its working in Madhya Pradesh, Panchayat Raj has brought considerable transformation in social relations. At one level, the traditional leadership has given way to elected leadership. Dalits and OBCs have challenged and displaced the upper caste hegemony. But

Panchayats also have become the ground where the social hierarchy tries its best to re-establish. At the other level, political decentralization has its own limitations. Political decentralization and breaking down of the upper caste hegemony does not necessarily mean social transformation. At best, it is the first step towards it. Different social and marginalized groups have gained access to decentralized governance but the battle for livelihood is controlled by the institution that do not fall in the purview of decentralized governance. Until the marginalized, because of exclusion, are tackled at the Gram Sabha, decentralization has little to offer for social and economic transformation.

Inequality and Social Poverty

The third link between economic growth and human development can be described in terms of reduction in social and economic inequalities as the result of the growth and expansion of the economy. Some idea about social and economic inequality in Madhya Pradesh can be made on the basis of inter-district disparities in selected indicators of economy driven development. An analysis of the values of Gini coefficient of inequality and of coefficient of variation at two points of time—around 1981 and around 2001—to assess the trend in inter-district disparities in selected indicators of economy driven development indicate following facts (Sah and Chaurasua, 2005). The findings reveal a mixed scenario; the inter-district disparities appear to have decreased over time in some dimensions of economy driven development but increased in other dimensions. For example, there is clear indication that the inter-district disparity in the proportion of net sown area irrigated has decreased over time. In case of per capita deposit in commercial banks also, a similar situation appears to have prevailed. However, in case of the value of agriculture produce per hectare at current prices, inter-district disparities appear to have increased over time. Similarly, inter-district disparities in the number of industries per 100 thousand population and surfaced roads per 100 sq km appear to have increased over time. Clearly, economic growth has only a limited impact in reducing inter-district disparities and in some dimensions of the economy that have direct relevance to human development, inter-district disparities appear to have actually increased. This increase in inter-district disparities indicates that the benefits of economic growth are getting accumulated in selected districts because most of the economic growth in the state is confined to these districts only. There is little industrialization and industrialization driven development in these districts; there are little work opportunities in these districts; there are very few human development institutions; and the population of these districts is growing at a rapid rate because of prevailing high fertility and high mortality. As the result, there is mass exodus of working age population from these districts in search of better livelihood and work opportunities. Poor performance of the economic production system has implications for the social production system, which in turn has a direct impact on human development.

Some idea about the impact of the economic growth and associated economic development on economic inequality can be made on the basis of the trend in the proportion of the population living below the poverty line. According to the estimates prepared by the Government of India, the proportion of population living below the poverty line in Madhya Pradesh decreased from 49.78 per cent in 1983 to 37.43 per cent in 1999–2000 (Government of India, 2002). However, the limited impact of economic growth on household income can be judged from the fact that the total population living below the poverty line in the state increased from 27.797 million in 1983 to 29.854 million in 1999–2000. In proportionate terms, poverty in the state appears to have decreased over time but the actual number of families living below the poverty line has actually gone up during the twenty years under reference. Majority of the households in absolute poverty are from the districts where the social and economic development remains poor. Remote tribal areas are one such group in Madhya Pradesh.

The tribal belt of Madhya Pradesh is characterized by resource poor, technologically stagnant, and remote from state and market where depletion of resources like land, forest and water has a history (Sah, 2003). In this situation, the livelihood struggles and coping with resourcelessness contribute to high incidence of poverty. About half of the population lives in economic poverty. Over a third of poor are chronic poor in tribal Madhya Pradesh.

Chronic poverty is not a product of economic forces alone; it manifests through social processes created by shocks or resourcelessness. The livelihood struggles end up creating a vicious circle of multidimensional 'unfreedom'; livelihood struggles undershocks prompt a social process of mortgage and asset losses, borrowing and inability to service debt, hunger and migration. This livelihood mechanism does provide sustenance but at the cost of freedom, in a multiple way, to the households. Their lack of freedom lies in their access failure to land and natural capital. But their livelihood struggles force 'unfreedom' on their family members;

they live in inhuman conditions at the destination, their access to education severed, their opportunity to develop skills adversely affected and health services and sanitation made poor by any standard; above all, they often have to face abuses. Cumulatively, all these affect adversely their self-esteem. Disturbing it may appear but the process is difficult to break without massive drive to create new opportunities in the economy. Conceptually, as the representative democracy fails to prevent the creation of such opportunities, whereby the macro processes subsume the micro-variability of the economy; most likely the participatory democracy is a feasible option to safeguard their interests. The participatory democracy has capabilities to convert cumulative 'unfreedom' to distributive 'unfreedom'; households may remain economically poor but the political and decision-making power still rests, in the process, with them. The newly acquired political power has a potential to create situations that may prevent further concentration of 'unfreedom'. Prerequisite for this process to succeed is closer interactions between civil society, community and the state. This interaction may not directly influence individuals' access to capital; it nonetheless brings attitudinal changes in the bureaucracy and elected representatives on the one hand, and developing better understanding of community's rights on the other. This engenders confidence and self-esteem among the marginalized, paving a way for improving the quality as well as their access to political, social and economic infrastructure.

Migration in absence of a sustainable livelihood has become unavoidable in remote rural areas. A shock or resourcelessness can push a household into a debt-trap and has to resort to migration as a coping mechanism. A way of reducing the incidence of migration is to intensify investment that conserves the soil-moisture and makes agriculture sustainable. Evidence reveals (Sah and Bhatt, 2004) that civil society initiatives in tribal areas have reduced seasonal migration significantly. Since migration in remote tribal areas is inevitable, the processes that facilitate migrants in the course of migration are as important as reducing migration. How to make the lives of migrants at the place of destination less stressful, provide them with amenities and make their position stronger in the labour market is as important as improving agriculture and increasing borrowing capacity of migrants at the place of origin. Access to institutional consumption credit, at low interest, is a soothing proposition compared to informal credit, at an exorbitant interest rate. Bringing such an institutional change may not reduce migration but shall certainly increase savings from migration. Breaking the debt-trap and strengthening agriculture of the area are two important interventions that may result in pulling people out of chronic poverty.

Public Spending

The fourth link between economic growth and human development may be traced through increased public spending in social sector. The growth of the economy results in increased income of the government through taxation and returns against the public services. Moreover, with the growth and expansion of the economy, the social and economic production system is controlled more and more by the market forces and less by the government initiatives and support so that more and more public resources are available for investments in the social sector. Increased investment in the social sector then results in improvements in human resources.

Information about the structure of public spending in Madhya Pradesh is given in Table 3 for the period 1980–81 through 2000–01. The good sign is that government spending in social sector as proportion to the total government expenditure has shown an increasing trend. However, this trend is significant only in case of education. The expenditure in the education sector accounted for 21 per cent of the total government spending during the period 1980–81. This proportion increased to more than 34 per cent during the year 2000–01. In contrast to education, increase in the proportion of public spending in health, social security and housing had not been so significant. For example, the public expenditure on health increased marginally from around 4 per cent of the total government expenditure in 1980–81 to around 7 per cent in the year 2000–01. Similarly, the proportion of government expenditure on social security and welfare services increased by less than 2 per cent points between 1980–81 and 2000–01 while in case of housing and other community amenities, the government expenditure increased by more than 4 per cent points during this period. On the other hand, the increase in the proportion of government expenditure in general public services has been very sharp—from around 14 per cent in 1980–81 to more than 20 per cent in 2001–02. By contrast, the proportion of public expenditure in economic services decreased very sharply from around 48 per cent in 1980–81 to just around 23 per cent in the year 2000–01.

Table 3

Public Expenditure in Madhya Pradesh

Purpose Classification	*1980–81*			*1991–92*			*2000–01*		
	Total	*Revenue*	*Capital*	*Total*	*Revenue*	*Capital*	*Total*	*Revenue*	*Capital*
Education	20.92	35.72	2.54	31.11	38.53	4.76	34.18	39.83	4.73
Health	4.47	7.62	0.55	5.09	6.20	1.14	7.12	8.11	1.98
Social security	2.78	4.62	0.50	3.82	4.73	0.57	6.27	7.24	1.24
Housing, etc.	8.22	3.29	14.34	9.48	3.92	29.18	7.93	3.98	28.52
General public services	13.96	24.95	0.29	16.62	20.67	2.23	20.23	23.02	5.71
Economic services	47.56	21.87	79.48	32.75	24.73	61.18	23.14	16.63	57.00
Other services	2.09	1.93	2.3	1.13	1.22	0.94	1.13	1.19	0.82

Remarks: Figures in the table are proportion (per cent) to the total public expenditure.
Source: Government of Madhya Pradesh.

One positive feature of public spending in Madhya Pradesh is that despite sluggish growth in the economy during the 20 years under reference, the share of public expenditure on human development services has increased, although, except education, this increase has been marginal in other dimensions of human development. This increase in public spending in human development activities, especially in education, has largely been influenced by the political commitment and initiative rather than derived from the growth and expansion of the economy.

Conclusions

Madhya Pradesh, like rest of India, has experienced the rhetoric of expansion of economic activities and social opportunities. But still the state mirrors the reality of stagnation, economic poverty and social deprivation. The per capita domestic product of the state is lower than national average and much lower in comparison to the better performing states like Punjab, Gujarat and Maharashtra. It has been argued that since a large part of the growth in the economy is because of rapid expansion of employment in service sector, including public administration that remained confined to well-to-do within the economy, the pattern of growth is unsustainable in influencing well-being of the people. As industrial performance of Madhya Pradesh is indifferent, growth and stagnation in agricultural production is responsible for bulk of the variations in the economic performance of the state. The agricultural sector of the state continues to be less developed, depends upon vagaries of the monsoon and high instability over the years. The growing instability in the agricultural production and productivity in Madhya Pradesh is attributed to declining capital formation in agricultural sector. The gains of new agricultural technology, owing to investment constrains, have remained confined to only a section of middle size irrigated farmers. On the other hand, labour-replacing inputs did reduce labour absorption in agriculture. This development strategy, evidently, excluded a large mass from economic opportunity in the state.

Madhya Pradesh with its near feudal agrarian relationship and skewed land holding pattern—where civil society is conspicuous by its absence in influencing public actions, where move to universalize elementary education have begun only a few years back, and where health services and food security has touched only a minuscule of population—social and economic well-being is low in state agenda. This needs to change. With land unable to sustain a large rural mass, making easy access to land may have been the strategy of social transformation in India, but there is hardly any significant association between land capabilities and social opportunities in Madhya Pradesh. As a hypothesis, therefore, one can argue that having a minimum land entitlement neither increases economic security nor improves bargaining power, if large mass of the economy is struggling for survival with non-land based livelihood. Would the ground realities change if the people were given opportunity to decide the contents and pattern of development? Would situation change if community participation were institutionalized in planning, implementing and monitoring the programmes that are made to change their lives?

The first step in this direction is to replicate successful water harvesting interventions in remote rural areas to make the agriculture sustainable in normal years. The cushions provided by good agriculture may be able to sustain a few shocks. The second step is to strengthen the borrowing capacity of the masses through group financing for ground water exploitation, creating production-oriented as well as consumption supporting self-help groups that augment institutional finance. The third task is to facilitate process of seasonal migration by reducing the cost of transaction and strengthening support that is traditionally provided by middlemen, like where to go, type of work, wage negotiations, etc. And lastly, providing support to migrants at the destination in terms of childcare, educational facilities, healthcare, drinking water and sanitation, living conditions and subsidized food supply would make the migrants' life less stressful. If these are the few important tasks that are obvious in remote rural areas to strengthen the coping mechanism of the people, evidences show that the state is ill equipped to undertake them. The role of civil society to facilitate the migration as well as restricting it cannot be overemphasized.

Multidimensional poverty is a complex interaction of resourcelessness, livelihood struggles and dishonest use of public funds. The nexus of political elites, bureaucracy and contractor disconnects the poor from development affairs of the village. Access failure to healthcare and education services to the marginalized section perpetually keeps them poor in terms of human capabilities. Multidimensional poverty is also a manifestation of asymmetrical command of resource and decision of their use in the village. Decentralized governance has failed to influence poverty owing to the nefarious nexus that encourages corruption and wasteful use of resources. The socially, economically and politically well-off vigorously try to reach significantly more to outside agencies. Their increasing trust on these agencies is a product of their desire to economically benefit from the newfound association. On the basis of such bridges, the always non-poor and transitory non-poor receive benefits of government schemes. But chronic poor, owing to their inability to bridge, have failed to get economic benefits. It will now be easy to understand why it was that the always non-poor received significantly more proportion in the resource redistribution than what they actually should. The political 'unfreedom' in the community is evident in the remote rural areas. The blame for this 'unfreedom' to decide what and how the local development should take place may be surmounted by: (a) initiating a new set of reforms that empower the community to exert pressures for participatory process to begin at the grass-roots level; (b) augmenting the quanta of financial allocation in order to meet the demands of the community; (c) introducing second generation of reforms to curb bureaucracy and the elected representatives, at higher echelons, to control the activities and finances of the Gram Panchayat; (d) replacing the existing forest laws that obstruct control of commons to be passed to community.

A corollary to decentralization is to further reforming the education and the health sectors. Poor are excluded from these facilities mainly because such people's participation in the monitoring and management of development is marginal. These systems are under severe bureaucratic control. Management and monitoring of education services has to be made community-centric. The elite healthcare system has no time to hear the voices of the people. There are not only pressing supply side constraints in the health system but also lack of 'the education and information campaign' on planning the family. More than anything else, it is this faith on decentralization that may endow the community with space it deserves in local affairs and preserves equilibrium in unequal power relations.

If community participation is that crucial for PRIs' performance, how to induce participation is worth debating. Indian development experiences have demonstrated that as long as Panchayats do not ask community to pay tax—house tax, electricity charges, business cess, water charges, livestock tax, charge for maintenance of commons, etc.—the community does not ask uncomfortable questions. Therefore, as a strategy, in order to encourage community participation, development should make people stakeholders and create a sense of ownership by asking community to contribute a token cost equitably. This shall force community participation in development. Alternatively, in order to alleviate poverty, it can be argued that a negative income tax should replace the PRIs investment all together. Such a strategy needs to be seen as a safety net for those unfortunate who are trapped in poverty. Negative income tax would transfer resources to most needy at much lower cost compared to the way it is being transferred at present. The strategy is worth pursuing despite the fact that in the era of liberalization and globalization, state egalitarian redistribution may be economically inefficient and self-defeating. But the faith that it can break the nefarious nexus and curb corruption provides strength to a policy shift from PRIs to negative income tax.

These are a few ways to strengthen the linkages between economic growth and human development in the state that have remained, at best, weak. At the one hand, economic growth and economy driven development appears to have contributed only marginally to human development processes. On the other hand, low levels of human development in the state appear to be a major stumbling block in spurring economic growth and economy driven development. The lopsided development puts a break on human progress; the lopsided human development inhibits rapid economic growth.

References

Acharya, S. (2003), "Access to Primary Education" in R., Govinda and R., Diwan (eds.), *Community Participation and Empowerment in Primary Education*, Sage Publications, New Delhi.

Bhalla, G.S and Alagh, Y. (1979), *Performance of Indian Agriculture*, Sterling Publications, New Delhi.

Bhalla, G.S. and Singh, Gurmail (2001), *Indian Agriculture: Four Decades of Development*, Sage Publications, New Delhi.

Bhalla, S. (1987), "Trends in Employment in Indian Agriculture", *Indian Journal of Agricultural Economics*, Vol. 42.

Chaurasia, A.R. (1999), "White paper on higher education in Madhya Pradesh", Bhopal, Government of Madhya Pradesh, Department of Higher Education.

Fei, JCH, Ranis, G. and Stewart, F. (1985), "Towards Viable Balanced Growth Strategies: A Locational Perspective", Paper prepared for United Nations Industrial Development Organization.

Govinda, R. (2003), "Dynamics in Decentralised Management in Primary Education" in R. Govinda and R. Diwan (eds.), *Community Participation and Empowerment in Primary Education*, Sage Publications, New Delhi.

Government of India (1985), SRS Based Abridged Life-tables 1976–80.

— (no date), Ministry of Home Affairs, Office of the Registrar General, Occasional Paper No. 1 of 1985.

— (2002), National Human Development Report 2001, New Delhi, Government of India, Planning Commission.

— (no date), SRS Based Abridged Life Tables 1998–2002, New Delhi, Government of India, Office of the Registrar General, SRS Analytical Studies Report No. 1 of 1985.

Government of Madhya Pradesh, (no date), Districtwise Development Indicators of Madhya Pradesh 1980–81 through 1983–84, Bhopal, Government of Madhya Pradesh, Directorate of Economics and Statistics.

— (1995), Estimates of State Domestic Product of Madhya Pradesh 1980–81 to 1993–94, Bhopal, Government of Madhya Pradesh, Directorate of Economics and Statistics.

— (1995), *Madhya Pradesh Human Development Report 1995*, Bhopal, Government of Madhya Pradesh, Department of Institutional Finance.

— (1998), *Madhya Pradesh Human Development Report 1998*, Bhopal, Government of Madhya Pradesh, Department of Institutional Finance.

— (2002), *Madhya Pradesh Human Development Report 2002*, Bhopal, Government of Madhya Pradesh.

— (2003), *Estimates of State Domestic Product of Madhya Pradesh 1993–94 to 2001–02*, Bhopal, Government of Madhya Pradesh, Directorate of Economics and Statistics.

— (2003), Districtwise Social and Economic Development Indicators of Madhya Pradesh 1998–99 and 1999–2000, Bhopal, Government of Madhya Pradesh, Directorate of Economics and Statistics.

Hulme, D. and McKay, A. (2005), "Identifying and Measuring Chronic Poverty: Beyond Monetary Measures". Paper presented in the International Conference on The Many Dimensions of Poverty Brasilia Brazil.

Kawadia, G. (2001), "Economic Growth and Structural Change in M.P. Economy" in Kawadia G. (ed.), *Development Dynamics of a Backward Economy*, Shree Sunit Prakashan, Indore.

Krishna, Anirudh (2003), "Falling into Poverty in High Growth State: Escaping Poverty and Becoming Poor in Gujarat", *Economic and Political Weekly*, Vol. 38 (49).

Kumar, G. (2003), "Promoting Public-Private Partnership in Health Services", *Economic and Political Weekly*, July 19.

Mehrotra, P.K. and Chaurasia, A.R. (2001), "Population and Social Development: Higher and Technical Education in India" in K. Srinivasan and M. Vlasoff (eds.), *Population and Development Nexus in India: Challenges for the New Millennium*, Tata McGraw Hill Publishing Company, New Delhi.

Minocha (2001), "Madhya Pradesh Economy: An Overview" in Kawadia G. (ed.), *Development Dynamics of a Backward Economy*, Shree Sunit Prakashan, Indore.

National Institute of Rural Development (1999), *India Rural Development Report*, National Institute of Rural Development, Hyderabad.

NCAS (2002), *Land and Life: Promises and Performance of Land Reforms in Madhya Pradesh*, National Centre for Advocacy Studies, Pune.

NFHS2, (1999), "Summary of Findings: Madhya Pradesh", *National Family Health Survey*, 1998–99.

Noronha, A. (2003), "Community in Charge: Shades of Experiences from Madhya Pradesh" in R. Govinda and R. Diwan (eds.), *Community Participation and Empowerment in Primary Education*, Sage Publications, New Delhi.

Rao, C.H.H., Roy, S.K. and Subbarao, K. (1988), *Unstable Agriculture and Droughts*, Vikas, New Delhi.

Rao, J.M. (1994), "Agricultural Development under State Planning" in T.J. Byres (ed.), *The State and Agricultural Planning in India*, Oxford University Press, Delhi.

Rao, J.M. and Storm, S. (1998), "Distribution of Growth in Indian Agriculture", in T.J. Byres (ed.), *The Indian Economy: the Major Debates since Independence*, Oxford University Press, Delhi.

Sah, D.C. (1999), "Pressure on Land, Employment and Migration", *Review of Development and Change*, Vol. 4 (2).

Sah, D.C. (2004) "Livelihood Struggles: Agriculture in Tribal Gujarat", in D.C. Sah and Y.S. Sisodia (eds.), *Tribal Issues in India*, Rawat Publications, Jaipur.

Sah, D.C. (2004a), "Markets and Democratic Decentralisation", *Indian Social Science Review*, Vol. 6 (1), January-June.

Sah, D.C. and Shah, Amita (2003), "Chronic Poverty in Remote Rural Areas of Southwestern Madhya Pradesh", mimeo, MPISSR, Ujjain and GIDR, Ahmedabad.

Sah, D.C. and Bhatt, A. (2004), "An In-depth Study of Chronic Poverty: Evidence from Southwestern Madhya Pradesh", mimeo, MPISSR, Ujjain.

Sah, D.C. and Chaurasia, Alok R. (2005), "Economic Growth and Human Development in Madhya Pradesh", mimeo, MPISSR, Ujjain.

Sen, A.K. (1984), "Rights and Capabilities" in A.K. Sen, (ed.), *Resources, Values and Development*, Harvard University Press, Cambridge, MA.

— (1985), *Commodities and Capabilities*, Elsevier Science Publishers, Oxford.

— (1990), *Development as Capability Expansion*, Oxford University Press, Oxford.

— (1999), *Development as Freedom*, Oxford University Press, Oxford.

Streeten, P., Burki S.J., Haq M., Hicks N. and Stewart F. (1981), *First Thing First: Meeting Basic Needs in the Developing Countries*, Oxford University Press, New York.

United Nations Development Programme (1991), *Human Development Report 1991*, Oxford University Press, Oxford.

Vaidyanathan, A. (1988), *Indian Agricultural Development in a Regional Perspective*, Orient Longmans, Calcutta.

Vaidyanathan, A. and Nair, P.R.G. (2003), "Introduction" in R. Govinda and R. Diwan (eds.), *Community Participation and Empowerment in Primary Education*, Sage Publications, New Delhi.

Verma, Vinod (1997), *Reference Madhya Pradesh 1996–97*, Deshbhandhu Publication Division, Raipur.

7 Issues in Socio-Economic Development of Backward States with Special Reference to Orissa

Basanta K. Sahu

Economic growth dynamics and inverted-U hypothesis advocate that regional inequalities within developing countries will be eventually reduced through factor mobility. Neoclassical growth theory highlights the mobility of supply side factors—like capital stock, technical change and labour, as the reason for the eventual reduction of such disparities. On the other hand dependency and structural change theories postulate that regional inequality is an inevitable outcome of development of capitalism. However, the proposition of convergence in recent growth literature has been of much appeal to the analysis of disparities amongst countries. Following Barro and Sala-i-Martin (1995) in the context of regional growth, there are two views on how the process of catching up and convergence can take place: β-convergence, where poor regions will tend to grow faster than the more developed regions (as the diminishing marginal returns to capital prevails in the latter regions) and s-convergence concerning cross-regional dispersion (inequalities) which would tend to decrease over time. Regions with better infrastructure can attract more capital and more activities through market when an economy is liberated and there is deregulation of investment. But applicability of conventional proposition and methodology to the analysis of regional disparities may not be enough in case of a diverse and large country like India where different groups of regions and sub-regions perform differently between and within the groups.

In India, regional disparity is alarmingly high and probably increasing. The extent of and trends in regional inequality and poverty across the states, particularly among backward states, is different from other states which often challenge several development policy actions initiated over period. In other words, the current pattern and structure of regional growth and poverty in the country pose a threat to future course of development actions to achieve the desired goals. However, major policy changes during last two decades had a clear impact on India's regional economic growth focusing on pattern and distribution of growth, poverty and human development. In India growth rate was low but stable for a considerable period but during 1990s the country experienced a sharp rise in economic growth rate followed by liberalization of economic policy and major structural changes—faster growth of service sector, rising growth rate, growing informal sector, casualization of rural labour and increase in wage rate, etc. However, the reorientation in growth rates was not experienced and benefited equally by all states and all sections in the country; rather it perhaps lead to the pattern of regional growth and the poverty distribution which was not desirable. A question may arise that if the regional growth patterns get stimulated by macroeconomic policy changes then why some backward regions become more backward than others, whether growth rates and human development in different regions would eventually converge or not.

Several studies found that the pattern of India's growth in the 1990s stimulated by liberalization exacerbated rural-urban and regional inequalities. Some recent studies have observed that the regional disparity has widened in India during post-reform period (Ahluwalia, 2000, 2002; Rao, Shand and Kalirajan, 1999; Shand and Bhide, 2000; Bhattacharya and Saktivel, 2004). This not only affects people living in the undeveloped regions and sectors most directly but it led to higher wage inequality that has tended to increase economic insecurity among poor and unskilled people. Wide regional inequalities may increase the costs associated with moving people out of poverty, low level income and from low productive to high productive activities.

There is rise in inequalities in the Indian economy: until 1993–1994, the all-India Gini-coefficient of per capita consumption expenditure was fairly stable but has shown a marked increase later. The magnitude and rate of change of inequalities is quite substantial as very sharp contrasts are evident between the rural sectors of the slow growing states and the urban sectors of the fast growing states. While rural inequalities have stayed the same in the 1990s as in the 1980s with few exceptions, urban inequalities have risen rather than fallen (Deaton and Dreze, 2002). During 1990s, inequalities seem to have risen between occupation groups too. Real agricultural wages have grown about 2.5 per cent while public sector salaries have grown at almost 5 per cent per year during the same period

(Deaton and Dreze, 2002). On the other hand, within manufacturing, employment in the organized sector has "declined significantly" (Sundaram and Tendulkar, 2003) despite high rates of overall growth while employment in the informal/unorganized sector has increased faster. Thus, wide disparity in wages, sectors, and skills across regions in the country seems magnified by an increase in regional inequalities.

The major problem of continuing poverty and rising inequalities in backward states arises out of a basic asymmetry between growth of the national product, SDP and individual income and employment. Though farm sector growth has immense influence on regional as well as national level growth because of its strong linkage with rest of the sectors, growth of productive non-farm employment and income has failed to lift more people from the low wage and low-income agricultural sector to the higher growing manufacturing or high performing service sector in backward regions. Because growth of non-farm sector in backward states like Orissa has largely become distress-induced (Sahu, 2003) farm and non-farm growth linkages have failed to drive backward regions out of the trap of low productivity, low wage and low income. Under this condition, the issues and the possibilities of addressing problems of emergent inequalities and poverty can be better realized if we understand the mechanisms and linkages between rising growth rates, its nature and patterns and socio-economic changes among the people living in poor and backward areas. Thus, it would be important to understand the factors that prevent people in a region from moving into better income areas and sectors despite of high national level growth rates, to know why regions having similar problems and potential yet performed in a different manner.

The poor states have different growth experiences over a period. The present paper highlights some of these issues with special reference to backward states, particularly Orissa. In the first section, this paper analyzes regional growth performance amongst major states in India. Some aspects of growth, poverty and human development for five poor states (Bihar, M.P., Orissa, Rajasthan and U.P.) vis-à-vis India has been highlighted with the objective to know if there has been any reduction in disparities during post-reform period (1990s). In the second section the analysis is extended to understand the nature, pattern and evolution of regional disparities in Orissa in details. The last section concludes with some policy suggestions.

I

In 1990s, while economic liberalization has reduced the degree of control exercised by the Centre leaving greater scope for states to initiate suitable actions, some poor states have become poorer, even when there were several special packages exclusively designed for backward states to accelerate their growth process. On the other hand, given the approximately similar initial conditions and constraints, some states have performed better than others. Regional disparity was also noticed during 1980s across the states when growth was achieved under a protective regime but it has widened significantly during reform period. From policy point of view it is important to discuss the performance of individual states, especially backward states, during 1980s and 1990s.

Performance of Major States vs. Poor States in India during 1980s and 1990s

In spite of lack of consistency and other limitations, State Domestic Product (SDP) data has been widely used for analysis of growth performance, both at national and sub-national level. Ahluwalia (2000) found a significant degree of variation in growth across the states and there was an increase in gini-coefficient after mid-1980s, which was fairly stable. Deaton and Dreze (2002) argued that there was a wide variation in the growth rate of average per capita consumption expenditure in 1990s. Using revised SDP[1] data and covering up to late 1990s, Bhattacharya and Saktivel found that growth performance and structural changes in SDP have been uneven across the states during the last two decades, especially in 1990s. The problem is compounded by inverse relationship between population growth and income growth. They also note that wide variations in regional growth rates and increasing gaps between advanced and backward states are discernible during the reform period. Another study found that growth has been concentrated in few states like Gujarat, Maharashtra, West Bengal and Tamil Nadu where industrial sector contributes relatively higher in their SDP. Regional variations across 16 states as shown by the coefficient of variation, increased from 18 per cent in the 1980s to 27 per cent in the 1990s. The coefficient of variation in per capita gross state domestic product increased from 25 per cent in the 1980s to 43 per cent in the 1990s (Shetty, 2003).

It may be seen from Tables 1 and 3 that with a few exceptions, all major states, including five poorer states—Bihar, M.P., Orissa, U.P. and Rajasthan had achieved more than five per cent SDP growth during the 1980s. Interestingly, Rajasthan, U.P. and Orissa reported higher growth rates than the all-India growth rate of 5.6 per cent per annum. Considerable variation in growth performance of individual states is evident from the data. Though some states have experienced a faster growth than the national level growth and others states during 1990s, it is important to note that extent of dispersion in regional growth has increased during this period. In spite of disparity across the states, regional growth seems more balanced during 1980s than in 1990s. While few industrial and better infrastructure states gained more in terms of accelerated growth during post-reform period, A.P. and Kerala, whose performance was less than the national average (average of major states) in 1980, improved their performance. Among the backward states, except marginal increase in SDP growth in M.P. from 5.18 to 5.45 per cent, others experienced a decline growth during 1990s. SDP growth drastically declined in Orissa, Bihar and U.P. from 5.85 to 3.60, 5.20 to 3.46 and 5.88 to 4.33 per cent respectively. However, growth rate in Rajasthan, though declined in 1990s, remained the highest among the poor states and higher than all-India average. What is important to note is that during 1990s deceleration of growth was sharper in backward states like Orissa, Bihar and U.P. than in other states like Punjab and Haryana where the base of growth was relatively high. This analysis shows that states reporting high growth could have managed to attract more capital investment during post-reform period but the backward states like Orissa and Bihar failed to do so. Interestingly, neighbouring state West Bengal performed remarkably high even though all of them have more or less homogenous conditions that prevail within eastern India.

Table 1

Growth Rate of SDP at Constant Prices (per cent per annum)

States	*1980–1990*	*1990–2000*	*1980–2000*
Andhra Pradesh	4.81	5.12	5.05
Assam	3.91	2.47	3.49
Bihar	5.20	3.46	3.85
Goa	5.71	8.23	7.47
Gujarat	5.71	8.28	6.80
Haryana	6.68	6.71	7.80
Himachal Pradesh	6.10	6.91	6.20
Karnataka	6.10	7.07	6.53
Kerala	4.50	6.00	5.97
Madhya Pradesh	5.18	5.45	5.89
Maharashtra	5.98	6.80	6.30
Orissa	5.85	3.60	3.90
Punjab	5.14	4.63	4.70
Rajasthan	7.17	6.46	6.95
Tamil Nadu	6.35	6.65	6.51
Uttar Pradesh	5.88	4.33	5.15
West Bengal	5.20	7.24	6.11
All India	5.60	6.03	5.66
Coefficient of Variation	0.14	0.29	0.22

Source: Bhattacharya and Saktivel (2004).

Similarly, inter-state variations in growth of per capita SDP during 1980s and 1990s reveal more marked regional disparity during later period. While increase in SDP per capita growth was faster during 1990s in many states as well as at all-India level, it declined in all backward states except M.P. The decline was sharper in U.P., Orissa and Bihar. This may be due to their demographic behaviour—high population growth especially in Bihar and U.P.. Relatively high population growth in these backward states seems to affect their per capita SDP growth. However, lower population growth reported in Orissa in comparison with national average is mainly due to high mortality rate. Bhattacharya and Saktivel (2004) found a positive but not significant relationship between population and SDP growth in 1980s, showing that the SDP growth was neutral of population growth, turned to reverse in 1990s. However, it is difficult to conclude any clear result from an inverse relation between income and population growth, especially for backward states like Orissa, as it may be noted that during the post-reform period the state experienced a decline in public investment and deregulation of private investment.

Regarding the sectoral composition and contribution to total growth, the experience of backward states widely varies with other states in nature, structure and the base of sectoral growth over period. It may be noted that in Orissa, primary sector contributed about half of its SDP in 1980s, but it reported sharp decline in the primary sector growth but slow declines in it (49.7% to 42% of SDP) in the 1990s. On the other hand, secondary sector registered a decline in growth in all poorer states except M.P. But Orissa reported a very high decline in secondary sector growth (from 7.4% to 4.3%) with no change in its share (23%) in the state SDP during 1990s.

Sectoral composition of growth and changes therein explain clearly about the growth behaviour across the states. As expected, most of the major states experienced decline in share of primary sector in their SDP during 1990s irrespective of the rate of sectoral growth. In case of backward states, the share of primary sector declined from about 60 to 46 per cent in Bihar and from 50 to 42 per cent in Orissa between 1980s and 1990s. However, the decline was sharper among industrially developed states. Considering the primary sector growth performance among backward states it was relatively better and impressive in M.P., U.P. and Rajasthan, whose overall growth performance was also better during 1990s as compared to 1980s. On the other hand, Bihar and Orissa suffered a major setback in primary sector growth during 1990s, which might have been instrumental in their low and declined overall SDP growth.

While industrially advanced states like Gujarat had improved in primary sector growth from –0.34 per cent in 1980s to 2.67 per cent in 1990s, Bihar became the only state to experience a negative primary sector growth of (–0. 93) per cent per annum during 1990s, which declined from 2.62 per cent in the 1980s. Orissa reported a drastic decline in primary sector growth from a respectable rate of 4.75 per cent per annum in 1980s to 0.65 per cent in 1990s—the highest decline by any major state in India.

Secondary sector contribution was about one-fifth of total SDP in Bihar, Rajasthan, and U.P. against 17 per cent in Orissa in 1980–81. But its share in SDP increased to 28.1, 30.2 and 26.4 per cent in Bihar, Rajasthan and U.P. respectively in 1999–2000. Drastic decline in primary sector growth and stagnant secondary sector share in Orissa's SDP is matter of serious concern (which has been elaborated later).

Relatively higher growth (around 8–9%) in tertiary sector and its increasing contribution (around 40%) to SDP in most of the states during 1990s has been widely discussed in current literature. Surprisingly, the share of tertiary sector in SDP was higher and faster in two most backward states of Orissa and Bihar (43.2 and 42.4% respectively) than some developed states like Punjab, Haryana and Gujarat in 1999–2000. While relatively high tertiary sector growth declined in many states during 1990s, among poor states only Orissa registered a marginal increase from 5.67 to 6.14 per cent growth. This does not explain much about the nature and sustainability of the sector in the state. Various factors like poverty, poor human development, performance of agriculture, poor pace of industrialization or all the above factors taken together may be responsible for the tertiary sector. Some of these issues are discussed henceforth.

Poverty and Human Development

One key message emerging from recent research is that higher growth can take care of poverty and achieving a policy environment conducive to growth interacts multiplicatively with human resource development (Datt and Ravallion, 2002). In other words regional disparity in terms of growth, per capita income or human development presumed to be narrowed down with human resource development, i.e., when poor states grow faster than rich states. But the growth experiences of states during 1990s, as discussed above, do not completely support this. National Human Development Report 2001 for India (2002) reveals vast differences in human development and poverty between the states of India. The report also notes that disparities among the states with respect to human poverty are quite striking. While there have been improvements in the human development index and human poverty index during the 1980s, the inter-state disparities have persisted through the decade of 1990s.

It appears that poverty in India is concentrated in a few states. The share of six states (Bihar, U.P., M.P., West Bengal, Orissa, and Assam) in total rural poor increased from 68.8 per cent in 1993–1994 to 74 per cent in 1999–2000. If growth is unevenly concentrated in some states, then one can analyze it whether the distribution of growth patterns is most conducive for reducing poverty and promote human development. Similarly, source of growth or composition of growth is also important from policy point of view. However, the regional pattern of agricultural growth in India seems to have not been pro-poor. The states experienced with higher growth rate in agricultural yields do not have higher share of India's poverty (Dutt and Ravallion, 2002). On the other hand the poorer states in India show a lower reduction in poverty and lower growth rates where role of

Table 2

Rural Poverty in Percentage during 1983 to 1999–2000

States	*1983*	*1993–1994*	*1999–2000*
Andhra Pradesh	26.53	15.92	11.05
Assam	42.60	45.01	40.04
Bihar	64.37	58.21	44.30
Gujarat	29.80	22.18	13.17
Haryana	20.56	28.02	8.27
Himachal Pradesh	17.00	30.34	7.94
Karnataka	36.33	29.88	17.38
Kerala	39.03	25.76	9.38
Madhya Pradesh	48.90	40.64	37.06
Maharashtra	45.23	37.93	23.72
Orissa	67.53	49.72	48.01
Punjab	13.20	11.95	6.35
Rajasthan	33.50	26.46	13.74
Tamil Nadu	53.99	32.48	20.55
Uttar Pradesh	46.45	42.28	31.22
West Bengal	63.05	40.80	31.85
All India	45.65	37.27	27.09

Source: Panning Commission (2001).

Table 3
Growth Performance of Backward States in India

States/Variables	*Period*	*Bihar*	*M.P.*	*Orissa*	*Rajasthan*	*U.P.*	*All India*
Growth Performance							
Growth Rates of GSDP (%)(at Constant Prices)	1980–90	5.2	5.18	5.85	7.17	5.88	5.6
	1990–00	3.46	5.45	3.6	6.46	4.33	6.03
	1980–00	3.85	5.89	3.9	6.95	5.15	5.66
Growth Rates of Percapita GSDP (%) (at Constant Prices)	1980–90	2.97	2.74	3.96	4.41	3.46	3.36
	1990–00	1.86	3.22	2.12	4.09	1.98	4.07
	1980–00	1.92	3.08	2.15	4.2	2.92	3.54
Sectoral Growth Rates of SDP (%)				**Primary**			
	1980–90	2.62	1.53	4.75	3.27	2.55	2.95
	1990–00	-0.93	3.28	0.65	3.08	3.7	3.33
	1980–00	0.38	2.92	0.98	4.27	3.3	3.25
				Secondary			
	1980–90	6.15	4.85	7.44	11	8.34	7.34
	1990–00	4.79	7.07	4.36	8.15	6.13	7.37
	1980–00	4.83	6.73	6.21	9.96	6.55	6.93
				Tertiary			
	1980–90	9.84	12.05	5.67	10.36	8.64	6.46
	1990–00	7.09	7.17	6.14	8.6	4.54	7.63
	1980–00	8.27	9.28	6.07	9.37	6.44	6.83
Sectoral Composition of SDP (%)				**Primary**			
	1980–81	59.93	50.71	49.79	51.9	49.53	39.64
	1990–91	46.52	38.43	42.43	42.72	36.47	32.91
	1999–00	29.59	30.79	33.78	28.88	34.68	25.2
				Secondary			
	1980–81	21.89	29.6	17.18	18.77	19.54	24.36
	1990–91	24.66	28.56	22.9	24.65	24.17	28.03
	1999–00	28.06	30.67	23	30.19	26.37	21.83
				Tertiary			
	1980–81	18.18	19.7	33.03	29.3	30.93	35.99
	1990–91	28.82	33.01	34.67	32.64	39.09	39.06
	1999–00	42.36	38.55	43.22	40.93	38.95	52.97
Population Growth	1980–90	2.14	2.41	1.84	2.53	2.3	2.44
	1990–00	2.43	2.05	1.49	2.53	2.3	1.94
	1980–00	2.28	2.23	1.67	2.53	2.3	2.16
Nos. Of Rural Poor (in Million)	1983	41.77	21.55	16.46	9.67	44.80	251.96
	1993–94	45.09	21.66	14.09	9.47	49.62	244.03
	1999–00	37.65	21.73	14.37	5.50	41.20	193.24
Rural Poverty Ratio (in %)	1983	64.4	48.9	67.5	33.5	46.4	45.7
	1993–94	57.9	40.7	49.8	26.4	42.4	36.8
	1999–00	44.3	37.06	48.01	13.74	31.22	27.09

Source: Bhattacharya and Saktivel (2004) and Planning Comm., Government of India (2002).

agriculture is vital. Table 2 provides some trend in rural poverty in major Indian states.

The rates of poverty reduction vary across states, with Kerala having the highest rate of poverty reduction and Assam the lowest with Orissa and Bihar close behind. In 1960s, Kerala had one of the highest poverty rates, along with Orissa but by mid 1990s, Kerala's poverty rate had fallen to about half that of Orissa. The fact that the four bottom states—Bihar, Uttar Pradesh, Madhya Pradesh and Orissa together have 55 per cent of all people living below the poverty line in India, illustrates the seriousness of the problem of regional disparities and the need to deal with this problem. In a study (Mehta and Shah, 2003) of chronic poverty in various states in India it was observed that better-off states remained relatively affluent and reduced poverty, while poorer states remained poor and made less progress in poverty reduction.

From the experience of poor states, it seems that inter-state inequality in poverty in India has become complex than the usually believed fact that rich got richer and poor got poorer. For instance, when poor states like Orissa, Bihar and U.P. failed to improve their performance in 1990s, Rajasthan and M.P. fared well, inspite of the high population pressure and other common constraints. In terms of rate of poverty reduction, it has been faster in the fast growing states including some poor states. In this regard, Orissa becomes worse off after 1993–94. Although the pace of poverty reduction during 1980s was modest in Orissa, but it could not sustain it further.

Human development is another critical determinant of the growth and poverty reduction. Economic growth and the composition of such growth assist in expanding the employment opportunities for the poor, who own very little physical and human capital. It appears that states that registered faster growth in 1990s have performed better in human development than others. For instance, the pace of female literacy in some poor states like M.P. and Rajasthan was better in 1990s than in 1980s but female literacy rate remains lower than national average of 54 per cent. On the other hand, gender gaps in education remain alarming in poor states in spite of there is an increase in the share of education in public expenditure in all poor states. There has been increase in the share of spending on secondary education in India compared to other countries in recent years.

Health sector is another critical area in the poor states like Orissa. But the share of health expenditure in total expenditure has declined over period. Deterioration of human development in backward states and their poor performance during 1990s is evident from the data. It has been found

Table 4

Performance Indicators of Development in Backward States in India

States	*Period*	*Bihar*	*M.P.*	*Orissa*	*Raj*	*U.P.*	*All India*
Human Development Index (Value/Rank among Indian States)	1981	0.237 (32)	0.245 (30)	0.267 (27)	0.256 (28)	0.255 (29)	0.302
	1991	0.308 (32)	0.328 (30)	0.345 (28)	0.347 (27)	0.314 (31)	0.381
	2001	0.367 (15)	0.394 (12)	0.404 (11)	0.424 (9)	0.388 (13)	0.472
Life Expectancy (2001–06)	Male	65.7	59.2	60.1	62.2	63.5	63.9
	Female	64.8	58	59.7	62.8	64.1	66.9
Sex Ratio	1981	948	921	981	919	882	934
	1991	907	912	971	910	876	927
	2001	921	920	972	922	898	933
Gross Enrolment (6–11 years) 2002–03	Male	80.7	98.6	106.1	101.6	106.9	5.33
	Female	65.6	91.2	99.8	92.4	108.8	3.39
Female literacy	1981	13.6	15.5	21.1	11.4	15.9	29.8
	2001	33.6	50.3	51	44.3	41.8	54.2
Mean Years of Schooling of Population (in years) 1998–99	Male	4.51	4.84	5.06	4.94	5.13	5.33
	Female	2.1	2.73	3.06	2.24	2.75	3.39
Share of Education Exp. In Total Public Exp. (%)	1980–81	13.19	10.82	12.35	13.07	13.15	2.7*
	1998–99	21.16	16.36	17.16	19.53	18.31	3.9*
Share of Health Exp. In Total Public Exp. (%)	1980–81	5.49	7.59	6.7	10.21	5.89	1.4*
	1998–99	4.81	5.8	5.58	6.42	4.1	5.78*
	*Central Govt.						
Infant Mortality Rate (IMR) Person	1981	75	133	125	87	99	77
	2001	67	97	98	83	85	71
Decline in Crude Death Rate	1980–82	7.8	13.28	5.69	8.79	16.04	12.5
	1990–2000	9.1	18.58	11.05	15.23	13.3	11.49
Population Covered by Health Facility (nos. of Health Centre) 1994	CHC/ Lakh people	5.87 (15)	2.66 (10)	1.79 (08)	1.37 (03)	4.50 (12)	
	PHC/ 000 people	33.96 (14)	43.01 (16)	26.02 (07)	23.59 (03)	29.74 (10)	
	Sub-Centre/ no. of people	5069 (11)	4268 (10)	4627 (09)	4242 (07)	5532 (14)	

Source: HDR India 2001 Planning Commission (2002) and Economic Survey 2004–05, Government of Orissa.

that 87 per cent of tribal and 83 per cent of illiterate women deliver at home (see NHFS–2, 1998). Data on access does not however seem to square with numbers of health centres per average population, where Orissa ranks average among Indian states, but the wide geographical spread of population enhances Orissa's challenges. Evidence given in Table 4 on some human development are self-explanatory.

II

Growth, Poverty and Regional Disparity in Orissa

From the above discussion it appears that no remarkable impact of growth on poverty reduction has been observed in Orissa during the last decade. Inter-sectoral linkages become low and localized. The growth of agriculture and allied sectors, key to poverty elimination, lagged behind due to decline in investment in agriculture and allied sectors. This has imprints on regional and sectoral growth.

As discussed in the first section, Orissa has recorded 5.85 per cent of SDP growth against 5.60 per cent at all-India level during 1980s, but registered only 3.60 per cent; nearly half of the growth at all-India level in the 1990s. The slow performance of the overall state economy during the 1990s perhaps affected its inter-regional growth. Similarly, per capita income growth declined from 3.96 per cent to 2.71 per cent against 3.36 to 4.07 per cent between 1980s and 1990s. Since growth of population was low in Orissa than the national level,[2] it seems that there has been divergence in the growth of per capita income of the state from that of the national average and the divergence has increased during the 1990s.

Regarding structure of growth, the share of primary sector declined sharply from 50 per cent of SDP in the early 1980s to 42.43 per cent during 1990–91 and 33.78 per cent in the late 1990s without much change in the share of employment. While share of secondary sector remains stagnant, tertiary sector contributed about 43.33 per cent to SDP during 1990s. This shows a typical structural problem in Orissa's economy suffering from weak inter-sectoral linkages over period. This might contribute to shaping the current inter-regional disparity in the state. It may be seen in the Tables 5 and 6 that primary sector, which suffered major setback in 1990s, is followed by a very low and declined growth of agriculture sector. On the other hand, high growth of mining sector (11.6% in 1990s) in the state did not contribute much to the SDP due to the nature and quantum of linkage it generates for local areas.[3] So the resource use pattern in mining sector perhaps does not improve the growth prospect of the local area that would reduce regional imbalances.

Table 5

Sectoral Growth Rates in Orissa and India

Sectors/Year	*Agriculture*	*Industry*	*Service*
		Orissa	
1980–81/1990–91	1.36	7.38	5.93
1993–94/2000–2001	-0.43	2.49	7.02
		All India	
1980–81/1990–91	3.12	6.60	6.48
1993–94/2000–2001	2.73	6.25	8.13

Note: Compiled from Report of the Poverty Task Force (2003).

Table 6

Sectoral Growth of SDP in Orissa 1980–81 to 2000–01

(Constant 1980–81 Prices)

Production Sector	*Average Share in*		*Growth Rate of SDP**	
	1980s	*1990s*	*1980–81/ 1990–91*	*1991–92/ 2000–01*
1	*2*	*3*	*4*	*5*
Agriculture and Allied Activities	46.1	32.7	1.37	0.55
Mining and Quarrying	2.9	6.5	10.47	11.60
Manufacturing	11.9	12.4	7.74	-0.12
Utilities	1.9	2.2	6.85	1.14
Construction	4.2	4.4	5.63	1.74
Trade, Hotels and Restaurants	13.5	16.4	4.80	4.82
Transport, Storage and Communication	3.4	4.8	8.04	6.08
Finance, Insurance and Real Estate	6.7	8.6	6.20	7.87
Community, Social and Personal Services	9.4	12.1	7.19	7.53
All Sectors	100.0	100.0	4.29	3.65
Primary	46.1	32.7	1.37	0.55
Secondary	20.9	25.5	7.66	3.08
Tertiary	33.0	41.8	6.11	6.39

Note: *Growth rates have been estimated by using the semi-log model.

Source: EPW Research Foundation, *Domestic Products of States of India: 1960–61 to 2000–01*, Mumbai, June 2003.

Table 7

Rural Head Count Poverty Ratio by Region and Social Groups in Orissa

	Rural Head Count Ratio			*Contribution to Total*			*Total*
	Coastal	*Southern*	*Northern*	*Coastal*	*Southern*	*Northern*	
		1999–00			*1999–00*		
ST	66.63	92.42	61.75	4.10	18.29	18.62	41.01
SC	42.18	88.90	57.22	11.15	5.15	6.43	22.74
Other	24.43	78.15	34.66	16.19	9.97	10.10	36.25
Total	31.81	87.14	49.84	31.44	33.40	35.15	100.00
		1993–94			*1993–94*		
ST	87.02	77.42	63.73	4.23	15.23	16.52	35.98
SC	51.03	58.75	41.42	9.82	4.29	4.41	18.51
Other	40.92	59.04	33.10	28.99	5.74	10.77	45.51
Total	45.33	68.84	45.87	43.03	25.26	31.71	100.00
		*1983–84**			*1983–84**		
ST	64.0	79.1	85.5				
SC	61.3	63.8	63.7				
Other	35.4	55.7	54.7				
Total	41.7	65.1	68.5				

Source: See Dev et al., (2003).

Note: The category 'others' include OBC.

The state is characterized by being highly calamity prone to unpredictable factors, which erode the existing use of resources. It also drains out substantial amount of resources (both of state as well as of households) to cope with the situation. While cumulative impact of calamities like drought is relatively high in Orissa, the state government has no long-term drought measures (Hirway and Sahu, 2004).

Similarly, high tertiary growth (above 6% per annum) over last two decades in the state is appreciable but how much it contributed to reducing regional disparity and poverty in the state is important to understand. Tertiary sector growth is largely contributed by service sectors and, by nature, these sectors tend to concentrate on relatively developed areas. However, the organized service sector in the state drains out a substantial proportion of resource of the state in form of payment of salary and pension. As a result the state is unable to spend adequate expenditure on social sector like education and health as well as on anti-poverty programmes.

The financial situation of the state is precarious. The growth of revenue expenditure has been rising and that of capital expenditure has been falling. During the 1990s very low amount of the state domestic product has been utilized for capital expenditure. As a result the state has been unable to spend on infrastructural development as well as on social sector development. Under this condition, the role of service sector growth in narrowing down regional disparity, especially in backward areas like southern and northern Orissa is under doubt and needs further detailed study.

Orissa's growth performance has been poor in 1990s in comparison with that of 1980s as well as in comparison with other backward states. A number of factors such as sectoral growth, distribution of poverty, human development, state finance and governance in regional perspective of Orissa might have contributed to this scenario. We have analyzed some key factors focusing on three regions—Coastal, Southern and Northern regions of Orissa.

Poverty in Orissa: Regional Perspective

Orissa has been one of the poorest states in India with high regional disparities. It is reported that about 47 per cent people were below the poverty line during 1999–2000 with wide variations in the distribution of poverty across regions and social groups. According to NSS data, during 1983–84 the poverty ratio was 65.1, 68.5, and 47.7 per cent in southern, northern and coastal areas respectively. It changed to 87.1, 49.8 and 31.8 in southern, northern and coastal regions respectively during 1999–00. While there was sharp decline in poverty in coastal area over a period, its regional share in the state poverty has been concentrated more in southern and northern areas in comparison with coastal area during the 1990s. Till 1993–94, more numbers (43%) of poor were from coastal region as compared to other two regions but the region improved its position. In other words, southern region shared disproportionately higher burden of poor during late 1990s. In fact poverty ratio has increased in other two regions, and more pronouncedly in southern region. However, it is to be noted that these two regions constitute about 70 per cent of the total tribal population of the state and about 79 per cent in northern and 85 per cent in southern regions are extremely poor.

The poverty level in Orissa was the highest during 1990s with wide variations in its incidence across all regions and socio-economic groups. It may be noted that whereas poverty has declined in coastal region across all groups, in southern region it increased sharply among SC/ST groups in 1990s. Incidence of poverty is high and concentrated among ST and SC population and is widespread in the southern region (undivided Koraput, Kalahandi, Bolangir and Phulbani) with sharp increase in poverty ratio in 1990s. The available estimates suggest that during 1999–2000 people belonging to STs and SCs contribute 64 per cent of the total poor in Orissa and a considerably large proportion of these poor are likely to be located in forest covered districts. Increasing poverty among backward castes in backward southern region indicates that it may have significant bearing on agriculture-led strategy for growth and poverty reduction in the state. The relatively stronger impact of the spatial characteristic of poverty needs to be seen in the light of the asset holding pattern of the community and agricultural productivity. Uncertainty about settlement of land that many SC/ST people operate on, followed by severe limitations to ensuring livelihood security from ownership of the forest-land remains the key factor for high poverty level and insecurity. Factors like access to forest based livelihood, type of land ownership and the prospects of agricultural-growth seem instrumental in slow or no reduction of poverty in the backward region of state.

It is often believed that the agricultural growth may create a significant pull effect for people from backward tribal regions to agriculturally developed regions. Though this kind of population movement is a fairly common phenomenon but it may not be true in the case of Orissa. In spite of wide variations in the population density (from 375.4 in coastal region, to 169.1 in Northern and 109.9 in southern region) there are large scale out migration from backward southern and northern region under distress conditions. Poor performance of agriculture, ever declining access to alternative livelihood modes followed by poor infrastructure and slow industrial growth are largely responsible for high incidence of poverty in backward tribal areas. This indicates weak linkage between the growth and poverty reduction in the state, particularly in southern Orissa where poverty is deeply concentrated.

Poor Performance of Agriculture

Agriculture remains the key source of livelihood for two-thirds of the people in Orissa and contributes a lion's share to total employment and state domestic product. The rate of growth of agriculture sector has been not only very low but it declined during 1990s in comparison to 1980s and became negative during later period: agricultural growth was positive (i.e., 1.36%) during the eighties but became negative (–0.43%) after the nineties (see Table 5).

Poor performance of agriculture sector in Orissa has been due to a variety of factors including reduction of capital formation in agriculture, poor credit delivery mechanism and farm insurance, traditional input use, agrarian structure, land ownership and recurrence of natural calamities like floods and droughts. The agriculture in the state is characterized by low growth with wide disparity in the development of infrastructure facilities in different regions. For instance, the availability of irrigation facility, adoption of modern inputs in southern and some northern districts are much below even the state average. Uncertain property rights in land for a substantial number of households make their access to resource problematic and discourage investment in farming. In such a situation it becomes difficult even for those households having certain resource (land) to utilize it properly in the absence of complementary resource (credit).

High agricultural productivity is crucial for reducing regional imbalances through accelerating growth in backward regions and extending bulk of the gains to the poor in terms of higher farm yield and higher real wages. In Orissa, except the coastal area and few areas in northern region such as Sambalpur and Bargarh, agricultural growth has a narrow base with limited spread—in terms of lower coverage and intensity in the use of water, due to poor and uneven development in rural infrastructure and inputs like irrigation, HYVs, new technology, credit, markets (see Dev et al., 2003). So accessibility to develop or progressive agriculture is not easy on the part of the poor in backward areas that lack resources, skill and entrepreneurship. The agrarian structure in the state has not been favourable enough to achieve a fairly high growth rate across the regions. High inequality in asset holding, lack of formal credit, high transaction cost, poor performance of institutions and other factors discourage many small and marginal farmers to invest in productive investment or make them unable to exploit growth-promoting opportunities. This accentuates regional disparity further.

Even in developed coastal area like Balasore, agricultural productivity is low despite availability of irrigation facility, because of inferior quality of soil, low use of chemical fertilizer and high incidence of tenancy (see Sarap et al., 2003). Another key factor for uneven regional agriculture growth in Orissa is the agrarian structure. Inadequate property right and poor access to land by weaker sections remain major constraints for regional growth.

The decline in capital expenditure in the agriculture and allied sector during 1990s as compared to 1980s has affected agriculture across the state especially in dry and semi-arid areas. It has declined from Rs 133 crores per year during 6th Plan (1980–81 to 84–85) to Rs 86 crores per year during 8th Plan (1992–93 to 96–97) at 1980–81 price. In term of per hectare of net sown area the capital outlay was Rs 266 per year during 6th Plan period which declined to Rs 137 per year during the period 8th plan (see Dev et al., 2003).

Similarly, growth in industrial sector suffered a major setback in Orissa, falling from 7.4 per cent to 2.5 per cent during the last two decades. Negative growth of manufacturing sector in 1990s poses a serious threat to the growth prospect of the state economy as well as reducing regional disparity.

Unfavourable Industrial Sector Growth

Orissa occupies the status of the least industrialized state among the major states of India during last two decades. Though the share of Orissa in all-India value added marginally increased from 1.7 per cent during 1980–81 to 2.4 per cent during 1997–98 per capita value added in manufacturing sector in the state was lowest among the major states (Rs 812 in Orissa against Rs 1789 at national level during 1998–99). The share of the manufacturing sector in the NSDP has declined from 7.22 per cent in 1993–94 to 5.31 per cent in 1997–98 resulting decline in the state's share in the country's industrial sector in terms of employment and value added.

The structure of industrial sector is dominated by growth of few mega public sector industries and mineral based extractive industries. It is accompanied by large number of sick/defunct small scale industries. Weak backward and forward linkages as well as weak infrastructure linkages characterize industrial sector in the state. The pattern of industrialization, especially mineral based industries, has marginal impact on the economic growth. However, in the process of industrialization, large-scale displacement of local population has taken place. They have been uprooted from their traditional source of livelihood (forest). But the provision of alternative source of livelihood is negligible.

Industrialization has been primarily concentrated in the natural resource based industries with very weak links with other regions and sectors. Ancillary industrialization is of very insignificant nature in the state. During the late 1990s (1997–98), more than 80 per cent of net value added and two-thirds of total industrial employment had come from few major industry groups like electricity, basic metal and alloys, non-metallic minerals and food products. Growth of engineering goods industry is negligible both in terms of its share in value added (3%) and employment (about 6%). Industrial structure of the state is characterized by regional concentration and absence of diversification (Vyasulu and Kumar, 1997). Thus, structure of manufacturing sector in Orissa hardly helps in reduction of regional disparity.

The state industrial policy has not been successful in correcting the existing industrial structure, nature and balance growth industry. Though growth of small enterprises was faster during 1980s and 1990s (the numbers increased from 9,119 in 1979–80 to 35,867 in 1989–90 to 52,709 in 1996–97) but it was concentrated in few districts in the coastal region (Cuttack, Puri and Ganjam) accounting for over 40 per cent of total units, and 45 per cent of capital invested. The tribal districts in southern regions remained left out from such development. It may also be noted that majority of the small-scale enterprises in the state remain sick and non-functional and exist on paper only.

In recent years, the state government has initiated development of industries through provision of several types of incentives, which makes Orissa as one of the preferred investment destinations in the country. Though most of these new ventures are limited to natural resources—mines based activities and huge investment is expected in these sectors especially by private sector, but given the absence of social and human capital development in the state, the common people of backward and tribal districts, may not be in a position to gain out of this kind of industrial development. Rather it may lead to further widening regional development gap in the state.

Forest

Forest is an important source of livelihood for more than one-third of population in the state but its contribution to the state domestic product is less than 5 per cent. It is important to note that forest dependent people constitute more than two-thirds of total poor people. After massive deforestation, development projects in recent years followed by stringent forest regulations in the state survival of the forest dependent people has become a serious problem in terms of income as well as access to human and physical capital. As a result, their contribution is marginal to the state level growth (see Sarap, 2004). Unfortunately, to a large extent, tribal development programmes do not account this fact with a thrust on improving these people's access to forest resources, especially NTFPs. Studies have gone into examining the scope and constraints in providing livelihood support to people in the forest based regions in the state. According to an estimate, there are about 10 million workers directly or indirectly engaged in forest related activities in the state (Sarap, 2004). Similarly, a study by Mallik (2003: 1) suggests that NTFPs constitute nearly 20–50 per cent of households' income in the forest based regions in the state though, the intensity of forest dependence has been found to be declining in the wake of increasing population and simultaneous depletion of forest resources.

Tribals are confronted with the single largest problem, that is they occupy land and cultivate land on which they do not have any recorded rights. Ill-defined property rights, absence of developmental opportunities and lack of transparency in the state controlled management of forest resources are key issues that are not attended properly. In fact, people's involvement through Joint Forest Management (JFM) and other participatory institutions do not work as devices to make the communities operate more as a protector rather than as beneficiaries of the resource regeneration. Similarly, prices and market access for NTFPs, remain problematic despite the efforts made in the past few years to improve marketing and processing of NTFPs in the state. The recent reforms for marketing of NTFPs are welcome efforts, but it may not be adequate income support that NTFPs could provide to the people in absence of systematic assessment of the resource availability over period when there is high decline in total forest area in the state.

A large number of development projects are recently coming up in the State of Orissa. Ironically, these development projects are coming up mainly in such areas where there is predominance of tribal population. Statistical figures indicate that more than 40 per cent of the displaced families in development projects in Orissa are the tribals. There are a large number of such Development Projects which are in pipeline and are likely to further displace many more tribals. It is true that the tribal displaced families have by and large failed to restore their pre-displaced living standards in the post-displacement stage and they have become further impoverished as compared to their former standards of living. This is precisely because the tribal families do not get compensated properly for their land and tribals are not getting successfully adapted to the non-forest based economy. While there is decline in investment in forest conservation and development, simple resource transfer or provision of unclear property rights may not be effective in assuring sustaining livelihood of forest dwellers. A recent study suggests that majority of the households in the backward region are facing scarcity of food and bio-mass for sustaining their livelihood (Mallik, 2003: 35).

Infrastructure Development

Development of basic infrastructure is a necessary factor for favourable regional growth. A dependable infrastructure base raises productivity and minimizes production and other costs. It also improves human development through reduction of transaction costs of delivery of different provisions. In Orissa there is wide variation in basic infrastructure across regions. Road transport being one of the key infrastructures has increased in length in the state over period. In fact, Orissa has relatively higher road density in comparison with many other states but it is unevenly spread across regions. The road density in tribal and other hinterland districts is petty low as compared to coastal area. Rural road connectivity is petty bad—only 49 per cent of villages in the state were connected by road as against 57 per cent at the national during 1996–97 and there is hardly any improvement later. Variation in quality of road is well marked between coastal and tribal regions. Poor maintenance of roads in backward rural areas affects regional growth process. Seven backward districts in the state have no railway connection at all. Similarly, telecommunication sector of the state remains poor and concentrated in urban or coastal areas. Tele-density is very low in southern and northern area due to poor tele-network and poor economic condition of consumers (*Human Development Report Orissa*, 2004).

Social Sector Disparity

Access to educational facilities in Orissa is pathetic in backward tribal areas. Spread of schools and educational institutions are highly skewed in the state. About 12,869 villages, mostly located in southern and northern regions, did not have schools in 2002–03, about 12,000 schools have only one teacher and in more than 22,000 schools do not have a room for each class. But the situation in developed coastal areas are better and improved.

While allocation of funds on primary education was very low (2.11% of NSDP) during 1990s, the progress of some popular programmes like mid-day meal and DPEP has been dismal in many tribal districts. This has reflected in the form of low literacy rate, especially female literacy at district level.

Similarly, health sector in the entire state, particularly in southern and northern districts is undeveloped and grossly neglected. There is concentration of health institutions in coastal and other developed districts with absence of basic medical facilities in backward areas. There is only one medical agency (all categories) per 92 sq km at state level, and in tribal area it was available per 123 sq km in 2002. With poor connectivity, tribal areas are worse affected in basic medical facilities including doctors and para-medical personnel.

Regional variation in health sector is well documented in terms of variation in infant mortality rate (IMR). IMR in Orissa is one of the highest in the country but varies from 87 at state average to 119 in Bolangir to 110 in Koraput. The high IMR has been persisting in many of these districts over a long period. Average government spending on health care is one of the lowest in Orissa over a period and has further declined later. Public expenditure on health was 3.61 per cent of total budget during the year 1990–91 which declined to 2.54 per cent during 2001–02.

The low expenditure on health and education sector is clearly discernible in poor human development in the state and the impact is perhaps reflected in terms of widening regional gaps in human development, poverty and overall growth. The quantum and pattern of expenditure and the rural urban differences in health and education sector seem pronouncedly in regional disparity in the state.

Special Problems of the State

Orissa has the third largest share of Scheduled Tribes of the country constituting 62 tribes out of which 13 are primitive. About 40 per cent of people in the state are from backward castes. Most of the tribal people have uncertain property rights on land and have no physical and financial source to support their survival. Given minimal development of human capital among them, they are excluded from the development process. Efforts of state intervention to improve their resource base and income generating avenues have met with marginal success. Rather, the process of industrialization and development strategies followed over a period have affected these communities. In large extent, these social and cultural factors are responsible for low level and uneven development across the state.

The state is characterized by highly fragmented nature of polity and society and is unable to articulate and involve in focusing the goals under changing environment. In such a situation the political process in articulating the development goal is weak. The state lacks an effective monitoring mechanism in ensuring the process of development. The success of different programmes initiated by the state, NGOs and others is very poor due to problem of poor governance and other institutional problems. Lack of coordination among different organizations and institutions and implementation of development programmes under existing political and bureaucratic efforts have resulted in very low social and economic change in the state.

III

Conclusion and Policy Implication

To conclude it can be inferred that regional disparities between states have persisted over a period and became more pronounced in recent years. Though overall Indian poverty seems to be declining steadily, the problems of backward states like Orissa are not simply explained by lack of economic development or SDP growth only; rather they are more complex and deep rooted. The current pattern of growth does not assure backward areas and weaker sections to seek a way out of their current economic conditions and social problems because of multiple inequalities and the trickle down effects of growth is limited to the margins of the developed high growing regions and upper classes.

It is natural that different states may grow differently due to several factors but for policy actions what is important to understand here is the pattern and structure of growth at sectoral and sub-sectoral levels and factors that encourage and prevent a particular region to materialize its full potential and to achieve the desired goals. Accommodating major structural issues in regional development planning is very important to arrest further regional disparity. In this regard, growth performance of Orissa vis-à-vis other poor states and at all India level during last two decades provides some important insights for better understanding of inter-state variations and policy actions.

Orissa has suffered setback in sectoral growth behaviour, pace of poverty reduction and improvement in human development. The backward districts in southern and northern parts of Orissa are caught in a vicious circle of poverty, insecurity and low level development. Poor human development and lack of social and economic infrastructure in backward regions discourage further investment and progress.

Despite the fact that Orissa confronts several problems the state has the potential to achieve a respectable level of development and to reduce the existing pattern of regional imbalance. With a different pattern of growth the state could have achieved higher poverty reduction than currently achieved.

While the political economy between states is different, the competitive regional (within state) politics did not make the state of Orissa to deliver better as the case of other states. The regional growth pattern may affect the overall and regional prospects of poverty reduction. The key areas for policy action are to address the issues relating to structural problems of the economy, poor infrastructure, poor human development, impact of natural calamities, poor governance and weak institutions. Unless the current state of regional disparity is improved, Orissa may further lead to concentration of poverty, vulnerability and deprivation of large number of its people.

Notes

1. GDP series with base 1993–94 have been revised by CSO and so have the SDP series for states and the revised data are available from 1993–94 only. New GDP and SDP series have changed base year in terms of price and revised production boundary.
2. For instance annual growth of population was 1.67 per cent and 2.19 per cent at Orissa and all-India level respectively during 1980s, which declined to 1.49 per cent and 1.84 per cent during 1990s. However, low growth of population during 1990s in the state is more due to high death rates than due to improvement in health care and nutrition status of people.
3. It may be noted that mining activities creates few casual labour employment for local people and there is hardly any local demand for the output. The state gets some royalty from mining.

References

Ahluwalia, Montek S. (2000), "Economic Performance of States in Post-Reforms Period", *Economic and Political Weekly*, May 6.

Ahluwalia, Montek S. (2002), "State Level Performance Under Economic Reforms in India" in *Economic Policy Reforms and the Indian Economy*, ed. by Anne O. Krueger, Oxford University Press, New Delhi.

Barro, Robert J. (1991), Economic Growth in a Cross Section of Countries", *Quarterly Journal of Economics*, 106, May 2.

Barro, Robert J. and Salai-I-Martin, Xavier (1995), *Economic Growth*, McGraw-Hill.

Bhattacharya B.B. and Sakthivel, S. (2004) "Regional Growth and Disparity in India: Comparison of Pre and Post-Reform Decades", *Economic and Political Weekly*, 29(10), March 6.

Datt, Gaurav and Ravallion, Martin (2002), "Is India's Economic Growth Leaving the Poor Behind", World Bank, Policy Research Working Paper.

Deaton, Angus and Dreze, Jean (2002), "Poverty and Inequality in India: A Re-Examination", *Economic and Political Weekly*, September 7.

Dev, M. et al. (2003), *Poverty Reduction Strategies in Orissa: Report submitted to PTF Cell,* Government of Orissa.

Government of India (2002), National Human Development Report 2001 for India.

Government of Orissa (2004), *Orissa Human Development Report.*

— (2003) *Orissa Development Report.*

Hirway, I. and Sahu, B.K. (2004), "Drought Policy in the Eastern Indian States: Orissa, Chhattisgarh and Jharkhand: An Assessment", A project submitted to the International Rice Research Institute, Manila.

Mallik (2003), "Tribal Livelihood and Forest Management Policy" (Unpublished), Nabakrushna Choudhary Institute of Development Studies, Bhubaneshwar.

Mehta, A.K. and Shah, A. (2003), "Chronic Poverty in India: Incidence, Causes and Policies", *World Development*, 31(3), pp. 491–511.

Mohanty, B.B. (2001), "Land Distribution among Scheduled Castes and Tribes", *Economic and Political Weekly*, October 6.

Nagaraj, R., Varoudakis, Aristomene and Veganzones, Marie-Ange (1998), "Long-Run of Reforms", *Economic and Political Weekly*, October 14.

National Family Health Survey (NHFS-2) 1998–99, International Institute for Population Sciences, Mumbai (IIPS, 2000).

Panda, M. (2002), "Poverty in Orissa: A Disaggregated Analysis", paper for the NCCDS workshop on poverty monitoring, Bhubaneswar, February.

PTF (2003), "Poverty Reduction Strategy for Orissa" (Draft Report), Task Force, Government of Orissa, Bhubaneshwar.

Rao, C.H. Hanumantha and Dev, S. Mahendra (2003), "Economic Reforms and Challenges Ahead: An Overview", *Economic and Political Weekly*, Special Issue on Andhra Pradesh, March 22–29.

Rao, M. Govinda, Shand, R.T. and Kalirajan, K.P. (1999), "Convergence of Incomes Across Indian States: A Divergent View", *Economic and Political Weekly*, March 27.

Sahu, B.K. (2003), "Growth of Non-farm sector in backward agriculture: A study of three region in Orissa" in a book titled *Non-Farm Employment*, Published by NIRD, Hyderabad.

Sarap, K. (2004), "Participatory Forest Management and Livelihood Among Forest Dwellers in Orissa" Report submitted to DFID through CESS, Hyderabad and Overseas Development Group, University of East Anglia, UK.

Shetty, S.L. (2003), "Growth of SDP and Structural Changes in State Economies: Interstate Comparisons", *Economic and Political Weekly*, December 6.

Shand, R.T. and S. Bhide (2000), "Sources of Economic Growth: Regional Dimensions of Reforms", *Economic and Political Weekly*, 38(50).

Sundaram, K. and Tendulkar, S. (2003), "Poverty among Social and Economic Groups in India in 1990s", *Economic and Political Weekly*, Vol. 38, No. 50, pp. 5263–5276.

Vyasulu, V. and Kumar, A.V.A. (1997), "Industralizations in Orissa: Trends and Structure", *Economic and Politiacal Weekly*, Vol. 32, No. 22.

Part II

Policies, Strategies and Programmes for Basic Amenities

8 Universalization of Education through Adult Literacy Programmes

Some Empirical Evidences

S.K. Pant

Water, water every where
All the board did shrink
Water, water every where
Nor a drop to drink.

—Colridge

Literacy has always remained an area of importance and also concern for our planners, policy makers and social activists. As a result of this it has always figured at the core of planning since the inception of five-year plans, soon after attaining political independence (Pandey et al., 1997). Perhaps the plausible reason for this could be its ability to reach, influence and mould the human capabilities from very low levels to unprecedented heights, from being an unknown unproductive class to becoming a highly competitive unit and from being a raw and uncultivated class to a highly refined value added finished product (Pant, 2005).

A perusal of Indian history shows that efforts to eradicate illiteracy persisted even in the pre-independence days also. There are many instances when the provincial heads of the states like that of Mysore, Travancore, Coimbatore, to name few, themselves took keen interest to promote and propagate the cause of literacy among their masses. Likewise, many social reformers and activists like Tagore, Gandhi, Rajagopalachari, Raja Ram Mohan Roy, etc., had also taken keen interest to address the issue of illiteracy. However, as their efforts were not in continuum and were also quite sporadic, undertaken with limited resources, as a result of which their impact remained largely localized (Rawal, 1998).

After independence, the tryst with education took a far more ambitious and dynamic form and many new and innovative initiatives were tried out. However, their impact has remained a mixed one. It could be called a saga of success and failures, triumph and disappointments and integration and marginalizations. The success, triumph and integration were achieved in the form of manifold increase in the number of schools, number of teachers, physical infrastructure, enrolment level of students and overall increased literacy rates whereas disappointments, failures and marginalizations were seen largely in the form of high drop-out rates, both at the primary and secondary level, dilution in the quality of education and increasing marginalization of the disadvantaged sections.

Table 1

Literacy Rates in India: 1951–2001

Year	*Persons*	*Males*	*Females*	*Gap in Literacy*
1951	18.33	27.18	8.86	18.30
1961	28.30	40.40	15.35	25.05
1971	34.46	45.88	21.97	23.81
1981	43.57	56.38	29.76	26.62
1991	52.21	64.13	39.29	24.84
2001	65.38	75.85	54.16	21.70

Source: Census of India, 2001.
Note: Literacy rates for 1951, 1961 and 1971 census relates to population age five years and above.

Perusal of Table 1 shows that the literacy level which stood at 18 per cent in 1951 subsequently enhanced to over 65 per cent in 2001. However, the gap between males and females which was about 18 per cent in 1951 has also inclined to about 22 per cent in 2001. In absolute terms, the number of illiterates which was estimated to be 300 million in 1951 subsequently went upto to 437 million in 1991. While women comprised 57 per cent of the illiterates population, the situation among SC/ST was particularly bad (Rahi, 1996).

Moreover, this discrepancy was not only confined to gender specific domain but spread well across caste and regional boundaries as well. For instance, the 2001 census estimates clearly show that while the level of urban literacy was worked out to be over 80 per cent, its level was hardly 59 per cent for rural areas, for urban males and females, the literacy level was reported to be over 86 per cent and 73 per cent respectively: in rural areas about 71 per cent of the males and 47 per cent of the females were found to be literate (Table 2).

Table 2

Rural-Urban Literacy Rates 2001

(in million)

Regions	*Persons*	*Males*	*Females*
All Areas	566.71 (65.20)	339.91 (75.64)	226.79 (54.03)
Rural Areas	336.67 (59.21)	226.27 (71.18)	140.39 (46.58)
Urban Areas	200.03 (80.06)	113.63 (86.42)	86.39 (72.99)

Source: Census of India, 2001.

Note: Figures in bracket denote percentage.

Similarly, the National Sample Survey Organization (NSSO) (52nd Round) data report that about 47 per cent of the children who drop out of school cite inability to cope academically and lack of interest in the studies as a predominant reason (Kaul, 2002). The latest census estimates show their number to be 350 million, which is more than the population of many developed countries. Though various studies show that the drop-out of the children at the primary level classes (I–V), over the period 1960–61 and 1997–98 has come down from 62 per cent to 38 per cent, yet it is still considered to be alarming. For middle stage, the drop-out rate has been 51 per cent.

What has come as a surprise is the fact that during all these years the government has been launching a host of new programmes taking initiatives to create various organizations, trusts and institutions to cater to the needs of different sections of the society. Today, perhaps India is one of the few countries that has a literacy programme for every section of the society be they infant, child or adults or physically disabled or challenged. It all goes to show that the leaders and social reformers were quite sensitive to the issues of illiteracy.

Adult Education and Its Relevance

Though elementary education is considered to be important in a person's life because it lays foundation of personality, attitudes, confidence, habits, learning skills and communication capabilities in individuals. Likewise, the basic skills of reading, writing and arithmetic are also acquired at this stage. It also helps them to internalize values and sharpen their environmental consciousness (Kaur, Singh and Gill, 1998), and even the investment on education at the elementary stage also seeks highest return as has been pointed out by various scholars. Yet adult education is also perceived to be equally vital, because lack of education permanently damages an individual's future prospects. An uneducated youth always ends up as an unskilled adult worker who is unable to escape the vicious cycle of deprivation and economic disadvantages (Majumder and Vaidyanathan, 1994).

Thus, it could be said that education acquired at whatever stage, is not only considered to be a key factor but also a powerful instrument that is capable of ushering socio-economic and intellectual development of any community and also of a nation. Besides this, it also helps the individuals to move up in socio-economic hierarchy (Chandra, 1989; Chitnis, 1996; Dhareshwar, 1992). In other words, it can be called as a basic concomitant of development and has a strong bearing on the quality of life indicators, viz., mortality, longevity, birth rate, in the age group of 15–19 years (Sharma and Ratherford, 1987).

Relevance

The relevance of adult education for our country is very vital because even after more than five decades of planned efforts nearly one-third of the population still remains illiterate. Now with the enhancement in the life expectancy from 55 years in 1981–85 to 61 years in 1993, improvement in the HDI from 0.302 in 1981 to 0.472 in 2001 (Tenth Plan, 2002–07), the proportion of adult population is also likely to go up. The magnitude of the problem could be gauged from the fact that in 1986–87 two-fifths of rural and one-fifth of urban children in the age group of 6–14 years was not found to be enrolled in schools (Visaria, Gumber, Visaria, 1993). Thus, it could be said that the problem of adult illiteracy will persist in future also and no nation, howsoever rich and powerful, could afford to ignore this fact. Further, with the onset of economic reforms whereby the outlays on social heads has been drastically reduced, the position of adult illiterates is likely to become more vulnerable pushing them further in the pool of abject poverty and wantlessness, unless adult literacy programmes are not revitalized. Hence it becomes critical for us to utilize the resources earmarked for them quite economically and judiciously so that their impact could be optimized (Table 3).

Table 3
Drop-out rate of School Going Children at Elementary Stage in India

Year	*Primary Classes (I–V)*			*Middle Classes (I–VIII)*		
	B	*G*	*T*	*B*	*G*	*T*
1960–61	61.7	70.9	64.9	75.0	85.0	78.3
1970–71	64.5	70.9	67.0	74.6	83.4	77.9
1980–81	56.2	62.5	58.7	68.0	79.4	72.7
1990–91	40.1	46.0	42.6	59.1	65.1	60.9
1997–98*	38.2	41.3	39.6	50.7	58.6	54.1

Note: *provisional figures ** B = Boys, G = Girls, T = Total
Source: Selected Educational Statistics (relevant years), DoE, MHRD.

Table 4
Expenditure Incurred on Education

(Rs crore)

Pre-Reformed Period	*Amount*	*Percentage*
1980–81	3859	3.20
1989–90	16905	4.10
1990–91	19791	3.87
Post-Reformed Period		
1991–92	21914	3.72
1994–95	32107	3.51
1996–97	43035	3.48
1997–98	49200	3.55

Source: Central Statistical Organisation, Selected Socio-economic Statistics for India 2000, Department of Statistics, Ministry of Finance, Government of India.

Adult Education Programme

Soon after independence and prior to the launching of First Five-Year Plan, the Central Advisory Board of Education (CABE) appointed a sub-committee under the chairmanship of Mohan Lal Saxena to report on the working of adult education. In the mean time the concept of 'social education' was evolved, which was nothing but a comprehensive programme that aimed at uplifting the community through community action. It primarily focused on educating man to understand the rights and duties of a citizen, improve his productivity and enable him to lead a fuller and richer life.

At a later stage social education became part of community development programme and included use of language, arithmetic, health and hygiene, etc. For propagating the programme, community centres and youth centres were established and five crore rupees were accordingly spent on literacy centres, community centres, libraries and Janata Colleges (Rahi, 1996).

This continued for other subsequent plans and by the end of third plan, the need for applying adult education intensively was also realized. It was also felt that for its successive implementation a different administrative structure and sufficient funds were necessary. Widespread illiteracy was seen as a real handicap in the way of both economic and social development. Hence it was decided to make adult literacy centres functional in character and link up with the work and life of people.

By the Sixth Plan, one of the most ambitious and revolutionary adult education programmes was launched in 1978 and a sum of Rs 200 crores was earmarked for it. Literacy was seen as an indispensable component of National Adult Education Programme (NAEP). In addition to basic literacy, the NAEP included two more components, viz., 'functionality' and 'awareness' which were included into its fold. Since literacy was visualized as the primary focus, NAEP was to be implemented through literacy centres that provided 350 hours of literacy instructions spread over a period of nine to ten months. Initially in the formulation of NAEP, the concept of Post Literacy (PL) and Continuing Education (CE) did not figure, except by implication. However, later on the recommendation of a committee, PL and follow up programmes were also accepted to be as important components as the literacy programme itself.

After the change of government in the Centre in 1980, the NAEP was greatly trimmed and converted into National Programme of Adult Programme (NAPE) and was subsequently linked to the already existing Rural Functional Literacy Programme. Similarly, the NAEP review committee's proposal for a three-year literacy programme was also shelved but in 1982–83, the government revived functioning of post literacy and follow-up programme (Daswani, 2002).

Adult education got a shot in the arm after the establishment of National Literacy Mission (NLM) in 1988 and Total Literacy Campaign (TLC) was subsequently launched. The plan allocations for adult education in the subsequent plans are summarized below:

Table 5
Plan-wise Allocation for Adult Education

(Rs Crore)

Plan Period	*Plan Allocation for Education*	*Plan Allocation for Adult Education*
First Five-Year Plan	153	5 (3.27)
Second Five-Year Plan	273	4 (1.47)
Third Five-Year Plan	589	3.50 (0.59)
Fourth Five-Year Plan	786	4.5 (0.57)
Fifth Five-Year Plan	912	18* (0.89)
Sixth Five-Year Plan	2,530	224 (8.85)
Seventh Five-Year Plan	7,633	4706 (6.16)
Eighth Five-Year Plan	8,522	718 (8.4)
Ninth Five-Year Plan	24,908	630 (2.5)

Source: 1. Madan Singh (1999), Companions of Adult Education, National Literacy Mission, New Delhi.
2. Mid-Term Approval of 9th Five-Year Plan, Planning Commission, New Delhi.

Note: *Only 9.0 crore was utilized.

What started as a time bound one shot affair on a modest scale in Kottayam, a city of Kerala, in 1989, soon grew into a massive movement first in Ernakulam district and then in the entire state of Kerala and many other states. The TLC model, thereafter, became the dominant strategy and approach of the government for adult literacy from Eighth Five-Year Plan grew out of Ernakulam TLC model.

The key ingredient for the success of TLC, based on the strength and weakness of earlier programmes, was identified as a national commitment and serious efforts were made to motivate learners, instructors and create positive environment and solicit people's involvement. It also emphasized the need of techno-pedagogic inputs and above all, efficient monitoring and management. However, the duration of TLC was reduced from 350 hours to 200 hours to be completed in six to eight months (Daswani, 2002).

TLC and Its Growth

The growth of TLC since its inception in 1988 has truly been impressive. From 1988–89 to 1992 even before the launch of Eighth Five-Year Plan, there were 22 TLCs working, which within the span of four months enhanced to 156. The Eighth Plan proposed to cover another 345 districts; that was about 75 per cent of the districts in the country under TLC.

By November 2003, there were 596 districts under the TLC of which 191 districts had graduated into post-literacy phase and another 238 districts into continuing education phase. It has so far covered over 150 million neo-literates in the age group of 9–35 years, through all NLM schemes of which over 71 per cent had been enrolled under the literacy campaign.

Administrative Structure

The total literacy campaign in the district is carried out by a registered body generally called Zila Saksharta Samiti, hereafter called the 'Samiti', which is headed by the District Magistrate or his nominee who acts as its president and one secretary, who is also a district level officer and is generally drawn from education or allied departments. Besides this, the other member of the body is a chief coordinator who is assisted by one

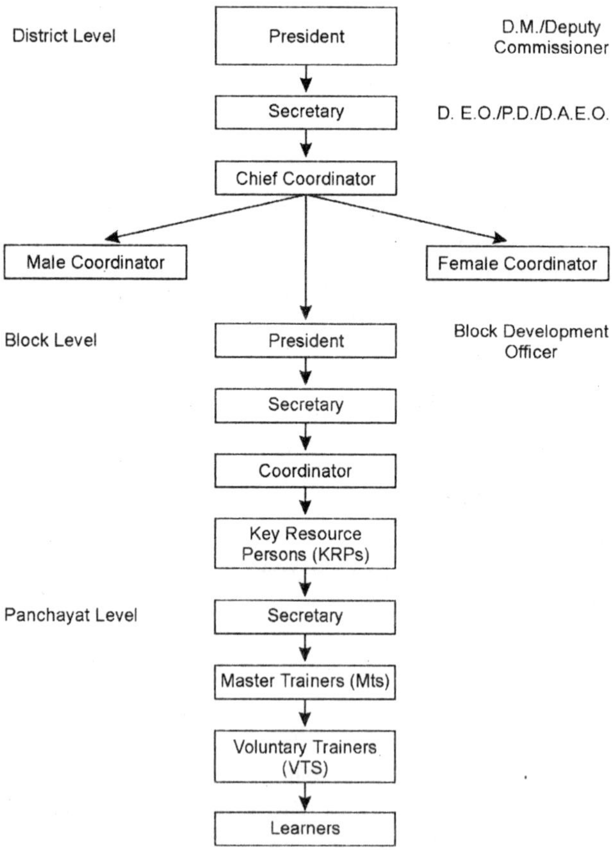

male and one female coordinator. This way the Samiti has a well defined three tier organizational structure which spreads across the district, blocks and panchayats.

At the block level it is headed by the block president and other functionaries, viz., secretary, coordinators and key resource persons are appointed mutually by chief coordinator and the president. The appointment is based on the experience and specialization of the concerned persons. Likewise at the panchayat level, it has a secretary, master trainer (MT) and voluntary trainers (VT). All the appointments are made by block president and block coordinators. The prime role of voluntary trainer is to provide literacy skills to the learners (adult illiterates), while the master trainer maintains a laison between a VT and block level functionaries. Besides this, he along with key resource persons is responsible for supervising the AE centres ensuring their smooth functioning, attending to the problems the VTs or of the AE centres that they face from time to time. Thus in the TLC administrative model the most crucial link is the VT, while the other functionaries provide supervisory and support services. The administrative set up of the Samiti could broadly be presented as:

Modus Operandi

The TLC is implemented in the district either in a phased manner or in the whole of the district at one go. However, prior to its launching, the Zila Saksharta Samiti undertakes base line survey to identify the magnitude or the volume of adult illiterates and subsequently identifies the targets to be covered under the programme. Accordingly, the process of recruitment of programme functionaries viz., master trainer and voluntary trainers also begins. The recruitment is done mutually by secretary and coordinator of the blocks respectively, keeping in view the candidates socio-economic background and experience. Preference is given to the candidates from backward sections and females.

Findings and Suggestions

The analysis of the working of TLC shows that their performance suffers on many accounts. The problems could be classified on the basis of their nature as (i) Administrative Level and (ii) Field Level.

Administrative/Organizational Level

On the theoretical plain it has been well documented that the Kothari Commission on Education as well as National Policy on Education (NPE) has categorically emphasized that the plan allocation on education sector should be at least 6 per cent of the GDP so as to give this sector a vital boost and make it vibrant, but nowhere has this commitment been honoured in practice in various plans (see Table 6).

Likewise, when the allocation is compared against the gross domestic product of the country, the level of allocation on education is quite low (see Table 7).

Table 6

Plan-wise Allocation of Resources on Education

Plan	*Percent of Total Plan*
First	7.76
Second	5.83
Third	6.87
Fourth	4.86
Fifth	5.04
Sixth	3.27
Seventh	2.70
Eighth	3.50

Source: Govinda, R. (ed.) India Education Report, Oxford University Press, New Delhi, 2002.

New Delhi 2002

Total Literacy Campaign in the district is approved by the National Literacy Mission, (NLM), New Delhi, when the concerned district submits a detailed proposal and financial budget highlighting the magnitude of the problem, the amount earmarked for each head or activity to be undertaken by them in the course of implementing the programme. These activities are conducting survey and environmental building exercise, distribution of reading and learning material, training of programme functionaries, monitoring and supervision of activities, etc.; all these inputs have a strong bearing on the performance of the programme. A perusal of the budget shows that:

Table 7

The Allocation on Education against GDP

Year(s)	*Per cent of GDP*
1950–59	1.2–2.3 (1.8)
1960–70	2.5–3.0 (2.8)
1970–80	3.1–3.5 (3.1)
1980–90	2.9–4.5 (3.2)
1990–96	4.9–4.0 (4.1)

Note: Figure in the bracket denotes the average value.

Source: Govind, R. (ed.) India Education Report, Oxford University Press.

1. The agencies, by and large, spent lesser amount than that was earmarked on many critical inputs like on training of the programme functionaries, supervision and monitoring activities and environmental building exercises. It may be reiterated that for the sustenance of the programme there is a need to step up investment on these heads.

2. It was also found that at the time of recruitment of VTs, many people, in the hope of receiving some honorarium, get enrolled into the programme and are provided teaching and learning material. However, when the honorarium is not provided (which is not stipulated in the programme), their interest dries out and subsequently the performance of programme also suffers. It is therefore recommended that utmost care be taken at the time of recruitment of VTs and MTs because they are the most crucial links in the entire programme. Only committed workers, who are the core spirit of the campaign, be enrolled and they be encouraged and publicly felicitated for their good work. Likewise, giving them priority in the other rural development programmes that are in vogue, if they apply for it, could also safeguard their interest. This gesture would go a long way to motivate other committed workers to join the programme.
3. The analysis also shows that the programme functionaries, particularly the VTs, were mostly trained but they were provided the training only once which was highly insufficient to cater to their demanding job. Hence, the concept of providing one time training to the programme functionaries should be done away with and efforts be made to provide training to the programme functionaries on regular and sustained basis. This will enable them to understand and comprehend the latest developments and problems in the filed of literacy and would also provide them motivation.
4. The NLM, New Delhi, has categorically stated in its guidelines that the evaluation exercise should begin when the implementing agency has roughly covered half of the district so that a quick feedback could be obtained that may help them to incorporate corrective measures, if so required. But this condition was never followed. The evaluation of the campaign in the district only begins by the time the implementing agency had already covered up the entire district and is waiting for the follow up leg of the programme. It was seen that a lot of time was being consumed and wasted on paper work, viz., writing to NLM, inviting the evaluating agencies from the panel given to them by NLM, negotiating the contract and signing the MOU, etc. In the meantime, in the absence of academic support activities, a majority of learners (adult illiterates), who have acquired learning skills gradually fall back into the illiteracy zone thereby defeating the whole purpose of the campaign. Hence, it is recommended that the implementing agency be given some share of autonomy to select the evaluating agency from the list given to them by the NLM so that time loss is

minimized. Further, after the completion of the campaign, when the district awaits for next phase of evaluation, some requisite amount of academic activities needs to be carried on, to enable the learners to retain the newly acquired skills.

At the Field Level

1. It was observed that adult education centres were largely managed by male voluntary trainers, and since they operated at odd hours like when the beneficiaries or the learners come back home after their daily jobs, the female participants, many a time, did not attend the centre or were quite irregular in their attendance. Hence efforts be made to recruit more female voluntary teachers so that female education may be given boost.
2. The distribution of teaching and learning materials at the AE Centres was also not satisfactory and at many centres all the three primers were not distributed timely. All this disrupted the teaching process, and no concerted efforts were made by the VTs to procure them, which clearly projects their inefficiency. This aspect could be taken care of once sincere, hardworking and committed project functionaries are deployed and effective monitoring and supervision is undertaken. This will ensure regular supply of materials to the centre.
3. The poor supervision and inspection of the VT Centres also contributed to the poor performance of the programme. It was found that on an average, about one-fourth of the centres were not being inspected or supervised at all. Even in the supervised category, as the frequency of inspection was quite low and no district level programme functionary was found to be visiting the centres, all this had also demotivated the committed programme functionaries. Hence it is recommended that it should be made mandatory for all supervisory staff to visit centres at regular intervals and the modalities of their visit could be decided mutually at the meetings.
4. Likewise, the progress report of the centres was also not sent regularly by the VTs which severely curtailed the flow of information to the district and it could not respond to the centres requirement timely. All this affected the performance of the programme as well as that of the beneficiary.
5. The programme did not have a standby operating mechanism/arrangement as a result of which more than 50 per cent of the centres faced closure as and when the VTs had to attend or perform some other work related or unrelated with the programme.

Hence, efforts be made to make some alternative arrangement like the MTs be asked in the event of eventuality, to ensure continuity of VTs centres by making alternative arrangement.

6. Environmental building exercise be carried out at the grass-roots level at regular intervals and on sustained basis to motivate and sensitise the people. If required, the help of some professional organization with requisite experience could also be taken.
7. Provision should also be incorporated to replace or call back the programme functionaries like VTs, MTs or even KRPs, whose working is not found up to the mark or is unsatisfactory.
8. Most of the committees constituted under TLC right from the district and village level were dominated by government officials and those who themselves were not aware of the real spirit of the programme and its basic objectives. It is, therefore, suggested that highly committed social activists, teachers and other prominent persons, who are well known for their social and community work, be nominated on these committees. Further, for the smooth functioning of the campaign, a coherent system of communication and cooperation among various committees and sub-committees be ensured so that inconsistency of any form can be ironed out.
9. It was also observed that in a majority of the AE Centres the teaching/learning method was being followed on traditional text book lines which many a times generated insipidness and monotony and discouraged the learners to come to the centres. In order to provide a conducive, thriving and vibrant environment at the centre, there is a need to provide regular training to VTs to equip and acquaint them with the latest techniques and methodologies in the field of pedagogy.
10. The content presented in the primers also needs to be revised by including more historical events, folk tales, cultural practices, etc., of the region and area to evoke interest of the learners. Irrelevant and routine types of syllabus also contributed to the high drop-out rates and low attendance at the AE centres. It is therefore recommended that the task of preparing primers be assigned to the district authorities who may solicit cooperation of learned people from various disciplines and institutions to make the primers interesting and need-based.
11. The campaign was also found to have suffered on account of resources crunch. The grant promised by the government was not released timely with the formal launching of the project. The initial

and subsequent delays in the flow of grant continued to haunt the performance of the campaign as the nodal implementing agency could not mobilize or generate internal resources. Hence it is suggested that once the project gets clearance from the government, the required amount should be subsequently released. However, to ensure the efficient functioning of the campaign, certain checks and balances may be incorporated.

12. It was also observed that the programme, many a times, lacked community support and was operating in isolation. It may be pointed out that no programme could survive without public support. Efforts, therefore, need to be made to sensitize and motivate prominent persons of the area, VEC members, panchayats functionaries and local community in general through vigorous environmental building exercises and other appropriate social intervention strategies. This could be achieved by holding rallies in support of the programme, by inviting common public to participate in the programme, by holding meeting at village levels and thereby introducing an element of transparency into the working of campaign. Through committed efforts, the project implementing agency, viz., ZSS could win back the support of the public.
13. It was found that generally the grass-roots public institutions like the VDC, VEC, Cultural Centres, to name a few were, lying defunct; largely they were infected with members who did not have any stake in the development of the area. Hence, efforts may be initiated to replace all such kinds of elements and only genuine and committed people be included in such people-friendly programmes.

References

Chandra, K.S. (1989), " Education and Social Change among Munda Community", *Journal of Rural Development*, Vol. 8(2), NIRD, Hyderabad, pp. 181–86.

Chitnis, S. (1996), "Educating Women for Development", *Journal of Education and Social Change*, April-June and July-September, Vol. X, No. 1 and 2, Pune, pp. 1–21.

Daswani, C.J. (2002), "Education beyond Literacy Changing Concept and Shifting Goals" in R. Govinda (ed.), *India Education Report*, Oxford University Press, New Delhi.

Dhareshwar, H. (1992), "Girls Education in India: A Situational Analysis", *Journal of Educational Planning and Administration*, NIEPA, New Delhi, pp. 133–140.

Kaul, Vinieta (2002), "Early Childhood Care and Education" in R. Govinda (ed.), *India Education Report*, Oxford University Press, New Delhi.

Kaur, M., Singh, S. and Gill, S.S. (1998), "Facets of Primary Education in Rural Punjab: An Appraisal", *Manpower Journal*, Vol. XXXIV, No. 2, July-September, pp. 67–68.

Kumar, M., Singh, S. and Gills, S.S. (1998), "Facets of Primary Education in Rural Punjab: An Appraisal", *Manpower Journal*, Vol. XXXIV, No. 2, July-September, New Delhi, pp. 67–68.

Majumder, M. and Vaidyanathan, A. (1994), "Access to Education in India: Retrospect and Prospect", *Journal of Educational Planning and Administration*, Vol. VIII, No. 4, October, New Delhi, pp. 353–403.

Pandey, J., Pant, S.K., Bhatt, K.N. and Singh, S. (1997), "Concurrent Evaluation of Total Literacy Campaign in Mirzapur District of Uttar Pradesh", *Project Report*, G.B. Pant Social Science Institute, Allahabad.

Pandey, J., Pant, S.K., Bhatt, K.N. and Singh, S. (1997), "Concurrent Evaluation of Learning Outcomes: Total Literacy Campaign in Ghaziabad District of Uttar Pradesh", *Project Report*, G.B. Pant Social Science Institute, Allahabad.

Pant, S.K. (2005), "Final Evaluation of Total Literacy Campaign in District Gumla, Jharkhand", *Project Report*, G.B. Pant Social Science Institute, Allahabad.

Pant, S.K. and Bhatt, K.N. (1999), "Final Evaluation of Total Literacy Campaign in Tikamgarh District of Madhya Pradesh", *Project Report*, G.B. Pant Social Science Institute, Allahabad.

Pant, S.K. and Bhatt, K.N. (2000), "Concurrent Evaluation of Total Literacy Campaign in Ballia District of Uttar Pradesh", *Project Report*, G.B. Pant Social Science Institute,

Rahi, A.L. (1996), *Adult Education: Policies and Programmes*, The Associated Publishers, Ambala.

Rawal, G.B. (1998), "The Gandhian Vision of Education", *Quarterly Journal of Peace Foundation*, Vol. 20, No. 2, New Delhi, pp. 225–29.

Sharma, O.P. and Ratherford, R.C. (1987), "Recent Literacy Trends in India", Occasional Paper No. 2, Census of India, New Delhi.

Visaria, P., Gumbar, A. and Visaria, L. (1993), "Literacy and Primary Education in India 1980–81 to 1991 Differentials and Determinants", *Journal of Educational Planning and Administration*, Vol. III, No. 1, January, New Delhi, pp. 13–62.

9 Land Degradation and Poverty in India

Evidence and Policy Implications

Amita Shah

> We should not take lightly the long-term economic threat of accelerating soil degradation. Historical evidence suggests that the economic decline of empires in Mesopotamia and the Indus Valley was due, at least in part, to widespread salinization and waterlogging of irrigated lands, while decline in ancient Israel, Lebanon, Greece and Rome was due to topsoil loss in the rainfed uplands of the Mediterranean ... . The difficulties of measuring and valuing soil quality changes and their effects should not deter economists and policy makers, but rather inspire them to focus greater attention on soil quality management as a central natural resource issue for sustainable agriculture in the developing world.
>
> — Sara J. Scherr (1999)

Land is one of the basic factors of production, and thus assumes special importance for promoting not only economic well-being but also socio-cultural identity in a spredominantly agrarian society such as India. Ownership and/or access to land are important sources of economic security, opening up larger range of options leading eventually to human development and dignity.

Various theories, mainly from neo-classical economic literature uphold the importance of land in determining the pace as well as composition of economic growth over different stages. While the physiocrats referred to the role of land in creation of land as mother of wealth, Ricardo pointed to the limited availability of good quality of land as a factor leading to diminishing returns to land. The neo-classical economists however, failed to take proper account of the multifarious functions performed by land, which is an exhaustible resource. It is therefore, essential that issues pertaining to management, access and use of land be discussed in the light of ecological economist perspective, which allows for appropriate valuation of land and identifies policy instruments for ensuring its sustainable use.

More recently, attention has been drawn to the adverse impact of soil on poor people's livelihood (Scherr, 1999; Jodha, 1986). Recent evidence from India suggests that land degradation is the single most important form of environmental degradation influencing people's livelihood (Ramachandran, 1990). It is due to the constraint of cultivable land that the growth of agricultural output could not exceed the pre-green revolution period, despite a significant increase in capital formation and technological advancement (Rao, 1994). In fact, the growth-limiting impact of land is reflected through limited availability of water or water-deficiency as observed in a recent study covering a large number of countries in different parts of the world (Kumar and Singh, 2005). According to available estimates, economic cost of land degradation accounts for about 2.82 per cent of the gross domestic product in India (Ramaswamy, 2004). Besides these there have been a number of studies that highlight the economic implications of soil erosion and soil loss (Kumar, 2004).

Overall, the understanding emerging from theoretical as well as empirical studies lend support to the fact that in an economy with large proportion of the (rural) workforce depending on primary production, land is by far the most critical factor, shaping up not only economic growth, but also poverty reduction. The basic proposition however, is that agricultural growth is at the centre of poverty reduction, where quality and access to land play a critical role. The present analysis seeks to adopt a two-staged approach by first examining the linkages between land and income poverty as well as human capabilities; next discussing various coping mechanisms for redressing livelihood constraints emanating from low quality as well as access to both private as well as public (common property) land.

It may be noted that the linkages between land degradation and poverty are mediated by a number of factors that arise not only at individual (household) level, but also at regional level. For instance migration is an important factor mediating the interface between land degradation and poverty. Similarly, access to irrigation has overpowering impact on poverty outcomes; the same holds good for sectoral diversification at region/state level (Shah, 2005; Shah and Singh, 2004). It is therefore, difficult to ascertain direct association between land degradation and poverty especially among households across regions/states, because of the constraints of appropriate data on some of the mediating factors like out-migration, intensity rather than extent of irrigation, and above all, quality of land (degradation). Given these limitations the paper tries to examine the interface between various dimensions of land and poverty across major states in India.

The paper is divided into five sections including the introduction. The next section presents changing profile of use, quality and ownership of land among the major states in India. This is followed by an analysis of co-relates of land, income poverty and human development across the states. Section four discusses major coping mechanisms, presently adopted by poor people, which address their future sustainability. Section five explores policy options for promoting more sustainable and equitable land use so as to provide livelihood support to the poor. The analysis is mainly based on secondary data pertaining to ownership, and quality of land; poverty and indicators of human capability; and other indicators influencing economic growth across major states in India.

Land Use: Degradation, Ownership and Access

This section aims at presenting a brief profile of some of the important attributes of land across major states in India and highlights important changes that have taken place over time.

Table 1

Change in Land Use

	1950–51	*2000–2001*
1. Land Under Forests	12.3	21.1
2. Land Not Available For Cultivation	14.5	13.0
(a) Under Non-Agriculture Use	2.9	7.1
(b) Barren and Unclearable land	11.6	5.9
3. Other Uncultivated Land excluding fallow	8.5	8.5
(a) Miscellaneous Tree Crops	6.0	1.0
(b) Pastures and Other Grazing	2.0	3.3
(c) Culturable Waste	7.0	4.2
4. Culturable Land	44.7	50.5
(a) Net Area Sown	36.1	42.92
(b) Other than Current Fallow	5.3	3.1
(c) Current Fallow	3.2	4.5
5. Data Not Available	13.5	6.9
6. Total Reported Area	100	100
Gross Sown Area	46.39	56.88

Source: CMIE (2005), Agriculture, Centre for Monitoring Indian Economy, Mumbai.

Land Use and Changes over Time

The total geographical area of India is 328.73 million hectares, of which reported area is 304.89 million. By the turn of the millennium, nearly 54 per cent of the reported area was available for agriculture, of which 46.1 per cent was under cultivation whereas 8.1 per cent of land was reported as fallow. On the other hand, 23 per cent of the remaining land area was under forest; 14 per cent was under non-agricultural use and unculturable land; and 9.1 per cent under pastures (plus miscellaneous trees) and culturable wasteland (see Table 1). It is pertinent that over time the land use pattern has changed for better in so far as area under forest as well as under cultivation have increased. Apparently, this has been achieved by improving the productivity of unculturable land and land under miscellaneous trees.

Wasteland and Degradation

Notwithstanding the positive shift in land use pattern, a large part of India's land is facing degradation thereby limiting the productivity and also potential for poverty reduction among people depending on these degraded/marginal lands.

According to the estimates prepared by the National Remote Sensing Agency (NRSA), wasteland constituted about 17.5 per cent of geographical area in the country. This was based on estimates of 241 districts covered 1986–1993 (Table 2). Recently, the second round of results has been published, covering 597 districts in the country. While the estimates suggest that the proportion of wasteland has remained more or less the same, there is however, significant variation across states in the level of degradation and changes thereof overtime. It may however, be noted that the estimates while indicating types of wasteland, do not capture intensity of degradation.

Alternatively estimates prepared by the Ministry of Environment and Forest (1989), provide information on extent of degradation caused by different sources. According to these estimates nearly 130 million ha. of India's land is degraded. This works out to be 42.2 per cent of the geographical area in the country (Chopra, 1996). Of the total degraded land, degraded forest land constituted 27.7 per cent; the remaining 72.3 per cent is non-forest degraded land, which is caused by salinity (7.6%), wind erosion (13.8%) and water erosion (78.6%), wind erosion (13.8%) (See Table 3). It is this component of India's land, which may have a direct bearing on loss of productivity resulting in poverty.

Table 2
Estimates of Waste Land

States	*Per cent Total Geo. Area (241 Districts)*	*Per cent to Total Geo. Area (597 Districts)*
Andhra Pradesh	19.8	16.5
Assam	57.2	17.9
Bihar	15.1	5.6
Gujarat	17.7	10.4
Haryana	7.8	7.4
Himachal Pradesh	37.7	50.9
Jammu & Kashmir	48.3	69.0
Karnataka	11.9	7.0
Kerala	4.9	4.6
Madhya Pradesh	15.7	18.5
Maharashtra	37.7	16.0
Orissa	13.7	12.2
Punjab	4.3	2.3
Rajasthan	25.2	29.6
Tamil Nadu	15.7	13.3
Uttar Pradesh	10.5	—
West Bengal	7.8	4.9
India	17.5	17.4

Source: Based on Waste Land Atlas of India.

The policy makers, therefore, are faced with dual tasks of regeneration of wasteland on the one hand and enhancing productivity of the degraded land other than waste land. In fact, both these tasks should be seen in conjunction with each other given the close interface between the two. The driving force behind the policy interventions should be the idea of land capability so as to ensure diversity in land use, which is crucial for environmental sustainability in the long run.

Private Land: Ownership and Size

Although, agriculture constitutes a major source of employment and livelihood for about 60 per cent of India's population, a significant proportion of rural households are landless (11.3%) and semi-landless

Table 3
Change in Average Size of Landholdings—All India

(hectares)

Category of Farmers	*1970–71*	*1976–77*	*1980–81*	*1985–86*	*1990–91*	*1995–96*
Marginal	0.41	0.39	0.39	0.39	0.40	0.40
Small	1.44	1.42	1.44	1.43	1.44	1.42
Semi-medium	2.81	2.78	2.78	2.77	2.76	2.73
Medium	6.08	6.05	6.01	5.95	5.90	5.84
Large	18.07	17.57	17.38	17.19	17.30	17.21
All Groups	2.30	2.00	1.84	1.69	1.57	1.41

Source: NSSO, 48th Round, Report on Land and Livestock Holdings Survey No. 399, July 1995, Ministry of Planning, Government of India, New Delhi.

(31.1%), i.e., having a landholding size of 0.002–0.2 hectares. Together, these two categories constitute about 42 per cent households in rural India. Prima facie, it may be argued that a large part of these land-poor households (i.e., landless + semi-landless) in absence of adequate income from non-farm activities, are likely to face severe deprivation in terms of income poverty, especially if these holdings consist of marginal land. In reality, however, semi-landless households also reflect high degree of pressure on land, which generally exists in areas with higher proportion of irrigated land or medium-high rainfall. Conversely, the land holding size is generally larger among dry land areas owing to low productivity hence, low density of population in these regions.

During mid-nineties, the average size of landholding was fairly small, i.e., 1.14 hectare, which was initially 2.3 hectare per household in 1970–71. This decline is mainly due to increased demographic pressure, which often leads to non-sustainable use and degradation of land in the long run (Table 4).

Over time, the average size of land holdings has declined due to increase in population. As a result, the proportion of land owned by marginal farmers (<1 ha.) increased from 8 per cent in 1961–62 to 17 per cent in 1992. On the other hand, the share of large holders (>10 ha.) declined from 28 to 14 per cent during the same period. Nevertheless, the concentration in land holding size has remained more or less the same over time. The Gini Coefficient declined from 0.73 during 1961–62 to 0.71 in 1971–72 and remained the same till 1992 (see Table 7).

Table 4
Average Size of Landholdings: States

(hectares)

States	*Marginal 1995–96*	*Small 1995–97*	*Semi-medium 1995–96*	*Medium 1995–96*	*Large 1995–96*	*All Groups 1995–96*	*Concentration Ratio 1992*
Andhra Pradesh	0.46	1.43	2.68	5.74	15.34	1.36	0.72
Assam	0.37	1.37	2.63	5.16	65.60	1.17	0.57
Bihar	0.34	1.32	2.73	5.57	16.52	0.75	0.70
Gujarat	0.54	1.47	2.80	5.90	14.81	2.62	0.71
Haryana	0.50	1.40	2.79	5.90	16.52	2.13	0.68
Himachal Pradesh	0.41	1.39	2.69	5.71	15.60	1.16	0.60
Jammu & Kashmir	0.39	1.38	2.66	5.39	0.00	0.76	0.51
Karnataka	0.48	1.45	2.74	5.87	15.03	1.95	0.66
Kerala	0.15	1.34	2.54	5.20	34.00	0.27	0.69
Madhya Pradesh	0.46	1.44	2.76	5.94	16.11	2.28	0.65
Maharashtra	0.49	1.45	2.73	5.76	16.20	1.87	0.71
Orissa	0.50	1.38	2.67	5.54	16.20	1.30	0.66
Punjab	0.60	1.31	2.60	5.73	14.97	3.79	0.77
Rajasthan	0.48	1.44	2.85	6.22	18.69	3.96	0.65
Tamil Nadu	0.37	1.40	2.70	5.68	23.37	0.91	0.75
Uttar Pradesh	0.39	1.41	2.73	5.54	15.54	0.86	0.63
West Bengal	0.48	1.48	2.74	5.27	203.00	0.85	0.68
India	0.40	1.42	2.73	5.84	17.21	1.41	0.71

Source: As in Table 3.

Common Property Land Resources: Access and Use

Given the property rights regime in India, the land-poor depended mainly on Common Property Land Resources (CPLRs), especially, pastures. In 1951–52, 2.3 per cent of the total reported area was under pastures, which increased to 3.9 per cent in 1981 and then declined to 3.3 per cent in 2000–01. CPLRs have been an integral part of the traditional socio-economic structure, where occupations and resource-use were determined by the hierarchy as well as interface between households, castes and classes. Livestock being an important component within an integrated farming system, village pastures used to play an equalizing role within an agrarian structure where ownership of private land is extremely skewed. In most cases, villages have allocated a part of the village land for pastures; the norm used for allocating such land was 0.4 acre (or 1 Begha) per adult cattle unit.

Over time, the CPLRs have declined both in size and quality (Jodha, 1986), mainly due to increased human as well as livestock population. Besides these, the pastures have also been used for distribution of land under the reform policies. Finally, the most critical issue concerning the CPLRs is encroachment by villagers, who converted the land for crops and other cultivation into land for private access. There are, of course, no systematic estimates of encroachment. The micro studies however observe this as a widely prevalent phenomenon, having positive association with the quality of pastures (Gulati and Chopra, 1994). This obviously reduced access to the CPLRs, which further marginalized the land poor (Iyengar and Shukla, 1999).

The NSSO in its 54th Round has estimated the size and access to CPLRs used for various purposes by village communities. According to this, 15 per cent of geographical area was under different categories. This works out to be nearly 50 million hectares, which is constituted by pastures and grazing land (23%), village forests and wood lots (16%) and other village sites on which villagers have legal usufructuary rights. This excludes government land under the jurisdiction of forests and revenue. Estimates indicate that the average size of CPLR is 0.31 ha. per household where the average size of owned land is 0.84 ha. which is somewhat lower than the average (i.e., 1.01 ha) of owned land during 1995. The average size of CPLR varies from 0.03 ha. in West Bengal to 2.04 in Rajasthan (see Table 5).

The estimates in Table 5 also provide details about various uses of CPLR and their contribution to monthly per capita income (MPCI) across major states in India. It may be noted that whereas average value of collection from CPLR is determined largely by the agro-climatic conditions, their contribution to households income (consumption expenditure) is relatively higher in some of the high poverty states such as Assam, M.P. and Orissa. The contribution is found to be particularly low in Kerala and Rajasthan thus, indicating a diverse pattern.

Land, Poverty and Human Development: An Interface

The poverty geography of India suggests concentration of high incidence of poverty in the central eastern parts, characterized by sub-humid to

Table 5

Extent and Use of CPLRs among Major States in India

States	*CPRl and per HH (ha)*	*Average value of Collections from CPR (Rs)*	*Ratio of Value of Collections Cons. Expd. (%)*	*Per cent of Hhs Reporting Collection*	*Possessing Livestock*	*Reporting Grazing*	*Percent of hhs Access to CPR (0.10 ha. more)*
A.P.	0.17	554	2.78	59	36	14	20
Assam	0.05	1071	4.89	44	62	24	5
Bihar	0.08	519	2.77	41	52	16	4
Gujarat	0.72	663	2.77	55	59	25	51
Haryana	0.05	1174	3.09	27	74	15	6
H.P.	0.33			56	81	35	4
J & K	0.14			33	81	25	15
Karnataka	0.25	635	2.90	53	56	25	25
Kerala	0.12	390	1.17	13	32	3	1
M.P.	0.74	984	4.93	56	68	42	28
Maharashtra	0.30	799	3.61	59	46	11	18
Orissa	0.28	929	5.59	62	58	35	8
Punjab	0.02	1057	2.76	24	55	1	4
Rajasthan	2.04	266	0.91	21	84	28	52
Tamil Nadu	0.16	667	3.65	61	29	9	16
U.P.	0.14	69.0	2.75	33	72	22	13
West Bengal	0.03	450	2.09	38	54	17	1
India	0.31	693	3.02	45	56	20	63

Source: NSSO, 54th Round, 1998.

humid regions with relatively better coverage of forest area. Strangely, these areas have a high potential for agricultural growth. On the other hand, dry land regions, consisting of large tracts of waste land, do not necessarily have high incidence of poverty. To a large extent this is due to factors like (a) high level of commercialization of agriculture; (b) larger land holding size; (c) sectorally better infrastructure and connectivity; and above all, (e) favourable agrarian relations (Shah and Guru, 2004).

The above scenario pertaining to rural poverty in India has been aptly described as follows: "Drier states (in the west) harbour lesser poverty proportions than the wetter ones (in the east). In general, the states, which were under zamindari regime and have experienced relatively ineffective agrarian and land reforms and thereafter green revolution, have been the losers, while those in the west have been gainers. Within these contours, if monsoon fails, all suffer and vice versa" (NIRD, 2000: 9). How far is rural poverty inter-linked with land and human development among major states across these two categories? This issue has been examined in the following analysis in this section.

Land: Occupation and Poverty among Rural Households

The literature on rural poverty in India has more than established the importance of land in determining poverty outcomes among rural households (Mehta and Shah, 2003). This is not surprising given the predominantly agrarian characteristics of Indian economy where majority of poor live in rural areas. What is however, less explored is the change in the nature of the interface that has taken place over time and the pattern of poverty among landless and semi-landless constituting a substantially large proportion (about 42%) of rural households as shown earlier in Table 6.

Table 6

Incidence of Poverty across Landholding Size Class: 1993–94

Landholding Size	*% of Rural HHs*	*% of Rural Poor HHs*
Up to 0.2	42.4	41.6
0.01–0.4	8.9	21.8
0.41–1.0	20.5	17.0
1.01–2.0	13.5	12.0
2.01–4.0	9.3	5.3
4.01 and above	5.4	2.2
All Hhs	100	100

Note: Based on Table 2.9 in Chelliah and Sundarshan (2001).

A recent analysis examining the land-poverty interface in rural India provides useful insights. It is observed that whereas rural households in the category of landless and semi-landless constituted about 42.1 per cent they accounted for a slightly lower proportion, i.e., 41.6 per cent of all the poor households in rural area. Contrary to this, the households owning very small holdings, i.e., <0.4 ha. (or 1 acre) of land have significantly larger proportion of rural poor households as compared to their share in total rural households (see Table 6). To a large extent, these households constitute a recently emerging category of landed community, which have shifted to the category of casual labour mainly due to very small size and/or low productivity of land holdings (Nayyar and Sharma, 2005).

Table 7

Poverty among Landless and Landed Households By Social Groups

Social Groups	*1983*		*1993*	
	Without Land	*With Land*	*Without Land*	*With Land*
Scheduled Tribes	50.6	61.6	49.2	54.2
Scheduled Castes	53.0	54.8	45.9	47.1
Other	32.5	37.7	34.5	31.1
All	40.4	43.4	39.5	36.8

Note: Estimated From Household Level Data on Consumption Expenditure Forum. 38th and 43rd Round of NSSO. For details see Shah and Yagnik (2004).

Table 7 presents estimates of poor households among Scheduled Tribes (STs), Scheduled Castes (SCs), and other communities during 1983 and 1993–94. The estimates clearly indicate that while households with land had higher incidence of poverty in all the three social categories during 1983, the pattern, however, changed in the later period. During this period landless and landed households in the other category experienced opposite pattern whereas poverty among landless belonging to other community registered an increase. As a result, poverty among all the landed households appeared to be higher than poverty among the landless. If we compare this for STs and SCs, landed households continued to have higher incidence of poverty as compared to the landless.

To an extent, the estimates in Table 7 reinforce the widely observed phenomenon of ownership of size of land owned by a large proportion of landed households among STs and SCs, thereby casting a poor impact on poverty reduction. The landless, on the other hand, may explore wider options in the casual labour market and/or get engaged as self-employed in non-agricultural sector especially, if coming from traditional artisan class, they happen to have special skills. Moreover, landless face relatively low level of social taboo to join the cadre of manual labourers around their villages whereas, a poor from landed households may have to migrate out for taking up 'low-status' manual work and perhaps, migrate to urban areas. It is likely that lower incidence of rural poverty among landed in the other category is partly an outcome of out-migration (rural-urban type) of the poor. It is in this context that urban—poverty and the associated deprivation (or adverse in-cooperation) of migrants in these areas deserve special attention.

Table 8

Decline in Poverty (HCR) Among Households Across Different Occupations

Occupations	*HCR*		
	1983	*1993*	*% Change*
Self-employed in Agriculture	38.99	27.11	-30.3
Self-employed in Non-Agriculture Sector	42.89	29.13	-30.2
Rural Labour in Agriculture	63.20	50.56	-19.9
Rural Labour in Non-Agriculture Sector	44.13	34.62	-21.5
Other	29.80	23.27	-21.6
All Households	46.80	37.70	-25.8
Female Headed Households	Na	32.70	Na

Note: Based on Table 2.2 in Chilliah and Sudarshan (2001).

Table 8 presents incidence of poverty among rural households engaged in different occupations. It is observed that households with the background of agricultural labour experienced the highest incidence of poverty; as 50 per cent of households in this category were poor during 1993–94. What is more noteworthy is that these households have experienced the slowest pace of decline in poverty between 1983 and 1993–94. In fact, self-employed households in non-agriculture sector experienced the steepest decline in poverty, (i.e., by 32.2%) which is higher than that recorded among cultivators (self-employed in agriculture). The incidence of poverty among the former is only slightly higher (i.e., 29.1%) as compared to that among cultivators (27.1%) during 1993–94.

It is plausible that a substantial part of the households in the category of self-employed in agriculture are semi-landless, having very small holdings. In that case, households in the category of landless, semi-landless and self-employed having non-farm activity are likely to do better than those having marginal holdings, without occupational diversification within the rural areas. The above phenomenon has been further substantiated by a recent analysis across different social groups (Shah and Yagnik, 2004).

Overall the evidence on access to land and rural poverty brings forth two important observations. First, while land ownership is an important condition for poverty reduction, it is not a sufficient condition; size and also quality of land have significant association with poverty reduction. And second, land-poor (landless + semi-landless) households may often have larger options for diversified sources of income and employment as compared to the marginal and small farmers; thus, the former may escape poverty by combining various opportunities, including manual labour in and around the villages.

Land and Income Poverty

Land, Poverty and Human Development: Correlates Across States

Table 9 presents results of correlation between the four sets of variables, viz., quality, size and access to land; agricultural productivity; sectoral diversification, and poverty as well as human development across major states in India. The important observations are:

- Land productivity has significant negative correlation with chronic poverty. Similarly agricultural labour productivity is also inversely correlated with rural poverty Head Count Ratio (HCR).
- More importantly, quality of land reflected through proportion of wasteland and non-forest as well as total degraded land have significant positive impact on chronic poverty. Strangely, these variables do not have significant correlation with poverty measured through HCR.
- Whereas, rural poverty (HCR) and chronic poverty do not have significant correlation with human development index (HDI), there is however, significant negative correlation between mal-nourishment and chronic poverty and also proportion of stunted children among poor. To an extent this is a tautology. It may however be noted that HCR is significantly correlated with malnourished children.
- Moreover, both female as well as total literacy are found to be positively linked to proportion of stunted and also mal-nourished children. More importantly, land productivity is linked to total literacy as well as IMR, and labour productivity is linked to IMR with negative sign.
- The interface between quality of and access to land, however, indicate significant positive correlation between land productivity and HDI, as in the case of chronic poverty. Equally important is the fact that labour productivity in agriculture has significant positive correlation with HDI, as in the case of poverty (HCR).

Table 9

Correlates of Land, Poverty and Human Development

Variables with Significant Correlation	*HCR*	*HDI (Rural)*	*% of Literate Population (1991)*	*IMR*	*Land Prod.*	*Ag. Labour Prod.*	*% HHS with Livestock*	*% CPR to Total Area*
Landless Households (%)							–0.513*	
Landless + Semi Landless		0.592*		–0.638**	0.500*	0.500*	–0.849**	–0.486*
Total Degraded Land (%)							0.542*	0.676*
Landholding Size (Ha.)					–0.593**		0.475*	–0.602**
% of CPLRs					–0.607**			
Non-Forest Degraded Land (%)**					–0.578*	–0.549*		0.623**
Hhs with livestock				0.578*				0.797*
Gross irrigated area (%)						0.543*		
Rural Poverty (HCR)						0.534*		
Chronic (very) Poor (%)	0.946**			0.531*		0.472*	0.722**	
Stunted Children (%)		–0.601*	–0.638**					
Malnourished Children (%)	0.606*	–0.675*	–0.542*			–0.576*		
HDI (Rural)			0.890**	–0.875**	0.672**	0.649**		
HDI			0.854**	–0.877**	0.620**	0.621**		
Land Productivity		0.672**	0.542*	–0.582*		0.758**		
Ag. Labour Prod.	–0.534*	0.649**		–0.516*	0.758**			
Rural Literacy 91		0.870**		–0.781**	0.542*			
Rural Literacy 01		0.822**		–0.682**		–0.504*		
IMR		–0.875**	–0.782*		–0.582*	–0.516*	0.578*	

- HDI however, does not have significant correlation with quality of land as noted in the case of indicators of poverty.
- With respect of CPLR, the results indicate that the proportion of CPLR in total geographical area is positively correlated to average landholding size (which is generally higher among dry land regions), and negatively co-related with proportion of landless and semi-landless households (indicating land scarcity) in a state.
- CPLR is found to have negative correlation with land productivity. Conversely it has positive correlation with degraded land. To an extent this indicates an overall adverse impact on income through lower productivity and smaller size of holding in land scarce areas.

The variable indicating proportion of households owning livestock indicates an interesting pattern. It is observed that the variable is negatively correlated with proportion of landless and semi-landless households but has positive association with land holding size, degraded land, and is also positively correlated with extent of stunted children. The declining role of livestock in enhancing income/well-being especially among the land poor is thus established.

The results thus, suggest a somewhat mixed picture with respect to the linkages between land, poverty and human development. What is however, important is the critical role of land productivity in influencing both income poverty as well as human development.

Coping Strategies

The above analysis suggested that land degradation and low productivity of land exert significant adverse impact on poverty and malnutrition, which in turn, reflects in poor human development. How do rural households especially poor, cope with these inherent limitations of low quality and productivity of land, and spread over large parts of the country? What is the implication for long-term sustainability of the existing strategies? These issues have been addressed briefly in the light of the evidence and insights emerging from the existing studies.

Three important and interrelated, strategies have been identified for discussion in this section. These are:

1. Livestock as supplementary source of income especially, in dry land and forest based (hilly) regions.
2. Out-migration
3. Increased irrigation through over-use of ground water.

Livestock and Land: Changes Over Time

The analysis of correlation in section 3 indicators suggested that ownership of livestock is inversely related with proportion of landless households across state. In turn, this implies that livestock economy, as an asset/income equalizer, may have started loosing its impact among land-poor households. The phenomenon is clearly depicted in the estimates of livestock ownership across land holding size classes at all India level. Table 10 reveals that whereas the number of cattle among 100 (<0.02 ha. of land) households is 228 among those having a land holding of 1–2 ha. The numbers of buffalo are eight and 90 respectively. These estimates substantiate the findings noted above.

Table 10

Ownership of Livestock and Irrigation Among HHs Across Landholding Size Classes

Size-class of Holdings (0.00ha)	*Nil*	*0.02–2.20*	*0.21–0.50*	*0.51–1.00*	*1.01–2.00*	*All*
			Livestock Owned per 100 HHs			
(a) Cattle Total	14	76	138	206	228	143
In Milk	3	19	24	33	38	26
(b) Buffaloes Total	8	33	45	59	90	59
In Milk	3	12	16	21	31	20
(c) Sheep and Goat	20	75	77	93	115	85
(b) Pigs	2	4	3	—	6	4
(e) Poultry	49	14	183	203	223	166
			Irrigation Equipment Owned per 100 Households			
(a) Pump	0.51	1.58	7.04	11.69	22.12	12.78
(b) Indigenous Water-Lift eqpt.	14.39	28.29	44.85	45.16	53.07	38.44
% of Rural HHs	21.84	20.06	13.31	14.66	14.21	100
Area per HHS	—	0.06	0.36	0.74	1.41	1.08

Table 2.7 in Chelliah and R. Sudarshan.

The phenomenon however, has deteriorated over time. This is reflected by a comparison of 1982 and 1992 (see Table 11). While the number of livestock has declined among the majority of households across land holding size, the changes reflect a U-shaped pattern with landless having the sharpest decline (58.8%) followed by the large farmers (51.3%) on the extreme end. In fact, households with the landholdings varying between 0.21–1.0 ha. experienced an increase over time; and households in this category accounted for 30 per cent of rural households during 1992.

Table 11

No. of Livestock per 100 Households in Each Landholding Size Class: 1982 and 1992

Landholding Size (Ha)	*No. of Livestock per 100 Households All India*		
	1982	*1992*	*% Change*
(I) Landless	68 (35)	28 (17)	–58.8 (–51.4)
(II) Unto 0.2	222 (85)	167 (77)	–24.7
(III) 0.21–1.0	265	289 (204)	9.0
(IV) 1.01–4.0	563 (382)	416 (293)	–26.1
(V) 4.01–10.0	863 (591)	494 (328)	–42.7
(VI) > 10.0	1523 (922)	741 (366)	–51.3
All	337 (205)	252 (179)	–14.8 (–12.7)

Source: NSSO 37th and 48th Round, Reports on Land and Livestock Holding Survey.

Prima facie, the 'U shaped' pattern noted in Table 11, could be explained by decline of CPLRs (for landless) on the one hand, and changing preferences for shifting away from highly labour intensive activity such as livestock among relatively better off farmers on the other. To a large extent, this is a reflection of increased pressure on land (hence degradation) on the one hand and encroachment of CPLRs on the other. This, combined with frequent failure of rainfall since the mid-eighties, seem to have driven out the land-poor from the arena of livestock as a supplementary activity. The result is further marginalization of poor from the land. On the flip side, however, this may have reduced livestock related migration among the land-poor as we discuss below.

Out-Migration: Impact on Access to Amenities and Entitlement

A plethora of studies in India have gone into examining the causes and stream of migration from rural areas. The studies, by and large, indicate three important features: First, a large proportion of out-migration is distress induced. Second, there has been an increase in rural urban migration. Third, adverse natural resource endowment influences the direction of migration from poorly endowed regions to better ones.

While the official statistics do not adequately capture these aspects, micro studies from different states in India substantiate the observations noted above. For instance, a recent study in the context of dry land regions in Gujarat by Shah (2005), observed that whereas degradation of private land did not appear as a significant determinant of out-migration from the region, degradation of CPLRs did emerge as an important factor. Of course, the estimates of degradation are mainly perception-based, hence are subject to further verification. What is, however, more important is that neither ownership nor degradation of land influence the migration decisions of households; rather, the decisions are critically mediated by access to irrigation, which in turn works as a compensatory mechanism of degradation of a part of the land operated by the households.

Chopra and Gulati (2001) on the other hand, highlighted the importance of institutional arrangements for managing CPLRs. Better management and hence better quality of CPLRs emerged as important factors influencing out-migration from arid and semi-arid region in the country. The literature also indicates adverse agrarian relations and forest dependence as one of the important factors influencing out-migration from some of the areas with skewed distribution of land, and limited access to forest resources in the states experiencing high incidence of poverty.

In fact, the pattern of out-migration from these lagging regions is likely to be different from the one from the dry land regions. It is likely that the former, given the limited financial, social and physical (infrastructural) facilities, may explore limited avenues for migration hence, the outcome is often less encouraging than for those from the dry land regions, who go longer distance, in search of non-farm activities and often get settled down in an urban destination. The study by Shah (2005) indicated that the differentiated pattern of migration also exists within the same micro-environment, with asset-poor and asset-rich having different trajectories.

Both short-and long-term migration are likely to exert an adverse impact among rest of the members of the migrating households due to uncertainties and instability in the lifestyle of income around a low mean. We do not have adequate evidence on this aspect. Nevertheless, it may be hypothesized that rural-rural migration is often for short duration and does not create additional disadvantages for the family member in seeking services of health and education. On the other hand, rural urban migration, especially on the lower end of the livelihood spectrum, may end up causing severe deprivation in terms of basic facilities.

Table 12 presents estimates of inter-state out-migration for short duration as well as total migration. It is observed that five major states, viz., Bihar, Rajasthan, U.P., Haryana and Punjab have larger share in the total number of short duration out-migration as compared to their share in the total population. In turn, this suggests higher incidence of out-migration among these states. The pattern is more or less similar except for Karnataka, which joins the category of higher incidence of inter-state out-migration. The results tend to substantiate the observation about differential pattern of migration among households (states) belonging to the two end points of a spectrum of economic well being/asset base. It appears that migrants from Bihar, U.P. and Rajasthan may be more distress induced as compared to those from Punjab, Haryana, Karnataka. The later are likely to be more of 'precautionary' nature rather than purely 'distress' type (Shah, 2005).

Table 12

Inter-State Out Migration and Impact on Projected Population

Major States	*% Share (1991)*			*Impact on Proj. Population Growth***
	Population	*Short Duration Migration **	*Total Migration**	
Andhra Pradesh	8.1	4.6	4.6	–0.1
Assam	2.7	1.4	1.3	0.1
Bihar	10.6	10.9	11.3	–2.3
Gujarat	5.1	2.7	3.5	3.0
Haryana	2.0	4.8	5.3	3.0
Himachal Pradesh	0.6	1.4	1.3	–
Karnataka	5.5	5.8	5.3	0.8
Kerala	3.6	3.2	3.6	–1.4
Madhya Pradesh	8.1	6.8	5.6	2.0
Maharashtra	9.7	9.6	6.6	3.4
Orissa	3.9	2.7	2.3	–0.4
Punjab	2.5	4.4	5.2	0.8
Rajasthan	5.4	7.8	7.3	–0.8
Tamil Nadu	6.8	5.9	5.5	–0.9
Uttar Pradesh	17.0	18.6	21.6	–2.9
West Bengal	8.3	3.4	4.3	3.0
India	100	100	100	–0.1

Note: *Based on Table 6 and 11 in Srivatsava (1998); **Based on Table 5.7 in Dyson (2004).

If we examine the flow of migrants in predominantly dry land and forest-based regions, we find that migration from a dry land region is more likely to be intra-state especially, in the case of Gujarat, Maharashtra, and Andhra Pradesh, given the highly developed secondary and tertiary sectors in the states. It was found that the flow of migrants towards Gujarat, Maharashtra and West Bengal work as magnets for migrants from a number of states. On the other hand some of the forest based economies such as Orissa, undivided M.P. and Assam do not show much of out-migration as noted in Table 12.

However, examining the net impact of inter-state migration, Dyson and Visaria (2004) noted that Maharashtra, Gujarat, West Bengal, Haryana and M.P. will have significant increase in the projected population for 2026, whereas U.P., Bihar, Rajasthan, TN, and Kerala will experience a decline due to migratory movements across state. It is thus, difficult to ascertain the causes and outcomes of migration, which is highly differentiated. Nevertheless, one may safely conclude that much of the distress migration has significant cost in terms of social identity, besides fragmentation of families, increased work burden on women and loss of educational achievements for children in the event of the entire family moving from not-so-remote rural areas to floating settlements at urban destinations.

Irrigation: Overexploitation

The above analysis suggested that land-productivity (rather than) irrigation per se, emerged as an important co-relate of both income poverty and human development. In turn, this may also check distress out-migration, given the fact that irrigation is the single most important factor determining households' decision on migration. There is also ample evidence, the world over, that irrigation, through its direct and substantial impact on land productivity, holds the key for poverty reduction. The Tenth Five-Year Plan for India has also echoed this perspective. Unfortunately, irrigation in large tracts of dry land regions, is found to be fairly non-sustainable because of the over depletion of ground water (Shah et al., 1998). In that sense, irrigation may work only as a short-term strategy, in absence of appropriate interventions for management of land and water through an integrated approach. Failing this, those not having adequate 'land + water' may have to shift out of the primary sector/rural areas so as to be able to prevent further deterioration in their income/livelihood.

On the other hand, people in the agriculturally high potential area suffer because of underexploitation of ground water, mainly due to lack of power supply, financial capital, and market institutional support to facilitate private investment in irrigation (Shah T., 2005). As a result, people from these areas also migrate out. In absence of effective interventions for management of water having critical impact on land productivity, the objectives of poverty reduction and human development are not likely to be realized.

Future Policy Directions

In the light of the analysis given above, some of the directions for future policy are given under the following heads:

Promotion of Livestock through Farming System Approach

It is important to reinstate the asset equalizer role of livestock sector, which may go hand-in-hand with economic diversification of the household village economy. This is particularly important as diversification in non-farm activities per se, may not be adequate for lifting a large proportion of the poor out of poverty. It is, thus, important to view development of livestock sector as complementary rather than as substitute for non-farm employment.

This kind of development however, may follow different trajectory of land use and market support in comparison to irrigation intensive and vertically linked dairying sector, flourishing mainly through intensive use of irrigation. The trajectory that needs to be evolved has to start by enhancing productivity of culturable wasteland including pastures in the context of promoting integrated farming system suitable to different agro-ecological conditions. The thrust should be on promotion of sustainable cropping pattern, emphasizing low water intensity. At the same time, pasture development should also have a share in the use of total water resources in the region. Obviously, institutional support is a precondition for promoting a comprehensive approach for land-regeneration.

Integrated Land and Water Resources Management

While there has been a fair amount of emphasis on Integrated Natural Resource Management, the actual practice is quite the contrary. It is imperative that the discourse on natural resources, poverty reduction and human development bring forth the required coherence among different natural resources. This is essential because neither natural resources nor people's interface with them exist as compartmentalized phenomena.

The issue is particularly true in the context of degraded land—both under crops and forest—on the one hand and water on the other. It has been increasingly recognized that improvement of degraded land, especially in low rainfall/dry land regions is critically contingent upon regeneration, allocation and sustainable use of water across regions, farms, households. For water, rather than land per se is the most scarce resource in these regions, which have large tracts of degraded land. The prescription therefore is to provide limited water to all land rather than only to crop land.

Watershed development programme symbolizes an integrated approach for natural resource based livelihood development. However, there are substantial gaps between the concepts and the practice. The need is to promote convergence in resource management to the extent possible and link that with the developmental objectives at regional as well as household levels.

Land Reforms: Completing the Unfinished Agenda

The recent discourse on structural change and development, by and large, has overlooked the issue of the unfinished agenda of land reforms. The argument has gained legitimacy mainly on the ground that: (a) with increasing population, there is not much of surplus land to be redistributed among the landless; and (b) it is the self-interest of the land poor to shift to non-farm employment rather than getting stuck in low productive land. The correlation exercise in section 3 also reflected absence of any significant association between ownership of land and human development at the state level, though the size of holdings may appear to be an important factor for poverty reduction and/or human development.

While there is some validity in the arguments put forward, what is often missed out is that: (a) there are a lot of deficiencies in the system of land records and legal title in the states where agricultural growth has been particularly low and poverty is glaring; and (b) agricultural growth is a precondition for promoting non-farm employment. In that sense, land reform is also critical for promotion of economic growth and diversification in the lagging regions.

Paving the way towards the above agenda is of course a huge task, requiring strong political will. The state alone may not be able to undertake the task without the requisite institutional support. The participatory institutions being created through various development programmes thus, may provide a platform for implementing the next phase of land reforms. It is imperative to recognize the critical importance of land not merely as a limiting factor for economic growth but more importantly as a basic precondition for facilitating development which is spatially balanced, socially equitable and environmentally sustainable.

References

Birthal, P.S. and Ali, J. (2005), "Potential of Livestock Sector in Rural Transformation" in R. Nayyar and A.N. Sharma (eds.), *Rural Non-Farm Sector,* Institute of Human Development, New Delhi.

Chadha, G.K., Sen, S. and Sharma, H.R. (2004), *State of the Indian Farmer*, Academic Foundation, New Delhi.

Chopra, K. (1996), "The Management of Degraded Land: Issues and an Analysis of Technological and Institutional Solutions", *Indian Journal of Agricultural Economics*, Vol. 51, Nos. 1 and 2, pp. 238–249.

Chopra, K. and Dasgupta, P. (2003), "The Nature of Household Dependence on Common Pool Resources: An Econometric Study for India", Working Paper Series No. E/232/2003, Institute of Economic Growth, Delhi.

Chopra, K. and Gulati, S.C. (2001), *Migration, Common Property Resources and Environmental Degradation*, Sage Publications Ltd., New Delhi.

CMIE (2005), *Agriculture*, Centre for Monitoring Indian Economy, Mumbai.

Das, S. (2000), "A Critical Evaluation of Land Reforms in India (1950–1995)" in B.K. Sinha and Pushpendra (eds.), *Land Reforms in India: An Unfinished Agenda*, Sage Publications Ltd., New Delhi.

Dyson, T. (2004), "India's Population: The Past" in T. Dyson, R. Cassen and L. Visaria (eds.), *Twenty-First Century India: Population Economy, Human Development and Environment*, Oxford University Press, New Delhi.

Government of India (1995), *Wasteland Atlas of India* (Vol. II), National and Eco-Development Board, Ministry of Environment and Forest, New Delhi.

Government of India (1999), Land and Livestock Holding Survey: 48th Round, National Sample Survey Organization, Ministry of Planning, New Delhi.

Government of India, 54th Round, National Sample Survey Organization, Ministry of Planning, New Delhi.

Gulati, S.C. and Chopra, K. (1994), "Population Redistribution, Environmental Degradation and Land Use Patterns: A District Level Study of Linkages in Semi-arid Zones of India", *Demography India*, Vol. 23, Nos. 1 and 2, pp. 1–14.

Iyengar, S. (1998), "Land Use Statistics: Implications for Environmental Data Base", Working Paper No. 97, Gujarat Institute of Development Research, Ahmedabad.

Iyengar, S. and Shukla, N. (1999), "Regeneration and Management of Common Property Land Resources (CPLRs) in India: A Review", Working Paper No. 110, Gujarat Institute of Development Research, Ahmedabad.

Jodha, N.S. (1986), "CPLRs and Rural Poor in Dry Regions in India", *Economic and Political Weekly*, Vol. 30, No. 27, pp. 1169–81.

Kumar, D, and Singh, O.P. (2005), "Virtual Water in Global Food and Water Policy Making: Is there a Need for Rethinking?", paper presented at Research Workshop organized by IWMI-TATA Water Policy Programme, Anand, February 24–27.

Kumar, P. (2004), *Economics of Soil Erosion*, Concept Publishing House, New Delhi, MSSRF (2001), *Food Insecurity Atlas of Rural India*, M.S. Swaminathan Research Foundation and World Food Programme, Chennai.

Mehta, A.K. and Shah, A. (2003), "Chronic Poverty in India: Incidence, Causes and Policies", *World Development*, 31(3), March.

Nadkarni, M.V. (1996), "Poverty, Dependence on CPLRs and Economic Development" in J. Parikh and Reddy, S. (eds.), *Utilization of Common Property Land Resources through Cooperation: A Step Towards Sustainable Development*, Indira Gandhi Institute of Development Research, Mumbai, pp. 100–111.

Nayyar and Sharma (eds.) (2005), *Rural Transformation in India: Role of Non-farm Sector*, Institute of Human Development, New Delhi.

Ramachandran, H. (1990), *Environmental Issues in Agricultural Development*, Concept Publication Company, New Delhi.

Ramaswamy, C. (2004), "Constraints to Growth in Indian Agriculture: Needed Technology, Resource Management and Trade Strategies", *Indian Journal of Agricultural Economics*, Vo. 59, No. 1.

Rao, C.H.H. (1994), *Agricultural Growth, Rural Poverty and Environmental Degradation in India*, Oxford University Press, New Delhi.

Reddy, D.N. (2002), "Changing Agrarian Relations and Rural Labour: Certain Emerging Issues", *Indian Journal of Agricultural Economics*, Vol. 45, No. 1, pp. 47–65.

Scherr, S.J. (1999), "Soil Degradation: A Threat to developing Country Food Security?, Food, Agriculture and Environment", Discussion Paper No. 27, International Food Policy Research Institute, Washington D.C.

Sengupta, R. (2001), *Ecology and Economics: Approaches to Sustainable Development*, Oxford University Press, New Delhi.

Shah, A. (2003), "Changing Interface Between Agriculture and Livestock: A Study of Livelihood Options under Dryland Farming Systems in Gujarat" (unpublished), Gujarat Institute of Development Research, Ahmedabad.

Shah, A. (2005), "Land Degradation and Migration in a Dryland Region in India", Working Paper No. 10, South Asian Network for Development and Environmental Economics, Kathmandu, Nepal.

Shah, A. and Guru, B. (2004), "Poverty in Remote Rural Areas in India: A Review of Evidence and Issues", IIPA-CPRC Working Paper No. 21, Indian Institute of Public Administration, New Delhi.

Shah, A. and Yagnik, J. (2004), "Poverty Among Economically and Socially Marginalised Households in Rural India: How Critical is Land-Base?" (unpublished), Gujarat Institute of Development Research, Ahmedabad.

Shah, M. et al. (1998), "India's Drylands: Tribal Societies and Development through Environmental Regeneration", Oxford University Press, New Delhi.

Shah, T. (2005), "Ground Water and Human Development", paper presented at the Research Workshop organized by IWMI-TATA Water Policy Programme, Anand, February 2005.

Shah, T. and Singh, O.P. (2004), "Irrigation Development and Rural Poverty in Gujarat, India: A Disaggregated Analysis", *Water International*, Vol. 29, No. 2, pp. 167–177.

Shenggan, P. and Hazell, P. (2000), "Should Developing Countries Invest More in Less Favoured Areas? Empirical Analysis of Rural India", *Economic and Political Weekly*, Vol. 35, No. 17, pp. 1455–64.

Srivastava, R. (1998), "Migration and Labour Market in India", *Indian Journal of Labour Economics*, Vol. 41, No. 4, pp. 583–617.

Vasisht, A.K., Singh, R.P. and Mathur, V.C. (2003), "Economic Implications of land degradation on sustainability and food security in India" South Asian Regional Conference on the Transition towards sustainable development in South Asia, 10–11 Feb., 2003, India Habitat Centre, New Delhi, pp. 179–187.

World Bank (India) (1998), *Wasteland Development Review*, Mimeo, New Delhi.

10 Paradox of Hunger

Shilp Shikha Singh

Food is one of the basic needs for human existence. Denial of right to food is not only a human rights violation but it also puts a question mark on the legitimacy of the state structures. It is a well known fact that inspite of the wide-ranging institutional changes and impressive achievements in food security at the national level, the Indian economy still houses a bulk of hungry and starving people. This compels one to enquire into the processes that generate and perpetuate hunger, and see to what extent democracy matters in hunger alleviation. In order to understand this dynamics let us first have a look on the severity of the problem of hunger?

Hunger

> Israwati has seven children, her youngest son is just six months old and is ill since birth therefore she always keeps him wrapped in her pallu. Her husband died four months back due to severe illness. Death due to illness is very common in the Bhotaha 'tola' of Sohagi Barwa village (one probable reason can be lack of immunity due to insufficient diet). She has been the sole bread earner before his death. She borrowed a sum of Rs 200 for his medical treatment but nothing could save him as proper cures are not available in the region. This place is surrounded by forest and watery streams from all sides. The local PHC is 60 km away from this place. They totally rely on quacks even for severe ailments. Israwati pointed towards her 12 yrs old (eldest) daughter who was peeping out from the darkness of the hut and told us that now she goes out for work "I am too weak and with a baby to feed, I cannot earn", says Israwati. She admitted though reluctantly that sometimes she gets poshahar from the Aganwadi Centre. Her lack of enthusiasm for being a beneficiary of Aganwadi Centre showed how disinterested she was to feed herself when

> she had seven unfed mouths back home. Moreover, just a handful of Sattu in a week is insufficient. She told us that she eats only once a day and her kids, if fortunate enough, sometimes manage to eat twice and those are the days to rejoice. Situation has deteriorated after her husband's death, now it is a normal practice in their household to remain on fasting for 10–12 days in a month. There are also days when after children are fed nothing is left for her to eat. The meager flesh on her body was testimony to that. The full diet of this lactating mother includes three chapaties or a handful of rice with chutney or a little bit of vegetable, which the creeper on her depilated hut provides. Three kilograms are consumed in a day when everyone is fed properly. This family is not a beneficiary of any food security schemes run by the government. It was the chairperson of the Musahar Manch (community based organization) of her 'tola' who came for her help after her husband's death and told her about various government schemes. She expressed her inability to run from one office to another in order to fulfil all the formalities in order to be chosen as a beneficiary as her baby was very ill. When she took out the baby for us to examine we found that the baby was extremely malnourished and was apparently suffering from Marasmas.

This is the tale of a Musahar family which lives in Sohagi Barwa village in the Nichalaul Tehsil in Maharajganj district of U.P.. Musahaar is the name of a community that lives in small and scattered hamlets alongside the banks of river Gandak in eastern Uttar Pradesh.[1] This Musahar belt extends from the neighbouring state of Bihar where they have a noticeable presence. In U.P. their population is densely concentrated in Kushinagar, Maharajganj, Deoria and Gorakhpur districts where they constitute the majority of Scheduled Caste population, though there is general consensus that given their life dependence on forest and lifestyle they should be classified under Scheduled Tribe.

The Musahar Community

As the name signifies Musahars have been traditionally identified as 'rat-eaters'. People are hesitant to give recognition to their presence around themselves. They are seen as a lazy community whose members will not work until even the last penny is spent. This is their constructed social image, which still dominates the village mind. The typical social classification based on a peculiar feeding habit accentuates their marginalization in society. Owing to this reason, if you ask a Musahar whether he eats rat or not, he will invariably reply 'No'. On much insistence they will tell that their ancestors used to eat rats, but that is an old story now, the present generation has not even tasted it. Whether rat eating is a myth or a reality is yet to be explored. The regular practice is that Musahars collect the leftover grain scattered in the field after the harvest. In the field rats are their only competitors and they are compelled at times to follow field rodents and glean grains from their burrows. From Sohagi Barwa the impression comes that now for fun one may roast a mouse and eat but it is not out of necessity.

In the Maharajganj district, Nichlaul is the tehsil and block where Musahar concentration is dense. Within Nichlaul tehsil in Sohagi Barwa and Shikarpur Gram Sabha, Musahars constitute the majority of population. There are 16 Musahar tolas in these two gram sabhas. These two gram sabhas are separated from the mainland of Nichlaul tehsil and is at a distance of 60 km. In order to reach the place one has to cross Kushinagar district, then enter Bihar and then again re-enter Nichlaul tehsil through the forest. It is difficult to approach this area because there are no proper roads and bridges to cross the watery streams. The forest has been declared as Reserved Forest and hence roads cannot be constructed. "Even for a small work, as to improve connectivity with the mainland, administration has to take Supreme Court's decision and hence job becomes tedious and the needs are often overlooked", says the Chief Development Officer of Maharajganj district. It is said that years back this area was covered with dense forest and some British officials used to come here for hunting. An old dak bungalow called 'Kath Bangla' in local parlance is still standing there which might have been used by these officials. In order to clean some patches of land, Britishers settled these hard-working Musahars in this area. These people cleared some forest land and started practicing shifting cultivation. "Only a Musahar could have done it as we have the traditional skill of judging the property and quality of soil", says Raju. The land being fertile and the population of Musahars settled in the area being small there was enough for everyone to eat unless hit by a natural calamity. Other forest produce also supplemented the diet. Though the level of poverty was never less but at least there was neither any exploitation nor a situation of extreme deprivation. Slowly, this fertile land attracted people from the neighbouring areas who, by giving petty allurements (a piece of cloth) to these innocent people, acquired large chunks of land. With the passage of time ownership of landholdings became more and more concentrated in the favour of upper class. Some of them left their traditional abode along the riverbank to settle wherever the local land/estate owner allowed them to stay in exchange of *begari*.

Musahars, the natives of this place turned into landless agricultural labourer. Whatever small amount of land was left in their hand was mortgaged due to increased vulnerability to shock and disaster. This area is prone to flood. It is worth mentioning that Musahars were never experts in agricultural techniques. Thus the outsiders came to the area, got the forest cleared thereby robbing Musahars of their homes. The irony of the situation is that Musahars helped in clearing the forest for the land/estate owners and in return their right over land was taken over by the estate owners. Since time immemorial, it has been easier for the dominant class to exploit and use Musahars, who on account of little knowledge and skill became accustomed to be dependent on their *sarkars* to such an extent that it became impossible for them to see a destiny beyond this relationship. Upper class people who came from outside, introduced new cropping pattern. Earlier only coarse grains were produced but now paddy and sugarcane are grown extensively. On the one hand it increased the productivity and profitability of the farm (all benefits accrued to the landlords) and on the other hand it brought about considerable change in the food basket of the poor. Now it mainly constitutes of rice and wheat which is to be bought from the market. It not only increased the dependence on market but also reduced the choice available with the poor, all coarse grain being absent from the scene. No work for the day means nothing in food for the family. During their stress period when work is scarce and so is food, they face hunger very often. They have in fact learnt to live with hunger.

> Rajawati (26 yrs) spends her day sitting in front of her small hut because her lower body part is paralyzed. Due to insufficient nutrition and health care her lower body part became weak after giving birth to her youngest son and 6 months back it stopped functioning all together. She cannot move on her own. Somehow she cooks the food early in the morning before her husband leaves home in search of work. There was nothing much in her hut, just a chulha surrounded with a little bit of utensils one containing some cooked rice (perhaps that was the lunch for this family of 5 on that day), a machan in the corner with some phus and shabby linen and rags to be used in place of quilt, few broken empty plastic containers and an open old steel box with few clothes untidily spread inside and outside it. In the centre of the hut one could see a half burnt wooden log which is used by almost all Musahars to fight the chilling cold waves. Surprisingly there was no mud container, which is used for storing food grains for longer period, and 2 kg of paddy was lying in a basket. It is to be remembered that this was one of the food secure

months. The family possesses 5 katha of land but it is all waterlogged throughout the year. She is aware of Ration Cards but complains she has none. Her husband Chanan earns Rs 30 a day when he gets some work. He cannot migrate outside for work like other people of his community because now Rajawati cannot take care of the family back home and his children are very small. Nanchu is just 2½ yrs old, Chanak 8 yrs and Manitwa is 11 yrs old. Manitwa helps her mother in the household work besides looking after the younger ones. Rajawati cannot go for medical treatment as she has no money. Though the entire income is spent on food still for 4–5 days in a month the entire family has to undergo fasting. Nanchu is too young to understand his family's agony and therefore cries whenever he is hungry, but like his brother and sisters when they were small like him, he only gets slapped on his face. Rest of the family has perfected the art of fasting.

Seasonality of Food Availability

Musahars are mostly wage labourers and in the absence of any durable asset[2] (like land or jewellery) food availability is closely linked with the availability of work. Since they have no land they are totally dependent on the market to buy every foodstuff.

Stress Period

The Musahars do not get sufficient agricultural work mainly during two months of the rainy season, i.e., *Sawan* (mid-July to mid-August) and *Bhado* (mid-August to mid-September); and two months of the winter season, i.e., *Pous* (mid. December to mid-January) and *Magh* (mid January to mid-February). In the rainy season, the adjoining fields and sometimes the entire village is inundated by the flood waters. "We cannot migrate out for work during this period because arrangements have to be done to keep our family and its belongings safe and secure. At times we migrate with our entire family on boats to the neighbouring areas of Bihar and remain there for 10–20 days and then come back to reconstruct our huts destroyed by the flood water", says Sanjay of Dharampur tola in Shikarpur gram sabha. In case there are no floods, then also the only work available at that time is repairing of houses with mud or laying of roof on huts. Living under dripping and shattered rooftops, they themselves lay the roof of others in the village in order to earn Rs 10–20. Further the area[3] in which rice is cultivated, in the month of July when rains fill the fields, rice saplings are sown in waist deep water. It is mostly done by females who get only Rs 20. Tolas which are nearer to forest like Musahari tola of Naksa baksa is heavily dependent on forest produce like Dhak leaves from which *pattal* are made or tolas of Ledi, Piparpati Baithwalia, and Katahari where people cut and sell headloads of wood, face immense problems in rainy season. During winters the temperature falls down to 3–4 degrees celsius making it very difficult to go out for work. In order to collect the forest produce, they go very early in the morning before the forest officials come or late in the evening just before it gets dark because in the day-light there is danger of being caught and harassed by forest guards and here again winters bring hardship. Moreover, they sell whatever they collect from the forest at throwaway prices.

Due to the scarcity of work during these months there is scarcity of food also. Fasting is the common practice that is imposed on them due to this scarcity. During these four distress months, on an average almost every Musahar family remains on fasting for 3–4 days a month and otherwise also the members barely manage one meal or not even that because there is no work available in the field.

Food Secure Month

On the contrary, the months when there is sufficient work are March to June and September to November. During these months they do not have any problem in obtaining sufficient work though minimum wages are not given. Males get Rs 30 to 35 and females get Rs 20–25. It is assumed that agricultural work is not as labour intensive as industrial or construction work (road construction, work in construction industry, looms, mills, etc.) and hence a minimum wage rate of Rs 58 is very high. Every member of the family who is above 12 years in case of girls and 15 years in case of boys goes out for work. Otherwise for a family of six, which is the average family size, it would be difficult to arrange two square meals. In the months of October and November, rice is harvested, while in February and March wheat is harvested. Since this area falls in the sugarcane belt of eastern U.P., sugarcane sowing in the months of May and June provides some work. From November to January cutting and peeling of sugarcane is the major wage labour. It is to be mentioned that at the time of harvesting they do not get wages in cash but in kind. This system is called *banihari*. For peeling and cutting of sugarcane, they get cash payment.

Coping Strategy

During stress period they are dependent on what they call *pani ke phal* or water fruits like Siurki,[4] Makhana,[5] Malkoka[6] and on the flesh of small creatures of ponds and rivers like Dhoka,[7] Dhoki,[8] and snails, which they collect manually. Women enter in shoulder-deep freezing waters during *Magh-Poos* to collect these. Cases have been reported where they have fallen ill and even have died after eating poisonous aquatic food. They also sell them to get some money. In winters, they bring from the jungle some wild roots namely Gethi,[9] Katarua[10] and Tevana[11] to eat (these have some medicinal value as well), but now it is difficult to find them due to changing vegetation in forests. Mostly, they take rice along with chutney of salt and chilli. Even wheat, pulses (Arahar which is the staple food of that region) and vegetables are unaffordable and luxuries for them. Children are slapped hard when they demand food. "We teach our children to live with hunger" says Tulsi, a 32 year old mother of three children. When they have nothing to eat they take credit from the local moneylender who charges an interest at the rate of 10 per cent. In order to repay this loan, they work almost as bonded labourers in the fields of moneylenders. Same strategy is adopted in case that they need large amount of money for meeting marriage or medical expenditure. The only difference in this case is that they have to keep their land as security. Nearly 33 per cent, i.e., 583 Musahar households out of 1,762 have mortgaged their land. On the whole, 898 Musahar households are indebted to moneylenders.[12] The most striking feature of this entire transaction is that indebtedness provides them a kind of job security. Though they are underpaid[13] by moneylenders but at least they have an available source of credit. The exploitation, toiling and humiliation it involves have been accepted by them as their fate. Indebtedness has become an indispensable part of their life. Indebtedness, mortgaging and landlessness together form the critical complex of Musahar's vulnerability.

Although migration was not very common among Musahars but now this trend is picking up fast. Normally youths migrates in groups leaving their families. Care is taken that at least one adult is left to take care of the family and earn for daily needs, but old parents are often left alone and in some cases abandoned by unmarried youths. They migrate to different states like Rajasthan, Gujarat, Punjab, Haryana and Uttaranchal. In Rajasthan they get work in cloth printing and dyeing industry, in Gujarat they get work in the textile and fertilizer industry, while in Punjab, Haryana and Uttaranchal they work as agricultural labourers. From tolas, which are nearer to Nepal border people, both male and female migrate to Nepal because of wage differential in agricultural work.[14] Since it is located nearby, often the entire family moves together. While parents and adult children have to work, employers make arrangements for free lunches for the younger ones. The travel expenses are also covered by the employer.

From the social angle, migration has brought about real change in their lifestyle and perspective towards life. Exposure to the outer world gives them a sense of lack of power and of inferiority in their status as a group. They have a growing understanding that their own identity as a social group instead of providing collective strength has become a causal factor for marginalization. This has led to the realization to bring about change in their habits for their acceptance in the society on their own terms. They cite seasonal migration for work as the main reason to leave the rat eating practice. Migration has also brought them closer to other caste groups who similarly undertake migration. Foreign surrounding has been acting as a precipitating factor for social cohesion. Out there, the common homeland builds a bond between them, which could never bloom on their original land due to a rigid social stratification.

Figure 1
The Paradox of Hunger

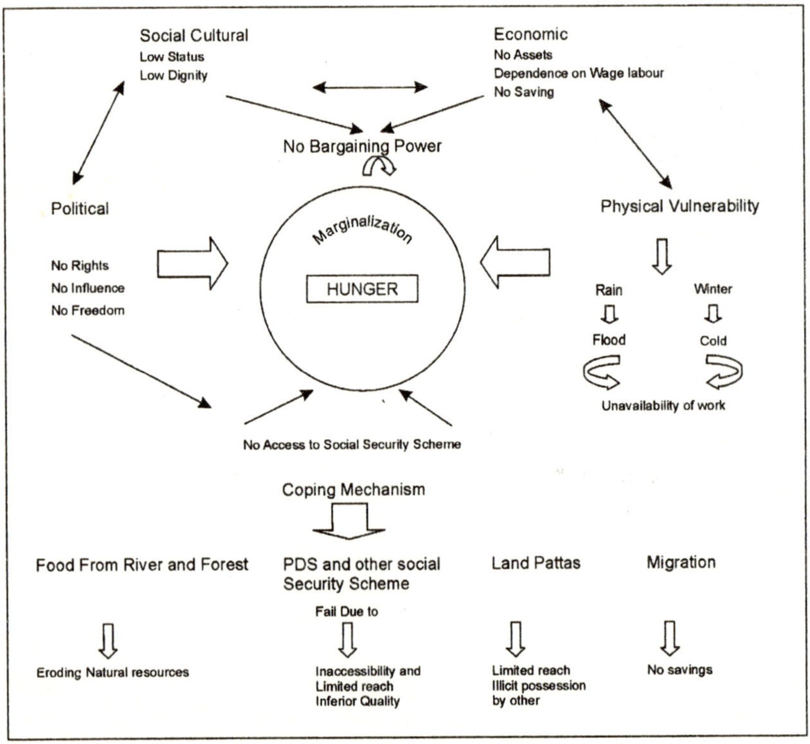

The Issue of Wages and Land

Land ownership among them is negligible. Out of 1,762 households, 647 households, i.e., 37 per cent of the Musahar families are without land.[15] Whatever ancestral land they had, has been kept on mortgage for small sums of money. They have been working almost as bonded labourers on their own land to repay the loan taken from local landlords in distress months. Though at the time of Mayawati government some land pattas were distributed in the villages, but fertile lands were cornered by other Dalit castes and in their share, came the infertile, waterlogged and disputed land. There are incidences of forged occupation of land. Kashinaresh owns approximately 400 acres of *benami* land in the Barhara Chargaha of Maharajganj district. Out of these, 60–70 acres is that land, which has been identified under ceiling limits for distribution, but the owner has taken stay orders from the court and about 150–200 Musahars are affected by it. These people have strong political nexus and they use their money and muscle power to nullify any opposition.

As has been mentioned earlier, employers do not consider agricultural work to be very labour intensive like industrial or construction work (road construction, work in construction industry, looms, mills, etc.) and hence Rs 58, which is the minimum wage rate, appears unjustified to be paid by them. Thanks to government schemes for road construction, which have popularized the minimum wage concept amongst these poor people, but only privileged ones get a chance to work there. Further there are big farmhouses in Maharajganj district on which Musahars are toiling like bonded labourers from last 4–5 decades and there is virtually no scope of resistance for demanding higher wages. Even the land on which their huts stand now is not owned by Musahars and this adds to their predicament. They are constantly threatened and compelled to work only on the farms of these big landlords accepting whatever is offered. In other cases, on demanding higher wages landowners have opted for mechanized farming and the use of combine harvester is increasing. During harvest time one can see groups of Musahars and other landless labourers silently witnessing the use of combine harvester which can do the work of 20 labourers in a day. There are also cases when the landowners do not honour verbal contracts and that makes Musahars to suffer.

> In the village of Barhara Chargaha a landowner struck a deal with 5 Musahars of neighbouring area to harvest the paddy standing on his field of 3 bighas on the payment of 7 men (280 kg) of paddy for each bigha along with two meals a day. Though they were never given the promised

meals even once, these people worked hard for 15 days and they harvested the entire paddy and also separated the husk from 3/4th of the harvest. One day when they came back on work after lunch they found that the owner himself was engaged in separating the husk from rest of the paddy and he straightaway refused to make payment for the work done until now by these five musahars.

The above figure unfolds the paradox of 'hunger'. Four causal factors of hunger have been identified viz.; Socio-Cultural, Economic, Political and Physical. Socio-Cultural and Economic factors weaken the bargaining power Political factor reduces the accessibility of the food security and other related social security schemes. These factors are further interlinked with each other which together lead to marginalization and precipitate into hunger. Coping mechanisms fail due to various reasons.

The Role of the State

Visible role of the state in alleviating hunger can be seen in the form of identified food security schemes[16] being run by the government. All the eight specified food security schemes are running in the area, but their functioning is marred by corruption and irregularities. About 58 per cent Musahar households have BPL cards, although all the 1,762 households are seemingly under absolute poverty. Out of these cardholders only 19 households have green (Annapurna) cards and 347 have red (Antyodaya) cards. Notably 39.5 per cent Musahars are without any ration cards.[17] BPL cards are called 'Oil cards' by them, since they take only kerosene oil on it as the price of food grain is equivalent to the market price and the quality is poorer, though the officials claim that there are only seasonal variations in purchases from the fair-price shops. At the time of harvest, when market is flooded with grains and prices are quite low, people prefer to buy from the market; otherwise purchases are made from the fair-price shops. It is to be noted that the kotedar lifts the entire quota including that of BPL in every season. "We have to pay Rs 6 per quintal for rice and wheat, Rs 25 per quintal for sugar and Rs 25 per barrel for kerosene oil as commission in the supply department where it is shared. Losses are also incurred due to various other expenditures, which are not covered by the official margin. In Antyodaya there is no profit at all. In order to compensate for these losses we sell the unlifted quota in the market at a price less than market prices because quality is not good and weights are also not appropriate", says a kotedar of Mithora block of Nichlaul tehsil. On the other side, the district supply officer says that, "BPL and Antyodaya schemes should be abolished altogether and only Annapurna scheme should be continued for the most deprived sections. Distribution of the foodgrain at half the economic cost under the Antyodaya scheme only creates a kind of dependency syndrome among able-bodied persons who tend to save their labour at such a heavy cost being borne by the state. The margin of Rs 5 on each bag, which the kotedar gets, is not enough to cover even the freight and other extra charges and hence they are forced to charge extra money from the beneficiaries. Although I am confident enough that no government can dare to abolish such populist schemes which are making the department bankrupt on account of vote bank politics." Besides price and quality differences there may be other reasons as well for dependence of Musahars on the market: one being the inability to make monthly purchases in one go (fair price shops are open only for two or three days a month). Mostly these people make weekly purchases when they get wages. These people have devised a strategy of rotating Antyodaya card amongst the members of the family and also within the tola to get maximum benefit out of it. Suppose there is one card in a big family where there are 5 sons who are married and live nearby with their wife and children, then whosoever is able to collect 105 rupees will take the card and make the purchase for his individual family. Likewise, if any card is lying free in the tola due to inability of the owner to save money and someone else has the capacity this month but doesn't have the card, then he will buy the card in Rs 20 from the owner and use it. "Five times on someone's else card I have bought 35 kg of ration", says Ramdhani. One more practice is that if a person has less than Rs 105 then he can keep his card with the kotedar who will make the entry of selling 35 kg and that person will purchase according to his paying capacity. Further, Pradhan takes bribe for this purpose ranging from Rs 100 to Rs 300 depending upon the paying capacity of the 'would be' beneficiary. There are hardly any Annapurna beneficiaries amongst the Musahars. Aganwadies or the ICDS centres are absolutely non-functional. There is complete lack of infrastructure and there is lack of supervision at these centres as they are far away from the Musahar tolas. The height of corruption is reflected from the incidence of selling the 'poshahar' in the market. People are not aware of National Old Age Pension scheme and the National Maternity Benefit scheme. Spreading of awareness with regard to existing government scheme has led to the selection of few Musahars for the National Family Benefit scheme. The status of Mid-day Meals scheme is somewhat better, in a sense that people know about it and it is being run in every school, but menu is never followed. In the name of food, only 'khichari' with a little bit of lentil and more of rice in it, is served almost daily. On all these the Pradhan of Naksa

Baksa says, "Cooking according to menu will take a lot of time because these village lads eat a lot. Further, we cannot refuse to give food to any child who comes during lunch time on moral grounds. All this increases the workload and kitchari seems convenient in that case". Students are asked to bring the utensils from their home and since at home one utensil is shared by many, so they have to go in the lunch time to bring it and go back to return it also. At some places they are even asked to clean those utensils in which food is cooked and thus a lot of time is wasted in this process, which adversely affects the learning at schools.

In spite of such a state of affair where not a single scheme is being run properly, people are not disenchanted with the state machinery. Though the issue of proper implementation is vital, but one larger question, which is often ignored, is whether food security can be ensured only by these schemes. Having analyzed hunger from various socio-cultural, economic and political angles it is difficult to assign central importance to these schemes. Hunger, where it is a group phenomenon, is the result of multiple marginalization, which is the reflection of larger societal set-up that demands more radical solution. It is in this light that I will examine the intervention by Action Aid for the cause of Musahars of Maharajganj district.

Action Aid Intervention

Musahars of Maharajganj and Kushinagar have been identified as a vulnerable community by Action Aid. The organization plans to have a long-term engagement to build the capacity of the community to fight for its rights especially the "right to food and livelihood". In Kushinagar, Nari Vikas Seva Samiti and one local activist were already working with Musahars (primary focus, land rights). Action Aid started its project in their collaboration in December 2002, but after some time it decided to directly intervene in the adjoining area of Maharajganj. The 18 months pilot project just ended in Maharajganj. The intervention is financially being supported by PACS/DFID[18] programme. In India PACS intervention is part of the efforts to achieve the Millennium Development Goal of halving the poverty by the year 2015. Maharajganj district is one of the poorest districts of PACS programme.

The initial focus of the initiative was on meeting the immediate poverty needs of the community under which food security was the foremost challenge, within the rights framework. Other objectives of the Action Aid Intervention are community institution building, consentization of non-Musahars, policy advocacy, liasioning with the government, community capacity building, research and media advocacy.

They started their work by conducting a baseline survey of the community. Slowly, they initiated the process of creating awareness regarding their rights. Through intensive interaction and small training session, the community was exposed to the developmental process in order to generate demand for learning skills to approach the state with their problems. This helped to bring confidence in Musahars and prepared them to initiate their collective struggle. The project has been successful in motivating Musahars to form their own Community based organization in the form of Musahar Manch at the tola level and a federation at the district level having representatives from each tola with an executive of 12 members. SHGs in each tola were formed to encourage entrepreneurial skills and to make them self-sufficient for day-to-day needs. In Sohagi Barwa, Musahar Manch of all the 16 tolas and SHGs of these tolas invested funds to start a crusher plant. It is running successfully and last year Rs 15,000 were saved when the plant was run for 90 days. In this crusher plant, 6–8 labourers of the Musahar community worked daily and earned Rs 50 per day. Further, a lot of money was spent by the organization (4.3 lakhs) to pay for releasing the mortgaged land on priority basis, which was decided by the community itself. By organizing various rallies, demonstrations and interface camps, attempts have been made to bring Musahars, hitherto unheard and unseen, on the forefront of public domain and also to make government machinery responsive and accountable towards them. During interface camps government officials were invited and made to hear the complaints and plights of the Musahars by the community itself. This gave them the first feel of empowerment, since to directly face the official and to be able to say something was in itself, an unusual experience for a Musahar. It had a catalytic effect. On the part of government officials the experience of going at the doorstep of Musahar hamlets, witnessing acute poverty, interacting with the most vulnerable amongst them, sensitized them towards their cause. Efforts yielded in the release of several government orders (GOs) instructing the line departments to accord high priority to Musahar dominated villages for all kind of developmental work. Block officers were directed to carry out a survey to assess the access of Musahars in government schemes. District Magistrate appointed a Nodal Officer to oversee the implementation of government-run schemes/programmes in Musahar hamlets. A coordination committee at the tehsil level (Nichalaul) was set up having heads of health, education, rural development, forestry and aganwadi departments as its members, to coordinate and monitor the efforts for Musahar empowerment through government support.

Creation of 49 grain banks, fully managed by the Manch at the tola level, is one of the biggest achievements of the initiative. The community itself contributed nearly 5,889 kg of wheat and 4,300 kg of rice in the grain bank. Action Aid has contributed 38,200 kg of wheat and 11,770 kg of rice in this. The average requirement of a family is 3–4 kg of grains daily. At present if 95 per cent of the total Musahar population is assumed to be in need of food grain from this bank in the distress months, then the grain bank can provide food security for one week or so with the present stock. The target is to make provision for two months assuming that two months can be managed by government run schemes and migration. Community food grain bank can, not only address their immediate needs but can also ensure food security during the distress months. It will go a long way in preventing hunger deaths. The community members understand the nature of revolving stock and have shown complete commitment towards sincerely returning the grain taken from the bank. Existing grain banks have already reduced the dependence of the community on moneylenders.

Another noticeable feature, which is the direct result of political mobilization of the community, is the existence of Musahar Pradhans. In the last term, there were two pradhans of Musahar community. During this election as many as 20 Musahars stood for various posts of pradhans and BDC (Block Development Committee). Out of these elected 6, 4 became pradhans and 2 got the BDC seat. Ramsaware, whose wife Girija Devi stood for the post of pradhan and lost, says, "The Musahar Manch supported us and gave financial assistance for the election, though we lost but we have still gained in another sense. Next time even if nobody would support financially we will fight from the general seat. Now at least we know what are the processes involved in it, how to campaign and most importantly the realization of misuse of a Musahar vote has come. This time we lost because just before election the big weights spread rumour about Musahar candidate being bought by some other influential person and is therefore only a proxy candidate. We didn't have time to counter-argue and since such a thing had happened in past, people easily believed it." This is a sign of political empowerment of the community. Up till now voting was considered as a routine exercise in order to maintain the citizenship. It was surprising to find that people were afraid that if they do not go to cast their votes their names would be deleted from the voter's list or what they called the "sarkari kagaz" (government paper) and this would cancel their entitlement for any government assistance at the time of crisis. A better understanding of the system resulting from mobilization has lead them to realize the significance of the ballot. Now they know that it is an opportunity to decide their own fate. This also necessitates liasioning with other non-Musahar dalits in the village.

The Slippery Ground

Musahar Vikas Pahal is a wonderful experiment beyond any doubt. In such a short span of two years, there are big achievements to their credit. But with the end of the pilot phase now it is time to pause for a while and ponder over the strengths which are to be built upon and the loopholes that are to be plugged. At times, conceived ideas show varied manifestations due to different permutations and combinations of existing factors of social reality. These deviations and mutant variety of expression need constant appraisal.

Let us see what happens when an outside organization intervenes in an area to act as a facilitator in the process of development by public action in particular, through community's collective endeavour. In the first or what may be called the nascent stage, there is the uphill task of rapport building, which is very crucial. Any fault with this can lead to the outright rejection of the facilitator by the community. Then comes the second stage, when both the sides, i.e., facilitator and the community impart knowledge to each other and there is mutual learning. This is also the stage of complete agreement, maximum enthusiasm and high expectation and hopes on both the sides. In the third stage, differences start surfacing and the existing social reality becomes an active element. This entire struggle or endeavour is to transform the structures of society, which until now have served to oppress the marginalized. The questions that arise in this stage are—whether people are capable of acting in a genuinely non-power seeking way; are people altruistic or are they essentially selfish, always tempted to free-ride on the achievements of others; to what extent can people in general be emancipated (or emancipate themselves); If they are emancipated from some forms of power, will other forms of power then emerge merely to create new constraints and forms of oppression? The fact of the matter is that any intervention as explained in the beginning attempts to disturb the temporary equilibrium. This equilibrium, however biased and tilted, was up till now running the system smoothly. For example, the dependence of Musahar on the landlords and moneylenders instead of being exploitative has been the only source of livelihood for them. Now the demand for minimum and equal wages is one of the factors leading to the increasing mechanization of farms turning Musahars into jobless groups. Food-for-work provides engagement of one month or so and though full wages are given, there is considerable delay in payments. If at this stage other poor and Dalit communities of the area are not included in this initiative, then this exclusionary tactic will prevent the Musahars from becoming a force to reckon with. Support of other groups in the village is not only desirable but becomes a necessity for the political empowerment of the community. When Musahars become capable of leading the struggle against poverty and hunger then the real transformation will come as Musahars are the most vulnerable poor groups in the village. Further, this inclusion is also necessary for maintaining social cohesion. Small and repeated conflicts at the village level and in panchayats can consume much energy of the community and they might reach the stage of bigger battles totally exhausted and tired. Though the winning of small battles provides confidence and raises the morale in the initial stages, efforts should be made that even those small victories are final since repeated fighting at the same level may be frustrating.

The conflict that emerges in the third stage can have two outcomes depending upon the extent of downward flow of future vision of empowerment of the community. If the community has properly imbibed this vision and there is realization of collective strength and common interest then every new emerging challenge finds automatic solution. Community based organization comes nearer to the state and interaction between them becomes smoother resulting in desired outcomes. Lack of such a vision due to improper sensitization leads to conflict of interests at the community level. The commitment for collective action decreases and self-interest takes precedence over community interest. Any support from outside creates a dependency syndrome and the existence of community-based organization comes under pressure. There is a sequential step-by-step decline and if remedy is not sought in the first stage the disease becomes incurable. For catching the symptom of this disease in the very beginning, even small failures have to be identified and reasons need to be located for that. This attitude is visible in the functioning of SHGs. Repayment rate is extremely low and on insistence some people start looking for excuses to come out of the group. Hence the revolving fund freezes at various points. Now such a situation has come that in every meeting and gathering the issue of money dominates the scene relegating other organizational and strategic issues to the background. Since the total amount of saving is very small therefore often it is not possible to cater to the needs of all the members and decision has to be taken on priority basis. The process of setting priorities through consensus calls for maturity and mutual understanding, which can function only when strong ethical foundation has been built.

Conclusion

The Rights Approach has facilitated self-help amongst Musahars and grain bank is an excellent example in this regard. It has publicized the prevalence of hunger and malnutrition in Musahar hamlets and has facilitated efforts to provide developmental assistance for the state to fight hunger. These are the direct outcomes of Action-Aid intervention. Increasing political participation is an indirect result, but is the most crucial aspect because the sustainability of the entire endeavour depends on it. Radical approaches bring about sudden ruptures in the social fabric. This is happening in the case of Musahars as well as their distance from other communities is growing. Crystallization of group identity and solidarity has led to further isolation. This can be harmful until power gains are optimized politically. Social attitude can change only when other people will realize that Musahars are a force to reckon with politically, then the vote bank politics will take a different turn and claims of Musahars will be given space socially.

Notes

1. Musahar settlements are also found in the districts of Banaras, Chandauli, Bhadohi, Gazipur, Jaunpur and Ambedkar Nagar.
2. Now they have started keeping some animals mostly goats, cock and hen on batai or contract (if an animal will give birth to two offsprings, then one will belong to the owner and the other will go to the person who has made a contract to rear the animal) .
3. Bangar is the land or soil which is good for cereals and Bhat is the land which is good for sugarcane cultivation.
4. White coloured stem which is boiled and then peeled to eat.
5. Prickly fruit that is eaten after splitting.
6. Stem of lotus.
7. The flesh is taken out from the shell, boiled in water, later cleaned with cold water and then cooked with turmeric, salt and other spices.
8. It is dipped in water and left overnight so that mud oozes out of its body and later in the day, after cutting the tail it is boiled to be cooked with turmeric, salt and other spices.
9. It is very bitter in taste; therefore, after peeling and boiling, it is kept in a basket and left overnight in the flowing stream of river. The next morning it is cut into fine pieces and again boiled then cooked with salt and spices.
10. Eaten after peeling and boiling.

11. Eaten after peeling and boiling.
12. Baseline Report, 2003, Musahar Vikas Pahal.
13. Males get Rs 30–35 and females get Rs 20–25.
14. In Nepal they get 5 kg of foodgrain for a day's work, while in India they get only 3 kg for the same.
15. Baseline Report, 2003, Musahar Vikas Pahal.
16. Targeted Public Distribution Scheme, Antyodaya Anna Yojana, Mid-day Meal Scheme, National Old Age Pension Scheme, Annapurna Scheme, Integrated Child Development Scheme, National Maternity Benefit Scheme and National Family Benefit Scheme.
17. Baseline Survey, 2003, Musahar Vikas Pahal.
18. PACS: Poorest Area Civil Society; DFID: Department for International Development (British Government).

11 Nutrition Deprivation at Household Level

Evidences from a National Survey

Rudra Narayan Mishra

Undernutrition in India has several dimensions. One such dimension is known as calorie poverty. Calorie poverty can be studied both at household level as well as individual level. A household (or person) is considered undernourished if it consumes less than the prescribed quantity of calorie per day (in case of person the norm is decided, given its age, sex and occupation). Household calorie requirement is nothing but the sum of the requirement of all the members of the household. However, the risk of the undernutrition may vary among members of the household depending upon their age, sex and occupation (above all it also depends on their place in intra-household hierarchy). It has long been argued that dependent population in a given household has the higher risk of facing undernourishment. These dependent populations consist of children, adolescents, women and the aged population. Many researchers have tried to capture this aspect of intra-household calorie deprivation at household level. In India around 55.2 per cent households suffer from calorie deprivation in rural areas. Whereas for urban India, the figure stands at little higher at 57 per cent (Source NSSO 55th Round, 1999–2000). According to different sources, almost three-fourths of the Indian population is believed to be undernourished (Singh et al., 2002, FAO, 2000, Meenakshi et al., 2003). The issue has attracted attention of various researchers to understand the root cause of the phenomenon. So given the high incidence of the calorie deprivation in India as well as associated gender dimension to the phenomenon, it becomes compelling to look into the type of the households where this deprivation concentrates and the composition of such households. The scheme of presentation of the paper will be the following. In section one, the conceptualization of the issue in hand has been done, both from theoretical and empirical perspective. In section two, issues related to the data and methodology are discussed. Then the third section is about the discussion of the results obtained and spell out the policy implications.

I

Why intra-household bias is important to understand the problem (phenomenon) called undernutrition.

India is always an interesting case for development researchers. It has traditional class differences between rich and poor. Along with this 'class' what we have is indigenous taxonomy of society in terms of 'birth', better known as caste. Certain sections are deprived of equal opportunities just because of their birth. They are not allowed to have equal access to available socio-economic opportunities. To make the situation further worse, there is gender discrimination of women across these class and caste groups. They are at the bottom of the power structure, both at societal and household level. So the denial of opportunities or access to resources have added barriers of poverty and social discrimination along with sexual discrimination for the women and female children from poor and socially marginalized households.

So coming to the question of 'intra-household bias' in Indian context, it is important to remember this complex structure of Indian socio-economic reality. Now we will discuss in detail; what are the dynamics of intra-household allocation of a given food basket, in a typical Indian family or household.

1. It is uni-modal in nature (following Baker's characterization of family). Where one individual (predominantly household head who is in most cases an adult male) decides about the utility trajectory of all members. In fact the households utility function is same as of that individual (Sen, 1984). Sen uses a very harsh term for this type of family 'a despotic family'. It is logically absurd to think that one individual's preference level is same for all. He points out to the fact that absence of 'individual entitlement' leads to capability failure among individual members of a despotic household (most of the Indian family). So lack of sensitiveness towards individual food requirement aggravates the problem of undernutrition in India. Bird (2004) and Laurence Hadad, et al. (1996) discuss the importance of intra-household distribution in ensuring nutritional outcome in detail. Bird has presented a literature review of different approaches to study the issue. According to him, relation to household head is

important to get a fare share of the available intake for the household as a whole.

2. Indian families are demographically large in size. Most of them have large dependent population. They may constitute women, children and the aged.
3. The persistent poverty in rural countryside (not to ignore the plight of urban poor either) make less resource (food is considered to be the most important resource) available to the household. So the distribution of the inadequate pie dependence upon urgency; in this case the earning members (preferably male) got the lion's share, because their physical fitness is thought to be crucial to the family's economic life. Culturally it becomes a norm that women, children and old will manage with little. Even among children there is practice of allocating higher amount for male ones who are thought to be economic assets of the family in future, (not to say about their ritualistic importance in the family).[1] The needs of lactating women, adolescent girls and seek old aged people receives low priority; when it comes to allocation of food.
4. There are some established cultural norms about dietic practices in India. Many households prefer vegetarian diets. There is inadequate consumption of fat, animal protein. But this scenario is changing slowly in terms of higher consumption of these nutrients, as evident from the successive consumption rounds reported by NSSO.
5. Coming to the issue of marginalization which is an integral part of any study on any form of deprivation in India; there exist a large number of studies which tells us that certain sections are deprived historically to access basic needs of life. They are on the periphery of our economic and social life for centuries. Those households are more likely to have limited resource (predominantly food).
6. The dependence of rural economy in India is predominantly on agriculture. It is a well known fact that, agriculture to a large extent is controlled by exogenous factors like monsoon; not to say about the endogenous factors (or the in-built bottlenecks) like infrastructure, credit and access to market. The uncertainty in agriculture gives rise to the phenomenon which is called 'seasonality'. Since agricultural activity is seasonal; it has implication in terms of fluctuation in rural employment opportunity and food prices. It is found that most of the rural poor are also likely to be agricultural labourers. Since casualization of Indian agrarian economy started (from 1970 onwards its peak pace), the nominal income of the agricultural labourers may

have increased. But several researchers have shown that the real income is declining. So in lean seasons when there are little agricultural activity and food prices are high, it is most likely that these casual labourers in agriculture or in rural agro-based industry face resource constraint to have adequate intake.

On this backdrop; what is attempted here, is to present some empirical findings in Indian context to support the theoretical construct of the issue presented above. There are many researchers in India who have already examined the issue from different angle. The foremost among them is Beherman (1988), Beherman and Deolalikar (1987). Taking in to account six ICCRISAT villages from Deccan (four from A.P. and two from Maharashtra) these studies found that there is discrimination in calorie allocation against the girl children in households. The discrimination is higher in the poor households belonging to scheduled caste and other disadvantageous groups. The discrimination (in terms of calorie availability to male and female children) reaches an alarming proportion in the lean seasons. The reason is clear. Boys are seen as productive assets of the poor households whereas girls as liability.

Sen's own empirical findings shows that in time of flood, incidence of under weight is higher among girl children, both in places at Kolkata and Bangladesh (Sen 1984). Even his findings show that the economic well being of the family might not trickle down to each member equally. He has found evidence from two Bengal villages that when in one village the land reform is successful (that means now poor families have some income generating asset with assumption that quality of distributed land is satisfactory and in Bengal; since it is on Gangetic Delta, quality of land does not differ much), the prevalence level of underweight among girls are identical to another village where land reform is not successful. But he found there is difference in prevalence of underweight among boys of two villages. It leads to conclude that in Indian context the intra-household distribution norms are very crucial to outcome such as nutrition. Then in the same paper he has demonstrated in the village where land reform is not successful, but there is some direct intervention through feeding programmes (albeit for tribal girls only), there is marked difference in prevalence of underweight among them from their counterparts in the other village with no feeding programme (though land reform is successful). It might indicate to the fact that state has a role to play (or for that matter some agency arrangement) to reach the deprived individual within the given family. Because family in this case is not a 'rational' distributive mechanism which will take care of 'individual needs'. The issue of gender discrimination in distribution of available calorie at household level is re-emphasized (Dreze and Sen, 1989).

The reduction in food availability for the rural households during natural calamities like drought is confirmed by the study of Shah and Sah (2004). Their study is based on the two villages from western Madhya Pradesh. The result confirms the proposition that food consumption declines considerably for the lower income households in the drought year compared to any normal year. This in turn has adverse effect on the diet intake of the dependent population in those households (Table 11, page 26). The study by Chakravarthy and Dand (2006) shows that tribal house-holds engaged as casual labourers are highly vulnerable to food insecurity; especially in summer and monsoon months. As it is mentioned earlier in summer, there is lack of agriculture activity and in monsoon there are generally high prices of food, owing to the fact harvest is not in near future.

Borooah (2004) found that in India still boys are favoured over girls as far as diet and health provision for children is concerned. The gender discrimination is found to be less in southern part of the country, compare to any other region in India.

The studies by J.V. Meenakshi and Viswanathan (2003) show that there is low calorie intake among the households who belong to Scheduled Caste and Scheduled Tribe households. But the study is at all-India level, not at state level. The fact is supported from another study by Radhakrishnan et al., (2004).

A study by Rajan (2004) shows 51.4 per cent of elderly are fully dependent for their survival. Among them male constitute 45.0 per cent where as females are of 58.2 per cent. For urban India he found the situation is the worst with 60.6 per cent of old age population who are fully dependent. Among males the incidence of full dependency is 55 per cent and for females it is 64.2 per cent. So there is gender dimension to dependency at the all-India level. A more detailed picture is given for all the major states in India (for details see page 37 of Rajan, 2004). There is no doubt that this population is at more risk for calorie deprivation.

Sudarshan and Bhattacharya (2004) have shown that women are most likely to take food at last. At least in 64 per cent of the households argue that the women take food at the last where as husband (in 25.61% cases) and male boys (in 46.95% cases) are most likely to get food at first. Only in case of 0.61 per cent households daughters get food first. The study is based upon three slums of Delhi.

In recent years there is a lot of discussion on the implication of the new economic policies followed by developing world towards their food security and nutritional goal. The downsizing of government, increasing importance of the market, declining spending towards social security net and intervention programmes, declining food subsidy are crucial to availability and accessibility of food at household level. It has also implication towards intra-household allocation as well. For example, due to liberal labour laws and downsizing of government spending; the employment in organized sector is declining. The situation is alarming in the unorganized sector. More and more jobs are done by contracting or sub-contracting. This uncertainty of employment has forced other members of the household to join labour force. Increasing food prices and other basic requirements must have accelerated the process. To meet the challenge, women are forced to join market where they are underpaid. They have to manage their household activity as well. But there is little evidence to show that on an aggregate, their social status and economic status along with their participation in 'decision making process' has a positive shift due to their participation in the workforce. They are getting unfair share of the food basket as well. This leads to a paradoxical situation where women are self-sufficient but still undernourished (for details see Laxmi Lingam, 2006).

The 'food security measure' in terms of creating a better buffer stock to meet the uncertain agricultural production is also going through rapid change. The recent incidence of wheat import shows how private players can distort the market and create artificial shortage to hike prices for self interest. The phenomenal rise in wheat price especially in states which are handicapped to self sufficient in food production has again justified the active role of the state to have complete command over it's food basket (Swaminathan, 2006).

So one can say, in India, the intra-household distribution of available food resources is a function of several factors ranging from class, caste, gender and age as well. It does not mean that other economic and policy related factors are not important.

II

Data and Methodology

The study has used information from the National Sample Survey 55th round which provide information on the calorie deprivation at household level. It is collected in the year 1999–2000. Since the data is collected at the household level; one cannot undertake intra-personal distribution of calorie intake analysis directly. Though NSSO 55th round does give information on the persons living in a sample household; the information on calorie intake is reported at household level; not at the individual level. So with given adult equivalents for 12 different age and sex combinations; one is not able to find out the actual calorie consumption at individual level. It assumes that all the members of a household are undernourished, if that household's calorie consumption is less than the norm. For this specific reason one cannot do any exercise to know the distribution of available (calorie) intake within the household, among adult males vis-à-vis adult females, male children vis-à-vis the female ones, adult vis-à-vis the old members, widowed, sick, etc.

But it does provide information on the age and sex composition of the members of the given household. A composite variable taking these two demographic characteristics, i.e., age and sex was developed. Then an attempt is made to find out those households where female children are more in number than male children. Another variable is also created to ascertain whether the number of dependent population is more than the number of male population in the household. The reason for such an exercise is that, as it is evident from literature, that the large households comprising more children and old age population are vulnerable to calorie deprivation. Since the distribution of the available food in typical Indian household is based on power relations and hierarchy; it is more likely that children and old people are the one who might get less attention. It is more likely that the adult male members of the household (in most of the case one among them is head of the household) who earn; get the lion share followed by the adult females, children (again among children the girls come next to their male sibling) and then comes the old (Bird, 2004).

NSSO also gives information on the occupation, social background of the households.[2] So one can compute to know in which occupation and social category combination, the vulnerability is higher. A similar attempt has been made here to ascertain the concentration of vulnerability of calorie deprivation across those households.

Since our dependent variable (incidence of underweight at household level) is dichotomous and its categories are mutually exclusive; a concept called 'group inequality measurement' is used to know whether the presence of more girl children or dependent population has any association with the outcome of calorie deprivation (Chakravarthy, 2001).[3] This measure of group inequality gives us a 'ratio of odds' or 'risk probability' for the affected group vis-à-vis the better one, which is not dependent upon the overall incidence level. Ratios of odds measure the relative degree of departure form homogeneity and qualify the desirability of scale independence.

The nutritional outcome is measured in terms of a dichotomous variable; where a household consuming below 2400 kcal (for urban areas the norm is 2100 kcal) is considered under-nourished or other wise. This particular norm has been decided by Gopalan et al. (1979), which is followed till today.

III

Results and Discussion

The results are discussed in two sections, viz., household characteristics and demographic composition of household.

Household Characteristics

Here an attempt has been to identify the vulnerable households for calorie deprivation. The identification is not just based on any one characteristic but a combination of relevant characteristics. It has considered their place of residence, social background and their occupational status together. It will help to answer following questions:

- to identify the undernourished households among given social group across states;
- to know which are the occupation where the concentration is most likely across states; and
- to find out intra-group and intra-occupation concentration of nutritionally vulnerable household in rural as well as urban India.

Our figures from Table 1 shows that 50–60 per cent of rural Scheduled Caste households engaged as self-employed in agriculture suffers from calorie deprivation in states like Andhra Pradesh, Maharashtra, West Bengal and Uttar Pradesh, whereas in states like Gujarat, Kerala and Tamil Nadu the incidence across same social and occupation category ranges between 80–90 per cent. In Assam 90 per cent of households belonging from scheduled caste and engaged in agricultural labour suffers from calorie deprivation. Gujarat and Tamil Nadu follow it where 70–80 per cent of the household suffers from calorie deprivation among scheduled caste agricultural labour household.

Among tribals in rural set-up, it is found that in most of the states except Orissa, the calorie deprivation in tribal households engaged in

Table 1

Nutritional Vulnerability across States at Household Level given their Place of Residence, Social Background and Occupation

Selected vulnerable categories		*50–60%*	*60–70%*	*70–80%*	*80–90%*	*Above 90%*
Social categories	*Occupation status*					
			Rural India			
Scheduled Caste hh.	self-emp. in non-agriculture	A.P., Maharashtra, West Bengal, Uttar Pradesh, All-India	Assam, Haryana	Gujarat, Kerala, Tamil Nadu	—	—
	engaged as agricultural labour	A.P., Maharashtra, West Bengal	Kerala, Karnataka, Madhya Pradesh, Orissa, All-India	Gujarat, Tamil Nadu	Assam	—
	self-employed in other labour	West Bengal	Gujarat, Haryana, Kerala, Karnataka, Maharashtra, Orissa, Tamil Nadu, All-India	A.P., Assam	Madhya Pradesh	—
	self-employed in agriculture	A.P., Assam, Karnataka, All-India	Kerala, Maharashtra, Orissa	Tamil Nadu	—	—
	self-employed in other labour	Madhya Pradesh, Maharashtra	Tamil Nadu		—	Karnataka

Cont'd...

Cont'd...

Tribal hh.	self-employed In non agriculture	Orissa, All-India	A.P., Assam, Gujarat, Madhya Pradesh, Maharashtra, Orissa, Uttar Pradesh	Bihar, Karnataka	—	Punjab
	engaged as agricultural labour	Orissa	A.P., Bihar, Madhya Pradesh, Maharashtra, Uttar Pradesh, All-India	Assam, Gujarat, Kerala, Karnataka, West Bengal	Tamil Nadu	Haryana
	self-employed in other labour	Bihar, Kerala, Orissa, Rajasthan	All-India	Assam, Tamil Nadu	Madhya Pradesh, Maharashtra	Haryana
	self-employed in agriculture	Assam, Bihar, Gujarat, Madhya Pradesh, Maharashtra, All-India	—	Bihar, Tamil Nadu		—
OBC hh.	self-employed in non- agriculture	A.P., Kerala, Orissa, Karnataka, All-India	Gujarat, Madhya Pradesh, Maharashtra, Tamil Nadu	—	—	—
	engaged as agricultural labour	A.P., Bihar, Karnataka, All-India	Assam, Gujarat, Kerala, Maharashtra, Tamil Nadu	Assam, Madhya Pradesh, Punjab	—	—

Cont'd...

Cont'd...

	self-employed in other labour	Bihar, Tamil Nadu, All India	A.P., Haryana, Kerala, Karnataka, Maharashtra	Assam	Gujarat	—
	self-employed in agriculture	Tamil Nadu	—	—	—	—
Other hh.	Engaged in agriculture labour	Gujarat	Assam, Bihar	—	—	—
			Urban India			
Scheduled Caste hh.	self-employed	Madhya Pradesh	Gujarat, West Bengal, All-India	A.P., Assam, Bihar, Maharashtra, Tamil Nadu	—	—
	having regular wage	A.P., Assam, Madhya Pradesh, Tamil Nadu	Gujarat, Maharashtra, All-India	Kerala	—	—
	self-emp. casual labour	Madhya Pradesh, Punjab	A.P., Assam, Bihar, Maharashtra, All-India	Gujarat, Karnataka, Tamil Nadu, Uttar Pradesh	—	—
	engaged in other jobs	Assam, Tamil Nadu	—	—	—	—
Tribal hh	self-emp.	A.P., Assam, Karnataka, All-India	Bihar, Haryana, Kerala, West Bengal	Maharashtra, Orissa	—	—
	engaged having regular wage	Karnataka, Madhya Pradesh, Orissa, All-India	—	—	—	Tamil Nadu

Cont'd...

Cont'd...

	casual labour	Madhya Pradesh	Bihar, Karnataka, Uttar Pradesh, All-India	Haryana	Gujarat, Maharashtra, Rajasthan, Tamil Nadu	Assam
	engaged in other jobs	Haryana	—	—	Bihar	—
OBC hh.	self-emp.	Madhya Pradesh, Uttar Pradesh, All-India	A.P., Maharashtra, Punjab, Tamil Nadu	—	—	—
	engaged having regular wage	Madhya Pradesh, Tamil Nadu	Kerala, West Bengal	—	—	—
	self-emp. casual labour	Uttar Pradesh	Maharashtra, Tamil Nadu, All-India	Bihar, Gujarat, Karnataka, Madhya Pradesh, West Bengal	—	Assam
Other households	engaged in casual labour	Bihar, Madhya Pradesh, Uttar Pradesh	A.P., Assam, Gujarat, Karnataka, Maharashtra, Rajasthan, West Bengal, All-India	Tamil Nadu, Uttar Pradesh	—	—

Source: SSO 55th round unit record data (computed by the author).

Note: Occupation categories are different for rural and urban India A household's occupation type is determined according to the major source of income. If the household earn at least 51 per cent of the annual income from a particular occupation, say for example, agriculture labour, then it is considered an agriculture labour household.

hh. household.

agriculture (either as self-employed or as agricultural labour) ranges from 60 per cent to 100 per cent. In Punjab and Haryana it shows that all the sample households from this social category are vulnerable to calorie deprivation.

Among Other Backward Caste households in rural India, the study found that in most of the sates the deprivation ranges from 50 to 70 per cent. However in case of 'agricultural labour' as occupation, it is found that in states like Assam, Madhya Pradesh, Punjab and Gujarat, calorie deprivation ranges from 70 per cent to 80 per cent. One thing is to note that among OBCs, the households associated with agriculture face high calorie deprivation. But those households which reported self-employed in agriculture reported below 50 per cent (except Tamil Nadu).

Among 'others' it is shown that only in three out of fifteen states; namely Gujarat, Assam and Bihar, calorie deprivation is found to be above 50 per cent in households engaged in agriculture. In all other occupation categories, it is well below 30 per cent, across all states.

This analysis thus indicates that in rural India, social groups like Scheduled Castes and Tribes are more vulnerable to calorie deprivation in any given occupation in comparison to the households from other social background. However, the result indicates that numbers of states are higher in rows, which represent calorie deprivation among Scheduled Caste and Scheduled Tribe households. These higher numbers (in terms of number of states) are also somehow concentrated in the rows associated with agriculture; given the social group of the households. Since majority of these marginalized groups depend upon agriculture or allied works without substantial land or asset of their own, it is most likely that they are engaged in jobs where cash reward is very low, which ultimately affect their consumption pattern and as a result in calorie intake.

For urban India it is found that across states the households where major earning is from casual labour are more vulnerable to calorie deprivation, given any social category. By social background it is found that households belonging to Scheduled Caste and Scheduled Tribe households are more vulnerable compared to any other social categories.

In 8 out of 15 states, 60 per cent of the scheduled caste households, who are self-employed, face calorie deprivation. In 10 out of 15 states, the Scheduled Caste and Scheduled Tribe households engaged in casual labour face calorie deprivation in 50–80 per cent range.

For OBCs the figure ranges between 50–70 per cent of the households for any given occupation except the casual labour.

Among the most advantageous social category, i.e., 'others' the prevalence of calorie undernourishment is above 50 per cent only in case of casual labour households in 12 out of 15 states. The result from urban India clearly shows that by occupation in most of the states the 'casual labour' household is vulnerable to calorie deprivation irrespective of the social class.

Household Composition

From Tables 2 and 3, it is evident that, households with higher number of girl children and dependent population are experiencing higher incidence of calorie deprivation. It is found that in rural India the gap in calorie deprivation is highest in Andhra Pradesh followed closely by Maharashtra and Tamil Nadu (well above 15 percentage point). Madhya Pradesh, Karnataka, Kerala and Punjab are the other states where gap is hovering around 12 to 13 percentage point. The group inequality (or risk) measurement also confirms the findings. In fact, the revised version of the measurement shows that in Tamil Nadu, Maharashtra and Andhra Pradesh the risk for calorie deprivation for the household having more girl children is twice than the households having lesser number of girl children than male ones (for details see Table 2; column 6).

The figures in bracket refers to ranks of the state at the original reported incidence level of the calorie under-nourishment from the report itself and the rank after revised group inequality measurement, in column 2 and 6 respectively.

In case of urban India it is shown that except Uttar Pradesh in all other states the gap is higher than 10 percentage point. In fact in West Bengal the gap in calorie deprivation in households having higher girl children than the male ones is highest (18 percentage point). The revised group inequality measurement shows us that in states like Bihar, Kerala, Punjab, Tamil Nadu and West Bengal the risk for the households are twice when compared to the households having lesser girl children. The all-India results also confirm the trend.

Coming to the households with more dependent population than the given adult male; it is found that the gap is highest in West Bengal, followed by Orissa, Madhya Pradesh, Karnataka and Andhra Pradesh. In all these states the gap is around 15 percentage points. The revised risk computation further reinforces the findings. It is evident from the study that the states where the overall incidence of calorie undernourishment is lower, the risk for the households with more dependent population is not necessary low. For almost all the states it is found that households with

Table 2

Calorie Undernourishment among the Households Having More Girl Children Compared to Male Children in Rural India

States	*Overall pre-valence of under nourish-ment*	*House-holds having lesser girl child than male child*	*House-holds having more girl child than male child*	*Gap between column 2 and 3*	*Simple risk measure-ment*	*Revised measure-ment*
			Rural India			
A.P.	59.1	53.59	70.56	16.97	1.19	2.08
Assam	73.6	70.95	76.65	5.70	1.04	1.34
Bihar	56.0	52.01	61.24	9.24	1.09	1.46
Gujarat	61.2	58.01	66.71	8.70	1.09	1.45
Haryana	43.1	42.99	38.49	–4.50	0.89	0.83
Karnataka	62.5	56.57	68.61	12.03	1.10	1.68
Kerala	58.0	53.70	66.43	12.74	1.15	1.71
M.P.	61.1	56.00	69.14	13.15	1.13	1.76
Maharashtra	61.9	56.13	72.78	16.64	1.18	2.09
Orissa	54.9	50.80	59.98	9.19	1.09	1.45
Punjab	41.5	36.86	49.67	12.81	1.20	1.69
Rajasthan	36.0	32.26	41.95	9.69	1.17	1.52
Tamil Nadu	69.6	65.10	81.54	16.44	1.17	2.37
U.P.	43.9	40.09	48.16	8.08	1.10	1.39
West Bengal	59.3	55.49	63.79	8.30	1.08	1.41
All India	55.8	51.80	62.20	10.40	1.11	1.53
			Urban India			
A.P.	59.50	54.38	69.77	15.40	1.17	1.94
Assam	60.00	57.56	59.29	1.73	0.99	1.07
Bihar	50.70	45.34	63.05	17.71	1.24	2.06
Gujarat	59.50	53.81	68.85	15.04	1.16	1.90
Haryana	57.40	53.19	63.85	10.66	1.11	1.55
Karnataka	59.80	53.70	61.20	7.51	1.02	1.36
Kerala	54.70	48.97	68.11	19.14	1.25	2.23
M.P.	54.70	54.37	69.46	15.09	1.27	1.91
Maharashtra	59.50	57.56	71.05	13.11	1.19	1.78
Orissa	44.50	57.94	50.43	10.73	1.13	1.55
Punjab	51.80	39.70	66.01	18.82	1.27	2.17
Rajasthan	47.10	47.20	54.17	12.98	1.15	1.69
Tamil Nadu	60.60	41.19	72.05	15.82	1.19	2.01

Cont'd...

Cont'd...

U.P.	56.30	56.23	60.14	6.73	1.07	1.32
West Bengal	56.3	53.41	71.08	18.35	1.26	2.20
All India	57.2	52.73	62.20	9.60	1.09	1.48
			All India			
A.P.	59.3	51.23	70.35	19.11	1.16	2.26
Assam	66.8	60.98	74.66	13.68	1.11	1.89
Bihar	53.35	47.11	61.45	14.35	1.02	1.79
Gujarat	60.35	55.15	67.46	12.31	1.25	1.69
Haryana	50.25	44.69	45.95	1.25	1.27	1.05
Karnataka	61.15	54.84	65.84	11.00	1.19	1.59
Kerala	56.35	52.34	66.87	14.53	1.13	1.84
M.P.	57.9	58.43	69.21	10.78	1.27	1.60
Maharashtra	60.7	53.70	72.17	18.47	1.15	2.24
Orissa	49.7	43.84	58.46	14.62	1.19	1.80
Punjab	46.65	39.81	54.82	15.01	1.07	1.83
Rajasthan	41.55	31.38	44.52	13.14	1.26	1.76
Tamil Nadu	65.1	59.37	78.25	18.88	1.09	2.46
U.P.	50.1	40.82	50.53	9.71	1.01	1.48
West Bengal	57.8	49.82	65.23	15.41	1.13	1.89
All India	56.5	52.00	63.10	11.10	0.92	1.17

Source: NSSO 55th round.
—Simple risk is calculated by dividing column 4 with column 1
—The formula for revised measurement is given by [column 4/(1-column 4)]/[column 3/(1-column 3)]
—The risk values are calculated for the column 4 with respect to the column 3

Table 3

Calorie Undernourishment Among the Households Having more Dependent Population Compared to Adult Male

Rural India

States	*Overall prevalence of under-nutrition*	*Prevalence of under-nutrition in the less dependent household*	*Prevalence of under-nutrition in higher dependent Household*	*Gap between Column 2 and 3*	*Simple measure of group inequality*	*Revised measure of group inequality*
A.P.	59.1 (7)	50.08	65.73	15.65	1.11	1.91 (5)
Assam	73.6 (1)	68.09	76.37	8.28	1.04	1.51 (12)
Bihar	56 (10)	47.40	59.35	11.95	1.06	1.62 (9)

Cont'd...

Cont'd...

Gujarat	61.2 (4)	54.06	65.73	11.67	1.07	1.63 (8)
Haryana	43.1 (13)	34.54	46.65	12.11	1.08	1.66 (7)
Karnataka	62.5 (6)	51.56	67.83	16.27	1.09	1.98 (3)
Kerala	58 (5)	53.35	60.30	6.95	1.04	1.33 (15)
M.P.	61.1 (8)	49.95	66.56	16.60	1.09	1.99 (2)
Maharashtra	61.9 (3)	54.55	64.81	10.27	1.05	1.53 (11)
Orissa	54.9 (11)	44.50	61.08	16.58	1.11	1.96 (4)
Punjab	41.5 (12)	35.50	43.33	7.83	1.04	1.39 (14)
Rajasthan	36 (15)	29.31	38.49	9.18	1.07	1.51 (13)
Tamil Nadu	69.6 (2)	64.16	73.68	9.52	1.06	1.56 (10)
U.P.	43.9 (14)	33.47	46.99	13.52	1.07	1.76 (6)
West Bengal	59.3 (9)	48.36	66.11	17.75	1.11	2.08 (1)
All India	55.8	48.40	59.30	10.90	1.06	1.55
			Urban India			
A.P.	59.5 (8)	49.43	68.43	19.00	1.15	2.22 (2)
Assam	60 (1)	58.25	57.38	–0.87	0.96	0.96 (15)
Bihar	50.7 (13)	38.79	60.03	21.25	1.18	2.37 (1)
Gujarat	59.5 (6)	50.69	65.21	14.52	1.10	1.82 (8)
Haryana	57.4 (11)	46.46	65.37	18.91	1.14	2.17 (3)
Karnataka	59.8 (7)	50.49	63.75	13.25	1.07	1.72 (11)
Kerala	54.7 (9)	47.07	61.88	14.80	1.13	1.82 (7)
M.P.	54.7 (5)	50.81	66.10	15.30	1.21	1.89 (5)
Maharashtra	59.5 (3)	54.32	69.78	15.47	1.17	1.94 (4)
Orissa	44.5 (14)	37.68	49.23	11.55	1.11	1.60 (13)
Punjab	51.8 (12)	44.45	59.24	14.79	1.14	1.82 (9)
Rajasthan	47.1 (15)	37.43	51.00	13.57	1.08	1.74 (10)
Tamil Nadu	60.6 (2)	54.48	66.49	12.02	1.10	1.66 (12)
U.P.	56.3 (10)	47.00	62.47	15.47	1.11	1.88 (6)
West Bengal	56.3 (4)	52.82	63.45	10.63	1.13	1.55 (14)
All India	57.2	49.30	63.70	14.40	1.11	1.80
			All India			
A.P.	59.3 (8)	49.89	66.45	16.56	1.12	1.99 (1)
Assam	66.8 (1)	66.38	74.64	8.26	1.12	1.49 (13)

Cont'd...

Cont'd...

Bihar	53.35 (10)	45.98	59.43	13.45	1.11	1.72 (6)
Gujarat	60.35 (4)	52.75	65.56	12.81	1.09	1.71 (7)
Haryana	50.25 (13)	38.94	51.64	12.70	1.03	1.67 (8)
Karnataka	61.15 (6)	51.12	66.55	15.42	1.09	1.90 (5)
Kerala	56.35 (5)	51.52	60.68	9.17	1.08	1.45 (14)
M.P.	57.9 (7)	50.19	66.47	16.28	1.15	1.97 (2)
Maharashtra	60.7 (3)	54.44	66.41	11.97	1.09	1.65 (10)
Orissa	49.7 (11)	43.07	59.49	16.42	1.20	1.94 (3)
Punjab	46.65 (12)	39.35	48.19	8.84	1.03	1.43 (15)
Rajasthan	41.55 (15)	31.66	41.05	9.40	0.99	1.50 (12)
Tamil Nadu	65.1 (2)	60.51	71.30	10.80	1.10	1.62 (11)
U.P.	50.1 (14)	37.31	49.84	12.52	0.99	1.67 (9)
West Bengal	57.8 (9)	49.80	65.63	15.83	1.14	1.93 (4)
All India	56.5	48.70	60.30	11.60	1.07	1.60

Source: NSSO 55th round

— Simple risk is calculated by dividing column 4 with column 1

— The formula for revised measurement is given by [column 4/(1-column 4)]/[column 3/(1-column 3)]

— The risk values are calculated for the column 4 with respect to the column 3.

more dependent population have the higher risk of calorie deprivation. The trend is not different in case of urban India. But severity in terms of revised risk does differ. In case of urban India it is found that Bihar has the highest gap as far as calorie deprivation is concerned, between the households with higher dependent population with given adult male and households with lesser dependent population with given adult male (21 percentage point). It is followed by Andhra Pradesh, Haryana, Maharashtra and Madhya Pradesh. Interestingly, in Assam where it is found that overall calorie deprivation is higher at aggregate level, the gap between the households with higher dependent population and households with lesser dependent population is lowest (in fact negative). Thus, one can say households where the dependent population is more than the given adult male members, the households is more likely to face calorie deficiency. The same trend is observed at all-India level as well (for details see Table 3).

Conclusion with Policy Implication

Thus, the study concludes that the calorie deprivation in India could be better understood if the focus will be on their characteristics and composition. Instead of studying isolate characteristics one should look at more composite characteristics of the household, which comprised of social backwardness, occupation and place of residence. The income criterion is deliberately avoided in the study for analysis purpose; since it is not universal across states and also it is a proxy for occupation. The composition of household helps us to know which section of the population may have higher vulnerability for the deprivation. If the undernourished household consists of more aged members, children; especially female ones, it is these age and sex combinations which are likely to face calorie deprivation.

Thus, one can conclude that any targeting for the reduction of nutritional vulnerability should not only focus on the households belonging to Scheduled Castes and Scheduled Tribes, but also on those households associated with agriculture (especially agricultural labour households). In case of urban India, households depending upon causal or other form of labour should be given priority. Since many of them are likely to be in the unorganized sector, where exploitation is higher in terms of low wage, state should enforce strictly the minimum wage rate policy. It will definitely have positive impact on those household's food security. While making intervention to eradicate undernutrition at household level, not only household's social and occupational background, but also the composition of such household must be taken into account. So those households where the number of girl child and other dependent population is higher need proper targeting mechanism through which a better intra-household allocation of food will be possible.

Notes

1. Here the term 'family and household' is used interchangeably. Though conventionally 'household' is used in sense of economic decision making unit. Some authors however prefer to use family and household synonymously; for example see Sen (1999: 369).
2. Here social groups are divided broadly into Scheduled Caste (SC), Scheduled Tribe (ST), Other Backward Caste (OBC) and others. The classification is taken from NSSO. No attempt has been made to reorganize the social groups, which is beyond the scope of the current paper. While SCs and STs are considered both socially and economically backward and discriminated, the OBCs are mostly distinguished in terms of their economic and educational backwardness. SCs are discriminated on the basis of their birth and occupations (mostly menial works termed as

polluted), while the STs by their very social structure remain in a closed society distanced from the mainstream. Though both are most disadvantaged groups of Indian society, both socially and economically; the reasons are different.

3. For more details please go through the "Measurement of Group Inequality" By Dr Achin Chakravarthy CDS working paper no. 315, Centre for Development Studies, Ullor, Trivandrum. This measure is applicable if the phenomenon under observation is a dichotomous one.

Reference

Beherman, J.R. (1988) "Intra-Household Allocation of Nutrients in Rural India: Are Boys Favoured? Do Parents Exhibit Inequality Aversion?", *Oxford Economic Papers*, Vol. 40, pp. 32–54.

Beherman, J.R. and Deolalikar, A.B. (1987) "Will Developing Country Nutrition Improve with Income? A case study for Rural South India", *Journal of Political Economy*, Vol. 95, No. 31, pp. 492–507.

Bird, Kate (2004), "Chronic poverty and Understanding Intra-Household Differentiation", CPRC-IIPA Working Paper No. 7, Indianan Institute of Public Administration, New Delhi.

Borooah, Vani, K. (2004), "Gender bias among children in India in their diet and immunization against disease", *Social Science and Medicine*, Vol. 58.

Chakravarty, A. (2001), Concept and Measurement of Group Inequality, Working Paper No. 315, Centre for Development Studies, Thiruvanathapuram, Kerala, India.

Chakravarty, S. and Dand, Sejal (June 3, 2006), "Food Insecurity in Gujarat: A study of two rural populations", *Economic and Political Weekly*, pp. 2248–58.

Dreze, J. and Sen, A. (1989), *Hunger and Public Action*, Oxford, Clarendon Press, Chapter 1–3, pp. 3–45, Chapter 9, pp. 65–77.

Gopalan, C., Rama Sastri, B.V. and Balasubramanian, S.C. (1989), *Nutritive Value of Indian Foods*, National Institute of Nutrition, ICMR, Hyderabad.

Lawrence, Hadad; Pena, Christine, Nishida, Chizuru; Ouisumbing, Agnes and Slack, Alison. "Food Security and Nutrition Implications of Intra-household Bias: A Review of Literature" (September 1996), International Food Policy Research Institute, Discussion Paper No. 19.

Lingam, Laxmi (May 20, 2006), "Gender, Households and Poverty, Tracking Mediation of Macro adjustment Programme", *Economic and Political Weekly*, pp. 1989–98.

Meenakshi, J.V. and Viswanathan, Brinda (2003), "Calorie Deprivation in Rural India, 1983–1999/2000", *Economic and Political Weekly*.

National Sample Survey Organisation (2001), "Nutritional Intake in India, Report No. 471 (55/1.0/9)", Ministry of Statistics and Programme Implementation, Government of India.

Radhakrishnan R., Rao, Hanumantha K., Ravi, C. and Reddy, Samby B. (2004), "Chronic Poverty and Malnutrition in India", CPRC-IIPA Working Paper No. 11, Indian Institute of Public Administration, New Delhi.

Rajan (2004), "Chronic Poverty among Indian Elderly", CPRC-IIPA Working Paper No. 17, Indian Institute of Public Administration, New Delhi.

Sen, A. (1984), *Resources, Value and Developement*, OUP paperback, New Delhi, Chapter 15 and 16, pp. 346–385.

Shah, Amita and Sah, D.C. (2004), "Chronic Poverty in South-west Madhya Pradesh: A Multidimensional Analysis of its Extent and Causes", CPRC-IIPA Working Paper No. 05, Indian Institute of Public Administration, New Delhi.

Sudarshan, Ratna M. and Bhattacharya, Rina (2004), "Chronic Poverty and Gendered Pattern of Intra household Resource Allocation: A Preliminary Enquiry", CPRC-IIPA Working Paper No. 12, Indian Institute of Public Administration, New Delhi.

Swaminathan, M.S. (2006) http://www.thehindu.com/2006/10/06/stories/2006100601651500.htm.

12 Employment Generation Potential in the Organized Retail Sector in Urban Areas

Seema Joshi

The Indian economy grew at a comparatively low rate of growth of 3.5 per cent from 1950 to 1980. The plethora of procedures, permits, bureaucratic controls and protectionist policies created under import substitution strategy (ISS) along with other factors landed us into economic crisis in 1991(Joshi, 2006).The New Economic Policy was launched in June 1991 with the objective that the regime of controls, quotas and licences which had put fetters on the development process would be done away with. It was hoped that these policy measures would help to boost growth of GDP on the one hand and would also result in significant employment expansion on the other. Although the reform process led to acceleration in the GDP growth in the post liberalization period yet there was no commensurate increase in employment; the withdrawal of public sector from various sectors due to privatization and retrenchment of redundant labour force halted employment growth in the public sector. It was expected that the organized private sector would help filling up this gap as this was expected to be the 'torchbearer' of economic reforms. But contrary to expectations, employment in the private sector could not grow at a faster rate. Therefore, the growth rate of employment of the economy sharply declined to less than one per cent during 1993–94 to 1999–2000 from two per cent per annum during 1983–1993–94. This was described by the critics of liberalization as the phenomenon of 'jobless growth' (Datt, 2002). After more than a decade of reforms in India, unemployment levels have increased as per 60th Round of National Sample Survey for 2004–05 (with a large sample for Jan-June, 2004). The rate of unemployment has been estimated to have reached 9.4 per cent in 2004–05 as against 7.3 per cent in 1999–2000.The mid-term appraisal of the Tenth Five-Year Plan estimated the unemployment rate at 9.11 per cent for 2004–05 (Datt, 2006).

Recognizing the problem to provide productive employment for the continuing increase in labour force, the Task Force on Employment Opportunities was established by the Planning Commission to examine employment and unemployment scenario of the country and to suggest strategies for employment generation for achieving the target of providing employment opportunities to 10 crore people over the next ten years, i.e., one crore on an average per year. The Task Force on Employment Opportunities, 2001 which was headed by the Deputy Chairman, Planning Commission had brought to forefront inter alia, the need for development of organized private services sector especially for generation of employment in the organized sector on the one hand and for improving the quality of employment on the other. The report emphasized that some of the traditional consumer services like small retail shops (e.g., kirana shops), low income restaurants, hair cutting saloons, tailoring, photographers, taxis and small truckers, etc., where most of the establishments were small, the scope for expansion existed. The Report further suggests that many of these services could be provided by organized establishments and this would lead to increase in the role of organized sector in employment generation.

An analysis of structure of employment in case of India shows that out of the total labour force of the order of 406.05 million in 1999–2000, only 7.08 per cent was engaged in the organized sector and the remaining (92%) was in the unorganized sector. The organized sector in India usually refers to employment in the public and private sector establishments employing 10 or more than 10 persons. These jobs are characterized by much higher levels of remuneration than those prevailing in the market for comparable skill levels and near total employment security, hence strong preference for organized sector jobs exists. However, an analysis of trends in organized sector reveals that organized sector employment is shrinking (see Table 1). There has been deceleration in its growth from 1.20 per cent per annum during 1983–94 to 0.53 per cent per annum during 1994–99. It is a matter of grave concern given the strong preference for such jobs. The deceleration in this sector is accounted for by slow down of employment in the organized public sector. But the trend noticed in case of organized private sector has been just the reverse. The latter grew at a rate of 1.83 per cent between 1994 and 99 as against 0.45 per cent per annum between 1983 and 1994 (Planning Commission, 2001).

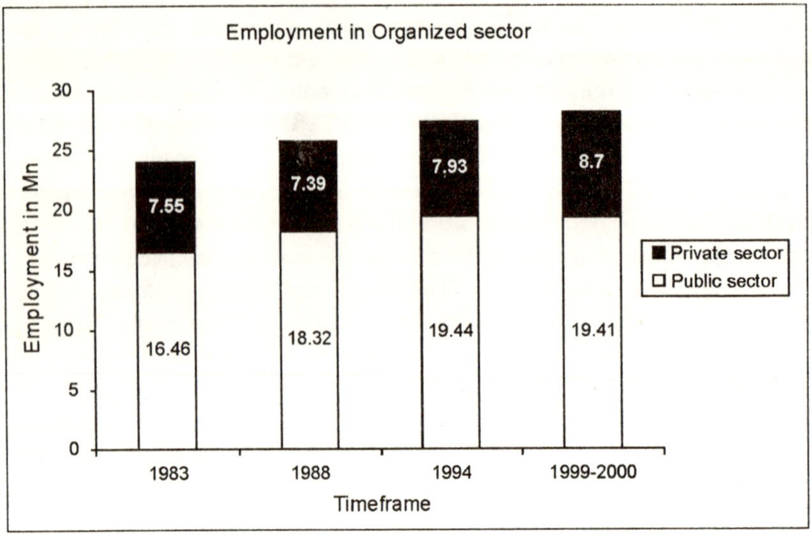

Table 1

Total Employment and Organized Sector Employment

S. No.	*Sector*	*Employment (million)*				*Growth (% per annum)*	
		1983	*1988*	*1994*	*1999–2000*	*1983–94*	*1994–2000*
1.	Total population	718.21	790.00	895.05	1004.10	2.12	1.93
2.	Total labour force	308.64	333.49	381.94	406.05	2.05	1.93
3.	Total employment	302.75	324.29	374.45	397.00	2.04	0.98
4.	Organized sector employment	24.01 (100.0)	25.71 (100.0)	27.37 (100.0)	28.11 (100.0)	1.20	0.53
5.	Public sector	16.46 (68.6)	18.32 (71.3)	19.44 (71.0)	19.41 (69.1)	1.52	–0.03
6.	Private sector	7.55 (31.4)	7.39 (28.7)	7.93 (29.0)	8.70 (30.9)	0.45	1.87
7.	4 as % of 3	7.93	7.93	7.30	7.08		
8.	2 as % of 1	43.0	42.2	42.7	40.4		

Notes: 1. Total employment figures are on Usual Status (UPSS) basis.

2. The organized sector employment figures are as reported in the Employment Market Information System of Ministry of Labour and pertain to 31 March of 1983, 1994 and 1999.

3. Figures in brackets indicate the percentage of employment in the public sector and private sector to total organized sector employment.

Source: Reproduced from Datt, Ruddar (2002): "Economic Liberalisation and its Implications for Employment in India" in Ashok Mathur and P.S. Raikhy (ed.) *Economic Liberalisation and its Implications for Employment in India*, Deep and Deep Publications, New Delhi, p. 17.

Further it can be observed from the figures given in Tables 2 and 3 that although women's share in the organized workforce has shown an increasing trend during the period 1981–99, yet women's participation in the organized sector is still very low as compared to men in organized sector as a whole and even in organized public sector. Therefore, there is an urgent need to find out avenues for employment for women especially in the organized sector where they constitute 50 per cent of population.

Table 2

Women in the Organized Sector (1981–99)

(figures in Million)

Year	*Women*	*Men*	*Total*
(1)	*(2)*	*(3)*	*(4)*
1981	2.8 (12.2)	20.1	22.9
1991	3.8 (14.1)	23.0	26.7
1999	4.8 (17.2.)	23.3	28.1

Note: Figures within parentheses indicate percentage to total.

Source: Reproduced from Tenth Five-Year Plan, 2002–2007, Vol. II, p. 234.

Table 3

Women in the Public Sector (1981–99)

(figures in Million)

Year	*Women*	*Men*	*Total*
(1)	*(2)*	*(3)*	*(4)*
1981	1.5 (9.7)	14.0	15.5
1991	2.4 (12.3)	16.7	19.1
1999	2.8 (14.5)	16.6	19.4

Note: Figures within parentheses indicate percentage to total.

Source: Reproduced from Tenth Five-Year Plan, 2002–2007, Vol. II, p. 234.

It is important to mention here that within the organized sector, the employment growth potential in public sector in case of both the central and state governments is limited because of the problems of excess staff, severe financial constraints and declining employment elasticity. Therefore, there arises a need to explore employment generation potential of the organized private sector. In this background an attempt has been made in this paper to examine the employment generation potential of

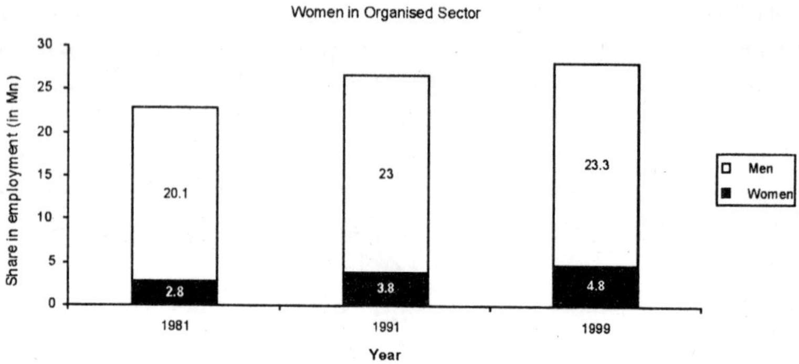

organized retail sector. Section II provides in brief an overview of retail industry in India. Section III deals with the debate on the issue whether FDI is desirable or not and Section IV gives conclusions and policy implications.

Retail Industry in India: An Overview

India has been called a nation of shopkeepers because of the huge number of retail enterprises in India. The number rose from 8.5 million in 1996 to 9.3 million in 2003, 12 million in 2004 and 15 million in mid 2005. India has been identified as the "topmost attractive destination" by A.T. Kearney from amongst the 30 emergent markets. Its contribution to the GDP is 14 per cent and share in employment is 7 per cent or 42 million (only agriculture employs more). It is the largest component of the service sector. The retail industry is divided into the organized and unorganized sectors. Organized retail refers to businesses employing more than 10 persons and comprises of corporate-backed hypermarkets and retail chains. It accounts for just two per cent of the trade and employs merely five lakh persons. Contrary to it , the unorganized sector refers to traditional formats of low cost retailing such as the local kirana shops, owner manned general stores, paan/bidi shops, convenience stores, handcart and pavement vendors , and employs over four crore persons. As much as 98 per cent of retailing takes place in this segment. This is highly fragmented with about 11 million outlets operating in the country and only four per cent of them being larger than 500 sq ft in size. This segment is highly labour intensive (Ramasubramanian, 2006).

Presently, in addition to neighbourhood unorganized retail outlets, 'mom and pop stores' (e.g., kirana shops), we are having organized retail outlets like Food World, Shoppers' Stop, Big Bazaar, Spencers Lifestyle, Westside, Pantaloon among others in India now. Many young men and women who had no hope of getting job earlier are getting absorbed in some of these outlets. Similarly, in organized coffee retailing brands like Café Coffee Day and Barista are in expansion mode. Some new entrants like Coffee World, Coffee-Not Just Craze, Gloria, Jean, Mahananda Dairy and Mr Bean Coffee Junction are planning to stimulate action across retail counters in India.[1] This trend will definitely have positive implications for employment generation in India. Exploring and generating new employment avenues for growing working-age population becomes all the more essential in view of the latest forecast of IMF (2005) which says that India would be one of the handful economies to have a growing working-age population over the next forty years. There is no denial from the fact that among services sector, ITES-BPO segment has been amongst the largest employment generator and high revenue generator segments within the country where 4,70,000 people got employment (NASSCOM). But India's Rs 3, 12, 180 crore largely unorganized retail trade segment employs even higher number of people which is approximately four crore (Bhargava and Anand, 2005). To develop and benefit the IT sector, 100 per cent foreign investment has been permitted but FDI in retailing is being opposed by some groups ignoring Chinese experience. The facts and figures point towards the huge potential of employment generation which exists in organized retail services segment.

One of the methods to generate employment in retail segment is through permitting FDI. There has been a lot of debate on the issue whether FDI in retailing should be permitted or not. There are two groups of people. One group has given arguments against FDI in retail and other one in favour of that. The next section focuses on the debate on FDI in retail.

Debate on FDI in Retail

Sceptics feel that FDI in retailing would lead to increase in unemployment by wiping out small retailers (like kirana shops) who cannot face stiff competition posed by MNCs and the outcome would be large scale displacement (Ramasubramanian, 2006; Datt, 2006). Secondly, they argue that global chains would squeeze suppliers more rather than deliver genuine supply chain improvements. Thirdly, proliferation of global chains and large stores will eventually harm consumers by encouraging skewed urban development (Bhargava and Anand, 2005). Fourthly, FDI should be welcome in infrastructure and heavy industry, in the energy sector, etc., which will help increasing productive capacity to have a GDP growth rate of 8–10 per cent on a sustainable basis. Opening up of this segment would enable the MNCs to legitimize their profits and would cater to the need of upper middle-class and affluent sections of our society and would be of no help to small retailers. Lastly, pointing towards the lackluster performance of some leading, modern retail outlets including pioneers like Shoppers' Stop and the collapse of another pioneer—the Delhi-based Nanz Chain of departmental stores, they argue that organized retail is just another bubble (Radhakrishnan, 2002).

The viewpoints of the supporters of FDI in retail (Radhakrishnan, 2002) have been summed up below.

First, their argument is that FDI in organized retail can indeed lead to job losses as some of the unorganized retail shops (kirana owners), which cannot withstand competition, will have to close down. However, pointing towards the worldwide experience, they emphasize that job creation will take place as organized trade will boost consumption, production and thereby generate employment.

Secondly, they argue that the phenomenon of job losses in cities with the setting up of big foreign stores would be accompanied by simultaneous job creation in villages and in small towns from where the retailers would source their farm and merchandise. Global retailers by moving jobs from cities to villages will help curbing the 'out-migration' from villages, towns and small cities as lack of employment is one of the major push factors for migration in India. This will further help checking the phenomenon of 'over-urbanization'. Instead of skewed urban growth, there would be balanced urban-rural growth as employment avenues would be there in rural or semi-urban areas.

Thirdly, organized retail will result in employment generation for those young matriculates and graduates, especially women, who may have low skills or no skills and have no hope of getting employment elsewhere. Consider the example of Shopper's Stop which employs those with a college degree. Another case in point is employment profile of Food World operations of RPG groups where in 2002, 70 per cent of employees were high school/graduates and were largely children of daily wage earners. "Today, they are on the threshold of a viable career opportunity and indeed many of the earlier recruits will be income tax payers in a couple of years" (Pillai, 2002). We can now envision India where today's unemployed will become tomorrow's productive corporate citizens—India will surely keep shining on the global map!

Fourthly, the argument of displacement does not seem to be valid in light of the fact that "... 98 per cent of the unorganized sector in retail is in the form of disguised unemployment" (Bhargava and Anand, 2005) [Nilotpal Basu, CPI (M)]. But in case of organized retail many career options are available at almost all levels. At lower levels customer service associates, supervisors, etc., and at middle levels store managers, merchandisers, area managers and marketing people are in great demand. Senior level people in all functions like marketing finance and human resources are being solicited with good offers. With absorption in retail segment, whether at the lower or middle or higher level, marginal product will definitely be high, not at all zero as is the case with unorganized retail because of disguised unemployment.

Fifthly, competition posed by private foreign retailers would boost small Indian retailers to reinvent them and the gainers would indeed be Indian consumers. For example, in Delhi itself many kirana owners have reinvented themselves by using various strategies to retain their customers. The techniques vary from offering personalized services to credit services to free home delivery. One spontaneously says, "Indeed competition is a wonderful thing!" (Radhakrishan, 2002).

Sixthly, another apprehension expressed by critics of FDI in retail is that lower prices to consumers will be offered by global retailers by virtue of their power to squeeze producers rather than through removal of inefficiencies in supply chain. The entry of organized retailers and distributors (both foreign and local) will remove many of these inefficiencies and result in cost savings also. The Left fears that a major share of those savings would be retained by global retailers by virtue of their size and purchasing power. However, the case studies on tomato and cauliflowers farmers in Hosakote and Kolar in Karnataka done by Professors S. Raghunath and D. Ashok (from IIM, Bangalore) shows "that modern distribution system increased the farmers realization by 22 per cent and brought down the price to consumers by 11 per cent". In fact, large retailers have built their businesses by making their suppliers more efficient. But misconceptions about large retailers regarding 'squeezing of suppliers' or killing them needs to be removed as this may be done by Indian retailers too. Therefore, instead of outrightly rejecting FDI in this segment, adequate checks to prevent monopolies should be evolved (Bhargava and Anand, 2005).

Conclusions and Policy Implications

Despite this debate on the desirability of FDI in retail and opposition from Left parties, which is the major constituent of the present U.P. A government in the Centre, government seems to be waking up now to the potential of the retail sector. That is why the concrete measure to actualize this potential has been announced by Union Cabinet on Jan 24, 2006. The GoI has opened up FDI floodgates by allowing 51 per cent FDI through the FIPB route in Single brand retailing. The debate on the desirability or otherwise of FDI in retail has taken a backseat and the question now is how to make the maximum benefit out of what has been done. Many brands which could not enter India because of old FDI norms would enter our economy. Many large brand owners like Benetton, Adidas, Gap, Ralph, Laureen , Zara , Old Navy and Banana Republic, etc., may like to start their exclusive outlets now. Earlier foreign retailers were not permitted to open their outlets and their products were sold by Indian shop owners through local franchisee. The recent government decision is going to have multiple effects on the economy. Chinese experience in retail is wonderful which started initially in 1992 permitting just 49 per cent equity in the form of joint ventures. It gradually dismantled restrictions for them and finally allowed them 100 per cent FDI in retail. Almost every major global retailer is present in China. But no large scale job losses took place there. In fact, the number of domestic retail outlets has increased by 32.35 per cent, while foreign funded ones by 21 per cent. It is only by allowing them it realized its potential of becoming local sourcing base for their global operations. For example, Wal Mart which had "Buy American theme" till 1992 sourced $15 billion worth of goods from China. Last year metro purchased 42 billion worth of goods from China. India too can stand to gain provided more FDI is permitted in this segment (Bhargava and Anand, 2005). This can be done gradually. Slowly FDI can be extended to food retail also. Then enormous amount of employment would be generated in high value crop production like agro-processing especially. Retail is a labour-intensive sector; therefore, huge potential for direct and indirect employment generation exists there. In addition, it would definitely make the consumers sovereigns by offering them wide range of choice and quality products at low prices. The farmers would gain because of better prices for their produce as improvement in supply chain would bypass intermediary system. Manufacturing (especially textiles) will also stand to gain. The gains will not stay limited to consumers, farmers or farm and manufacturing sectors, but services sectors like real estate, tourism, IT too would be amongst the beneficiaries. With latest move of GoI (51% FDI in retail), mall revolution is likely to get a boost. At the one end this will provide a push to the growth of real estate services and on the other this can help enhancing governmental revenue. The large, unused pieces of land owned by the government can be put to effective use by giving them on lease to the big foreign retailers for building up departmental stores in upcoming shopping malls. Lease rent would help raising governmental revenue. The retail trade can also help promoting tourism industry also. Well developed shopping environment to the tourists in India will help developing many of the cities as tourist destinations and bring in revenue for government. Indian ethnic brands can get noticed and promoted worldwide and would help earning forex. Further, IT industry would also grow because of inter-sectoral linkages. As per NASSCOM (2005), "the offshore IT and BPO industries could support an estimated 1.5 million to 1.75 million retail employees in 2010 as an estimated 80–90 per cent of employees' spending would be on food, recreation, clothing and footwear, utilities, transport, etc." (p. 85). Organized retail services sector can provide various entry points for women's employment and have vast employment generation potential for women. For example, 70 per cent of the people working in RPG stores are women and it provides them a very respectable source of earning money. This can surely create paths towards the elimination of poverty of women and help their economic empowerment. It is widely recognized now that real national development cannot take place by bypassing women who are the pillars of society and constitute almost 48.3 per cent of total population as per the 2001 Census. Economic empowerment of women of current generation can help in generating socio-economic benefits for the future generations in the form of lower fertility rate, slower population growth, better nutrition, better health and educational attainments, better quality of life and active role in decision-making, etc.

To sum up, opening up of retail trade segment to FDI will result in huge benefits for the economy as a whole which would be simply difficult to quantify. However, there is a need to examine the constraints faced by small retailers and to provide them safety nets as has been done in Thailand and other countries in Asia.

Note

1. See *Business World* (2005). The growth of cafeteria services would promote growth of BPO segment also. As has been mentioned in NASSCOM (2005, p. 16) one of the challenges India's offshoring industries are dealing with is in the form of urban infrastructure bottlenecks ranging from power to cafeteria services.

References

Bhargava, Anjuli and Anand, M. (2005), "Is the Left Right?", *Business World*, October 3.

Business World (2005), "Business Brews for Coffee Chains", November 14.

Datt, Ruddar (2002), "Economic Liberalisation and its Implications for Employment in India" in Ashok Mathur and P.S. Raikhy (eds.) *Economic Liberalisation and its Implications for Employment in India*, Deep and Deep Publications, New Delhi.

— (2006), "Single-Brand Retail FDI: Rhetoric and Reality", *Mainstream*, February 10–16.

International Monetary Fund (2005), *World Economic Outlook.*

Joshi, Seema (2006), "Impact of Economic Reforms on Social Sector Expenditures in India", *Economic and Political Weekly*, Jan 28-Feb 23, Vol. XLI, No. 4.

NASSCOM-MCKinsey Report (2005), *Extending India's Leadership of the Global IT and BPO Industries,* PS Press Services Pvt. Ltd., Noida (India).

Pillai, Raghu (2002), "A Case for Retail Consolidation", *Praxis, Business Line*, Vol. 3(3), January.

Planning Commission (2001), *Report of Taskforce on Employment Opportunities.*

— (2002), Tenth Five Year Plan , 2002–2007, Government of India, Vol. II.

Radhakrishnan, Sankar (2002), "Retail Detail", *Praxis, Business Line*, Vol. 3(3), January.

Ramasubramanian, R. (2006), "FDI in Retail: Major Arguments", *Mainstream*, February 10–16.

Sharma, E.A.S. (2006), "Need for Caution in Retail FDI", *Economic and Political Weekly*, November 12.

13 The Strategy of Zoning amidst Resource Degradation

William Joe

Blooming natural-resource base is a requisite for mankind's development and especially for the poorer section of the society; resource base forms a significant means of livelihood. Literature on natural resources widely discusses about the close nexus between poverty and environmental degradation especially in communities which solely depend upon natural resources for their livelihood. In this regard Kerala's marine fisheries sector gains significance because for a major chunk of the population in Kerala (recognized as the traditional fishing community), the fisheries resource continues to be the only means of livelihood. This traditional sector is characterized by relatively low capital commitment, low levels of production and higher levels of employment for a given amount of capital (FAO, 2001). For communities with such immense dependency upon natural resources, any detrimental effect upon the resource can bring about further impoverishment in their standard of living.

In this context this paper discusses the intensification of income deprivation and filth among the traditional fishermen community of Kerala because of stagnating fish catch during the 70s and early 80s. Overfishing by the mechanized sectors was proving to be detrimental for the resource base. The modernization model of fisheries development, which focused upon the capital intensive mechanized fishing, adversely affected the labour intensive traditional sector. The stagnation intensified due to the alarming increase in the size of the fishing vessels, gears, engine power and unrestricted and destructive fishing practices like mini-trawling along the inshore waters (Kurien and Achary 1988). The adversely affected traditional fishermen firmly agitated against this and demanded state action. Consequently the policy of zoning was adopted which provided specific zones of territorial seas for traditional fisherman and trawlers, and the banning of trawling during the monsoon.

Zoning is a redistributive strategy, and enquiry into the long-run impact of such natural resource management policies on welfare of the people becomes inevitable. A few studies such as Nair et al. (2000), Kurup (2001), Shahjahan (2000) have looked into the impact of monsoon ban upon the fish harvest but they do not discuss in any theoretical context on the need for zoning and also ignore the long-term consequences of the zoning strategy.

This paper intends to explain the theoretical rationale for zoning in the sea and examines its effectiveness on the fisheries sector especially upon resource conservation and its distribution. Economists have argued that the distribution of income is a critical determinant of economic development and it plays an adhering role in the society. The pattern of income distribution determines the extent of poverty, which has significant impact upon economic growth. Therefore, distributive policies need to be designed carefully so as to provide sufficient income to the poorer sections of the society.

The rest of the paper is organized as follows: the next section gives the distribution of marine fish catch and discusses the emergence of the distributional problem. Section III discusses the theoretical rationale for the strategy of zoning in the sea. Section IV examines the effectiveness of the zoning policy on the distribution of resources in the fisheries sector. Section V demonstrates that this welfare enhancing policy cannot avoid the re-emergence of the open access crisis because of certain institutional difficulties. Section VI concludes.

Pre-Zoning Scenario

The state of Kerala has a coastal belt extending over 590 kilometres and nature has endowed it with abundant marine resource potential in comparison to other coastal states of India. The stretch of coastline from Quilon up to Manjeshwari in the northern tip of the state is dotted with many protected bays, estuaries and natural harbours, which, except in the peak monsoon months of June, July and August, provide excellent facilities for launching and landing of fishing craft. It is therefore not surprising that the fishermen of the state are also well distributed over the entire length of the coast (Kurien, 1978). There are 222 marine fishing villages where fishing and related activities provide livelihood to a vast majority of the population.

Adoption of any technique basically depends upon certain economic, socio-cultural and ecological factors. In case of fisheries the nature of marine resources and the ocean topography are the most influencing factors on the development of certain traditional technique of fish harvesting. Until early 1950s the fisheries sector of Kerala comprised only traditional crafts and techniques of harvesting. This traditional sector can be viewed as a closed circuit of activities because of very little dependence on the outside economy for inputs and markets (Kurien, 1978). The initiative to modernize the fishing crafts of Kerala was taken up by the Indo-Norwegian Project in 1954–55, which first introduced small 25 footer-mechanized boats with 16–24 HP diesel engines. Activities in the modern sector incorporate more technology and capital. The need for foreign exchange and the potential of seafood exports to the world markets brought about rapid changes in the fisheries sector of Kerala. The rapid development and expansion of the mechanized sector characterized these changes, and their number increased from 160 in 1960 to approximately 3,000 during early 1980s.

Graph-1 depicts the fish catch trends before the implementation of the policy of temporal zoning (monsoon ban) for trawlers. It is evident that until mid 1970s the total fish-catch was increasing and the bulk of the catch was appropriated by the traditional sector. The mechanized sector was at its infancy in terms of share in total catch. After 1975 the total fish-catch showed a decline and its direct impact was felt upon the

Graph 1

Trends in Fish-catch before Temporal Zoning

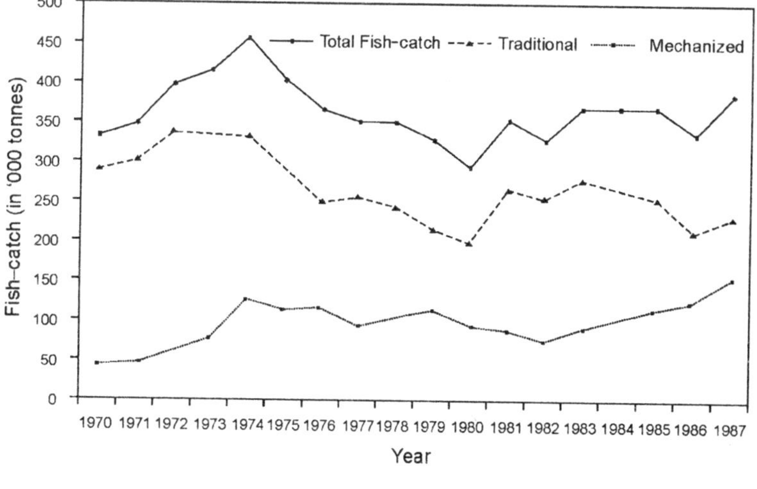

traditional sector whose share in the total fish-catch also declined. During this period the mechanized sector was harvesting almost a constant amount of fish but its share in total fish-catch showed improvement. This was mainly because of its better appropriation capacity and increased encroachment, which helped in grasping the catch of the traditional sector. During 1980s the overall level of harvest declined and the reasons for it can be attributed to excessive harvesting along the inshore waters. For a given level of harvest by trawlers the aggregate fish catch declined because of increasing externalities and the problem emerged.

Table 1

Average Annual Fish-Catch, Number of Crafts and Catch per Craft

Year	*Traditional Sector*			*Mechanized Sector*		
	Catch	*Crafts**	*Catch/ Craft*	*Catch*	*Crafts**	*Catch/ Craft*
1971–75	319300 (79)	31,089	10.27	84,480 (21)	2,151	39.27
1976–80	232840 (69)	32,615	7.14	1,04,390 (31)	2,500	41.76
1981–87	251320 (70)	34,770	7.22	1,06,790 (30)	3,116	34.27

Source: Estimated from Kalawar et al. (1985) and CMFRI cited in Paul (2003).

* Time series of crafts data is obtained through linear interpolation from the data of fishing crafts provided by Government of Kerala in its various fisheries reports.

Note: Figures in parentheses give the percentage share of catch by the respective sector in total fish-catch.

Table 1 shows that during early 1970s over four lakh tonnes of fish were harvested every year, where the traditional sector had a share of approximately 79 per cent and the mechanized sector appropriating approximately 21 per cent of the total fish catch. But in the latter part of 1970s the average fish-catch declined by almost 16 per cent in comparison to 1971–75. The traditional sector was the worst hit as its average annual catch declined by almost 27 per cent during this period. In comparison to 1971–75, during 1976–80 the total catch by the mechanized sector increased by around 24 per cent. After 1980s the average annual fish-catch for both the sectors showed a slight recovery but it was still a significant decline in comparison to the early part of 1970s.

The problem had begun to emerge mainly in the form of total decline in the fish-catch and it was further aggravated by the drastic changes in the share of the catch for traditional sector. The traditional sector was now able to appropriate approximately 70 per cent of the total fish-catch, which was a decline of almost 10 per cent in comparison to early 1970s. The mechanized sector had rapidly increased its share in total catch and was harvesting almost 30 per cent of the total fish catch. It is important to note that the average annual fish catch by the mechanized sector did not increase significantly but its share had increased. Here the real problem was that the mechanized sector was appropriating a larger share in total fish-catch at the expense of the traditional sector.

Kurien and Achary (1988) have pointed out the major causes leading to the crisis. First and foremost there were no licensing procedure or registration requirements for the mechanized boats. The state government provided subsidies and soft loans to fishermen co-operatives to purchase mechanized boats. Consequently it led to the rapid expansion of the mechanized trawlers whose number increased from a couple of hundred in 1966 to around 2,800 in 1985. Excessive trawling destroyed the sea bottom eco-niche and indiscriminate and non-selective purse-seining destroyed the whole shoals of pelagic fishes.

Second, the increased demand for prawns in the international market exerted extra pressure on the trawlers to make quick profits and thus promoted indiscriminate trawling. The growing fishermen population exerted pressure on the sea and reduced the coastal sea area available per fisherman. When trawlers are harvesting along with traditional crafts in coastal waters certain detrimental externalities are unavoidable. For instance, bottom trawling can affect juvenile fishes and fish spawning grounds thus reducing the overall harvest.[1] Often excessive trawling near the coast can lead to destruction of gears of traditional fisherman and can result in conflicts. During this period there were increasing instances of gears entanglement and often its destruction by the trawlers. This resulted in conflicts between these two sectors and finally required an appropriate strategy to deal with the situation.

The Need for Zoning

Baumol and Bradford (1972) have demonstrated that theoretically such problems can be conceived as of arising due to the presence of non-convexity.[2] For any pair of technologies one of which interferes with the harvest of the other non-convexity in the feasible set is unavoidable. The problem with the non-convexity is that market equilibrium cannot be relied on to exist when production sets are non-convex. This is illustrated with the help of Figure 1. Here OTM represents the set of fish harvest combination attainable by the mechanized and the traditional sector in the absence of externalities. Let 'w' denote the strength of externality, which signifies the proportion of decline in fish harvest when an intense mechanized operation further, degrades the resource stock. The strength of the externality is determined by endogenous as well as exogenous factors such as the number of mechanized and traditional crafts in operation, etc.

Figure 1
Fish Harvest Possibility Set

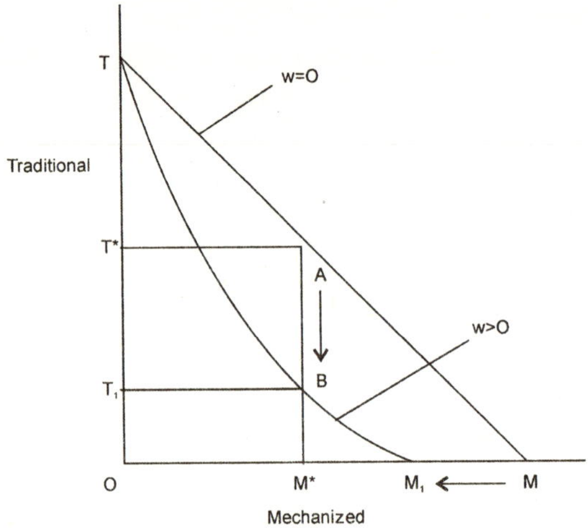

Algebraically, the fish harvest possibility set (F_n) current time period 'n' can be given by:

$$F_n = m+t - w\,[(mt/(m+t)) + F_{n-1}]$$

Here 'm' and 't' represent the fish caught by the mechanized and the traditional sectors such that both of them are greater than or equal to zero (to avoid negative values). In the absence of any external effects fish can be harvested along TAM. Because w=0, therefore $F_n = m+t$ will give the output. As the externalities increase (w>0) except T all other points on the locus shift downward. T remains totally unaffected because there is no detrimental externality generated in the absence of mechanized operation. The location of M varies with w because as the strength of externalities generated increases this shrinks the resource base. This is captured by the last component of the equation given above. Here TBM_1 depicts the harvest possibility set when the externalities grow serious. Let OM* depict the fish harvest of the mechanized sector in the absence of any externalities the traditional sector will be able to harvest OT*. But when the externality becomes severe then point A shifts downward to some lower point B, and the entire possibility locus becomes TBM_1. This increase in 'w' implies that with a given quantum of harvest by mechanized boats (OM*) smaller and smaller quantity of fish can be harvested by traditional sector (OT_1). Also the harvest possibility set becomes non-convex when it gets pulled below the line TAM.

The curvature of the harvest set shows the effect of externalities on the catch performance by the traditional sector. This is because of the increased intensity of operations in the coast where the continuity of operations slowly erodes the productivity of the bottom and more juvenile fishes caught can bring down the net recruitment rate. The curvature in the fish harvest possibility set also arises because the externality is also a function of the operational levels of the mechanized sector. Therefore the decline for the traditional sector will be lower initially but it will increase as the effort by the mechanized sector will increase. The rate of decline in the catch by the traditional sector reduces for low values of T. This is because there are parts of coastal sea which are difficult to be accessed by the mechanized boats and only traditional techniques can be employed at such place.

A fishery is an open access resource mainly because of large number of resource users and such resource can have problems because of heterogeneous techniques involved. Ostrom et al. (1994) classify the problems associated with common property resources into appropriation problem, technological externalities and assignment problem. Appropriation problems arise primarily because of the resource subtractibility. This implies that if a user harvests a certain quantity of resource stock, then the resource stock available for the rest of the users will decline. Therefore, there is a high possibility that fisherman can get trapped into the prisoner's dilemma and proceed to deplete the resource stock. Technological externalities are generated because of the employment of certain harvesting techniques for instance trawling, which is detrimental for the resource stock and users of other techniques. These technological externalities can be classified as direct and indirect externalities. In case of fisheries direct externalities would mean instances like physical interference entangling or destruction of fishing gears. Whereas destruction of fish spawning grounds which can reduce the future harvest is a sort of indirect technological externality. Assignment problem arises because of the spatial and temporal pattern of resource stock. For instance, some species are available at a particular time period and at a particular geographical space. However, Baland and Platteau (1996) argue that assignment problem is an outcome of the appropriation problem only.

Theoretically, zoning is done in order to overcome the non-convexity problem arising due to the presence of detrimental externalities when two technologies are operating simultaneously. Baumol and Bradford (1972) demonstrated that a lower bound to the degree of non-convexity in the social production set arising from detrimental externalities is provided by the possibility of separating the generators and their victims geographically, i.e., moving the trawlers from the vicinity of the traditional canoes.

In Figure 2, OTM represents the pre-zoning harvest possibility locus for trawlers and traditional canoes in the absence of any detrimental externality. Now assume that the externalities generated by mechanized operation have grown serious therefore the strategy of zoning is adopted. After the implementation of zoning, harvest possibility set shifts from OTM to $OTCM_Z$. Now TM_Z represents the levels of harvest for traditional canoes when trawlers are disallowed to harvest in a certain zone. Zoning will lead to reduction in harvest area available for trawlers hence all of TM_Z lies below TM. The end point T which corresponds to harvest capacity of traditional fisherman is unaffected by zoning regulations. Now if the mechanized sector harvests OM* of fish, traditional fisherman can obtain $OT_Z(>OT_1)$ amount of fish. This amount is greater than what could have been harvested in the absence of zoning. Thus, by separating the two operations of both the sectors the harvest of traditional fisherman can be increased by T_1T. Thus, zoning provides a lower bound ($TCDM_1$) to the fish-catch possibility locus and restricts it from moving closer to the origin. Thus sufficiently severe externalities make zoning of ocean space economical. In this process the feasible harvest region ($OTCDM_1$) becomes non-convex, as the lower bound must lie below line TM.

Figure 2

Fish Harvest Possibility Set After Zoning

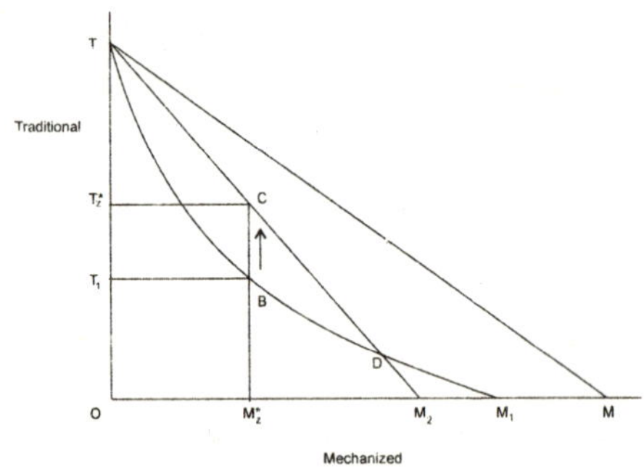

Therefore, if such resources are degraded, there is a good ground for state interventions that enable these poor users with their subsistence needs. The Government of Kerala adopted this policy of zoning to address the plight of the fisheries sector and especially the traditional sector. The Kerala Marine Fishing Regulation Act (1980) was framed which restricted fishing by mechanized boats—in particular the trawlers and the purse-seiners—to a depth outside the 20-fathom depth contour line in the coastal sea (spatial zoning). Because of its ineffectiveness[3] the government had to impose monsoon ban (temporal zoning) on mechanized fishing.

Effectiveness of Zoning

The theory of zoning argues that because of separation of two detrimental activities the wastage can be minimized and we can maximize the potential output. Here we are applying this theory in the case of a renewable resource which has the potential of actually increasing its stock. It was quite possible to observe a significant increase in the fish-catch if there was complete ban on mechanized fishing. After the successful implementation of temporal zoning it was expected that the average fish-catch would increase. Paul (2003) analyzes the performance of the Kerala Marine Fisheries Regulation Act and finds that the monsoon ban was the only regulation effectively enforced. He also found that the policy has helped to mitigate the conflicts in the coastal fisheries and the conflicts between the traditional fisherman and the trawler owners have fallen considerably.

Graph 2 shows the annual fish catch, segregated into pelagic and demersal fishes,[4] for the pre- and post-zoning periods. It can be concluded

Graph 2

Fish-Catch: Pre and Post Temporal Zoning

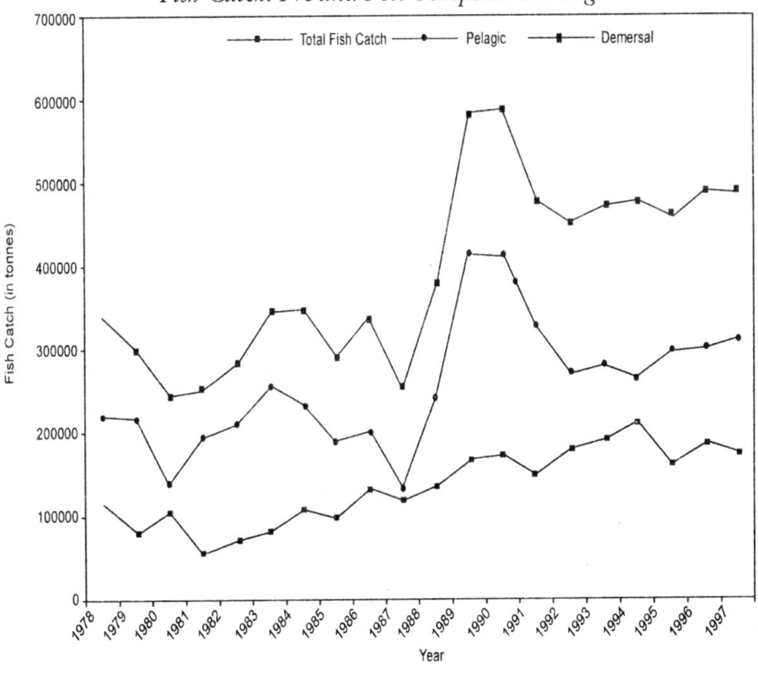

from the graph that there has been a trend break after the introduction of temporal zoning. The total fish-catch has increased by almost one and a half lakh tonnes and would thus give a stronger support for the success and continuation of temporal zoning.

But if we segregate the total fish-catch into pelagic and demersal resources we find a trend, which is different to the trend of the aggregate marine fish-catch. It can be seen that there is a minor trend break in the case of demersal fishery but the catch has increased over time at a constant rate until settling down at its threshold level. In the case of pelagic resources, a level shift occurs after introduction of temporal zoning. This level shift was mainly due to bumper harvest[5] of sardines and mackerels during the years 1989 to 1991. But in late 1990s the average catch of pelagic fishes settles at a higher average rate in comparison to the pre-zoning period.

In recent times both mechanized and the traditional sectors share equal quantity of overall fish harvest. Table 2 depicts the results of the regression analysis to test the trend and structural break in the catch of major marine species in Kerala. The following regression equation has been used:

$$\text{Fish-catch} = a + \beta_1(\text{time}) + \beta_2(\text{ban}) + e$$

It shows that ban has significant impact on the total fish-catch in Kerala. If we classify the total resources into pelagic and demersal resources we see that ban had a significant impact upon the catch of pelagic resources, whereas the catch of demersal resources has increased not only due to ban but also due to time.

The time element would include technical progress, demand generation, or even excess catch effort. It is important to note that after the ban, oil sardines have shown decline in the catch compared to pre-ban period. The catch of tunas and prawns showed significant increase due to operation of ban. Shahjahan (2000) found that the traditional sector in Kerala was able to catch more prawns during the post-monsoon ban. He concludes that increase in fish catch by traditional sector has led to increase in income of the traditional fisherman. The catch of cephalopods has also increased over time and the impact of ban also is significant on it. This is because of the growing export demand for this particular species as well as technical efficiency gained in catching such species. But the catch of a few major demersal species such as elasmobranchs and catfish has showed gradual decline with time.

Table 2
Trend and Structural Break Analysis of Major Marine Species

Species	*Coefficient time*	*t-stats*	*Coefficient ban*	*t-stats*	*Adjusted R2*
Pelagic	**-4164.2**	-1.07	**153961.2**	**3.42***	0.561
Seer fish	-96.65	-0.67	1979.14	1.20	0.103
Tunas	-245.26	-0.60	10173.74	2.15*	0.323
Mackerel	2155.58	1.37	37991.98	2.10*	0.696
Carangids	2510.24	1.84	24590	1.56	0.686
Oil sardines	-9335	-2.48*	64417	1.48	0.237
Lesser sardines	4.206	0.01	10226.94	1.37	0.228
Anchovies	547.439	0.57	10870.4	0.90	0.244
Demersal	**3518.7**	2.17*	**40724.3**	**2.18***	0.784
Elasmobranchs	-232.82	-2.38*	429.4	0.38	0.442
Catfish	-671.13	-3.38*	-1015.20	-0.44	0.744
Perches	1857.69	2.03	12833.69	1.21	0.665
Sciaenids	361.06	1.38	1157.06	0.38	0.343
Soles	524.53	1.53	3158	0.80	0.492
Prawns	-500.00	-0.60	24485.46	2.54*	0.438
Cephalopods	1602.97	4.24*	7282.17	1.67	0.873
Total	**2682.64**	0.92	**153657.8**	**2.95***	0.647

*at 5 per cent level of significance.

The importance of trend variable in the analysis of demersal fish-catch hints at the rapid technical progress (as depicted in Table 3) in the mechanized sector. After zoning the rate of expansion of the mechanized sector was slowed down, as there is an administrative ceiling upon the number of registered boats which restrained the growth of the mechanized sector. Nevertheless, there are around 4,510 (2002–03) mechanized boats operating in the coastal waters of Kerala. During the decade of 1990s most of the investments were made to upgrade the technology and increase the capacity of the boat. There was drastic restructuring in the harvesting technology of the marine fisheries sector in Kerala, resulting in widespread use of over-efficient harvesting technologies during the post-trawling ban period. As a result we can see that the number of crafts have not increased much but the length of the boats have increased significantly. During the period of early eighties, almost more than 95 per cent of the mechanized crafts were less than 35 feet in length but during late nineties data suggests that most of the trawlers are above 40 feet length.

Table 3

Structural Changes in the Trawling Sector–1980s and 1990s

Details	*1980s*		*1990s*	
	30	*32*	*40*	*42*
Length Overall (metres)	9.14	9.75	12.19	12.80
Fish hold capacity (ft3)	150	175	260	260
HP of engine	30–35	40–45	70–90	100–225
Number of crew	4	4	5	5
Endurance/Normal range (hrs/day)	20–24	24	3 days	3 days
Depth range of operation in fathoms	15	20	25	25

Source: Shahjahan (2000).

From mid-eighties, trawlers started venturing into new deeper areas in the sea. The introduction of high opening bottom trawling enabled trawlers to catch more cephalopods, an exportable demersal species of fish. Trawlers slowly started staying overnight on sea to reduce operational costs. Synonymous with this power of engines began to grow. Boats, which were using 40–65 HP engines, began using engines of 100–225 HP for bottom trawling. After ban the trawlers witnessed loss of income during monsoon season. At this juncture Marine Products Export Development Authority (MPEDA) stepped into the scene to provide financial assistance to the trawlers to enable them to modify and enlarge the trawlers thereby making them fit for offshore and deep sea fishing. MPEDA also took initiative in providing electronic equipment aimed at increasing fishing efficiencies such as echo-sounder, etc., at subsidized price (Shahjahan, 2000).

In the decade of nineties a spectacular increase in the number of motorized boats was observed. Apart from the conversion of non-motorized crafts into motorized, government policy of zoning has also led to the rapid expansion of this sector. Zoning regulations created extra capacity in the sea, which was to be exploited, and initially the high catches by these motorized crafts must have attracted investments in this sector. The opportunity cost of trawler during monsoon ban is zero so it was beneficial for the fishermen to buy motorized boats and appropriate a larger share of the resource. In the traditional sector the craft gear technology using motorized planks built crafts and ring seines was widespread. The most dramatic change took place in the use of outboard motors on the fishing crafts. During the mid-eighties a major share of the engines used were of 8 HP to a maximum of 25 HP. But in the decade of nineties outboard motors having an engine power of 40 HP were available for the motorized boats (SIFFS, 1999).

The increment in the number of crafts had resulted in increased area of operation for the fishermen; as a result more fishes were caught. Hence, the role of technology has to be acknowledged for much of the increase in catch after the post-ban period. Also the fact that due to their increased export demand of cephalopods (mainly squids and cuttlefish) trawlers have began to catch more of these species. These species were not caught earlier by the trawlers and now they constitute almost around seven per cent of total fish catch.

Re-emergence of the Open Access Crisis

Zoning is a welfare enhancing policy as it distributes the resources among a larger section of the fishermen community. But it is important to understand the long-term implications of this policy upon the fisheries sector. In the mechanized sector after zoning the profitability of the mini-trawlers declined and this sector had to look beyond the inshore areas. Administrative regulations pertaining to ceiling on the number of trawlers were also deterring the growth of the mechanized sector. As a result the rate of growth of trawlers declined after monsoon ban. After zoning the annual average catch per craft in the mechanized sector increased significantly (Table 4). This is mainly because of the technology upgradation and increasing export demands. The expansion in the number and capacity of mechanized boats also forced them to cover more fishing area. This is a good sign for the fisheries development in Kerala as most of the deep-sea resources are under-exploited.[6]

The real problem arises in the traditional sector, which demands greater attention as it includes a major chunk of the fisher-folk engaged for their subsistence requirements. Zoning ensured that the income of the traditional sector will increase and it acted as an incentive to invest more. From Table 4, it is evident that after zoning there has been a 50 per cent increase in the number of traditional crafts. If viewed in a disaggregated fashion the growth was mainly due to the rapid expansion of the motorized crafts in this sector. During the imposition of monsoon ban there were less than ten thousand motorized boats in operation but within a decade and half the number has tripled and is just under the thirty thousand figure. Huge investments were made in the motorized sector to reap the benefits of zoning. A larger area of the ocean was available for the motorized sector and the monsoon ban was not restraining this sector.

Table 4

Average Annual Fish-Catch (in tonnes), Number of Crafts and Catch per Craft

Year	*Traditional Sector*			*Mechanized Sector*		
	Catch	*Crafts**	*Catch/ Craft*	*Catch*	*Crafts**	*Catch/ Craft*
1981–87	2,51,320(70)	34,770	7.22	1,06,790 (30)	3,116	34.27
1988–91	3,59,010 (63)	38,227	9.40	2,12,760 (37)	3,742	56.86
1998–2001	2,98,950 (52)	49,126	6.09	2,76,310 (48)	4,099	67.41

Source: Estimated from Kalawar et al. (1985) and CMFRI cited in Paul (2003).

* Time series of crafts data is obtained through linear interpolation from the data of fishing crafts provided by Government of Kerala in its various fisheries reports.

Note: Figures in parentheses give the percentage share of catch by the respective sector in total fish-catch.

Another factor that contributed significantly to the growth of the motorized sector was the availability of soft loans for this sector. The Kerala State Cooperative Federation for Fisheries Development Limited (MATSYAFED) was the main agency responsible for the development of marine fisheries in the state. They arranged loans for fishing equipments like canoes, engines, gears, etc. They also assisted fishermen in getting loans from commercial banks for Yamaha outboard engines (Balasubrahmaniam et al., 1989). With technical progress achieved in the motor power and new gear designs, investment became profitable in this sector.

It must be remembered that the natural reserve of fish is a viable capital. The exploitable stock of fish is subject to changes depending upon the intensity of fishing. Therefore, increase in the returns to the fishermen is subject to the exploitable reserve of fish. As Gordon (1954) argues that:

> ... if a species were in ecological equilibrium before the commencement of commercial fishing, man's intrusion would have the same effect as any other predator. This can only mean that the species population would reach a new equilibrium at a lower level of abundance, the divergence of the new equilibrium from the old depending on the degree of man's predatory effect and effectiveness.

The increased catch per craft was mainly due to plentiful fish resources in the inshore waters. But as the number of crafts increased this resource base was appropriated by a larger number of fishermen thus providing a declining average catch per craft. During 1998–2001, the average catch per craft had reached to a level of six tonnes, which is lower in comparison to the average catch during the crisis period. Though increase in prices of fish might have saved the traditional sector but it cannot have a serious impact on the profitability because of the increased operational costs (mainly in the cost of fuel required for engine propulsion).

The other component of the traditional sector, i.e., the non-motorized sector has also become unprofitable and their numbers declined over the decade of 1990s. The share of the non-motorized sector in total fish catch has also declined (presently just over one per cent).[7] There was no incentive to enter into traditional sector because of excessive fishing by other type of crafts. This non-motorized sector is incompetent as compared with the motorized and the mechanized sector. Apart from the conversion to motorized fishing, some of the traditional fisherman might have given up the traditional fishing crafts and looked for alternative source of employment. Nevertheless still a large number of non-mechanized boats are operating in Kerala. This is because the fishermen do not have any other alternative or incentives to move beyond this field. These non-motorized crafts are mostly concentrated and operating in the southernmost tip of Kerala coast because of the topographical reasons, which disallow the fishing by the trawlers or motorized crafts.

With the growing size of the sector there is emergence of open access equilibrium. This will result in declining income of the motorized sector and it will have its implications upon their welfare. The re-emergence of the open access crisis is arising mainly due to the appropriation problem. Now, despite of declining average catch there will not be any protests and struggles in the fishing community because this is not due to any exogenous factor (mechanized sector) because it is evidently *tragedy of the commons.*

Paul (2003) argues that the non-motorized sector is the most vulnerable one and there is an urgent need to frame regulations to protect them from the externalities of the motorized segment. The alarming increase in the size of the fishing vessels, gears and engine power and destructive fishing practices like mini-trawling and the problem of marine pollution are serious problems demanding urgent regulations. But it is very difficult to regulate this sector because of the engagement of a large section of people and certain institutional difficulties in regulating and monitoring them. This difficulty arises because of the nature of the resource and large number of resource users. These resource users seem to be trapped in the prisoner's dilemma and despite understanding the importance of resource conservation are helpless and resort to the depletion route. This signifies that the distribution of income through the policy of zoning in itself cannot assure long run prosperity if it is not guided by appropriate investment in human capital, which can fetch higher returns in the long run. But these measures have to be well supported by the government.

The traditional fishermen have to find alternative means of livelihood or this sector has to undergo structural changes so as to earn profits. Signs of such structural changes have already emerged in Kerala's traditional fisheries. There is emergence of a new range of fishing boats called the In-Board Engine Vallams having huge capacity. This craft being evolved in the traditional sector, they do not abide by the zoning regulations.

There is a need for further studies to provide solution for this problem. In the common property resources literature argues co-management strategy to be one solution to the problem (Baland and Platteau, 1996). But this strategy also has problems especially because of the demographic developments within the sector, which can exert pressure upon the resource. Buyback strategy can prove beneficial for the resource users if the payment ensures adequate provision of educational opportunities and placement in alternative employment sectors. The fisheries sector requires active government support to encourage human capital accumulation in this sector. The standard literacy scale is inadequate until it converts itself into effective literacy. The labour mobility[8] has to be stepped up in the fisheries sector otherwise it could have detrimental effect upon the fishing community that had enjoyed a decade of good harvests after zoning.

Conclusion

The indiscriminate trawling during the late 1970s and early 1980s led to the emergence of the open access crisis in Kerala's marine fisheries. This problem emerged due to the presence of detrimental externalities leading to non-convexity of the fish harvest set and was not a result of over-exploitation. Consequently the strategy of zoning was adopted as a measure to overcome this non-convexity problem. This policy was successful in raising the aggregate fish harvest and also helped to raise the income of the traditional sector. Because of restriction on inshore fishing by trawlers this sector underwent changes mainly in capacity building and with the help of new technologies were able to harvest even greater quantity of fish.

Zoning provided an incentive for the motorized sector to earn profits, which led to over-investment of capital and labour. Resultantly this sector is presently approaching the open access crisis with continuous decline in the fish harvest and profitability due to large size of the sector and increased costs of operation. In order to overcome this problem there is a need to find alternative institutional arrangements for efficient management of the resource. At the same time labour mobility from the fisheries sector to other sectors has to be encouraged through active government support.

Notes

1. Bottom trawling is proving lethal to the existence of the living communities because it increases turbidity and consequently reduces the oxygen content in the marine ecosystem. Sudden alteration of the marine milieu can have detrimental effect on the growth and development of eggs, larvae and juvenile fishes. Thomas and Kurup (2005) have discussed and studied this aspect.
2. A convex set is a set in which a straight-line segment connecting any two points in the set lies entirely within the set; if not, then the set is defined as a non-convex set.
3. Paul (2003) finds that the ineffectiveness was mainly due to the monitoring and implementation difficulties involved.
4. Pelagic fishes are found near the surface of the sea whereas fish species dwelling on the seabed are termed as demersal fishes.
5. The combined harvests were almost more than double of the average harvests of approximately 1.2 lakh tonnes.
6. Ramchandran (2004) provides the estimates of the exploitable capacity of the fisheries in the different depth zones.
7. Rajasree and Kurup (2002).
8. Rajan (2002) finds that the probability of labour moving outside the fisheries sector is very low.

References

Baland, J.M and Platteau, J.P. (1996), *Halting Degradation of Natural Resources: Is there a Role for Rural Communities?*, Oxford, Clarendon.

Balasubrahmaniam et al. (1989), "In the Shadow of the Gulf: Case Studies in Poverty Alleviation in Kerala" in R.P. Slater, J.R. Watson and R.N. Tripathi (eds.) *In the Shadow of the Gulf: Case Studies in Poverty Alleviation in Kerala*, National Institute of Rural Development, Hyderabad.

Baumol, W.J. and Bradford, B.M. (1972), "Detrimental Externalities and Non-Convexity of the Production Set", *Economica*, Vol. 39.

FAO (2001), "Understanding the Cultures of Fishing Communities: A Key to Fisheries Management and Food Policy", FAO Fisheries Technical Paper No. 401, Food and Agricultural Organization, Rome.

Gordon, H.S (1954), "The Economic Theory of a Common Property Resource: The Fishery", *Journal of Political Economy*, Vol. 62, Chicago.

Government of Kerala (various years), Reports published by Department of Fisheries, Trivandrum.

Hardin, G. (1968), "The Tragedy of the Commons", *Science*, 162.

Kalawar, A.G., Devaraj, M. and Parulekar, A. (1985), "Report of the Expert Committee on Marine Fisheries in Kerala", Department of Fisheries, Trivandrum and Central Institute of Fisheries Education, Versova, Bombay.

Kurien, J. and Achary, T. (1988), "Fisheries Development Policies and the Fishermen's Struggles in Kerala", *Social Action*, 38.

Kurup, B.M. (2001), "Experiences from the Seasonal Closure of Bottom Trawling in Kerala (South India) on the Exploited Marine Fisheries Resources", in S. Goddard, H. Al-Qufi, J. McIlwain and T.M. McIlwain (eds.), Proc. 1st International Conference on Fisheries, Aquaculture and Environment in the NW Indian Ocean, Sultan Qaboos University, Muscat, Sultanate of Oman.

Nair et al. (2000), Report of the Expert Committee for Fisheries Management Studies, Kerala, Government of Kerala, Directorate of Fisheries, Trivandrum.

Ostrom, E., Gardener, R. and Walker, J. (1994), *Rules, Games and Common Pool Resources*, Ann Arbor, Michigan, The University of Michigan Press.

Paul, A. (2003), "Evolution and Performance of Institutions in Common Pool Resources Management: A Study of Kerala's Marine Fishery", CDS, Unpublished Ph.D. Thesis, Trivandrum.

Rajan, J.B. (2002), "Labour Mobility in the Small Scale Fisheries Sector of Kerala", Discussion Paper No. 44, Kerala Research Programme for Local Level Development and Centre for Development Studies, Trivandrum.

Rajasree, R. and Kurup, B.M. (2002), "Status of Exploited Marine Fishery in Kerala with special reference to the Effects of Conservation and Management Measures Imposed in Providing Respite to Fishstocks", *Sixth Indian Fisheries Forum*, 17–20 December, 2002.

Ramchandran, C. (2004), Teaching not to Finish: A Constructivist Perspective on Reinventing a Responsible Marine Fisheries Extension System, CMFRI, Kochi.

Shahjahan, K.M. (2000), "Impact of Ban on Monsoon Trawling on the Marine Fishery Resources and Income Levels of Marine Fishermen in Kerala", in Report of the Expert Committee for Kerala Fisheries Management Studies, (Chairman: Balakrishna Nair), Directorate of Fisheries, Gevernment of Kerala, Trivandrum.

SIFFS (1999), A Census of the Artisanal Marine Fishing Fleet of Kerala-1998, South Indian Federation of Fishermen Societies, Trivandrum.

Thomas, J.V. and Kurup, B.M. (2005), "Impact of Bottom Trawling on Sediment Texture and Organic Matter Along Inshore Waters of Kerala (South India)", *Fishery Technology*, Vol. 42(2).

Part III

Decentralized Governance and Responsive Administration

14 Evolution of Panchayat Raj in India

An Analysis of Development from Independence to Post-73rd Amendment Scenario

Yatindra Singh Sisodia

India, an ancient civilization, witnessed the panchayats as an integral part of Indian society and polity since ages. Indian villages have organized and maintained social order through panchayats since ancient times. The informal institution of panchayat was responsible for maintaining and governing village society in accordance with the socio-political norms of their times (Kashyap, 2003). Indian villages, remote and disconnected from the centres of power decided with a sense of autonomy their agenda of development and management of society and its resources with the institution of panchayat.

Historically, the institution of panchayat has been an integral part of rural Indian polity and society. Traditionally, panchayats have operated at two levels in the villages. The first level was that of the caste panchayats and the second was gram panchayat. Caste has been the predominant social reality of India, which dictated the organizing principles of polity and society. Panchayat is no exception to this social reality. Different castes in the villages have different panchayats of their own. This tradition of caste panchayats is still prevalent on a large scale in India. However, issues having wider ramifications beyond the caste group were also discussed threadbare in the Gram Panchayats. These traditional panchayats played the vital role of maintaining socio-ethical norms and order, and dispensing justice. It also resolved, with all its inherent limitations, unforeseen crises and disputes, and took decisions on behalf of the village community for the welfare and development of the villages. Nevertheless, the process of decision-making was participatory and very often a 'democratic' consensus emerged due to the mediation of the panchayat. This apparent 'democratic' consensus was obviously limited and restricted within the framework of a hierarchical society divided on feudal and caste lines. Significantly, the panchayats derived their legitimacy from the support of the village community and its decisions were accepted as binding on the community.

Forces of modernism, coupled with the penetrative reach of the modern administrative paraphernalia under the colonial state, started drastically altering the cultural, socio-political and economic profile of Indian villages. This deeply affected the village institutions including the panchayats. The modern state with the support of the instrumentalists of the bureaucratic framework slowly delegitimized informal institutions depriving them of their inherent legitimacy through informal channels. The growing functions of the state and its ever-increasing sphere also reduced the space of the panchayats. At this time, the Indian nationalist critique of colonialism emerged largely from a modernist paradigm and it largely used non-traditional instruments and strategies for the national movement. The cumulative result of the emergence of such forces of modernism was that the panchayats were reduced to playing a marginal role in the village society.

The Indian national movement was deeply influenced by Gandhi's leadership and by his philosophy of non-violent and mass programmes of civil disobedience, but the task of nation building was not undertaken in accordance with his philosophy. Gandhi's doctrine for nation building and national development was based on the concept of a confederation of villages; in fact, the model derived its roots from the traditional panchayat system. He envisaged greater autonomy to villages under a five-tier system of village panchayats, taluka panchayats, district panchayats, provincial panchayats and all-India Panchayats. His concept of administrative/state system was based on a pyramid model whose broad base was composed of numerous village communities of India. The higher panchayats would help the village panchayats in areas where the village panchayat needed help and guidance for improving the system of public service. The fundamental unit of administration was village panchayat; the model suggested a bottom-up approach where the power flowed upward from the smaller units to the higher one.

The sad experience of partition and the centrifugal political forces during the struggling days of Indian independence forced India to adopt a strong two-tier federal structure with a tilt towards centralism. Pursuing a modernist paradigm, independent India's first Prime Minister, Pandit

Jawaharlal Nehru, started creating and establishing new modern institutions and structures. His approach to nation building and national reconstruction was primarily top-down and for this he assigned a central role to the state. According to Nehru, the state could take on the task of nation building and also be the agent of social change. His faith in socialism and the process of planning led ultimately to a system, which was based on centralization of power and authority. As a result the Gandhian paradigm of development, discussed above, was marginalized. Another important reason for this marginalization was Dr Ambedkar's views on Indian villages. He was primarily responsible for drafting the Constitution; he condemned the villages as "a sink of localism and a den of ignorance and narrow mindedness and communalism" (Ambedkar, 1948). Dr Ambedkar felt that the Gandhian notion of village republics would adversely affect the country, therefore the idea of panchayats as fundamental unit of governance was rejected.

A middle path between these conflicting ideologies was devised and a mere formal acceptance of the idea of local autonomy and local self-governance was reflected in the incorporation of village panchayats in the Directive Principles of the Indian Constitution.

Initiatives for Panchayat Raj Since Independence

Independent India inherited in 1947, local self-government as a small wing of the local level of the governmental system. The central unit was the district administration, which was a complex of field offices and agencies of the then existing provincial government. District administration had evolved as a structure with its powers and functions over long years during the decades of the eighteenth century. It is now studded with manifold responsibilities relating to general administration, regulatory administration, revenue administration and development administration.

During this period most of the provincial governments passed fresh laws for providing democratization of structure and substantial enhancement of the powers of the local bodies. Administrative action also began to expand substantially the number of local bodies so as to cover increasing parts of the country. Several princely states then in existence in India also began to set up gradually local bodies, though with partial democratic structures and limited powers (Khanna, 1994).

Rural Local Self-Government During First Decade in Independent India

First decade of Indian Independence was mainly devoted to reorganization of states and to development and enactment of certain legislative and administrative measures with a view to expanding and developing rural local self-government. In this connection three main influences tended to make an impact upon policy-makers. One was the viewpoint of Mahatma Gandhi who had been pleading over the years that village panchayats should be treated as the primary units of grass-roots democracy. Another was that of newly framed democratic Constitution of the country in which there was a concrete provision about state's duty to develop panchayats as local self-governing units. The third was that of the viewpoint of the recently launched Five-Year Plans (1951 onwards) that people's participation should be promoted in management of rural development through local representative institutions. These three influences have continued to motivate, of course with fluctuating intensity, the policy-makers and public leaders even subsequently.

A very significant influence with regard to development of rural local self-government over the years on government and public leaders has been of Mahatma Gandhi, the father of the Indian nation. In his writings and statements he always drew attention of the people and government to the urgent need for rebuilding the villages as self-sufficient and self-reliant entities with the village panchayat playing the central role in encouraging and supporting constructive and creative activities among the people. His dictum was "greater the power of the panchayat, the better for the people"; he believed that true democracy "has to be worked from below by the people of every village".

The Constitution of India promulgated in January 1950 for setting up a democratic and semi-federal political system, included Article 40 relating to the panchayats. Though the draft Constitution did not include any mention about panchayats, some prominent members of the Constituent Assembly, influenced with Gandhian philosophy regarding self-governing villages, succeeded in getting it included in the final draft. Article 40 in the chapter on Directive Principles of State Policy states that "The state should take steps to organize village panchayats and endow them with such powers and authority as may be necessary to enable them to function as units of self-government". This Constitutional directive tended to inspire the Union and state governments to think about adoption of measures for development of the panchayats in the country. During the first decade of independent India, fresh laws were passed in many states to democratize the structure, devolve more powers and expand the spatial coverage of the panchayats. More recently, this constitutional directive has been interpreted as empowering the government to provide constitutional sanction for important features of not only village panchayats but also of local self-governing bodies above it.

The era of planned development in India started in the fifties with the launching of the First Five-Year Plan in 1951–52. Since then Development Plans have been growing in dimensions, scope and diversity and complexities. Certain administrative changes within the governmental system have been brought about for their formulation and implementation at national, state and local levels. One of these changes relates to devolution of politico-administrative powers. These include strengthening of local self-government to play a meaningful role in local development processes. People's participation through representative local bodies is envisaged to energize these processes and also make them more relevant and responsive to people's needs and expectations.

Community Development Programme (1952)

As a part of the planned development initiated in the country, the first major rural development programme, named as Community Development Programme (CDP), was launched by the state governments at some places in 1952 and later extended to many parts of the country in a phased manner. The basic premise on which CDP rests is to motivate the rural people to undertake self-reliant community-based approach for the improvement of economic and social condition of their life and environment. The government is expected to provide general guidance and technical-cum-financial assistance for reinforcing the community welfare programmes and activities, as need be. A few years later a programme with limited scope and funding named as National Extension Service (NES) was introduced as a prelude to the launching of CDP in the remaining parts of the country.

A new basic administrative unit below the district level, named as development block, was created in an increasing number to cover most parts of the country. Headed administratively by a block development officer and comprising several subject specialist extension officers, this new administrative unit was to serve as the locale of the CDP and NES under the overall direction of the district administration. For providing people's participation in local planning and implementation of these two programmes, advisory committees of nominated persons were set up at the development block and another at district level of the districts. Certain administrative changes were also brought about at the level of the state government, which had the main responsibility for these programmes under the overall guidance, support and review, by the Union Government.

Genesis of Panchayat Raj (1957–61)

During the closing years of the decade of the fifties it began to cause increasing concern to Union government that due care was not being taken in avoiding wastage of funds in implementation of community development and allied programmes. This wastage was attributed to inefficiency in the implementation process. The National Development Council appointed a committee on plan projects to look into this problem. The Committee appointed a Study Team in 1956 under the chairmanship of a senior legislator, Balwant Rai Mehta, to review critically the community development projects and national extension service and suggest measures needed for effecting economy and improving efficiency in their implementation. The Team was also asked to examine: "the extent to which Community Development Movement has succeeded in utilizing local initiatives and in creating institutions to ensure continuity in the process of improving economic and social conditions in rural areas".

The Planning Commission had already been advocating that village panchayats should be strengthened and linked with popular organization at higher levels and that this new democratic set-up should gradually be given responsibility for taking over development administration and even some aspects of general administration within a district. The Mehta Committee kept this plea in view while formulating its own recommendations about reorganization of institutional arrangements for community development and allied programmes. In summary form these were the main points of the report: The PRI structure, which was introduced in most parts of the country, as a result of this report, however, did not develop the requisite democratic momentum and failed to cater to the needs of rural development. There are various reasons for this such as: (i) political and bureaucratic resistance at the state level to sharing of power and resources with the local level institutions, (ii) the takeover of these institutions by the rural elite who cornered a major share of the benefits of the various welfare schemes, (iii) the lack of capability at the local level, and (iv) the absence of political will of the grass-roots leaders.

In 1958, the Standing Committee of the National Development Council agreed broadly with the recommendations of the Team. It also recognized that since conditions varied in different parts of the country, the state government concerned should be free to decide about the exact application of the concept of democratic decentralization and its institutional set-up. The Union Government tried through holding meetings of state ministers and administrators as well as through convening conferences of All India Local Self-Government Council and community development administrators to persuade, guide and support the state government to establish the proposed system with any minor modifications as need be. The main purpose was to switch over to an institutionalized participative approach for rural development at local levels. Starting with the setting up of the new system by three state governments in 1959, it was established in most of the existing states, with some variations in its structure during the early part of the sixties.

V.P. Naik Committee Report (1961)

In the State of Maharashtra a committee was set up by the state government under V.P. Naik to recommend institutional set-up suited to the state for practical application of the concept of democratic decentralization. The Report pointed out that people had yet to realize the importance of their role in "building up of the nation and its material prosperity". In order to enable them to play this role appropriately, local bodies at village, block and district levels should be set up. These bodies should be responsible to the people, enjoy their full confidence and be capable of enlisting their real, whole-hearted and determined support. Development functions needed to be separated into a local sector and a state sector. Popular local bodies at the village, block and district levels should play "a vital role" in the local sector of development functions. It was the Committee's view that powers and resources should be largely devolved upon the local body at the district level, i.e., Zilla Parishad, as at that level mature representative leadership and adequately trained administrative personnel would be available. The Zilla Parishad, according to the Committee, should be broad based in composition through providing for a majority of its members to be directly elected. All district level development departments would have to be transferred to its control to provide administrative assistance. The panchayats would continue to function at village levels, revamped as need be, under the overall guidance of the Zilla Parishad. The Panchayat Samiti would act mainly as a statutory committee of the Zilla Parishad for implementing programmes assigned to it by the Parishad.

Since the end of 1959, a network of Panchayat Raj Institutions was built by most of the state governments guided and supported by the Union government and inspired as well by the Planning Commission. The three-tier panchayat raj system with powers largely devolved upon the Panchayat Samiti (the intermediate level body) with some adjustments became popular, by and large, with state governments. After 1961, however, the recommendations of the Naik Committee of Maharashtra tended also to influence to a varied extent the decisions of some state governments regarding distribution of devolved powers among the three levels within the panchayat raj system. However, most of the state governments did not accept the Mehta Team's recommendations about district collector being the chairman of Zilla Parishad. By 1964–65 panchayat raj began to function in most of the rural areas of 12 out of 15 states of India. Hardly any headway was made in the then existing Union Territories, except in one.

The lead in establishment of the panchayat raj was taken by the states of Rajasthan, Andhra Pradesh and Tamil Nadu in 1959. Prime Minister, Jawaharlal Nehru, went himself to Rajasthan to inaugurate it. This lead in panchayat raj was followed by a number of other states during the next few years, as the result of growing enthusiasm among the state governments for the panchayat raj, which was expected to contribute significantly to the economic and social transformation of the depressed classes of rural life and environment. In Assam, Karnataka, Orissa, Punjab and Uttar Pradesh, it was established in 1960–61 by the governments concerned with some adaptations to suit their local needs. Next came Maharashtra, Gujarat, Bihar, Madhya Pradesh and West Bengal for launching it. The states of Kerala and Jammu and Kashmir, however, decided not to have the multi-tiered panchayat raj and only devolved some more powers to the existing village panchayats to perform a few developmental functions, besides the usual civic functions.

Stagnation and Decline (1965–85)

During the next two decades, however, panchayat raj began to stagnate in the first few years (1965–70) and then started even declining in efficacy of its role in promotion and management of development processes in the rural areas. This trend continued till 1985. Its public image and credibility began to suffer a set back. Its powers and functions were reduced by executive orders of the government on grounds of inefficiency.

The growing indifference of the state governments and also of the Union government with regard to development of panchayat raj was also attributable to certain happenings. One of these was that with the demise of Prime Minister Nehru in 1964 and also of several other panchayat prone political leaders and ministers, panchayat raj began to lose its ardent supporters. Several new ministers and many legislators began to develop increasing allergies with regard to the panchayat raj, as they tended to apprehend a challenge to their position from the emergent panchayat raj leadership, particularly at the Zilla Parishad and Panchayat Samiti levels.

Another reason was that the growing concern for improving the foodgrains production in the food-deficit country led to introduction of some new agriculture programmes. These were the Intensive Agriculture District Programme (1961), Intensive Agriculture Areas Programme (1963) and the High Yielding Variety (HYV) Programme (1965). These programmes were not entrusted to panchayat raj institutions but were administrated directly by the agriculture department with the support of the district collector. Even the existing agricultural personnel deputed to work under panchayat raj for promoting agricultural production as a part of Community Development Programme were withdrawn by the state government department of agriculture. Thinking that development targets could be achieved faster through bureaucratic administration under ministerial direction in the agricultural sector, a trend emerged within the state governments to start withdrawing several other developmental functions along with their assigned personnel from the panchayat raj. This resulted in the weakening of the status and authority of the panchayat raj and steep falling off in its budget and staffing strength. Thus, panchayat began to drift into background in the context of growing sectoral development programmes promoted by governmental agencies.

During the decade of the seventies (even in 1969) the political situation underwent a change. There was an atmosphere of 'political uncertainty'. There was some weakening of political stability of state governments in the country. Several state governments and individual ministers concerned about stability of their office began to perceive increasingly serious challenges to their position from the ambitions of Panchayat Samiti, more so of Zilla Parishad members and chairmen. To ensure support of the legislators for their position, they tried to please them by repressing the role of the panchayat raj leadership of which these legislators began to be jealous politically.

Another cause of this decline of panchayat raj, was growing resentment of the common people against elite domination of it who tried to grab, by and large, benefits accruing from its working. As political awareness began to grow among the people on account of political processes at work with increasing intensity over the years, they began to resent elite domination and pleaded to keep them aloof from these institutions. Thus, panchayat raj was getting alienated from the majority of people in many states. Even in Maharashtra and Gujarat wherein panchayat raj had built a good image and credibility, it started stagnating to some extent. Luckily, however, in one state the moribund panchayat raj began to be gradually rejuvenated from 1978 onwards. The Left Front government in West Bengal started this process of rejuvenation partly to help the common people and partly to consolidate its own position politically.

In 1977 the Janata Party replaced the ruling Congress Party in the states as well as at the Union level. The Janata Party government appointed a high level committee under the chairmanship of an eminent legislator, Ashoka Mehta, to inquire into the causes of decline in the working of panchayat raj with a view to recommending appropriate measures to reform and rejuvenate it.

Ashoka Mehta Committee (1977–78)

The Committee headed by a distinguished public leader like Ashoka Mehta was appointed by Janata Party government at the Centre in 1977 to inquire into the working of Panchayat Raj Institutions and suggest measures to strengthen them, "so as to enable a decentralized system of planning and development to be effective". The Committee submitted its report next year. It mentioned that panchayat raj had been weakened due to certain adverse factors. Its structure was inadequate and government support meagre to enable it to perform developmental role effectively in a changing socio-economic environment since its inception in the early part of the decade of sixties. In Maharashtra and Gujarat, however, Panchayat Raj Institutions were performing their role well on account of structural adequacy and appropriate state government support. Elsewhere, degrading factors like political factionalism, oligarchic domination, corruption, inefficiency, parochial loyalties, power intoxication and political and bureaucratic apathy and arbitrariness had diluted its performance, efficacy and public credibility.

The Committee made a number of recommendations to reform and revitalize panchayat raj based upon the central premise of "linking institutions of democratic decentralization with socially motivated economic development". The panchayat raj structures, powers and functions and also relation with the government as well as with various relevant local institutions should be reviewed periodically and revised to enable it to perform its role effectively in the changing social and economic environments.

Though the recommendations of the Committee were not accepted by the Union government due to change again in the ruling party within it, some of these did exercise varying influence upon the working of panchayat raj in a few states. Some years later (1983–85) Karnataka and Andhra Pradesh remodelled by and large their respective panchayat raj systems under this influence.

Renovation and Revival Since 1985

Since the middle of the decade of the eighties there has been growing interest within the Union Government and within several state governments in reviving the role of the panchayat raj, which had been languishing for a long time in many states in the country. The Planning Commission also reiterated its plea in the Five-Year Plans (Seventh and Eighth) for expanding and energizing the role of panchayat raj in the promotion and management of rural development, which was now growing considerably in scope, diversity and complexity. Effective people's participation through panchayat raj in rural development according to the Commission, would contribute to better responsiveness to people's needs and aspirations and also to the coordinated and accelerated progress of this development.

One important step was taken by the Union government in 1984: the Prime Minister wrote to chief ministers of state governments to take appropriate action without further delay for holding of overdue elections to Panchayat Raj Institutions as well as for revitalizing their functioning. Another important step taken by this government was to appoint two committees successively in 1985 and 1986 respectively to suggest ways and means for strengthening panchayat raj as vibrant local institutional set-up for playing an active and purposeful role in management of local services and appropriate development programmes. One committee under the chairmanship of a senior administrator (G.V.R. Rao) reported in 1985, suggesting appropriate improvement in the representative character and strengthening of the capability of both the people's representatives and the administrative personnel in the panchayat raj institutions so as to equip them to play a more active, equitable and efficient role in promoting and managing rural development and local affairs.

The other committee under the chairmanship of a distinguished jurist (L.M. Singhvi) advocated that panchayat raj should primarily be viewed as the local self-government system. It should be strengthened so as to serve better as one of the foundation stones of the country's democratic political system. Its secondary role of much importance was to continue to be that of an administrative agency for promotion and management of rural development. In order to strengthen the status of panchayat raj, its main features should be mentioned in the Constitution itself. The existing constitutional provision (Article 40) is too general and also of discretionary nature to provide appropriately a firm basis to panchayat raj system which had been weakened largely on account of neglect and unscrupulous politicking in various states (Singh et al., 1997).

The Union government also convened workshops of senior administrators concerned with panchayat raj affairs to provide opportunity to them to express their views about reinforcing and reorienting panchayat raj for undertaking increasing responsibility for management of local development and local affairs.

The administrators agreed that panchayat raj based upon the concept of democratic decentralization within the country's governmental system needed to be revamped suitably to improve its working for accelerating responsive and equitable development processes as well as for contributing to development of citizenship standards.

Conferences of panchayat raj leaders (including women) were as well arranged by the government to elicit their views about reorganization and strengthening of panchayat raj. In these conferences the demand was for debureaucratization of the control of panchayat raj as well as for devolution of more powers and resources to it.

Taking into account the views of these committees, workshops and conferences, the Union Government decided to amend the Constitution of the country in order to provide a firm constitutional basis to the essential features of the panchayat raj. This was intended to provide substantial protection to panchayat raj against negligence or arbitrary action by state governments, which had been contributing to its emasculation in many states over the years. It is as recently as 1992 that the government finally succeeded in getting the amendment approved by the Parliament. The state governments were required to take appropriate action under it.

Re-establishment of PRIs (1992)

As described earlier, in the 1990s, there had been growing serious concern in the country with regard to the weak status of the panchayat raj in most of the states. It was widely recognized by the government, public leaders, intelligentsia that the panchayat raj institutions were not able to "acquire the status and dignity of viable and responsive people's bodies". The main reasons mentioned by the government and others for this were: "absence of regular elections, prolonged super sessions, insufficient representation of weaker sections like Scheduled Castes/Scheduled Tribes and Women, inadequate devolution of powers and lack of financial resources".

Though Article 40 of the Constitution has directed the Indian State to organize and empower village panchayats to enable them to function as "units of self-government", most of the state governments have actually tended to pay only half-hearted attention to this directive. The Union government therefore has stated the imperative need to "enshrine in the

Constitution certain basic and essential features of the panchayat raj institutions to impart certainty, continuity and strength to them".

The 64th Constitutional Amendment Bill suggested setting up of panchayats in every state at the village level, intermediate level and district level. The intermediate level was not obligatory in the states with a population of less than 20 lakhs. This bill was passed in the Lok Sabha in 1989 but could not be passed by the Rajya Sabha. The 73rd Constitutional Amendment Bill (1990) was introduced in the Lok Sabha and recommended that Gram Sabha should be constituted in each village in addition to the panchayats at three levels. The bill recommended that the elections to the village panchayat should be direct and at other levels at least 50 per cent of seats should be directly elected. This bill also lapsed.

For this purpose the 73rd Constitution Amendment Act, 1992 was passed by the Union Parliament. In the Constitution, Part IX and Schedule XI have been inserted to contain certain provisions for the panchayats from the village to the sub-district and district levels.

The 73rd Amendment

After Independence efforts have been made to create the units of self-governance at grass-roots level but all in vain since they could not produce the desired results. During the Gandhian era and afterward a debate was going on for the strengthening of panchayat raj institutions at local level and central government's initiative came out with 73rd Amendment for the establishment of panchayat raj institutions in India.

The 73rd Amendment Bill was passed by the Lok Sabha and the Rajya Sabha with near unanimity on the 22 and 23 December 1992 respectively. This bill was ratified by 17 state assemblies in 1993 and came into force as the 73rd Constitution Amendment Act from the 24 April 1993 (Mahipal, 1997). The Act provides constitutional status to the panchayats and gives it uniformity by making the three-tier system a permanent feature. The key features of the Act are as follows:

- Panchayats shall be constituted in every state at the village, intermediate and district level. However, the states with a population not exceeding 20 lakhs have been given the option not to have any intermediate level Panchayat.
- There shall be a Gram Sabha in each village exercising such powers and performing such functions at the village level as the legislature of a state may provide by law.
- Members of panchayats at all levels will be elected through direct elections. The election of the chairperson at the intermediate and

district level will be through indirect elections and the mode of election of the chairperson of the village panchayat has been left to the respective states.

- Seats are reserved for Scheduled Caste (SCs) and Scheduled Tribes (STs) at all levels according to their population at each level. Not less than one-third of seats are reserved for women and these may be allotted by rotation. The office of chairperson will also be subject to this provision.
- A uniform five-year term has been granted to the panchayats. In case of dissolution or being superseded, elections should be held within six months of the date of dissolution.
- State legislatures have the legislative power to confer on the panchayats such powers and authority as may be necessary to enable them to function as institutions of self-governance. They may be entrusted with the responsibility of (i) preparing plans for social justice and economic development; (ii) implementation of schemes for social justice and economic development; and (iii) in regard to matters listed in the 11th Schedule. The list contains 29 items, such as land improvement, minor irrigation, fisheries, education, women and child development.
- State government has the power to authorize the panchayats to levy, collect and appropriate suitable local taxes. The government can make grant-in-aid to the panchayats from the consolidated fund of the concerned state.
- Review of the financial position of the panchayats will be undertaken by a finance commission, which shall be constituted every five years. It will also make recommendations on the distribution of funds between state and local bodies.
- A State Election Commission shall be constituted to ensure free and fair elections to the panchayats.

The 73rd Amendment was inserted in Part IX of the Constitution, containing Article 243 to 243-D. Local government is an exclusive state subject under entry 5 of List II of the Seventh Schedule, therefore the Union just provides the outline of the panchayat system, which would be implemented by the states by making laws or amending their existing laws to bring them in conformity with the provisions of the 73rd Amendment. It was binding on the states that the implementing legislation should be undertaken within a year of the commencement of the 73rd Amendment Act.

The 73rd Amendment to the Constitution of India not only gives a constitutional status to the panchayats; it also provides uniformity and formal structure to these traditional institutions of self-governance for the sake of their effective functioning. The earlier attempts at institutionalizing the panchayats were half-hearted and failed due to the absence of supportive constitutional measures and lack of political will (Behar and Kumar, 2002). The 73rd Amendment initiates a fundamental restructuring of governance and administrative system of the country, based on the philosophy of decentralization and power to the people. The new panchayat raj institutions have the potential to usher in a new era of change and development in accordance with people's needs and priorities, and to revitalize a deeply troubled system of democracy.

The enactments of the 73rd Constitutional Amendment Act and the subsequent statewise panchayat raj Acts in India have brought to frontline the significance of grass-roots democratic processes. This change in the Indian political system is the result of a growing conviction that the big government cannot achieve growth and development in a society without people's direct participation and initiative. This experience has brought home the lesson that the success of the new panchayat raj system largely depends on the congruence of perception and commitment of people, their leaders and the officials and about the role to be played by them in the new system. Contextually and theoretically too, the new panchayat raj system has been created as a model of self-governance (Sisodia, 2005).

The objectives of decentralization are to execute and implement schemes and programmes to meet the local needs, mobilize people, channelize their energies towards socio-economic reconstruction and to involve them in all the activities of the communities through the new institutions. Its objectives include also to reduce the size of work of the higher level government and leaving the responsibility to the people to decide their destiny as per the new dispensation. Decentralization is a much-debated issue in India and other countries with federal system of governance. Though there are various arguments for and against decentralization, arguments in favour of decentralization far outweigh those against it because of the inherent potential of democratization in the decentralized federal system through proper empowerment of people at the grass roots level.

A decade of panchayat raj in India has been a matter of debate and speculation about its performance and impact. All the major states have completed at least one round of panchayat elections, and in majority of cases at least two successive rounds. Almost three million people including one million women and a sizeable number of SCs/STs took part in these elections. The sizeable presence of under-privileged and poor as representatives through reservations in the grass-roots political institutions is a landmark development in the rural politics of the country. This significant development has special meaning because a decade earlier in most parts of rural India these groups were excluded from public life and political participation. This is also a matter of serious debate as how this excluded lot after their inclusion in active politics at grass roots would effectively tackle local power equation and set the agenda for development. Yet, the fact remains that these backward and so far ignored classes have heralded their arrival on the political stage of the country in the countryside.

The responses of state governments to the implementation of panchayat raj varied significantly and it is very difficult to generalize about this issue on the basis of their functioning for the last one decade or so. Only a few states like Maharashtra, Gujarat, Kerala, Karnataka, West Bengal have had a track record of panchayats since 1950s and the exemplary lead taken by the state of Madhya Pradesh after 1993 brings together a total of six states only that took steps to strengthen panchayat raj institutions. On the other hand, states of Bihar and Jammu & Kashmir are considered prominent examples among states where little or no progress had taken place over the last one decade; even regular panchayat elections were inordinately delayed in these states.

A perusal of state profiles would show that panchayat raj reforms have certainly taken place with vigour and zeal in some western and southern parts of the country, which are relatively sound from the point of view of economy, vibrant socially, and have active civil societies. On the contrary, the northern states with the greatest degree of poverty and inequality and deep schisms of caste and low pace of governance resulted in weak panchayats (Robinson, 2005).

Despite the recognition of the fact that without direct and active participation of the rural people the situation of development will remain dismal, the progress made by the states is not very satisfactory. Only few states showed their willingness and commitment to make the institutions of self-governance viable and functional with the required funds and functions.

The period under review witnessed that even the states have tried to de-recognize the very institution of panchayat. For the development purposes parallel structures were created in states, e.g., Janmabhoomi in Andhra Pradesh and village development committees in Haryana. These states were not interested to provide funds for development to panchayats.

The purpose of creating parallel structure was to bypass the role and responsibility of panchayat in development works and thereby creating an apathy among people towards panchayats. Thus, instead of strengthening PRIs, these efforts tend to weaken them.

It is realized and understood that the 'top down approach' of development is not capable enough to work and therefore the urgent need is to adopt the 'bottom up approach' (Sisodia, 2002). It is also pertinent that the delivery system has remained faulty and it could not deliver in the preceding decades and this situation has put forward strongly the need of people's direct participation in the delivery system. Another prerequisite of local governance is the accountability, which in the earlier stages of evolution of PRIs rested with upper echelons of bureaucracy, was frittered away the unhappy result was that the rural masses, for whom the panchayat raj system was inaugurated, remained far away from these institutions. The process of decentralization and globalization in India started almost on the same point of time. It has been argued that how these two processes can proceed together. It is assumed that post-1990 scenario is of globalization and market is a very important factor in decision-making and as a result of this, the policies and programmes of the nation are reformulated. Therefore, it is envisioned that state can no longer remain welfare oriented exclusively and the conditions imposed on the state are mandatory. This may lead to the shrinking role of the state. It is foreseen that in this changing scenario the role of state can be confined to the maintenance of law and order and against this situation, the local political institutions have to be made vibrant, comprehensive and self-sustainable to work independently as units of self-governance.

In this premise it is important to understand that decentralization provides opportunities to the people to participate in governance. The existence of grass-roots political arenas makes it easier for common people to participate and exert influence in areas of self-governing institutions. When power is brought closer to the citizens, the political process becomes more tangible and transparent where more people are involved freely in the process. Decentralization paves way for an open political system as decision-making powers rest with the people. It promotes popular participation and bestows controlling function on the representative institutions. Thus the greater degree of political inclusiveness becomes helpful in resolving crises of local self-governance.

After 73rd Amendment, Indian states have responded in different pace and patterns while introducing new panchayat raj in their states. The initiatives of states are certainly different yet a common thread of institutional similarities are discernible across the states; they are:

- Representation of Marginalized Sections of society
- Women in Panchayat
- Special Provisions for Scheduled Areas
- State Finance Commissions
- District Planning Committees
- Emergence and Strengthening of Gram Sabhas
- Regular Elections

It is certain that this mandatory position of panchayat raj along with sustained efforts of state, civil society and rural masses will pave the way for the little republics of Gandhi's dream. It is hoped that these little republics will work for the greater equality for all to create a society of the equals in India.

References

Ambedkar, B. (1948), Speech in the Constituent Assembly on November 14, 1978 in Vasant Moon (ed.) *Writing and Speeches*, 13, 61-61, Department of Education, Government of Maharastra.

Behar, Amitabh and Kumar, Yogesh (2002), "Decetralisation in Madhya Pradesh, India from Panchayati Raj to Gram Swaraj (1995 to 2001)", Working Paper 170, ODI, London, UK.

Hanumantha Rao, C.H. (1989), "Decentralised Planning: An Overview of Experience and Prospects", *Economic and Political Weekly*, February 25.

Kashyap, Subhash C. (2003), *Blueprint of Political Reform*, Shipra Publications, Delhi.

Khanna, B.S. (1994), *Panchayati Raj in India (Rural Local Self Government)*, Deep and Deep Publications, New Delhi.

Mahipal (1997), "Panchayati Raj in India: Issues and Challenges", *Kurukshetra*, August.

Robinson, Mark (2005), "A Decade of Panchayati Raj Reforms: The Challenge of Democratic Decentralisation in India" in L.C. Jain (ed.) *Decentralisation and Local Governance*, Orient Longman, New Delhi.

Singh, S.S. et al. (1997), Legislative Status of Panchayat Raj Institutions in India, IIPA, New Delhi.

Sisodia, Yatindra Singh (2002), "Decentralised Geovernance in Madhya Pradesh: Experiences of the Gram Sabha in Scheduled Areas", *Economic and Political Weekly*, October 5.

Sisodia, Yatindra Singh (2005), " A Decade of Panchayati Raj System in Madhya Pradesh" in Yatindra Singh Sisodia (ed.) *Functioning of Panchayati Raj System*, Rawat Publicattions, Jaipur.

15 Panchayats: Relevance, Potentials and Demonstrations

G. Palanithurai

In the Indian context, after the enactment of the 73rd Amendment to the Constitution, questions have been raised as to what extent the objectives of decentralization of powers have been realized? If not why? Whether obstacles and barriers have been identified? If they have been, why they are not removed? Given the background and the powers and the resources devolved, what changes have been created in governance and in the process of development? For the past one decade discussions have been held in different fora on the powers devolved, functionaries transferred and finances given to the grass-roots institutions to achieve what decentralized governance has to achieve in terms of development. Institutions have been created, frameworks for local governance have been evolved through legislation, elections have been conducted, elected representatives are in position and activities are being carried out through these institutions.[1] Against this backdrop one has to visualize to what extent the newly created institutions have started functioning in the way as expected and whether the leaders who have come to power have performed their functions.

For any role to be performed perfectly the role has to be perceived properly by the performer. Further, the same role has to be perceived properly by the clients.[2] In the process of decentralization of powers, one is likely to have a conflicting perception of the role to be performed by the grass-roots institutions. Primarily panchayat institutions are considered an extension of the government and as such are expected to have the characteristics of the government. There is a counter argument that it is not a government as there is no law making function and the activities listed in the 11th Schedule as these subjects are not the subjects of the IV list.

Further, the panchayat is perceived as an extension of the community and so expected to have flexibility in its functions. As governments failed in delivering the services to the people to their satisfaction, a new mechanism was evolved and it has to deliver the basic essential services to the communities. Thus, panchayat institutions are considered service providers or agents of the both central and state governments to carry out the programmes and schemes of the above governments.[3] In the given situation panchayat institutions have to work with a variety of strings and obstacles. Panchayat leaders are viewed as a threat and a power centre by the bureaucracy and the MLAs and MPs as they are in the community and they attend to the needs of the community directly.[4]

As a result, the bureaucracy, the MLAs and the MPs would see that adequate powers are not devolved to them. Knowing fully well that these barriers and obstacles would be created in the devolution process, the leaders have to assume responsibility and perform their duties. To work in the disturbed system, the leaders at the grass-roots should have capacity, skill and capability. Otherwise it will be very difficult to manage the system. People, while electing a leader to the panchayat, never consider the capacity as a factor and they elect their representative on a different set of considerations. But the elected representatives have to be oriented, sensitized and conscientized on the issues of the society and development.[5] Their skills and capacity have to be enhanced. Panchayat leaders have to build their perspective to manage the system and to work on issues of development. When the above-mentioned requirements are fulfilled the system will deliver the goods. Against this background, one has to visualize the potential available in panchayat institutions for taking initiative for achieving social development based on the experiences in the panchayats in Tamil Nadu. Before exploring and explaining the potential, it is necessary to have a look at the relevance of such an institution at present to achieve social development.

Relevance

Panchayat institutions have brought people's representatives closer to the people. For the past several years below the state government there was no representative democratic institution close to the people. Below the state government level, it was the rule of the bureaucracy. It is a well known fact that the expansion of bureaucracy would alienate the people. Middlemen establish links between the people and the bureaucracy and thereby brokerage becomes the accepted formula for all development activities.[6]

Now elected representatives are placed in all the areas and people can approach them easily. People will raise questions in the Gram Sabha. If water is not sufficiently available, people can raise the question face to face in the Gram Sabha. If the medical staff from the primary health centre are not visiting villages periodically people will question the panchayat leader. Likewise, if the primary school teacher is not regular in reaching the school, it can be raised in the panchayat.[7] When they raise questions, the leaders cannot shirk the responsibility by saying that they have no power or resources. They have to seek power and finance for which they have to work hard and purposefully.

In the whole process, people have developed the attitude that these are the functions to be attended to by the government for which the panchayat leaders have to work. Panchayat leaders have developed the attitude that in the absence of required power and finance to fulfil the needs and demands of the people, people have to be mobilized to exert pressure on the government to get things done for the people. In the whole process, people are being mobilized by the Panchayats. Mobilization is being done in many ways of which the Gram Sabha is one and an important one. No doubt in India people are mobilized for cultural activities, religious activities and political activities periodically by various groups and the political parties. But they are not mobilized for development work. But now Panchayats are mobilizing the people for development activities. It is true that the Panchayat leaders are drawn from the place wherefrom MLAs and MPs are drawn. But MLAs and MPs can keep themselves aloof from the community. Panchayat leaders have to live with the people and in the community and hence they have to be responsible and responsive to the communities. Provision has been made in the structure so that the marginalized and women can find a place legitimately in the institution for governance. Women and Dalits, who never had any experience in governance, have come to power. They want to be transparent because the community has a hold over them. Hence, there is always a conducive atmosphere for transparent governance by women and Dalits which can serve as a model for others.[8] Women have started attending the Gram Sabha meetings. A large number of SHG members attend the Gram Sabha meetings and they raise a lot of developmental issues in the meeting as they are oriented in social development activities by the NGOs. As a result, even the process of governance at the grassroots will be changed.

Electing a good leader is in the hands of the electorate. Shaping a leader and making him good lies in the hands of everyone. The leaders at the grassroots have to be conscientized on development and their skill and capacity have to be enhanced for proper management of institutions to achieve development and social justice. Once the leaders are properly trained, they will deliver the goods to the level of the expectations of the masses.

Potential Demonstrated

Leaders come to the panchayat with different aspirations and levels of commitment. To make the leaders work for the society for its transformation and upliftment, they have to be conscientized on the roles to be performed and sensitized on the real issues of development. To manage the institutions they require management skills. To manage and mobilize the community for development work they need communication skills. To manage development the leaders need constant flow of information on all aspects through all tracks pertinent to development. As communities are uneven in terms of their socio-economic conditions, the leaders have to face several hurdles and, to overcome all those hurdles, they need a supportive structure. When the above requirements are fulfilled, the leaders will achieve what they wanted to achieve and then they will be recognized by the community. Once they win the recognition of the community, the leaders are recognized as path finders. They become visible in the media. They constitute the core group of potential performers.[9] They are visited by government officials, panchayat leaders of other districts and leaders of political parties. They spread success stories and they become role models. When MPs and MLAs do not address social development issues who else will address them is the main question. It is the panchayat leaders who are addressing social development issues. Everyone is looking for such kind of panchayat leaders. Such panchayats are now visible in the society though their number is not large. Now the success stories are spreading through media. The media plays a predominant role in this regard. From our experience in Tamil Nadu, one would strongly argue that panchayats are capable of tackling all the social development issues provided the needed support is ensured. Representatives of the people assume responsibilities and perform their role and functions. Ten Gram Panchayat Presidents have demonstrated this by their constant attention to the services provided, enrolment of eligible boys and girls in school, reduction of drop outs in schools, ensuring antenatal care and postnatal care, family welfare, adoption of family planning methods, protecting the environment, establishing good sanitary conditions, providing safe drinking water, banning sale of illicit liquor, clearing channels which bring water to drinking water ponds and tanks for irrigation purposes.[10] The above activities were carried out by the Gram Panchayat Presidents with the support of the communities. These activities were the result of the Population Foundation of India project executed in Dindigul district. It was made possible by the continuous training given to the Gram Panchayat Presidents, Vice-Presidents, community leaders and self-help groups. The ten Gram Panchayat Presidents visited the Gram Panchayats in Kerala under the interface programme conducted by the Rajiv Gandhi Chair for Panchayat Raj Studies and acquainted themselves with the process of achieving social development. The Kerala visit provided enough input for them to work on social development issues. There are cases where the Panchayat Presidents have taken up the issues pertinent to social development on their own because of the commitment and the continued support of various development agencies.

Ms. Ponni Kailasam first took up the primary health centre issue. She made the doctor come regularly and made the paramedical and nursing staff visit the panchayat. She made the staff of the PHC accountable to the people in the Gram Sabha. She first had discussion with the doctor and listed the problems and the same was discussed with the District Collector. With the intervention of the District Collector, she sorted out the problems in the primary health Centre. The primary health centre doctor recognized her as a leader only after she sorted out the problems faced by the PHC through the intervention of Collector. Further, she made the staff affix her signature in the Visitor's Book of Panchayat as evidence to show that she visited the panchayat area. The PHC was surrounded by an area meant for open air defecation. She made efforts to clean the entire area and removed all the bushes with the help of the youth group and placed the area under the supervision of the same group. Now the PHC is functioning properly. To perform this task she had to struggle. Yet she did it, and this brought recognition among the people to the effect that she is capable of doing things. Next the same leader identified the massive encroachment of common lands and she got orders from the District Collector and removed all the encroachments in the inflow channels of tanks.[11] After the removal of the encroachment, all the *ooranies* and tanks filled up during the rainy season because all the low channels had been cleared and as a result they brought rain water to the tanks. But she had to face a lot of problems during encroachment removal. She took earnest steps to put an end to the production and sale of illicit liquor in her panchayat premises. All these activities were carried out with struggles. While experiencing the problems and struggles in the panchayat activities, she thought that this should not happen to other women leaders. Hence, for collective action, she initiated steps to form a federation of elected women representatives at the Gram Panchayat level as in the other tiers the women necessarily act on behalf of their party. This elected women representatives' federation constantly mobilizes the women leaders to work together to sort out their issues.[12] When they meet periodically they discuss their administrative problems and put them in a petition and submit the same to the Secretary and the Director of Rural Development, after submitting the same they meet the press also. The proceedings of the press meet used to appear in newspapers and hence the officials responded to their request. This outcome made the federation stronger. Further, they started discussing the issues of women in their forum. Thus, she was responsible for the critical action initiated at the panchayat level.

Mr Panneer Selvam of Keerapalayam Gram Panchayat of Cuddalore district provided toilets to all the households including those of daily wage earners. The entire village is clean and neat. He got several awards. His village is a total sanitation village. He mobilized the people for this public action and the people were sensitized. He was concerned about the utility of such facilities. So he developed a toilet culture in his village. He was supported by the DANIDA. It is an eye opener for many leaders, academics and bureaucrats.[13]

Ms. Rani Sathappan, President of K. Rayavaram Gram Panchayat of Pudukkottai district, successfully abolished polythene usage in her village. The Government of Tamil Nadu abolished the use of plastics but revoked the same as there was public pressure. But she did it with the support of the community. The village is clean and neat. With the approval of the community she slapped a ban on the sale and use of polythene in the Panchayat area.

Ms. Sahaya Mary of Kakkanur Gram Panchayat President established a village based management system for drinking water supply. In fact, she collected money from the people to manage the system. Her concept is that water should be given to all and should be brought very near to the people so that women's burden can be reduced. She collected water charges from the public and it is being managed by the people themselves. Her activities were also supported by the DANIDA. She constituted committees to look after the quality of the water supplied to the people. A separate bank account was opened for the management of water supply.

Ms. Jesu Mary of Michealpattinam Gram Panchayat established 100 per cent rainwater harvesting structure in her Panchayat area long before the Government of Tamil Nadu made it mandatory in every house. She was an eye opener for many and especially for the government.

Mr Irudayam, President of Karisalpatti Gram Panchayat, fought with the community for establishing toilets in the streets for public use and in schools for students' use. There was no scheme at that time. With the help of the nuns who used to undergo internship programme in the convent, he created awareness among the people about the implications of sanitation. The Panchayat President asked the ANM to stay in the sub-centre. She did not do so as she has got the support of the local minister. So he passed a resolution in the Gram Sabha and sent the same to the minister. Knowing fully well the implications of the resolution the local minister asked the ANM to obey the order of the panchayats.[14]

Mr Sreerangam, President of Komberipatti Gram Panchayat eradicated the bad practice of arranging marriage for girls at the age of 14 or 15 in the Kurumbar community. It was an age-old practice but it was stopped because of the intervention of the President. He even threatened them that he would inform the police. As a result he was defeated in the next election but he was happy that he stopped the age-old practice of a community.[15]

Ms. Jamruth Beevi, President of Devipattinam Gram Panchayat in Ramanathapuram district, took a firm decision to kill pigs in her Panchayat area despite the opposition of hundreds of families that are responsible for rearing pigs. Based on the advice of the doctors and health inspectors, 146 pigs were killed and the Panchayat was made a clean Panchayat. She initiated yet another step to make compost manure out of the waste collected in the village with the help of an NGO. She was responsible for spreading the clean village concept.

Women Gram Panchayat leaders of Tamil Nadu have formed a federation with the objective of highlighting their problems in managing the Panchayats and to take up the issues related to the life of women. This federation is gaining momentum as they adopt a proactive approach. Many of the women leaders in the federation are drawn from self-help groups and hence they are already oriented in social development issues. Whenever conventions are organized, they invite women activists to discuss the issues of women and to evolve strategies to combat the problems faced by the women through the Panchayat Raj. They pass resolutions and declarations for their future action.[16] The women leaders invite consumer forum activists to explain to the members of the federation, the methodology to be adopted to supervise the service providers. Further, they demand activity charts showing how the service providers could be managed by the local body institutions and what powers the panchayats are enjoying in this regard and, if the service providers do not comply with the request of the leaders what action can be initiated. All these details are discussed in their meeting.

Mr Ramanathan, President of Naalukkottai Gram Panchayat in Sivagangai district, ensured proper delivery of provisions to the poor through the ration shop by handing over the responsibility of the management of the ration shops to SHGs. It is a well-known fact that the ration shop is yet another institution to help the poor by supplying the basic needs of food material. It is also true that corruption keeps the poor away from it. He fought with the district administration and got it for an SHG. Now quality products in correct quantity are being supplied to the poor. SHG members are also earning from this service. This has now become a role model for others.

Ms. Chinnammal, President of Orathupatti Gram Panchayat, made it clear in her plan document that providing a nail cutter and mats and constructing a baby toilet in the balwadi was the priority work. Since the balwadi is located in a Dalit hamlet, she had a vision that all Dalit children should lead a decent human life, which, she feels, they are not leading now. Further she feels that the school is not clean and neat now. Such conditions have to be changed. Ms.Veera Kalaiarasi, President of Veppankulam Panchayat of Sivagangai district, explained that attending to the needs of the disabled, the destitute, widows and orphans is the priority work as she experienced torture at the hands of her husband and because of poverty. She feels that normally attention is not paid to the above sections. Hence she wants to pay much attention to these segments.[17]

With a sense of commitment to work for Dalits, Mr Ponnusamy, President, Semmipalayam Gram Panchayat started his work in water supply and transformed the life of the Dalits in his Panchayat area. His concern is the self dignity of the Dalits. By locating the sources of water at the places of the Dalits, he made them independent in getting water for their use. Their cleanliness, personal hygiene and sanitation are the other works of this Panchayat. This Panchayat has taken steps to activate the primary health centre and the sub-centre as they are the institutions of the poor. He tried to provide needed facilities to public schools as they are the institutions of the poor. His transparent, innovative, technology-oriented activities drew the public towards the Panchayat and the Gram Sabha. Equally, he attracted the attention of the government. For the district administration his Panchayat serves as a testing ground of experiment with innovative programmes. It has emerged as a model Panchayat which attracts the attention of the other Panchayat leaders. Many Panchayat leaders and officials from various places have been visiting this Panchayat in streams.

Mr Elango, President of Koothambakkam Gram Panchayat, a Dalit youth turned Gandhian constructive worker, has taken up the major task of stopping the brewing of illicit liquor and the drinking of the same by the youth in his Panchayat area. For this, the village youth had to be provided with alternative employment opportunity. With great difficulty he provided such an opportunity to the youth. By evolving and adopting appropriate technology, employment opportunity was provided to the Dalit youth. By his innovative approach, he made his Panchayat hut free. He has developed a growth model by linking the activities of Koothambakkam with those of other Gram Panchayats. His Panchayat has been marked for generating employment opportunity. Though he is an educated person he had to face a lot of problems from the administration and the society. He has proved beyond doubt that a Panchayat can work for Dalits.

Grandline Gram Panchayat is known for many activities of which working for the marginalized and the aged is one and significant. His work for the SHGs and Dalits made him popular. Eviction of encroachment, creating public library, establishment of park and garden got him recognition among the people. Transforming waste into wealth brought a name to the Panchayat president. Desilting of ponds and creation of hydraulic gym drew the youth close to him. He introduced a new scheme, feeding the poorest of the poor, and it is this scheme which attracts every one. In his Panchayat a provisions store is being run by the Gram Panchayat. It is also unique in this Panchayat.

Veerapandiapattinam is known for cleanliness. The President hailing from the fishermen community, wanted to transform the Panchayat into a clean Panchayat as it is fully dominated by fisher folk. With great difficulty he made it possible. Now the entire area is clean, neat and tidy. He wanted to create a new culture of cleanliness. By establishing a management system for delivery of services, he started delivering services according to the needs of the people. Having realized the potential of the Panchayat, government departments extended their full support to this Panchayat. His aim is to create a sanitation culture, not confined merely providing toilets and in his attempt he has succeeded. The people have been conscientized on hygiene, sanitation and cleanliness.

Mr Nattuthurai is the President of Keeranur Panchayat. He first worked out a strategy of mobilizing the people for social action, for which he started his work in a temple. Being a progressive farmer, he knew the problems involved in mobilizing people for social and political action. His Panchayat is known for water works, common property resource management and work for the marginalized. By attending to works related to the livelihood of the people, delivering proper health services and attending to the marginalized he won a name and support. He has also launched an innovative programme to distribute rice to the poorest of the poor. Nattuthurai emerged as a role model and hence Panchayat Presidents of his district and other districts are visiting this Panchayat.

Ms. Pappa is a rural revolutionary leader known for her fight against the existing social order and bureaucratic system and she has emerged as a force to reckon with not only in the Panchayat area but also among the Gram Panchayat women leaders. She moved into social service much before she moved into the Panchayat. Setting right the public institutions is the first step in ensuring delivery of services to the poor. She responded to the challenges from the upper caste and the bureaucracy and on all the occasions she fought against them. She is the President of the Dalit Women Gram Panchayat Leaders of Tamil Nadu. She is a good trainer and she takes classes in training programmes. She is a role model for Dalit women.[18]

The above stated cases demonstrate the potential of the panchayat institutions. The achievements projected here are the achievements of the leaders. How are these leaders able to achieve such results? They are sensitized, conscientized and capacitated leaders. They establish contact with their community, NGOs and government officials. They establish contact with the media also. Government officials are taking these success stories to various places for dissemination. The message they want to spread across the state is that with the limited resources, powers and functionaries, they are able to achieve this much. Why cannot others do the same by following these role models? The officials know pretty well that there is no political will and in the absence of political will they want to do something for Panchayats by which the leaders who want to break new ground can get the support of the higher level officials. Many of the higher level officials feel that Panchayats are competent to achieve social development provided needed support is given to the Panchayats.[19] The cases quoted here are a few examples which have registered remarkable achievements. Likewise, Panchayat leaders are breaking new ground in many areas and they are to be documented. Now the Government of Tamil

Nadu has decided to form a training team and to conduct training classes for the Panchayat leaders. While sharing their experiences they can motivate others to do such things in the Panchayats. At present these leaders are identified and they are provided needed support individually, not through a system. Panchayat leaders want an activity manual.[20] It is very difficult to create political will on the part of the leaders at the state level. But making the leaders perform by assuming responsibilities in achieving social development is possible. When the Government of Tamil Nadu announced a 15 point programme to make Tamil Nadu the number one state in the country, the Women Panchayat Presidents Federation convened a meeting and discussed all the major issues contained in the 15 point programme and they fixed the responsibility of the Panchayats in implementing the 15 point programme in the rural areas. They submitted a memorandum to the Minister, the Secretary and the Director of Rural Development, Government of Tamil Nadu. By sensitizing the masses through the Gram Sabha about the rights of the people vis-à-vis over the service providers, the people were prepared. By doing so, people can be mobilized through the Panchayats for social development activities. How can the above mentioned activities be done?

Process

The leaders who have broken new ground had a sense of firm commitment. They were in search of supportive structures and they were supported by many institutions. They enhanced their capacity and fixed targets for accomplishments. They developed their vision regarding the development of the community. They perceived their roles and responsibilities properly as they had undergone training continuously. By putting up exemplary performance they have developed contacts with higher level officials. To manage the problems of the middle level officials, they have built alliances with the media and formed a network with NGOs and other leaders. Because of their achievement the leaders have established strong contacts with communities.

Communities are drawn towards the Panchayats by the transparent administration of the Panchayat Presidents. They cross the boundaries of caste and political parties for Panchayat work. When their achievements are brought to light they develop their self-esteem. Thus devolution for social development can achieve personal evolution. All social indicators can be achieved through evolution. Every village Panchayat is a manageable administrative unit. All social indicators can be achieved at the micro level by enhancing the capacity of the Gram Panchayat leaders. By extending support to such leaders, their achievements will be increased to the next level. Their achievements are brought to light by the media as the media is constantly sensitized by The Hunger Project though its media workshop on building the perspective to cover the stories of Panchayats and women's empowerment. Panchayats ensure entitlements. People can claim their rights through Panchayats. By shaping a leader at the micro level, social development can be achieved.

Conclusion

Panchayats are instruments of the people created for governance with the participation of the people to achieve development. Though Panchayat leaders are drawn from the place wherefrom MLAs and MPs are drawn they cannot adopt the attitude and behaviour of the MPs and MLAs as they have to work with the community closely. By increasing their capacity and sensitizing them on developmental issues, Panchayats can be prepared to achieve development and social justice. Capacity building, continuous support extended by the support structure, forming network with the media and NGOs and providing needed information could make them achievers and pathfinders. If state governments really want to achieve social development, it can be achieved through the Panchayats. People should be mobilized to participate in the development process. In the long run people will assert and claim their rights and entitlements through the Panchayats.

Notes and References

1. Rajiv Gandhi Foundation, *Panchayati Raj in India: Status Report*, New Delhi: Rajiv Gandhi Foundation, 2000.
2. G. Palanithurai, *The Role Perception of Legislatures: A Case Study of Tamil Nadu*, New Delhi: Konark Publications, 1991.
3. G. Palanithurai, "Towards Participatory Governance at Grassroots: Synergisation of Rural Communities and Institutions", *South Asian Journal of Socio Political Studies*, Vol. 4, No. 1 (Dec, 2003).
4. Rajiv Gandhi Chair, *Problems faced by the Gram Panchayat Leaders*, Gandhigram: Rajiv Gandhi Chair for Panchayati Raj Studies, 2000.
5. G. Palanithurai, *Capacity Building for Local Body Leaders*, New Delhi: Concept Publishing Company, 2001.
6. G. Palanithurai, *New Panchayat Raj System: Status and Prospects*, New Delhi: Kaniska Publications, 1996, pp. 57–64.

7. Rajiv Gandhi Chair, *Functional Efficiency of Gram Sabha,* A Report submitted to II State Finance Commission, Gandhigram: Rajiv Gandhi Chair for Panchayati Raj Studies, 2000.
8. G. Palanithurai, *Evaluation of Process and Performance of Gram Panchayat Women and Dalit Presidents in Tamil Nadu*, Gandhigram: Rajiv Gandhi Chair, 2003.
9. The Hunger Project, Report on the Workshop on Panchayat Raj: Trials and Triumphs, Gandhigram: Rajiv Gandhi Chair for Panchayati Raj Studies, 2003.
10. G. Palanithurai, *Panchayats, Communities and Social Development*, Gandhigram: Rajiv Gandhi Chair for Panchayati Raj Studies, 2003.
11. G. Palanithurai, *New Panchayati Raj System at Work: An Evaluation*, New Delhi: Concept Publishing Company, 2000.
12. G. Palanithurai, "Building Alliances and Capabilities among the elected women representatives of Grassroots institutions", *Womens Link*, Vol. 10, No. 1 (January-March 2004), pp. 18–25.
13. Rajiv Gandhi Chair, Evaluation of Process and Performance of Gram Panchayat Presidents in Tamil Nadu (A Report submitted to UNICEF), Gandhigram: Rajiv Gandhi Chair for Panchayati Raj Studies, 2004.
14. Ibid.
15. Population Foundation of India, Empowerment of Panchayat Raj Institutions on Issues Related to Population, Health and Social Development, A Final Report, New Delhi: Population Foundation of India, 2001.
16. When they met on 26th and 27th October in Gandhigram 700 Gram Panchayat women leaders made a declaration. The following is the declaration:

    We, the elected women representatives who are gathered here at Gandhigram Rural Institute on this 27th day of October 2002, declare that we will address the following issues in the next one year:

    (i) All the eligible children (girls and boys) will be enrolled in schools.

    (ii) We will strive to remove malnourishment amongst children in the age group of 0–5 years. As elected representatives we shall ensure that no underweight babies are born in our villages. The mothers will be given proper nourishment before and after delivery.

    (iii) Better anti-natal and post-natal care will be provided for all the women in our Panchayats.

    (iv) Any injustice against women in our Panchayats will be dealt with firmly. As a collective we will fight against domestic violence and also any other form of violence against any women in our Panchayat.

    (v) We will ensure that child labour is abolished in our Panchayats.

(vi) We will ensure equitable access to and distribution of Panchayat resources among all the people in the Panchayats and guarantee at least the provision of the basic minimum requirements for the poorest. The PDS system will be improved with our intervention.

(vii) Problems faced by the women Panchayat leaders and women in general will be addressed collectively by making alliance with supportive institutions and organizations.

(viii) The newly implemented sanitary complexes meant for women will be effectively managed by women's groups with the support of the Panchayats.

(ix) Our Panchayats will not suffer from lack of drinking water. Everyone will be entitled to safe drinking water.

(x) We will ensure that Gram Sabhas take place regularly and more and more people take part in these meetings. We will ensure that a minimum of 50 per cent of the total women in the Panchayat attend the meetings and that their issues are properly heard.

(xi) We commit ourselves to the implementation of the 15-point programme prepared by the Tamil Nadu government and request the state government to devolve necessary powers to the Panchayats and local bodies for the same.

17. G. Palanithurai, *Development Role Reversed: From Government to People*, Gandhigram: Rajiv Gandhi Chair for Panchayati Raj Studies, 2003.
18. G. Palanithurai, M.A. Thirunavaukkarasu, G. Uma, *Leadership Matters: Change Makers at Grassroots*, New Delhi: Concept Publishing House, 2006 (in print).
19. The higher officials, Director and Secretaries, Government of Tamil Nadu while participating in a workshop on Panchayat Raj: Trials and Triumphs highlighted the potentiality of the Panchayats and indicated the problems faced by them.
20. The following is the activity manual given to the Panchayat leader:

Good Governance and Social Development in Gram Panchayat Indicators

S. No.	*Activities*	*Responsibility*	*Outcome*
1.	100% enrolment of eligible children	President, Vice-President, ward members, PTA, SHG members, youth clubs, NGO, retired officials	Increase in literacy, human resource development

Cont'd...

Cont'd...

2.	Reduction of dropouts	President, Vice-President, ward members, PTA, SHG members, youth clubs, NGO, eetired officials	Increase in educational standard
3.	Ensuring protected drinking water supply to School	President, Vice-President, ward members, school teachers	Improvement of students's health, reduction of absenteeism of students
4.	Providing toilets to school	President, Vice-President, ward members, school teachers	Increase in health of children
5.	Utilizing the toilets by the school students	President, other members of the Panchayat council teachers	Toilet culture developed
6.	Cutting the nails of the students every Monday in Balwadi and school	Youth club, SHG, Panchayat ward members, school teachers	Health education, reduction of diseases, improvement of nutrition
7.	Planting of saplings in the school premises	President, teachers, agriculture departments	Environment awareness, eco-development, income to school
8.	Creating a school garden	President, teachers PTA, Youth clubs	Education, increase in nutrition
9.	Keeping the Balwadi clean and neat	Balwadi teacher, President, Vice-President, ward members	Health education, increase in status of health
10.	Providing a toilet in the Balwadi	President, Vice President, ward members	Education, increase in health status
11.	Bringing toilet culture among the kids	Balwadi teacher	Health education, increase in health status
12.	Adding vegetables to the noon meal by getting donations and getting the vegetables from the school garden	President, Vice-President, Balwadi teacher	Nutritive food for students
13.	Taking steps to prevent the practice of child labour	President, Vice-President, ward members, school teachers, PTA, NGO, SHG, Youth club	School enrolment, literacy, HRD

Cont'd...

Cont'd...

14.	Cleaning overhead tanks	OHT operators, under the instruction of panchayat regularly	Health status, productivity
15.	Creating awareness among the people about the consequence of alcohol and stop brewing and selling the same in the panchayat premises	President, Vice-President, ward member, health committee, SHG, youth club, NGO	Economic status of poor, status of women and children, health of individuals and reduction of social problems
16.	Creating awareness among the people about family welfare	PHC staff, President, Vice-President, ward members, health committee, SHG, youth	Livelihood security
17.	Identify the vulnerable families and ensure food security to them and constantly monitor them with the help of government schemes	President, Vice-President, ward members, SHGs	Income generation, reduction of poverty, status of women
18.	Building the skill of the women through training	Presidents, Vice-President, ward members, training institution, Social Welfare Department at the District Women Development Corporation	Income generation, reduction of poverty, status of women
19.	Establish link between the skilled persons and banking sector for the establishment of business venture by the women	President, Vice-President, ward members, planning committee members, NGO, Banks, SHG	Development of rural economy, and status of women
20.	Building the skills of the youth through training	President, Vice-President, ward members, training institutions, NYK	Human resource development, economic eevelopment
21.	Establish link between the skilled persons and Banking sector for the establishment of business venture by the youth	President, Vice-President, ward member, planning committee members, NGOs, Banks, NYKs	Development of rural economy

Cont'd...

Cont'd...

22.	Ensuring proper functioning of PDS	President, Vice-President, ward members and SHG, officials of Civil Supply	Food security
23.	Prevent open defecation in the villages by creating awareness and constructing toilets in each and every house	President, Vice-President, ward members, SHG, youth club, NGO, project staff, TRSP, retired employees	Improvement in health, sanitation environment
24.	Creating awareness about RCH by printing a card and giving it to every family	President, Vice-President, ward members, health committee, NGO, staff	Improvement in women and children health, economic status
25.	Ensure the delivery of services from sub-centre and PHC to the people through the schemes available for prenatal and postnatal care	PHC staff, President, Vice-President, ward members, SHG, NGO, health committee	Increase in health status and economic status
26.	Creating awareness about growing medicinal plants and make it a business by involving SHG and youth clubs	President, Vice-President, ward members, SHG, planning committee, youth club, NGO	Increase in health, income generation productivity
27.	Creating awareness among the importance of water management	President, Vice-President, ward members, community leaders, planning committee members, NGO	Rational utilization of water
28.	Creating a common burial ground into grave yard in the villages	President, Vice-President, ward members, SHG, youth club	Social justice
29.	Taking steps to manage the solid waste and earn money from it for panchayats	President, Vice-President, ward members, planning committee, NGO, SHG	Environment development, income generation, better agricultural practices
30.	Organize workshop for pregnant women to disseminate the needed information akin to ANC PNC	PHC staff, SHG, President	Increase of health awareness, health status, economic status, reduction of infant mortality, new born babies are in exact weight

Cont'd...

Cont'd...

31.	Conducting medical camps for poor and school children	President, Vice-President, ward members, NGOs, SHG, nearby Rotary and Lions Club	Improved health status
32.	Make the SHG and youth clubs take up Panchayat works instead of employing contractor	President, Vice-President, ward members, SHG, youth club, NGO	Employment opportunity, quality of work, reduction of expenditure, local needs
33.	Regularly conducting Gram Sabha meetings.	President, Vice-President, ward members	Peoples participation, good governance
34.	Ensuring 60 per cent attendance in Gram Sabha meeting.	President, Vice-President, ward members, all eligible members, SHG members, NGOs working in the Panchayats.	Transparency, accountability of panchayats
35.	Ensuring women/Dalit participation 50 per cent of attendance	President, Vice-President, ward members, SHG, NGO	Social justice, status of weaker section
36.	Information disseminations Income/Expenditure display Report on schemes implemented display List of schemes proposed to be implemented List of beneficiaries	President and Panchayat clerk	Transparency, accountability credibility of Panchayat, better participation
37.	Participatory decision making opportunities for discussion to all communities Equal status to all in seating Developing consensus	President, ward members, community leaders/retired government officials, school teachers, planning committee members, dalit leaders, NGOs and other association members	Generation of collective wisdom, social justice
38.	Develop a system of communication to give information about Gram Sabha meeting	President, clerk, ward member, SHG, youth clubs, NGOs	Transparency, accountability

Cont'd...

Cont'd...

39.	Provision of water supply to Dalit hamlets	President and the concerned ward members, committee for water supply	Communal harmony, status of Dalit, productivity of Dalits
40.	Removal of untouchability by Preventing the two tumbler system. Participating in temple festival	President, ward members, SHG, youth clubs, community leaders.	Social justice, communal harmony
41.	Training to Dalit youths in skill development	President, youth clubs, NGOs, education institutions	Economic development, social justice
42.	Availing THADCO schemes	President, NGOs, Vice-President and ward members.	Economic development of Dalits, social harmony
43.	Identification of all CPR verifying the status of encroachment details	Panchayat President, Vice-President, ward members, government officials, police, department	Environment development social justice, income generation
44.	Removal of encroachments	Panchayat President, Vice-President, (Revenue and Police department)	Productive use of resources, equity, income generation
45.	Utilizing the common properties and developing the same.	Panchayat president, ward members, NGO, SHG, youth groups	Environment development, income generation
46.	100% house tax collection	President, clerk, Vice-President, ward members, SHG, youth	Financial status of Panchayat more government funds
47.	Panchayat functioning as a system	President, clerk, Vice-President, ward members	Integrated development
48.	Records maintenance/transpare ncy	President and clerk	Good governance
49.	Preparing a perspective plan through village planning forum	President, ward members, planning committee	Planned development Better use of resources
50.	Formation of Statutory Committees	President	Efficiency of panchayats accountability
51.	Old age, physically and mentally disabled, destitute, orphan and other vulnerable sections	President, ward members, SHG, NGO, government, and planning committee	Social security, social harmony

Key Assumptions

— Harmony prevails in Panchayat

— Panchayat is perceived as development space.

— Community supports the Panchayats.

— Panchayat leader has got commitment.

— Panchayat leader has vision.

— Panchayat leader has got skill and capacity.

— Panchayat is not leader-centric.

— Panchayat is people and system centric.

Part IV

Development and Issues of Trade, Agriculture, Industry and Environment

16 India's Development and its Trade Dynamics with SAARC

Ganesh Kawadia and Gunjan Malhotra

India is a fastest growing country of the world. It is growing at an average of 7 to 8 per cent per annum. The economic reforms undertaken since 1991 have influenced both India's industrial policy and external economic relations which include the trade, foreign investment and financial relations. Import quotas were removed (fully only in July 2001), tariffs came down slowly, currency was devaluated, the foreign investment policy was liberalized and various external financial transaction were eased. As a result, India's share of foreign trade in GDP has increased from 15.6 per cent in 1991–92 to 25 per cent in 2004–05. This expansion of trade must have developed better trade linkages with the members of SAARC countries. Though the SAARC was formed to accelerate the process of social and cultural cooperation, but because of globalization, now the member countries are promoting economic cooperation. India is not only a big economy in the SAARC but also a fast growing economy. Their trade dynamics are thus important in the SAARC region for overall development of the region. This paper is an attempt to understand the trade dynamics of India with its poor partners particularly after the policies of liberalization.

India is the largest country in terms of size of population, geographical area and economy within the SAARC. All SAARC members belong to low-income category and have suffered from basic socio-economic problems like low per capita income, large population pressure, massive unemployment, acute deficit in balance of payment, high incidence of poverty, external debt and fiscal imbalances. SAARC members have a population of around 1.5 billion which constitutes 22 per cent of the world population. However, region's aggregate GDP, at about 932 billion dollars, unfortunately is less than 2 per cent of the world's GDP. The highest GDP growth rate is observed to be 9 per cent for Maldives and lowest at 4 per cent for Nepal in 2004, whereas in 2000 it was highest for Bhutan at 7 per cent and recorded the lowest GDP growth rate at about 4 per cent for both India and Pakistan. This is an area of interest for policy makers to initiate effective and rapid economic growth by shifting from import substitution industrialization strategies to export orientation strategies in the SAARC region.

In any regional cooperation, trade plays a very key role and SAARC is no exception with the expansion and liberalization of intra-regional trade, establishment of SAARC Preferential Trade Agreement (SAPTA) in 1995 was signed with the objectives to facilitate trade through tariff and non-tariff concessions within the region. Further, SAARC nations established South Asian Free Trade Agreement (SAFTA) in 2004 to reduce import duties to 20 per cent by 2006 and between 0–5 per cent by 2013 and allowed less developed economies by 2016. Although SAARC has been in existence for 20 years, intra-regional trade is still around 4 per cent of their total trade (ITS, 2004). This has raised an alarming situation to initiate suitable actions with determination and sincerity towards economic progress and prospects in the entire South Asian Region.

The diplomatic move of the political leaders has worsened the intra-regional trade disparity. Raipuria and Mehta (1990), Naquvi and Samad (1992) state that there is no trade linkage system explored for SAARC region. Waqif (1987) mentions that all SAARC countries have the potential to increase their respective trades with their partners. Moreover, economic linkages are explained to induce autonomous and self-generating growth among the cooperating members. Kochanek (1996) has laid emphasis for radical shifts in India's economic policies towards a more open competitive economy. On the other hand, Kishore C. Dash (1996) reveals that quantitative economic analysis of any national economy within SARRC should allow its conscious efforts towards demonstration of political will with respect to intra-regional trade by lowering traffics with member nation without delinking from extra-regional and global economic relations in South Asia.

Further, Amal Sarkar (2004) has analyzed trade linkage system for SAARC and indicates role in intra-SAARC trade flows except India and thereby suggested various safeguard measures to the policy makers for improving the economies of SAARC with other trade blocks. The estimation of country specific models were done by Mohammad Mafizur Rahman (2006), who indicates that difference in production and consumption pattern, investment behaviours, tax and non-tax structure prevails within the SAARC region. Thus, stressed on the need to expand intra-SAARC trade based on comparative advantages to each members. Guru-Gharana (2000) states that lack of sufficient quantitative assessment about the implications of further economic integration especially on the volume and direction of trade, income and employment situation, GDP and inflation, etc., may be the reason for slow economic cooperation within SAARC. Many other economists are of the view that South Asian countries are importing certain products from outside the region while the same products are being exported by neighbouring South Asian countries to the outside world. Therefore, in the present paper an attempt has been made to study India's development and trade dynamics with other SAARC members. We have also attempted to analyze the shift or acceleration in India's foreign trade within the SAARC region after the policies of liberalization and globalization.

The paper has been developed keeping in view the following objectives: to analyze India's bilateral trade with member countries; to examine the shift in the intra-regional trade with India, if any, during the period of liberalization; to study the export potentials of India within SAARC region; to examine the impact of globalization on the trade dynamics with member countries; and to examine export/import of major commodities of India with SAARC member countries.

Research Methodology

The present paper pertaining to total exports of India to SAARC members is completely based on the secondary source of data published by Reserve Bank of India (*RBI's Handbook of Indian statistics*), World Bank (world development indicators), International Monetary Fund (*International Statistical Year Book*) and by domestic and international journals and periodicals. The period under study is 1985–86 to 2003–04, except for Bhutan where it is from 1990–91 to 2003–04 due to lack of data availability. The total export/import of India (Y) has been regressed on total export/import of the buyer country (X_1) and price index of export/import of India (X_2), The regression model used is given below:

$$Y_t = \beta_1 + \beta_2 X_{1t} + \beta_3 X_{2t} + U_t$$

where

Y_t = dependent variable (the export/import of India to member countries)

X_{1t} & X_{2t} = independent variables

$\beta_{1,}$ β_2 & β_3 are regression coefficients

In order to find out the period of acceleration or shift in India's total exports to SAARC region, the estimation of multiple linear regression equation with dummy variable has been used. The year of shift is taken as 1993–94 as in this year the policies of liberalization came into momentum. We have used the following equations to examine the shift in the intercept coefficient after liberalization:

$$Y_t = \beta_1 + \beta_2 + \beta_3 + \beta_4 D + U_t$$

where ß's are regression coefficient; β_4 represents coefficient of dummy variables. D is the dummy variable which is zero for the period prior to the shift and one otherwise. Thus, the model before and after the shift will be as follows:

Before shift (D=0) $\quad Yt = \beta_1 + \beta_2 X_{1t} + \beta_3 X_{2t}$

After shift (D=1) $\quad Yt = \beta_1 + \beta_2 X_{1t} + \beta_3 X_{2t} + \beta_4$

Data Analysis

Socio-Economic Conditions among the SAARC Countries

SAARC region presents a diverse set of socio-economic condition. They not only express diversion in geographical areas but also in most of the socio-economic indicators. We have categorized these countries into high status and low status in relation to India. The classification is given in Table 1. The position of Maldives and Sri Lanka is better in terms of per capita income, literacy rate, life expectancy and HDI. The status of other countries in terms of per capita income, HDI, literacy rate and life expectancy is poorer than India. It is interesting to note that the status of Bangladesh and Pakistan is poor in most of the socio-economic indicators but Bangladesh could manage higher growth rate while Pakistan could manage lower inflation rate. Thus, it can be said that among SAARC countries, India is not only the larger economy but very comfortable in most of the socio-economic indicators. The trade dynamics of India is therefore important in the overall development of SAARC region.

Table 1
Status of Member Countries in Relation to India

	High	*Low*
Real GDP Per capita (PPP $)	Maldives Sri Lanka	Bhutan Bangladesh Nepal Pakistan
GDP Growth Rate	Bangladesh Sri Lanka Maldives	Nepal Pakistan
HDI	Sri Lanka Maldives	Bhutan Bangladesh Pakistan Nepal
Literacy	Sri Lanka Maldives	Bhutan Bangladesh Nepal Pakistan
Poverty	Bangladesh Pakistan Nepal	Sri Lanka
Life Expectancy	Sri Lanka Maldives	Bhutan Bangladesh Nepal Pakistan
Infant Mortality Rate	Pakistan Nepal Bhutan	Bangladesh Sri Lanka Maldives

India's Bilateral Trade with SAARC Members

India's export and imports with SAARC region has not shown any uniform pattern during these years. India exported worth of US$ 143.7 million to Bangladesh in 1987–88, which was highest among the region followed by US$ 79.7 million to Sri Lanka and lowest of US$ 2.3 million to Maldives. During the same period India imported worth of US$ 33.9 million from Nepal, this was highest among the region followed by US$ 21.6 million from Pakistan and lowest of US$ 8.8 million from Sri Lanka.

In contrast, during the period 1993–94 India exported worth of US$ 430.2 million to Bangladesh, which was maximum among the member countries followed by US$ 288 million to Sri Lanka and lowest of US$ 7.9 million to Maldives. Moreover India imported worth of US$ 43.6 million from Pakistan, which was highest among the region followed by US$ 28.9

million from Nepal and lowest of US$ 0.3 million from Maldives. Further, during the period 2003–04, India exported worth of US$ 1740.7 million to Bangladesh, which was highest among the region followed by US$ 1319.2 million to Sri Lanka and lowest of US$ 42.3 million to Maldives. On the other hand India imported worth of US$ 286 million from Nepal, which was maximum among the region followed by US$ 194.7 million from Sri Lanka and lowest of US$ 0.4 million from Maldives.

India's Major Exports and Imports with SAARC Members

India has relative advantage in exports to SAARC members in comparison to imports from the member countries. It is observed that India has strong trade ties with Nepal, Pakistan and Sri Lanka among the region. The major exports and imports of India with SAARC members are presented in Table 2.

Table 2

India's Export/Import of Commodities with SAARC Member Countries

Country	*India's Exports*	*India's Imports*
Bangladesh	—Cement	—Raw Jute
	—Coal	—Fish
	—Machinery	—Newsprints
	—Unmanufactured tobacco	—Sea food
	—Raw cotton	
	—Cotton yarns	
	—Cotton textiles	
	—Books	
Bhutan	—Mineral products	—Hydroelectricity
	—Machinery and mechanical appliances	—Gypsum
	—Base metal and base metal products	—Calcium Carbide
	—Cereals	—Ferro-silicon particle board
	—Fruits	—Portland cement
	—Nuts	
	—Coffee	
	—Prepared foodstuffs	
	—Transport equipments	
	—Chemical products	
	—Animal products	
	—Vegetable oil	

Cont'd...

Cont'd...

	—Plastic products	
	—Rubber products	
	—Textiles	
	—Wood and wood products	
	—Indian vehicles	
Maldives	—Foodstuffs	—Fish and fish products
	—Petroleum products	—Clothing accessories
	—Consumer goods	
	—Rice	
	—Wheat flour	
	—Sugar	
Nepal	—Mechanical equipments and spare parts	—Vanaspati
	—Medicines	—Toothpaste
		—Jute goods (Sacking,Twines,Hessian, etc.)
	—Transport vehicles and spare parts	—Polyester and Acrylin yarns
	—Cotton Textile	—Pulses
	—Cement	—Hides and skins
	—Cotton thread	—Herbs
	—Chemicals	—Cardamon
	—Electrical equipments and goods	—Rice Bran oil
	—Rice	—Ginger
	—Baby food and other milk products	—Oil cakes
	—Agricultural equipments and parts	—Noodles
	—Tobacco	
	—Vegetables	
	—Coal	
	—Writing and printing paper	
	—Synthetic textile	
	—Cumin Seeds and pepper	
	—Sugar	
	—Books and magazines	
Pakistan	—Oil meals	—Rice
	—Drugs and pharmaceuticals	—Frutis and Nuts (excluding cashew nuts)
	—Spices	—Sugar
	—Chemicals	—Textile Yarns
	—Dyes/intermediates	—Fabrics and made up articles

Cont'd...

Cont'd...

	—Coaltar chemicals	—Leather
	—Rubber manufactured products except footwear	—Cotton
	—Paints/enamel/ varnishes	—Electronic goods
	—Plastic and Linoleum products	—Crude Minerals
	—Inorganic/organic chemicals	—Spices
	—Agro chemicals	
Sri Lanka	—Cement Grey	—Agriculture and agro-based products
	—Printing and writing paper	—Organic and inorganic chemicals
	—Books printed	—Paper and paper boards
	—Bus and truck tyres	—Iron and Steel
	—Insulators	—Machinery and Mechanical Appliances
	—Glazed Ceramic tiles	—Electronic and electronic appliances
	—Sanitary wares	—Natural rubber
	—Clinkers	—Spices
	—Asbestos cement sheets	—Ores and metal scrap
	—Granite polished slabs/tiles	
	—Drugs and pharmaceuticals	
	—Metal manufactures	
	—Textiles and garments	
	—Machinery and transport equipments	

The above table indicates that India exports mostly cement, machinery and mechanical equipments, textiles and garments, electrical equipment, transport equipments to SAARC countries and in comparison imports power, fish, ores and metals from SAARC members. It can thus be concluded that India has potentials to exports value added and finished goods to SAARC nations while imports mainly raw material, sea food and mineral ores. We also import electric power from Bhutan. India thus has a very comfortable position for exports of goods to SAARC nations.

India's Export Linkages to SAARC Members

It is therefore evident that Indian economy is expanding its trade linkage with member countries of the SAARC. We have used regression analysis to identify the factors of India's export to member countries with total imports from buyer countries and export price index of India. We have run the regression equations with all the six countries and the results are shown in Table 3. All the regression results explain good explanatory power except for Nepal. In all, these regression estimates the coefficient of total imports from buyer country is positive and significant whereas the coefficient of export price index of India is statistically insignificant. It is thus clear that export from India is mainly determined by the imports from the buyer countries. More the imports from the buyer countries more are the exports from India to these countries. The trade dynamics of India is thus completely of bilateral nature with the member countries and other variables are not affecting much to the exports of India.

In order to estimate the impact of globalization we have used dummy variable with 1993-94 as the shift year. The estimates with dummy variable are also shown in the Table. It is interesting to note that the coefficient of dummy variable for all these countries is statistically insignificant. In other words the policies of globalization and trade reforms in India is not supporting much for promoting exports of the country.

Table 3

India's Exports to SAARC Countries

US $ Million

Country India exports to	*Year*	*Interceptß1*	*Total imports of Buyer country ß2*	*Export price index of India ß3*	*Dummy variable ß4*	*R2*
Bangladesh	1987–88 to	–680.96391	0.184553	2.929353		0.83722
	2003–04	(832.85244)	(0.028347)	(6.552109)		
	Shift year	–689.84512	0172285	3.222084	73.390209	0.83962
	1993–94	(858.145978)	(0.040346)	(6.781851)	(166.55877)	
Bhutan	1990–91	–150.68786	0.440359	0.978639		0.52017
	to2003–04	(103.075491)	(0.143998)	(0.8083805)		
	Shift year	–203.04294	0.4418464	1.3713962	12.612726	0.55102
	1993–94	(122.167725)	(0.1461019)	(0.9471637)	(15.215976)	
Maldives	1987–88 to	22.0466943	0.057083	–0.218334		0.58922
	2003–04	(32.863427)	(0.020486)	(0.266687)		
	Shift year	23.595236	0.0697566	–0.238271	–4.2323506	0.59983
	1993–94	(33.764127)	(0.03301085)	(0.275263)	(7.210794)	
Nepal	1987–88 to	128.312871	0.218442	–1.976493		0.46013
	2003–04	(472.560680)	(0.088209)	(3.737667)		
	Shift year	170.6355014	0.362534	–2.983757	–149.966495	0.514301
	1993–94	(466.472187)	(0.147846)	(3.7729269)	(124.5453409)	
Pakistan	1987–88 to	70.79 76053	0.026793	–2.084109		0.77189
	2003–04	(153.005493)	(0.0053175)	(1.125923)		
	Shift year	90.8133613	0.0312357	–2.4949034	–27.817978	0.78171
	1993–94	(153.515296)	(0.00793002)	(1.2629221)	(36.374479)	
Sri Lanka	1987–88 to	244.3863	0.15106037	–4.671972		0.72348
	2003–04	(791.533572)	(0.0365834)	(6.1879512)		
	Shift year	81.784188	0.2401051	–4.9686815	–328.097265	0.764701
	1993–94	(765.34942)	(0.0686181)	(5.9269183)	(217.423986)	

Note: Values in parenthesis are standard errors.

India's Import Linkages with SAARC Members

Analysis suggests that India has a very strong bilateral trade links in terms of exports from India with rest of the SAARC countries. We have also tried to examine India's import link with SAARC countries through regression model with exports of the country and import price index of India as independent variable. This regression analysis explains the variation of India's imports from SAARC countries. The regression analysis suggests that India has a better bilateral linkage in terms of imports with Bangladesh and Nepal. These trade links are very poor in relation to Pakistan and Maldives. In all these estimates the coefficient of import price

Table 4

India's Imports from SAARC Countries (US$ million)

Country	*Year ß1*	*Intercept*	*Total imports of Buyer country ß2*	*Export price index of India ß3*	*Dummy variable ß4*	*R2*
Bangladesh	1987–88 to 2003–04	32.322978 (40.678855)	0.0166118 (0.0032527)	–0.363932 (0.3150664)		0.78704
	Shift year 1993–94	-8.6040054 (51.5326148)	0.01219114 (0.0047539)	0.0042444 (0.4261704)	22.555345 (17.991585)	0.81001
Bhutan	1990–91 to 2003–04	-22.151511 (38.329699)	0.47015056 (0.1568548)	–0.0376774 (0.2719787)		0.52462
	Shift year 1993–94	-110.0070113 (64.476859)	0.3004817 (0.1791599)	0.70780617 (0.5212749)	31.8772633 (19.480427)	0.62503
Maldives	1987–88 to2003–04	0.336767 (0.4708015)	0.0021982 (0.0014449)	–0.0022921 (0.0045214)		0.22443
	Shift year 1993–94	–0.440658 (0.9229121)	0.00122408 (0.00175636)	0.0041498 (0.0079831)	0.2065188 (0.2107047)	0.30758
Nepal	1987–88 to 2003–04	-210.27399 (139.059655)	0.5509136 (0.0778634)	0.8877999 (1.0909692)		0.82207
	Shift year 1993–94	-134.902441 (188.866335)	0.584752 (0.097247)	0.2559564 (1.5264486)	-32.84369 (54.104485)	0.82698
Pakistan	1987–88 to 2003–04	80.293094 (135.328045)	0.0028686 (0.0065256)	–0.346657 (0.9552254)		0.04353
	Shift year 1993–04	205.5928833 (166.824789)	0.01190605 (0.0096978)	–1.70 69732 (1.4423576)	-73.573612 (59.292594)	0.14481
Sri Lanka	1987–88 to 2003–04	–152.843 (110.5288807)	0.02568001 (0.0082608)	0.9934108 (0.8271011)		0.43835
	Shift year 1993–94	-163.208632 (131.814129)	0.0239189 (0.01399485)	1.0976629 (1.0791646)	8.0555319 (50.628423)	0.43944

Note: Values in parenthesis are standard errors.

index of India is negative except Nepal and Sri Lanka. However, all these coefficient are statistically insignificant. The coefficient of exports of supplier country is positive and significant only in case Bangladesh, Bhutan, Nepal and Sri Lanka. It is interesting to note that the coefficient of exports of the supply country is insignificant in explaining imports of India in case of Pakistan and Maldives. We have also tried to analyze the impact of globalization by introducing dummy variable with 1993–94 as the year of shift in order to examine the variation in imports of India from the supply countries. It is interesting to note that the coefficient of dummy variable is positive except Nepal and Pakistan but all these coefficients are statistically insignificant. It is thus clear from this analysis that import links of India are good only in case of Bangladesh and Nepal. Most of these links are bilateral because other parameters are not affecting imports of India from SAARC countries. The export links of India are much stronger than import links with the SAARC countries. It is therefore suggested that India can search good markets in the SAARC region by improving its economic and political relation with member countries.

Conclusion

India's socio-economic cooperation has accelerated the trade linkages with SAARC members in the region. Thereby it has helped to create trade dynamics and accelerated development process within the SAARC region. India has expanded the trade relations after globalization and liberalization with many European and American countries but failed to improve trade relations with the SAARC countries. This might be basically because of the economic and social poverty among the member countries which is not helping to create demand for exports from India. Moreover its poor political relations might be causing hurdles in trade development. India's import links are comfortable only with Bangladesh and Nepal. The export's links of India are much stronger than import links with SAARC members. Moreover, the political relations with Pakistan, Bangladesh, and even with Nepal are not supporting India's trade links with the SAARC countries. Improvement in the political relations with SAARC countries can boost India's trade links with member countries.

References

Dash, Kishore C. (1996), "The Political Economy of Regional Cooperation in South Asia", *Pacific Affairs*, Vol. 69, No. 2.

Guru-Gharana, and Kumar, Kishore (2000), "Macro Economic Modeling of South Asian Economies with Intra-SAARC Trade Link", Final report submitted to South Asian Network of Economic Institutes, IIDS, Nepal.

Kochanek, Stanley (1996), "Liberalisation and Business Lobbying in India", *Journal of Commonwealth and Comparative Politics*, 34(3), November 1996, pp. 155–73.

Mafizur Rahman, Mohammad (2006), *Prospect of Intra-SAARC Trade Expansion: An Empirical Analysis*, University of Sydney, NSW 2006, Australia.

Naqvi, S.N. and Samad, S.A. (1992), *SAARC Link: An Econometric Approach*, Oxford and IBH Publishing Co. Pvt. Ltd., New Delhi.

Raipuria, K.M. and Mehta, R. (1990), "Towards Trade Link Modelling for SAARC", *South Asia Journal*, Vol. 4, No. 2, pp. 167–180.

Sarkar, Amal (2004), "A Trade Linkage System for SAARC", *Foreign Trade Review* (Quarterly Journal of Indian Institute of Foreign Trade, July-September, 2004, Vol. XXXIX, No. 2.

Waqif, A.A. (1987) "Regional Cooperation for Industrial Developement in South Asia" in A.A. Waqif (ed.), *South Asian Cooperation in Industry, Energy and Technology,* Sage Publications, New Delhi.

17 Indian Agriculture at the Crossroads

Challenges and Prospects

Yogesh Bandhu Arya

Agriculture continues to remain the predominant sector of Indian economy even though its share in national output has declined from more than 50 per cent in the initial years after Independence from colonial rule in 1947 to less than a quarter in the recent years. In terms of employment and livelihood, still around 58 per cent workforce is engaged in agriculture as their principal occupation. Due to its importance in national output and employment, agriculture was given special attention by India's policy makers and development planners which helped this sector to play an important role in economic development of the country and in improving income and living standards of vast population dependent on agriculture. During last one and a half decade, several challenges have surfaced in Indian agriculture which became more and more severe with the passage of time. These relate to growth of output, efficiency, equity and sustainability. The biggest challenge for Indian agriculture is to reverse the sharp decline in growth rate experienced by this sector after mid 1990s. The growth rate of agriculture sector has become lower than the growth in population dependent on this sector implying that per capita income in agriculture is falling. This is considered to be a major factor responsible for large scale rural distress and large number of suicidal deaths of farmers in various parts of the country. Another big challenge is to ensure sustainable use of natural resources. While the need for accelerating agricultural growth is obvious, natural resource base in the country is shrinking. There are also signs of degradation of land and overexploitation of water in the country, especially in regions, which once headed the green revolution in India. This brings forth the second biggest challenge which is to ensure sustainable use of natural resources. Post-WTO period has thrown serious challenges in front of Indian agriculture, as domestic prices of several commodities have become higher than international prices. This has made imports attractive and has adversely affected exports. The situation calls for improving competitiveness of Indian agriculture through improvement in efficiency in agricultural production, marketing, transport, etc. This is the third challenge before Indian agriculture. The equity concerns with respect to sectors, regions, classes of farmers and gender are also important.

Over the last decade there is decline in the contribution of agriculture sector to GDP but hardly any significant change has surfaced in the proportion of the workforce depending on agriculture. While the importance of agriculture is not likely to diminish for sometime to come, there are so many reasons which justify continuous emphasis on agricultural growth in the country's development strategy. Some main concerns are: food security, full employment and availability of wage goods (Vyas, 2003). Therefore, at least in the near future agriculture will remain an important source of livelihood for the rural households and, an important instrument for alleviating rural poverty.

Key Domestic Policies and their Impact on Agriculture Development

In the last five decades, the government's objectives in agricultural policy and the instruments used to realize these objectives have changed from time to time, depending on both internal and external factors. Agricultural policies at the sectoral level can be further divided into supply side and demand side policies. The former include those relating to land reform and land use, development and diffusion of new technologies, public investment in irrigation and rural infrastructure and agricultural price supports. The demand side policies on the other hand, include state interventions in agricultural markets as well as operation of public distribution systems. Such policies also have macro effects in terms of their impact on government budgets. Macro level policies include policies to strengthen agricultural and non-agricultural sector linkages and industrial policies that affect input supplies to agriculture and the supply of agricultural materials. During the last five decades Indian agricultural policy can be broadly distinguished into three phases.

The period from 1950–51 to mid-1960s can be called the pre-green revolution period which witnessed tremendous agrarian reforms, institutional changes and the development of major irrigation projects. Intermediary landlordism was abolished; tenant operators were given security of farming and ownership of land. Land Ceiling Acts were imposed to eliminate large-sized holdings and cooperative credit institutions were strengthened to minimize the exploitation of cultivators by private money lenders and traders. Land consolidation was also resorted to reduce the number of land fragments. Expansion of cultivable area was the main source of growth in the pre-green revolution period. Since the scope for area expansion is limited, therefore increase in productivity became the main source of growth in crop output.

Further, the country faced a severe food shortage crisis in the early 1960s which forced the policy makers to realize that continuous reliance on food imports and aid would impose heavy costs in terms of political pressure and economic instability (Rao, 1996). In a desperate search for a quick breakthrough in agricultural production government took decision to import the HYV of seeds for wheat and rice which required the intensive use of fertilizers, irrigation and other inputs. This marked the second phase in the agriculture policy of the country. The strategy produced quick results as there was a quantum leap in yield. Consequently, in a short span of 6 years between 1965–66 and 1971–72, wheat and rice production witnessed an increase of 30 million tonnes which is 168 per cent higher than the total achievement in the 15 years following 1950–51. The biggest achievement of the new agricultural strategy, also known as the green revolution technology was the attainment of self-sufficiency in food grains. As the green revolution technology involved the use of modern farm inputs, its spread led to a fast growth in the agro input industry. Agrarian reforms during this period took a back seat while research, extension, input supply, credit, marketing, price support and spread of technology were the prime concerns of policy makers (Rao, 1996).

The next phase in Indian agriculture began in the early 1980s. While there was a clear change in economic policy towards delicensing and deregulation in the industry sector, agriculture policy by contrast lacked direction and was marked by confusion. There has been a considerable increase in subsidies and support to the agriculture sector during this period while public sector spending on agriculture for infrastructure development started showing a decline in real terms but investments by farmers kept moving on a rising trend (Mishra and Chand, 1995; Chand, 2001). The output growth, which was till now concentrated in very narrow pockets, became broad-based and got momentum. The rural economy started witnessing a process of diversification which led to a growth in non-food grain output like milk, fishery, poultry, vegetables, fruits, etc. This accelerated a largely market driven growth in agricultural GDP during the 1980s.

The decade of the 1980s did not see any major policy initiative for agriculture as wider spread of improved technology was the main factor for output growth. Towards the late 1980s, some adverse consequences of the new technology started emerging. Some pockets of the green revolution areas started showing signs of strain on natural resources like land and water. The mounting burden of subsidies put a pressure on the fiscal resources and after 1980–81, public investments in agriculture started declining.

Though the green revolution has been widely diffused in irrigated areas throughout the country, the dry land areas have not yet benefited from the technological breakthrough as witnessed through the green revolution technology. Of late, improved varieties of oilseeds and coarse cereals have provided some opportunities for productivity growth in dry land areas. A new phase started in India's economic policy in 1991 that marked a significant departure from the past. Government initiated a process of economic reforms which involved deregulation, reduced government participation in economic activities, and liberalization measures. Though these reforms were not directed at the agriculture sector, the sector was affected indirectly by a devaluation of the exchange rate, liberalization of external trade and dis-protection to industry. At the international level there was a new trade accord and the WTO required the opening up of the domestic market. Initially, there were strong apprehensions about the impact of trade liberalization on Indian agriculture which later turned out to be real for several commodities produced in the country. All these changes raised new challenges and provided new opportunities that required an appropriate policy response. The price intervention of the last two decades had a very limited coverage, and there was a sort of policy vacuum. Therefore, there is a strong pressure on the government to give new direction to agriculture in the new and emerging scenario.

New Economic Policies, Trade Liberalization and Indian Agriculture

The new economic policies of LPG (liberalization, privatization and globalization) since the beginning of the 1990s have direct and indirect effects on farmers' welfare. The presumption was that freeing agricultural markets and liberalizing external trade in agricultural commodities would provide price incentives leading to enhanced investment and output in that sector, while broader trade liberalization would shift inter-sectoral terms of trade in favour of agriculture. But the economic reforms totally overlooked this sector and did not include any specific package specifically designed for agriculture. However, there were changes in patterns of government spending and financial measures which also necessarily affected the conditions of cultivation. In particular, fiscal policies of reducing expenditure on certain areas especially rural spending have adverse impact on cultivation and rural living conditions. The LPG policies leading to economic reform strategy involved measures like; actual declines in central government revenue expenditure on rural development, cuts in particular subsidies such as on fertilizer in real terms, and an overall decline in per capita government expenditure on rural areas, reduction in public investment in agriculture, research and extension, very substantial declines in public infrastructure and energy investments that affect the rural areas, particularly irrigation, financial liberalization measures, including redefining priority sector lending by banks, which effectively reduced the availability of rural credit, and thus made farm investment more expensive and more difficult, especially for small and marginal farmers.

In recent years, most state governments were in fiscal crisis and did not have funds for capital expenditures. This has been especially important, since state governments are responsible for areas critical for farmers such as rural infrastructure, power, water supply, health and education. Meanwhile, at the central government level, capital expenditure as a share of national income declined and all public expenditure directed towards the rural areas fell both as a percentage of GDP and in terms of real per capita expenditure. India's financial liberalization strategy was made to relieve financial repression by freeing interest rates and allowing financial innovation, to reduce directed and subsidized credit, as well as to allow greater freedom in terms of external flows of capital in various forms. These measures, especially reduced emphasis on priority sector lending by banks, effectively reduced the availability of rural credit and thus made farm investment more expensive and more difficult, especially for small farmers. In addition to declining credit-deposit ratios in rural areas, the shift of banks away from crop lending and term lending for agriculture; the reduction in the number of rural bank branches and less manpower for rural service provision meant that the formal sector was increasingly unable to meet the requirements of cultivators. Farmers were therefore forced to turn more and more to private moneylenders and get involved in more exploitative relationships. This has brought back the problem of interlinked markets in which control in one market (say, credit) allows control also in other related rural markets (such as those for agricultural inputs and crop prices, as well as the labour market).

Trade liberalization process affecting Indian agriculture accelerated since late 1990s, in tune with WTO agreements, and involved liberalization of export controls, liberalization of quantitative controls on imports and decontrol of domestic trade. All quantitative restrictions on imports and exports were removed from April, 2000. Almost all agricultural products are now allowed to be freely exported. What is significant is that tariff rates have been relatively stable despite tremendous volatility in world trade prices, so that Indian agriculturalists have to deal effectively with all the volatility of world prices. This implies that as the uncertainties related to international price movements have become directly more significant for Indian farmers, so progressive trade liberalization and tariff reduction in these commodities have made their market relations more problematic.

In addition to this, government was persistent on reducing subsidies, which affected both agricultural producers and consumers, and the reduction of public expenditure which affected cultivation. However, these strategies, which involved raising the prices for consumers of both food and fertilizers, had undesirable and even counter-productive effects, leading to paradoxical results of reducing consumption and increasing subsidies simultaneously. Throughout the 1990s and even subsequently, there have been attempts to raise other user charges of public services and utilities relevant for farmers, such as irrigation water charges, power, etc. While these measures are typically under the control of state governments, the fiscal crunch of such state governments and the general atmosphere of reducing subsidies led many state governments to increase various user charges, especially on the use of power for agricultural consumers. In fact, government policies did not adjust in ways that would make the transition easier or less volatile. Thus, there was no evidence of any coordination between domestic price policy and the policies regarding external trade and tariffs. In the absence of such minimal protection, Indian farmers had to operate in a highly uncertain and volatile international environment, effectively competing against highly subsidized large producers in the developed countries, whose average level of subsidy amounted to many times the total domestic cost of production for many crops. Also, the volatility of such prices has created uncertain and often misleading signals for farmers who are forced to respond by changing cropping patterns.

Challenges of Globalization

Indian agriculture is facing multiple and complex challenges since the beginning of 21st century. These challenges can be grouped into four categories relating to: (i) growth, (ii) sustainability, (iii) efficiency, and (iv) equity. There are also other important concerns like food security, livelihood, employment, yield and income risks, improvement in farm incomes and standard of living of agricultural population.

Globalizing agriculture has the potential to transform subsistence agriculture to commercialized agriculture and to improve the living conditions of the rural community. But the experience of liberalization of agriculture in past fifteen years does not support this hypothesis. It was anticipated that the opening up of the agricultural sector to foreign trade, the move to a market determined exchange rate and reduction of protection for industry would, over time, benefit the agricultural sector. A significant observation of this process among stakeholders is that the expected increase in exports due to liberalization simply did not occur. India's share in world exports was 0.6 per cent in 1997; India had to aim for at least 4 per cent by 2005 in order to meet the growing import demands for capital goods, raw materials and crude oil as well as to meet her external financial commitments (Kaliranjan et al., 2001). For the last decade or so, India's share in world exports of agriculture has been between 2 per cent and 3 per cent. Furthermore, India is not as competitive as the other countries and calculations show that India's crop yields have increased at a slower rate over the 1990s. In addition, the agricultural sector's output growth decreased to 2.9 per cent during 1992–1993 to 1998–1999. Two important reasons for the slowdown are that there was no major breakthrough in developing new high-yielding varieties during the 1990s and there was a decline in the environmental quality of land which reduced the marginal productivity of the modern inputs. What could this mean in terms of the effectiveness of the policies of reduced protection to industry, a market determined exchange rate and the opening of the agricultural sector to foreign trade?

First, although the reduction in protection of industry is substantial, there is reason to believe that the reduction was not necessarily sufficient to benefit the agricultural sector whose tariffs were also drastically reduced. Hence, the expected shift in resources to agriculture did not occur. Second, is the apparent ineffectiveness of the market determined exchange rate in boosting exports? This is, however, not surprising as the exchange rate may not be a key factor in determining agricultural export demand for India. In general, unlike manufacturing industries, agriculture did not benefit much from these two policies because the share of imported inputs in the value of agricultural production is small. Third, in opening up the agricultural sector to foreign trade, India has taken major steps towards trade liberalization since 1991, partly on its own initiative and partly due to its commitments to WTO.

But the benefits from trade liberalization have been slow to come. One reason is that prospects for growth in agricultural exports depend partly on domestic policies and partly on the removal of protectionist policies pursued by developed countries such as US and members of the European Union (EU). The developed countries continue to support agriculture and these protectionist practices do not seem to come to an end. The implications of these protections are that, the food exports from India may not show a large increase given the international environment which has clouded the possibilities of increasing Indian exports. Another problem faced by Indian agricultural exporters is the prevalence of protectionist measures in the form of non-trade barriers that developed countries use to restrict market access. This is done by tightening standards of quality, testing and labelling, and imposing anti-dumping and countervailing measures.

Effects on Farming Community and Rural Livelihoods

The impact of trade liberalization on farmers' welfare works through various channels such as volatile prices, problems in imports and exports, impact on livelihood and other employment opportunities, etc. For farmers, perhaps the single most adverse effect has been the combination of low prices and output volatility for cash crops. While output volatility increased especially with new seeds and other inputs, the prices of most non-food grain crops weakened, and some prices plummeted for prolonged periods. This reflected not only in domestic demand conditions but also in the growing role played by international prices due to greater integration with world markets in this sector. These features, in turn, were associated with growing material distress among cultivators. In a closed economy, lower output is normally accompanied by some price increase. Therefore, coincidence of lower production with lower terms of trade was very rare until recently. This phenomenon reflected the effect of the growing integration of Indian agriculture with world markets, resulting from trade liberalization. As both exports and imports of agricultural products were progressively freed, international price movements were more closely reflected in domestic trends. The stagnation or decline in the international prices of many agricultural commodities from 1996 onwards meant that their prices in India also fell, despite local declines in production. It reflects in distress sale by small and marginal farmers at ground level. This throws the farmers into a vicious circle of debt trap and costs the life of thousands of farmers.

On the other hand, volatility of prices in international market faced typically by Indian exporters of agricultural commodities has very little to do with domestic harvest conditions and much more to do with international prices. Cultivators were exposed to volatility which not only added greatly to the uncertainties associated with farming, but also generated price signals that were wrong or misleading. Since Indian farmers are known to have very elastic responses to relative price signals in terms of changing average; this caused large and often undesirable shifts in cropping pattern which ultimately rebounded on the farmers themselves. The inevitable uncertainties associated with weather fluctuations were compounded by further problems of extremely volatile crop prices, which were no longer inversely related to harvest levels but followed an international pattern. Further, this dramatic volatility of output prices and the stagnation/collapse of some harvest prices from 1997 onwards—has been associated with continuously rising prices of inputs.

Such exposure to global price volatility has been associated with a growing reliance on private debt because of the lack of extension of institutional credit, coupled with growing inability to meet debt service payments because of the combined volatility of crops and prices. This in turn, has led to loss of assets, including land, by the small peasantry. This has been so marked that the proportion of rural households without any land increased dramatically over the 1990s, and by 1999–2000 accounted for around 45 per cent of rural households according to National Sample Survey data. The pervasive agrarian crisis has been most harshly illustrated by the increase in suicides by farmers, which amounted to nearly 50,000 cases across India by the end of May, 2006. In addition, there has been a deterioration of conditions of food security associated with the shift away from cultivation of traditional staples towards cash crops, as well as a sharp decline in per capita food grain absorption to the low levels last seen only in the late 1930s and again in the early 1950s, which were both periods of extreme rural distress. It is evident that both output and availability have fallen, but the decline in per capita availability has been sharper for output. Consumption data based on the National Sample Surveys suggest that both foodgrains consumption and total calorie consumption have declined substantially over the period, on the aggregate level and even for the bottom forty per cent of population in terms of expenditure classes. While the falling viability of cultivation has been an important reason for this, the collapse of rural employment opportunities, especially in agriculture but also in non-agriculture, has also been a major factor in the pervasive agrarian distress. The 55th Round of the National Sample Survey on

Employment and Unemployment, held in 1999–2000 indicates a dramatic decline in the rate of employment generation in the current period. In both rural and urban areas, the absolute number of unemployed increased substantially, and the rate of unemployment went up as well. A significant part of this collapse of employment occurred in agriculture and was related to both growing mechanization of agriculture and shift in cropping pattern.

The fall in rate of employment can partially be attributed to the decline in public spending on rural employment programmes since the mid-nineties. Expenditure on both rural wage employment programmes and special programmes for rural development declined as a percentage of GDP from the mid-1990s. The total central allocation for rural wage employment programmes was already only 0.4 per cent of GDP in 1995–96, but it declined further to a minuscule 0.13 per cent of GDP in 2000–01. This is probably why employment generation has emerged as not only the most important socio-economic issue in the country today, but also as the most pressing political concern. The mandate of the recent elections is clear on this, that the people of the country have decisively rejected policies which have implied reduced employment opportunities and reduced access to and quality of public goods and services and overlooked the agriculture sector.

The Way to Budge

India has shown commitment to stay on the bandwagon of globalization. Having realized that globalization is a necessary but not a sufficient condition for high growth production, India has undertaken economic reforms, both internal and external. It is quite apparent at this stage, that there is little observable evidence of gains to India's agricultural performance after liberalization. However, benefits could have been accrued but easily have not yet surfaced, or are yet to be identified and perhaps too difficult or intangible to measure. Therefore, it must be ensured that these reforms should be synchronized so that the pace of both internal and external reforms is set right in order to work hand in hand to promote agricultural growth. There is a growing concern that if the problems facing agriculture are not addressed urgently and effectively, then it would be very difficult for India to raise growth rate of its economy. This is because agriculture will remain an important source of livelihood for large number of Indians, either directly or indirectly, for a long time to come, as the majority of workforce remains engaged in farming and related work.

Moreover, most poor Indians live in rural areas, so broad-based agricultural growth must be at the centre of strategies to reduce poverty and achieve food security. There is serious concern about viability and future of smaller and marginal land holdings which constitute the entitlements of majority of farmers in the country. The present state of dismal picture of agriculture in the country is a result of several factors. The foremost is lack of clear policy on agriculture since long. The country did not change institutional mechanisms and regulatory framework to create environment conducive for agricultural growth, which was essential for adjustment with changes in domestic and global environment. The second reason is neglect of infrastructure and diversion of resources to populist measures. Third reason is slowdown in the technology reaching potential region and weakening of extension system used for dissemination of technology. Unless drastic reforms are implemented in agriculture sector it would not be possible to revive output growth on sustainable basis and mitigate rural distress.

It needs reorientation of our policies and large amount of public investment. Key investment targets include less-favoured areas, agricultural research and infrastructure especially roads and storage. Agricultural research must make use of all relevant tools, including molecular biology, conventional approaches, and better utilization of farmers. In conjunction with these public investments, agriculture will have to become more market oriented, with better targeted safety nets to assure that the transition from controls and subsidies does not leave poor people worse off. Safety net programmes and agricultural and rural development programmes alike need to be designed and implemented with the participation of the intended beneficiaries, rather than in a top-down bureaucratic manner. Greater attention must also be paid to sustainable use of natural resources. Globalization can be shaped to benefit poor people. The needed shifts in domestic food and agricultural policy would go a long way in assuring that small land owners and other rural poor people have a stake in export opportunities. These shifts in politics include ensuring access to infrastructure, inputs, credit, markets, and organizations such as cooperatives that can facilitate the participation of these stakeholders in markets and enhance their political voice.

Training the farmers and educating them appropriately to change their mindset and reorienting them to take up new challenges is of utmost importance. Also, with domestic economic reforms, more care needs to be exercised in drawing up state-specific corrective reform measures to maximize their benefits. Lastly, we have a number of policies for each and every problem but simultaneously we have failed to execute and implement these policies properly. So for successful globalization, one crucial element in the implementation of these reforms is the need for good governance.

Select References

Acharya, S.S. (1998), "Agricultural Price Policy and Development: Some Facts and Emerging Issues", *Indian Journal of Agricultural Economics*, Vol. 52, No. 1, pp. 1–47.

—. (2004), *Agricultural Marketing, State of the Indian Farmers*, Vol. 17, Academic Foundation, New Delhi.

Ahluwalia, M.S. (1996), "New Economic Policy and Agriculture: Some Reflections", *Indian Journal of Agricultural Economics*, Vol. 51, No. 3, pp. 412–426.

Chadha, R. (1999), Trade and Balance of Payments, National Council of Applied Economic Research (Mimeograph).

Chakraborty, Debashis (2005), Food Security in India: Policy Challenges and Responses, Briefing Paper ASP BP 05/02, Rajiv Gandhi Institute for Contemporary Studies, New Delhi, February 2005.

Chand, Ramesh (2001), "Emerging Trends and Issues in Public and Private Investments in Indian Agriculture: A State-wise Analysis", *Indian Journal of Agricultural Economics*, Vol. 56, No. 2, pp. 161–184, April-June 2001.

— (2005), "India's Agricultural Challenges and their Implications for Growth of It's Economy", Paper submitted for international symposium on "Regional Integration in Asia and India", organized by IDE–JETRO, Tokyo, Japan, December 8, 2005.

Desai, M. (1999), "What Should be India's Economic Priorities in a Globalized World?", Indian Council for Research on International Economic Relations, New Delhi.

Gulati, A. and Sharma, A.N. (1995), "Subsidy Syndrome in Indian Agriculture", *Economic and Political Weekly*, September 30.

Ghosh, Jayati (2005), "Trade Liberalization in Agriculture: An Examination of Impact and Policy Strategies with Special Reference to India Background", Paper for HDR.

Kalirajan, K.P., Mythili, G. and Sankar, U. (eds.) (2001), *Accelerating Growth through Globalization of Indian Agriculture*, Macmilan, India.

Kruger, A.O., Schiff, M. and Valdes, A. (eds.) (1991), *The Political Economy of Agricultural Pricing Policy*, Vols. 1 and 2, Baltimore, John Hopkins University Press.

Mahadevan, R. and Kalirajan, K.P. (1999), "On Measuring Total Factor Productivity Growth in Singapore's Manufacturing Industries", *Applied Economics Letters*, Vol. 6, pp. 295–298.

Mishra, S.N. and Chand, Ramesh (1995), "Public and Private Capital Formation in Indian Agriculture: Comments on the Complementarity Hypothesis and others", *Economic and Political Weekly*, Review of Agriculture, Vol. 30, June.

Nair, K.P. Prabhakaran (2005), "Is India Inching Towards a Hunger Trap?" *Financial Daily* from The Hindu group of publications, Tuesday, June 21.

Planning Commission, Government of India, (2006), Data posted at <http://indiabudget.nic.in>, accessed March 18.

Rao, V.M. (1996), "Agricultural Development with a Human Face", *Economic and Political Weekly*, 31(26): A-50 to A-62, June 29.

Rao, M. Govinda, Kalirajan, K.P. and Shand, Ric (1999), "Convergence of Incomes in Indian States-A Divergent View", *Economic and Political Weekly*, March 27-April 2.

Schumacher, Jr., A., (2000), "International Agricultural Trade at a Crossroads", *Economic Perspectives*, An Electronic Journal of the US Department of State, March 2000.

Singh, M. (1995), Inaugural Address Delivered at the 54th Annual Conference, *Indian Journal of Agricultural Economics*, Vol. 50, No. 1: 1–6.

Vyas, Vijay Shankar (2003), "Indian Agriculture: The Unresolved Issues", special feature, *ADB India Economic Bulletin*, June 2003 Vol. I, No. 2.

WTO (World Trade Organization), 2006. http://www.wto.org, accessed March 18.

18 The Problem of Industrial Displacement in Jharkhand

A Case Study of Bokaro Steel Plant

Binod Narayan

In recent years, one social issue that has caused intense debate among academics, social activists and planners is the involuntary displacement of people from their productive assets particularly land and homes, due to industrial and infrastructure projects. Though the process of acquisition of land for setting up mining, irrigation and transportation mega-industrial projects (mostly in the public sector) is not new, the intensity of adverse effects was never comprehended in the past as it is today (Sharma, 2003).

The liberalization of the economy, growing needs of infrastructure in fast-growing cities and new partnerships in industrial/economic sectors have threatened traditional sources of sustenance of people. More and more agricultural lands are being depleted for setting up industrial/infrastructure projects. All this has unleashed a situation where more and more people are being displaced from their communities and traditional ways of life. How many of them are co-opted into the new economic order and how many remain victims of the new model of development, remains unknown. However, there is a growing awareness of the sweeping powers of government, under the Land Acquisition Act of 1894 (now amended Act of 1984), which empowers it to acquire private lands and properties in 'public interest'. Along with the growing pace of development under the process of 'liberalization' the intensity of displacement has also increased. The past few decades have witnessed rapid economic growth in the country and the process forms a part of 'planned development'. This is manifested in the setting up of large-scale projects in power generation, mining, industry, infrastructure development and irrigation and even in creating new urban settlements. This entails large-scale land acquisition and even demolition of homesteads.

State induced land alienation leading to displacement negates the fundamental tenets of the Fifth Schedule of the Constitution and also questions the control and ownership of land and natural resources recognized in Provisions of the Panchayat (Extension to the Scheduled Areas) Act, 1996, particularly clauses (i) and (m) of Section 4. Alienation of land also leads to alienation of the surrounding livelihood resources on which the tribals depend. While setting up various development projects (mining, industries, hydel, irrigation, etc.), the concomitant impacts have hardly been taken into account or compensated. The idea that industrialization would lead to corresponding improvement in economic life of the tribals has proved almost mythical. In reality the tribals have been marginalized from the resources, which they enjoyed, and the rights, which they exercised. A conspicuous fallacy in our development paradigms in tribal areas has been that all projects in tribal areas have been considered as serving 'public purpose', so much so that even private mining has been brought within the purview of public purpose.

It is high time for the people and the Government of Jharkhand to reformulate the proper Resettlement and Rehabilitation (R&R) policy because there are so many industrial and developmental mega projects in the pipeline. According to Xavier Dias, spokesperson of JMCC, the Jharkhand government had signed over 42 MoUs with investors including Mittal Steel, Tata Steel, Jindal Steel and Power Company Limited worth about Rs 1,69,198.26 crore ever since the Jharkhand state was carved out five years ago. These projects would certainly require a whopping size of land. Dias claimed that approximately 47,445 acres of land would be required for the projects only in Kolhan Region, which was likely to affect about 10,000 families and cause deforestation of 57.15 sq km land. The required land can only be had by displacing the peoples of Jharkhand, especially tribal people, as we have seen in the past in the cases of industrial complexes like Jamshedpur, Bokaro, Hatia, and mining areas like Central Coalfields Limited, Bharat Coking Coal Limited, and dams like Maithan, Masanjor, Panchet, Tilaiya, Field Firing Range of Netarhat and so many other projects. Many of these projects started more than 20–30 years ago, but the cases of rehabilitation could not be settled as yet which has engendered anger and dissatisfaction among the oustees. Displaced persons of the Jharkhand feel that they have been cheated in the name of development. Due to bitter experiences of development-induced displacement in the past, the people of Jharkhand are opposing big projects and displacements.

The other side of the coin is the fact that without displacement any society can-not think of industrial and infrastructure development.

The present paper seeks to understand the nature of development-induced displacement and their consequences in Jharkhand with special reference to Bokaro Steel Plant. The paper is based on interviews, ethnographies among the displaced persons, leaders of different trade unions and associations associated with displacement issues. Secondary data has been collected from the office of Director Projects and Land Rehabilitation, Bokaro and review of some pertinent literature.

Why a New R&R Policy in Jharkhand?

The Jharkhand government has not with serious criticism and opposition from the affected people and public at large as well as the tribal groups ever since it started signing MoUs for setting up units in the mineral-abundant state.

Tribal outfits and political parties in mineral-rich Kolhan region of Jharkhand are outraged against development projects, including industries, fearing they would result in large-scale displacement of inhabitants and loss of their sources of livelihood. The outfits and parties, including Jharkhand Mukti Morcha, have launched a series of agitations and demonstrations protesting the MoUs signed between the Jharkhand government and prospective investors since the creation of the state in 2000.

A massive demonstration was organized recently by various organizations, including Bhoomi Raksha Gramin Ekta Manch, Moolvasi Adhikar Morcha, Adivasi Adhikar Morcha and Jharkhand Mines Area Co-ordinations Committee in the district headquarters in Kolhan region comprising areas of east and west Singhbhum and Saraikela-Kharswan to oppose the projects.

Addressing a massive *ulgulan* (revolution) rally in Chaibasa, headquarter of west Singhbhum district, Jharkhand Mukti Morcha (JMM) chief Shibu Soren called on tribals to be prepared to sacrifice their lives to protect their *Jal, Jungle, Jamin* (water, forest and land) and charged that the Jharkhand government was bent upon "displacing them from their own lands on the pretext of development". He was not categorically opposed to displacement but demanded a proper rehabilitation policy before any displacement. He threatened to launch *padyatras* (marches) across the state against the 'anti-people' approach of the government and said it should promote agriculture sectors and small-scale industries instead of big industries, if it was serious about development of the state.

Like Soren, Salkhan Murmu, the chief convenor of Adivasi Adhikar Morcha (AAM), which has been organizing rallies and demonstrations across the state to mount pressure on the Jharkhand government to implement Panchayat (Extension to Scheduled Area) Act, 1996 (PESA-1996), said AAM was not opposed to development of Jharkhand, but certainly not at the cost of tribals' interest. He further said that 'AAM' would file public interest litigation in the Jharkhand High Court by November-end against the investors' move to acquire tribal land for the proposed industries. He also suggested that land owners ready to vacate their land for the industries be made shareholders in the proposed company with ownership right of their land in return of their approval for setting up the industries. He said that hundreds of adivasi families had been leading miserable lives and are forced to migrate to other states in search of livelihood after they had been displaced from their own lands for development projects in the past.

Murmu, a former parliamentarian, said, "In fact, Jharkhand does not need big industries for the next two decades, but the agriculture sector and agro-based industries need to be promoted for the benefit of tribal masses". He advocated an honourable 'rehabilitation act' in the state instead of a rehabilitation policy, which has been 'proved anti-tribal' in the last five decades. The tribal leader said that any forcible acquisition of tribal land in the Scheduled Area would be violation of the Constitution as well as the 1997 judgment of the Supreme Court in a case between a non-governmental organization 'Samatha' and Andhra Pradesh government.

Various other organizations have announced their course of action against the development projects in the region. Bhumi Raksha Gramin Ekta Manch alongwith AAM and Moolvasi Adhikar Manch have announced a 'janata curfew' in Kolhan belt in protest against the possible groundbreaking ceremonies to be performed by investors.

While the tribal organizations have adopted an aggressive posture vowing to sacrifice their lives to protect their land rather than vacate it for development projects, JMM advocated promotion of agriculture sector and agro-based industries in the state.

Senior Bharatiya Janata Party leader Shailendra Mahato, who is also the president of the Lok Adhikar Morcha, has declared that not an inch of land will be given to investors for setting up their plants and threatened to launch 'Jamin Chipko Andolan' . Mahato further said that the movement will begin from Tentaposhi village in Saraikela-Kharswan district where Tata Steel has proposed to set up a 12 million green field integrated steel plant at a cost of Rs 53,000 crore in phases. He expressed apprehension that residents of two villages, which were likely to be acquired by the Tata Steel for its new plant, would be rendered homeless and their livelihood snatched as the Jharkhand government did not have any concrete rehabilitation policy as yet. He also said that Jharkhand government should rather focus on backward districts like Simdega, Gumla, Latehar and Santhal Paragana region where development projects were necessary.

State and the district administrations have, however, been trying to convince the villagers, activists and political leaders concerned that the development of the state was not possible without investments and projects.

It has been widely felt, in particular, that due to lack of a sufficiently holistic perspective all the relevant issues in this area have not been identified and addressed.

In the circumstances mentioned above, it is imperative to act now and formulate a comprehensive, convincing and holistic R&R Policy. Further, the new R&R issue needs to be taken more seriously than they have been in the past.

The displacement in Bokaro Steel Plant area is the most complicated case in Jharkhand, as is evident from thousands of displaced persons fighting under various organizations for their rights even after 40 years of the establishment of the plant. Various court cases in High Court are still awaiting their disposal. The present paper tries to look into the various problems and issues related to displacement in Bokaro.

Displacement in India

Estimating the number of internal displaced persons (IDPs) in India is problematic. Regular monitoring is not possible in such a huge country, which lacks a central authority responsible for coordinating data from central and state governments. The nature, frequency and extent of the causes of internal displacement in India are so varying that it would be a Herculean task to monitor and record them. Political sensitivities at state level prevent release of data on the exact nature and extent of displacements.

There is thus huge variation in estimates of the numbers of IDPs in India. The latest World Refugee Survey (2000) put the total number of IDPs in India as 507,000; the Indian Social Institute in Delhi and the Global IDP Project place it at 21.3 million (Fernandes, 1998).

The Mid-Term Appraisal of the Ninth Five-Year Plan document (2000) of the Planning Commission cites 50 million people as having been displaced since 1950 because of various development projects: of them more than 40 per cent people, i.e., approximately 25 per cent of the total

ST population has been thrown out of their homes and hearths. The Report of the Working Group for Empowering the Scheduled Tribes during the Tenth Five-Year Plan (July 2001) mentions a figure of 85.39 lakh tribals as having been displaced. There are other estimates. It seems, however, that scientific research studies in this regard are scarce. Overall, it seems that displacement has occurred on a large scale primarily due to acquisition of land by the state for various development projects like mining, industries, hydel, irrigation, educational institutions, health institutions, townships, etc. By and large, the benefits of the development projects have not reached the people who have been displaced. Even rehabilitation efforts have been inadequate and the displaced families continue to be in crises.

Displacement in Jharkhand

Orissa, West Bengal, Jharkhand and Andhra Pradesh have together more than 100 lakh displaced persons (DPs), or 50 per cent of 213 lakh (Fernandes, 2004).

A conservative estimate of the total number of persons and tribals displaced by various development projects in Jharkhand during 1951–1995 as compiled by Ekka and Asif (2000) has been given in Table 1. As per this estimate, about 15 lakh persons displaced in Jharkhand up to 1995, which comprised about 6.2 lakhs (41.28%) STs, 2.1 lakh (14.16%) SCs and 6.7 lakhs (45.01%) people of other categories. As there is no significant displacement after 1995 in Jharkhand, his estimate is relevant even in present time.

Table 1

Total Number of People Displaced in Jharkhand 1991–1995

S. No.	*Type of Project*	*STs*	*%*	*SCs*	*%*	*Others*	*%*	*Total*
1.	Water Resource	175127	75.2	17554	07.5	40287	17.3	232958
2.	Industries/Quasi Industries	22483	34.0	15006	22.7	28548	43.2	66087
3.	Mining: Coal	79568	29.6	42268	15.7	146752	54.6	268588
4.	Mining Non-Coal	3975	N A	21084	N A	73324	N A	134294
5.	Defence Establishments	237147	89.7	18529	07.0	8677	03.2	264353
6.	Wildlife Sanctuaries	80867	15.8	87601	17.1	339266	66.5	509918
7.	Grand Total	620372		212892		676575		1503017
	Per cent	41.28		14.16		45.01		100.00

Source: Ekka, A. and Asif, M. (2000) pp. 95.

Majority of Displaced are STs

Out of the 17 lakh DPs by 119 central and state government schemes a staggering 8 lakh persons, i.e., more than half were tribals. Mines have displaced over 21 lakh persons during the past 40 years, which includes 14 lakh tribals (Mohammed, 2000). A 1987 Government of India report claims that 85 lakh tribals have been displaced at least once (SARINI, 1997). Another estimate suggests that the total number of displaced persons and project affected persons in India between 1951–91 is 213 lakh and nearly 85 lakh of them are tribals (Fernandes, 1998). In Jharkhand also more than 41 per cent displaced peoples belong to ST category (see Table 1).

Details of displacement caused by the major projects in Jharkhand and estimate of affected villages, families and peoples alienated from land and habitat since 1960 have been given in Table 2. However, these figures are only estimates from various sources, and not accurate figures.

Table 2

Alienation of Land since 1960 (in acres)

Name of project	*Number of villages*	*Number of persons*	*Area in acres*	*Per cent of displaced tribals*
Netarhat field firing range	245	2,35,000	6,25,000	N A
Koel Karo Dam	250	2,50,000	66,000	88
Sankh Dam	208	46,694	19,000	75.3
HEC Ranchi	12,990 families	64,950	7,711	N A
Bokaro Steel Plant	23,957 families	62,435	34,227	15
Damodar Valley Project	N A	N A	28,837	N A
Adityapur Industrial Area	N A	N A	34,432	N A
Chandil Dam	120	37,600	43,500	87.92
Icha Dam	5,600 families	30,800	21,000	80
Maithon and Panchet	N A	93,874	N A	56.46
Masan Reservoir	N A	3,700	N A	31.00
Central Coalfields Ltd.	32,751 families	1,63,755	1,20,300	N A
TISCO	7,000 families	35,000	N A	N A
Subarnarekha Multi-purpose Project	68,400 families	3,42,000	85,000	N A
Tenughat Thermal Power	76,300 families	3,81,500	97,843	N A

Source: Compiled by the author from different sources, e.g., Singh 1997, and some Internet sites.

According to Mr Stan Swamy, a social activist, agricultural and forest lands are the sole sources of sustenance for the Adivasis/Moolvasis. When their land is forcibly taken away from them, the Adivasi/Moolvasi people become as orphans. What the government calls 'national development' is, in reality, the impoverishment of the Jharkhandi people.

Bokaro Steel Plant: A Case Study

Having built three steel pants with foreign collaboration in Rourkela, Bhilai and Durgapur, the Government of India decided to set up a fourth as a public sector enterprise with maximum indigenous content in equipment and enterprise in 1955. Conceived largely as a 'swadeshi' undertaking, the plant was set up at Bokaro with Russian collaboration. The government started the ball rolling on January 25,1965 when it entered into a collaboration agreement with the erstwhile USSR. Work on the project began in 1965, and the Bokaro Steel Plant was inaugurated on October 1972 by Mrs. Indira Gandhi, the then Prime Minister of India. Capital expenditure required for purchase of sophisticated facilities not available indigenously amounted to only 11.1 per cent of the total cost as on March 31, 1987, thereby justifying the claim of Bokaro being a 'swadeshi' plant. Apart from fulfilling its role of indigenous public sector steel production, the BSP provided jobs to lakhs of people. But for those displaced from the project site, it was a curse.

The Bokaro Steel Plant, conceived by the government as an instrument of the country's economic growth, was set up amidst a massive dispossession by local people, whose land and homes, falling within the project site area, were appropriated.

Loss of Land

A total area of 17,864.80 hectares in districts of Dhanbad and Hazaribagh was notified under the Land Acquisition Act by the Government of Bihar for establishment of the Bokaro Steel Plant (vide notification no. B/VII-498/52-5059R dated 9 August, 1956). Subsequently, an area of 114.29 hectares was acquired by HSL in 1959 for the construction of an airstrip and camp. A Directorate of Project Lands and Rehabilitation was established, to deal with land acquisition and rehabilitation of people, under Mr P.P. Nair, at Dhanbad in 1961.

BSL management notified the acquisition of land in different stages during 1956-1982, without preparing the list of the displaced. According to DPLR Bokaro of total 35,344.035 acres of land acquired, as on 19-05-2001, consisted of 29,873.04 acres of land as *Rayaiti*, 4,598.225 acres of land as *Gairmajarua Khas* or *Aam* and 872.77 acres of land as forestland of the Forest Department. Out of 35,344.035 acres of acquired land, 34,513.475 acres was transferred to BSL but 830.56 acres of land is still to be transferred in want of deference money as per Section 28(A) of Land Acquisition Act.

The 64 villages so far acquired for the site can be classified into two categories: Category I, consisting of villages from which both land and houses were acquired, and Category II, consisting of villages from which only lands were acquired.

Acquired Land Lying Unused

Initially the government planned for an 8 million tonnes of ingot steel per annum capacity, but finally only a plant of 4 million tonnes of ingot steel per annum capacity was installed. The land acquired for 8 million tonne plant, i.e., as per initial plan, therefore a vast unused tract still remains unused or misused by the BSL management by leasing out illegally.

According to DPLR records, land acquired by displacing 18 villages in north area and land near Garga dam, about one-third of total acquired land is still lying unused. Besides these, many small or big plots in or around the different sectors can be seen unused.

The displaced people of Bokaro paid an enormous price in terms of the loss of their ancestral land, with which their lives were closely linked. For construction of Bokaro Steel Plant, the cargo reservoir, railway yard, small industries, market complex and colonies for housing officers and other employees (mostly non-locals), a vast area of land belonging to the local inhabitants (now so called displaced persons), had been acquired by the government.

It turned out to be much more than what was actually required for the project, with the excess leased to the friends of officials and politicians for facilitating setting up of co-operative farms, petrol pumps, small industries, shopping centres, cinema halls, etc. There is need for a provision in the Land Acquisition Act requiring acquired land not to be used other than for the purpose specified, if so, it should be returned to original owners. Ways of stopping practice of acquiring excess land for a project and leasing it out to others must be found as well. In such circumstances, various associations demand back their unused land. As per Department of Industries, Patna Letter No. 17327-dated 12.10.1979, displaced population should be given priority in allotment of commercial plots. In a meeting with different associations of displaced, the Deputy Commissioner, Bokaro agreed on 60 per cent reservation for the displaced in allotment of commercial plots, but the BSL management denies any reservation.

Bereft of local employment, many from the ranks of the displaced left their homes and lands to go to the brick kilns, stone quarries and tea gardens of West Bengal, Uttar Pradesh and Assam, as well as to other places in search of a livelihood. The massive influx of outsiders seeking to take advantage of the economic and employment opportunities engendered by the Bokaro Steel Plant was thus paralleled by an outflow of dispossessed peoples who migrated away in pursuit of livelihood and survival.

Categories of Displaced Families

As per records of DPLR Bokaro, there were 23,957 families displaced as on 30.07.01. The distribution of these families has been given in Table 3.

Table 3

No. of Families Affected by Displacement by BSL

Category	*No. of ST families*	*No. of SC families*	*No of total families*
I	1,976	1,039	12,031
II	1,384	322	11,926
Total	3,360	1,361	23,957
Per cent	14.03	5.68	100.00

Displaced families have been put in two categories:

Category I : Those families whose arable as well as homestead lands were acquired.

Category II : Those families whose homestead lands only were acquired.

Records reveal that even in 2001 the family register was not finalized. A total of 36,057 awardees were declared but only 23,957 families were registered in the family register and remaining more than 11,000 awardees did not apply for inclusion in the displaced family register. Of 2,357 families , 4,248 families , comprising of 2,490 families of category I and 1,758 families of category II , were registered after 1995 (Table 4).

Table 4

Displaced Families Registered in the Register as on 30-07-01

No. of villages	Category I			Category II	Remaining employable families	
	Families as on 1995	Families added after 1995	Total families	Families as on 1995	Families added after 1995	Total families
64	9,541	2,490	12,031	10,168	1,758	11,926

So far as employment of the displaced is concerned, it is the most complicated matter. As per the records of DPLR, Bokaro, a total of 15,352 persons of 12,210 families were given employment as on 30.07.01. But 7,212 families were employed as on 1995 and 11,460 families were without any employment as on 2001(Table 5). Out of these 11,460 families, 287 families has no eligible person for employment. Most of associations of the displaced are regularly demanding employment for the remaining displaced. Various cases have been filed in courts.

Table 5

Employment in BSL of Displaced Persons as per DPLR

Category I		Category II		Remaining employable families	
Families employed of category I	Persons employed	Families employed of category II	Persons employed	As on 1995	As on 2001
8,486	11,213	3,724	4,149	7,212	11,460

Regarding the situation of displaced ST families, the records of DPLR, Bokaro, reveals that 3,034 ST families were displaced which comprised 1,976 families of category I and 1,384 families of category II. Total 3,034 persons of 2,475 families were given employment, but 885 families still remain without any employment. (Table 6)

People and communities evicted from their homelands on account of acquisition of land for Bokaro Steel Plant include, chiefly, the Santhals, Munda, Kumhar, Koiri, Kurmi (Kudmi) Teli, Gope (Yadav), Bhuiyan (Ghatwar), Napit (Hazzam), Rajwar, Dom, Hadi, Kahar, Medi, Mahli, Mochi, Dhobi, Malhar, Ghinna (fisher folk), Jolha and Ansari—mainly indigenous peoples. Also affected were the landed gentry such as the

Table 6
No. of ST Families Affected by BSL

	Category I	*Category II*	*Total*
Total ST families affected	1,976	1,384	3,360
Total ST families employed	1,632	843	2,475
Total ST families unemployed	344	541	885
Total no. of employed persons	2,083	951	3,034

Labana (Mishra), Bhumihar, Brahmin, Rajput, Sundi, Jain, etc., most of whom had been brought here as settlers by the Ramgarh and Panchkot Rajas. Inhabitants of region displaced by the steel plant also include a sizeable number of soldiers of the Punjab Regiment who revolted against the British during the Sepoy Mutiny of 1857, deserted the Ramgarh Military Cantonment, and settled down in nearby areas. These various communities coexisted in the region for centuries with great emotional integration with the non-tribal groups assimilating with the culture, festivals, dance, songs and rituals of the tribal people.

The lot of the displaced people of Bokaro remains the same as that of people who find themselves confronted with similar developmental projects in other parts of the country. The basic phenomenon that characterizes their situation is dispossession. These people were systematically and methodically dispossessed of the ownership of their means of production, product of their labour and thus of the very means of human existence. They were now being dispossessed of their culture, their values and their very identity. Their communities were being broken up in the name of progress and national interest.

In 1979, BSL management asked names of ex-service men registered in the employment exchange for recruitment against 300 posts of Khalasis. DPLR informed the Sr. Personnel Manager BSL through the Special Secretary, Ministry of Labour, Bihar that the posts of 4th grade employees reserved exclusively for the displaced has a large number of displaced waiting for job and their economic conditions are not good. The process is going on for giving a job per family, in this circumstance filling up the jobs reserved for displaced through ex-service men is against governments decision and it may cause resentment among the displaced.

Social and Cultural Impact of Displacement

The drastic change from subsistence to a cash economy, precipitated by dispossession of land of the locals and the monetary compensation paid by the government, has led to destruction of culture and social organization of the affected people. Their family life disrupted, they are losing their traditional social controls, and social tensions are increasing. Many incidents of social morbidities such as alcoholism, crime, suicide, prostitution, dowry, delinquency, gambling and despair have risen sharply.

With the loss of traditional practices, beliefs, customs, and certain values associated with them (for instance, when people begin to work for wages in place of the exchange labour commonly practised in shifting cultivation), people are losing their livelihood and their ability to cope with such drastic changes.

Language is the main cementing factor that expresses the identity of a given community. The language of the displaced and local people is mainly Khortha Bengali. But we find that there is a hidden policy to suppress their language and to impose on them dominant languages like Hindi, Bhojpuri, Maithili, etc.

Political Impact of Displacement

In our system of representative government, MLAs and MPs are elected by numerically dominant sections of their constituencies. With the construction of the Bokaro Steel Plant, outsiders concentrated in Bokaro Steel City, whereas displaced peoples dispersed to different regions, mainly to Dhanbad, Giridih, Hazaribagh and Purulia (West Bengal) districts. Due to the dispersion of the local population and the influx of outsiders (mainly from north Bihar), most of the political leaders now represent the interests of the outsiders. As a result of these developments, the displaced and local people have become politically powerless, marginalized and exploited by the dominant society. In order to preserve the interests and identity of displaced and local people, MLA and MP seats of this area should be reserved for them.

Associations and Trade Unions

It is surprising that even after forty years of the project, there are dozens of associations and trade unions with issues related to R&R fighting against the plant management and the government.

The trade unions, functioning at Bokaro Steel Plant, have tried their best to seek hold on the displaced persons relating to their employment in BSL, compensation for their land, etc. To achieve this end these unions formulate agitation plans in their own way. Besides, the displaced persons have formed their own associations/committees with several nomenclatures. These associations, too, organize meetings and plan agitational steps to pressurize the management either separately or jointly. Some of them are as follows:

Bokaro Kisan Mazdoor Sangh

This 'Sangh' is functioning under the guidance of Shri Aklu Ram Mahto (MLA) and the displaced persons of Ranipokhar, Mahuar and Ramdih More support it. They demand employment, development of rehabilitation sites, etc.

Jharkhand Mazdoor Samaj (JMM-Soren)

Some of the displaced persons have their allegiance to this 'Samaj' and fight for their demands under its banner. The displaced persons of Lebatand (Sec-XI), Dhandabra, Bhatua, etc., are very much supporters of this union. At present the displaced persons of the villages around Ash Pond area are agitating for their employment.

Bisthapit Kalyan Samiti

Shri S.K. Rai, Gen. Sec., Bokaro Karmachari Panchayat guides this union. However, they have not staged any active programme in recent past for the displaced persons.

Visthapit Sangaharsh Morcha

This 'Morcha' is related with CPI and Shri Gulabchand Thakir plays active role in highlighting the problems of displaced persons and formulating the agitation Programme.

Vananchal Mukti Sangathan/Visthapit Sangram Samiti

The displaced persons of Ranipokahr, Chaufand, Balidih, Jaina More, etc., are the supporters of this Sangathan, which is being led by Shri Samresh Singh (ex-MLA). At present, this Sangathan is active in Ash Pond area for the employment of displaced persons.

Visthapit Yuwa Chhatra Sangh (DYSU)

The followers of this 'Sangh' claim that their association is not affiliated with any trade union/political party. They say that they have already been interviewed and undergone medical test but only some of them have been provided employment. Remaining members formulate agitation programmes now and then to invite more members as this association has lost its strength.

Visthapit Kranti Morcha

The followers of this 'Morcha' say that management has issued interview letters but not conducted it. To achieve their demand they have filed a case at Ranchi High Court.

Visthapit Vikash Samiti

Sri Sadhu Sharan Gope is the main founder leader of this Samiti. The inhabitants of Chas, Sonatand, etc., are supporters of this Samiti. Shri Sadhu Sharan Gope has joined 'samajvadi party' due to which the Samiti has not shown any activity for the last few years. They may prepare plans in near future for their demands of employment, etc.

Visthapit Shramik Sahyog Samiti

Shri Hari Ram Manjhi, Secretary, says that their association has been registered to obtain contract work from BSL for the displaced persons.

Visthapit Sangharsh Morcha

Shri Rait Ram Manjhi is guiding this 'Morcha' and they mainly demand employment for the displaced persons. They remain very much active in Slab Dump area.

Visthapit Samanvaya Samiti

Shri Kamesh Thakur of Visthapit Sanykta Morcha, Shati Bharat of Visthapit Kranti Morcha, Sadhu Sharan Gope of Visthapit Vikas Samiti, Anil Kr. Goswami of Sanskritik Vikash Manch, and Praksah Manjhi of Visthapit Naujwan Sangharsh Morcha had tried their best for the formation of above Samities but they could not succeed in their mission. There are few more associations among displaced persons but they are defunct.

Displaced Youth Students Union (DYSU)

At present, this Student Union is most active and organizing *Dharnas* and demonstrations under the leadership of a displaced Debu Lal Mahto on regular basis for employment in the plant for remaining more than two thousand displaced families.

Besides these, there are other associations fighting for different causes or different areas of displacement. These are:

1. Bokaro Berojgar Visthapit Sangh
2. Visthapit Mahapanchayat

3. Bokaro Zila Visthapit Berojgar Morcha
4. Visthapit Sangh
5. Visthapit Lok Shakti Samiti
6. Visthapit Ekta Manch
7. Visthapit Sahjukta Morcha
8. Visthapit Hind Fauj

Inadequacies of Rehabilitation Programme

1. Inadequate Compensation

The policy of compensation adopted by the government has been very unjust and inequitable. Displaced persons were paid compensation in terms of money for the land acquired and the calculation of compensation was governed by the broad principles laid down in the Land Acquisition Act. The Act provides for determination of the market value and compensation amount based on sale deeds for lands in closest proximity and similar to that being acquired. The sale deed however does not reflect true market price of land, given the general tendency among transacting parties to undervalue land prices to save stamp duty. The 'market price', arrived at on the basis of the sale deed is therefore often low as compared to calculations based on 'capitalizing' on net profit of the land'. Again, the sale price varies from village to village and so compensation rates differ accordingly. This too was not taken into consideration.

Further, displaced people were paid compensation for their 'pucca' and 'katcha' houses based on cost of construction and depreciation in value. Equitable compensation should however be based on the value of construction in the year of notification and site placement, calculated by a qualified engineer. Compensation for wells and tanks must also be calculated along these lines. Further, in many cases it was found that the compensation was given only for the land on which tanks were built, with nothing being paid to cover constructions costs. In many cases, compensation was given for wells and tanks only. No compensation was paid to displaced people for the loss of trees, schools, places of worship, cremation grounds, graveyards, garugeat (places where cattle generally rest), cattle farms, irrigational facilities standing thereon, etc., for which investments had been made. Finally, it might be pointed out that rates of compensation were far lower than those of the Central Coal India Limited (CCL), Bharat Coking Coal Limited (BCCL), Subarnarekha Multipurpose Project (SMP), etc. Table 7 gives an indication of the magnitude of the discrepancy.

Table 7

Rates of Compensation Paid by Bokaro Steel Plant and Bharat Coking Coal Limited (BCCL)

Type of land	*Compensation rate (in rupees per acres)*	
	Bokaro Steel Plant	*BCCL*
Don I	3,000	32,000
Don II	2,000	28,800
Don III	1,000	22,400
Tanr I	1,800	23,600
Tanr II	600	19,200
Tanr III	160	12,800
Fallow	62	6,400

2. Problem of Cash Payment: Compensation in cash was detrimental to the interests of displaced persons in the following ways

(i) Since most displaced people were illiterate, they were cheated by intermediaries and *dalals* and even by the officials who made the payments. Again, cash payment was made only to those who could stake a claim to land ownership. While having lived in and around forests and vacant lands for centuries, many could not provide legal proof of land ownership. No compensation was paid to them as they were deemed to be living on public land.

(ii) Cash compensation created mistrust and division in many families, which were otherwise living peacefully. Some clever and stronger family members misappropriated the compensation rightfully due to weaker ones, e.g., widows and old women. This is believed to have been done in connivance with officials whose collusion was purchased with bribes.

(iii) While compensation paid was meagre, the price of land in the region shot up because of the demand for it by displaced people. Under such circumstances, most of the displaced people could not purchase land. Moreover, since the only skill they had, was that of farming, they could not put their compensation money to commercial uses.

(iv) In many instances, wily landholders cheated displaced persons who bought land around the project area and at times even the land under notification of the forest Department was sold to them.

(v) Land was basically non-transferable under the provisions of the Chotanagpur Tenancy Act. It could not be transferred and sold in the market. The Act allowed a limited and restricted transfer with the permission of the Deputy Commissioner. The displaced people of Bokaro, illiterate, unskilled and with skill of cultivation only, invested all their money in purchasing land in surrounding areas. Most of this land belonged to Adivasis. Later, the then Government of Bihar, implementing the Land Restoration Act in Chotanagpur, ordered the return of the land purchased from the Adivasis during twelve preceding years, without any compensation to the purchaser. Thus, as a consequence of government policy, Bokaro's displaced people lost their land without getting any compensation in return.

3. Provision of homestead land: The Government of Bihar decided recently that each family displaced by the Subarnarekha Multipurpose Project (SMP) will be provided, free of cost, a 25 decimal plot of homestead land with a house of two rooms at an estimated cost of Rs 20,000. However, in the case of families displaced by the Bokaro Steel Plant, 95 per cent of them were provided only 5 decimal plots of homestead land, for which they had to pay the cost price.
4. Employment for displaced persons: The state government had laid down that displaced persons would be given due preference in jobs according to their qualifications and experience and that class IV posts would be reserved only for them. It was also stated that they would be given due preference in allotment of shops and stalls in the township. But what eventually happened was vastly divergent. With the foundation of the Bokaro Steel Plant, many outsiders drawn into the region formed organizations to help the local people (but that was only in name), as their actual interest was only to obtain maximum employment for people of their own region.
5. Schooling for displaced persons: Not only in the Steel Plant itself, but also even in schools and colleges, it is the outsiders who are dominant. It was decided that Bokaro Steel Limited (BSL) would undertake only the responsibility of school education, leaving the nursery and college levels to independent private agencies or to the state government. It was also decided that about half of the requirement of the schools would be met by BSL and that these schools would be in Hindi medium, while the other half would be open to private enterprises. As stipulated, half of the schools in Bokaro Steel City were thrown open to private enterprise with infrastructural facilities and

recruitment was made from among the outsiders. It was the same story in colleges.

Though the people's struggles do not reject totally any sort of possibility of displacement and resettlement, all the ongoing and future displacement should be considered in the light of the displacement and experiences of resettlement hitherto. The major criterion regarding resettlement should be the public purpose of the development project and the accompanying displacement (Patkar, 1998).

Summary

The Bokaro Steel Plant, conceived by the government as an instrument of the country's economic growth, was set up amidst massive dispossession of local people, whose land and houses, falling within the project site area, were appropriated. Inadequacies in the rehabilitation of the local populace being what they are, the massive influx of outsiders seeking to take advantage of economic and employment opportunities in the steel city has been paralleled by an outflow of dispossessed refugees migrating away in pursuit of livelihood and survival. Ensuing changes in Bokaro's population composition have made local politicians attuned to the sensitivities of numerically preponderant outsiders, whose interest generally projected as the interests of society, have formed a basis for the legitimization of projects such as the Bokaro Steel Plant.

If, in the state, land for land is not available, should a share in the new enterprise (like industrial project) not be assigned to displaced ST families? In the Report of the Working Group for Empowering the Scheduled Tribes during the Tenth Five-Year Plan (July 2001), suggestion has been made that tribal families should have 15–20 per cent share in the enterprise in addition to having a lead-time to prepare for employment before the proposed undertaking becomes operative. Further, the community should be deemed to be the owner of 50 per cent share in its favour by virtue of its allowing the industry to use the local resources and being established. Land should be taken on lease from ST families, instead of being acquired. Land Acquisition Act should be amended in consonance with the provisions of the PESA Act, 1996 so that the rights of the tribal people are protected.

References

Asif, Mohammed (2000), "Why Displaced Persons Reject Project Settlement Colonies", *Economic and Political Weekly*, June 10–16, pp. 2005–8.

Ekka, A. and Asif, M. (2000), *Development-Induced Displacement and Rehabilitation in Jharkhand,* Indian Social Institute, New Delhi, 2000.

Fernandes, Walter and Thukral, E. (1989), *Development Displacement and Rehabilitation Issues for National Debate*, Earthscan Publications Ltd., London.

Fernandes, Walter (1998), "Development Induced Displacement in Eastern India" in S.C. Dube (ed.), *Antiquity and Modernity in Tribal India: Continuity and Change Among the Tribals*, Vol. 1, Inter-India Publishers, New Delhi, pp. 251–265.

Fernandes, Walter (2004), "Rehabilitation Policy for the Displaced", *Economic and Political Weekly*, March 20–26, pp. 1191–93.

Patkar, Medha (1998), "The Peoples' Policy on Development, Displacement, and Resettlement: Need to Link Displacement and Development", *Economic and Political Weekly*, September, 19–25, pp. 2432–36.

SARINI (1997), Indigenous Peoples in India, SARINI Occasional Papers, No. 1, Solidarity Action Research and Information Network International, Bhubneshwar.

Sharma, R.N. (2003), "Involuntary Displacement: A Few Encounters", *Economic and Political Weekly*, March 1.

Singh, S. (1997), *Taming the Waters*, Oxford University Press.

Srinivasan, N.R. (1988), *The History of Bokaro,* Bokaro Steel Plant, SAIL.

Walter Fernandes and Hampton, J. (eds.) (1998), *Internally Displaced People: A Global Survey*, Earthscan Publications Ltd., London, 1998.

19 Patterns of Development and Environment Quality in Gujarat

Hansa Jain

The concept of development may be taken to imply an improvement in the material and cultural well-being of the people of a region. The development of a region can be identified with the increase in employment opportunities, availability of infrastructural facilities, amenities and services, proper distribution of resources, increased production, investment and consumption and so on (Verma, 1989). Thus, development refers to an improvement in all the sectors of economy and social and cultural growth. The pattern of development thus depends upon how these important sectors of the economy behave in the changing development scenario for raising the quality of life of the people.

The development process of any region or country depends on its land and other natural resources, population (its composition and health status), technological development and organizational skills of its people (Nigam, 1993). On the other hand, the utilization of these resources depends upon the pattern of development adopted by the country. Hence, there is a bi-directional relationship between developmental process and environment, demography, technological and organizational factors.

After independence, there has been a massive increase in population in the country. The increasing demand for food and shelter exerts greater pressure on the available natural resources. For raising the agricultural productivity, more and more amount of land is brought under cultivation. This has reduced the forest area and also pasture and fallow land. Besides, the injudicious use of fertilizers and irrigation for intensive cultivation increases soil salinity and alkalinity in agricultural regions and thus converts the arable land into wasteland.

Besides this, the technological innovations have induced rapid industrialization and subsequent urbanization. The tremendous increase in the demand of wood for various purposes, ranging from domestic to industrial consumption has led to large-scale deforestation during the last few decades. The area under forest has declined at an alarming rate posing great threat to our environment. About 40 to 50 per cent of the forest area has become denuded and degraded (Nigam, 1993). The loss of these forests, in turn, has resulted in land erosion, flooding of rivers and siltation of water bodies. There is an urgent need to plan very carefully and judiciously strategies for the optimal use of our natural resources.

The present study deals with Gujarat state which is usually celebrated as the locale of one of the advanced and dynamic regional economies of India. At the turn of the 21st century, Gujarat was indeed the second most industrialized, the third most urbanized state and the fifth richest state (in terms of per capita income) among the major states of India (Bagchi, Das and Chattopadhyay, 2005). Today it is one of the prosperous states of India with about 50 million population (in 2001) spread over 196,000 sq km. The state has less than 5 per cent of the population, it contributes about 7 per cent of the production and about 15 per cent of the industrial output (Gujarat Human Development Report, 2004). Though Gujarat has done a marked progress in terms of economic development, but in terms of environment it has experienced severe degradation. It is one of the forest deficit states in the country. During the past decade, there has been a severe depletion and degradation of major natural resources which has adverse effect on health, nutrition, literacy, education and livelihood. Since the sustainability of growth depends upon the sustainability of environment and natural resources, it is necessary that a policy should be framed which could strengthen the relationship between environment and development. For this, it is necessary to analyze the pattern of development in Gujarat and to find the factors which are responsible for the deteriorating quality of environment and the forest area.

Objectives

The objectives of the present study are as follows: to study the development pattern in Gujarat; to determine quality of environment in Gujarat; to study the relationship between development pattern and environmental quality and deforestation in the districts of Gujarat; and to identify the factors responsible for environmental degradation and deforestation.

Methodology

The study is based upon the secondary sources of data. The data are mainly collected from Economic Survey (2005–06), Statistical Outline of Gujarat

State (2003), Gujarat Human Development Report (2004), Gujarat Economic Review, CMIE (February 2006) and Socio-economic Review of Gujarat State (2003–04). The position of Gujarat in Indian economy is determined from the 3-yearly averages of per capita Net State Domestic Product of 15 major Indian states. The trend of the sectoral development in the state is measured on the basis of NSDP at factor cost by economic activity at constant prices (1993–94).

To determine the pattern of development in Gujarat, the indices of income, education, health, housing, participation and basic services is directly taken from the Gujarat Human Development Report, 2004. Agricultural development index is prepared from percentage of gross irrigated area, fertilizer consumption kg per ha., value of agricultural production Rs per ha. and value of agricultural produce Rs per capita. The industrial development index is constructed from percentage of registered factories and average number of workers in secondary sector. These indices are constructed on the basis of the methodology adopted by UNDP. The indicators are made scale free by applying the formula

$$I_{ij} = \frac{X_{tj} - \min X_{ij}}{\max X_{tj} - \min X_{ij}}$$

where I_{ij} is the factor score for the jth district with respect to ith variable, $\min X_{ij}$ is the minimum value of the ith indicator and max X_{ij} is the maximum value of the ith indicator. The overall index is computed from the formula:

$$I_j = \frac{\sum_{i=1}^{n} Iij}{\sum_{i=1}^{n} i}$$

Environmental degradation is obtained by deducting the environmental index from one. Since the forest area plays a major role in balancing the environment, the rate of deforestation is also taken into consideration. Deforestation rate is measured by percentage change in forest area for 1991–2001. An attempt is made to explain the variations in these two variables through regression analysis.

In order to explain the variation in environmental degradation(E), the following variables are used as explanatory variables:

1. Agricultural development index (X_1): To fulfil the demand of the increasing population, more agricultural product is required. Hence

both extensive and intensive cultivation is practised. Extensive cultivation results into an expansion of the net sown area by decreasing the forest and pasture land. Intensive cultivation involves the use of more fertilizers and irrigation to raise productivity without disturbing the forest area. But the unbalanced use of fertilizer decreases soil productivity. Hence there should be a two-way relationship between agricultural development and environmental degradation. Up to a certain limit it should have a negative relationship ($dE/dX_1 < 0$) and after a certain limit when it results into deforestation and environmental degradation, the relationship should be positive ($dE/dX_1 > 0$).

2. Industrial development index (X_2): Since agriculture suffers from the uncertainty of monsoons, industries play a major role in raising the national output and per capita income. But the development of industries needs extraction of raw materials from the nature. The ruthless exploitation of natural resources and the lavishly cutting of forests disturb the ecological balance and thus create a threat for the sustainability of environment and development. Besides the liberation of toxic gases and the disposal of wastes pollutes the air, land and water. Therefore, a greater number of industries should mean a greater deterioration of environment. Thus, there should be a positive relationship between industrial development and environmental degradation ($dE/dX_2 > 0$).
3. Income index (X_3): Higher per capita income results into an increase in per capita expenditure. This results into an increase in demand for goods and services in the market. To fulfil this demand, more and more amount of goods and services are produced by exploiting the natural resources. Hence, there should be a positive relationship between income and environmental degradation ($dE/dX_3 > 0$).
4. Square of income index (X_4): This variable is taken to test the validity of Environment Kuznet Curve (EKC) in Gujarat. If the square of income is negative, it would mean that after a certain level of income, the environmental degradation should decrease ($dE/dX_4 < 0$).
5. Education index (X_5): Education has a multidimensional impact on the development of a nation. On the one side, it provides educated and skilled man power for the development of a country and on the other side, it is of great instrumental value in generating awareness in favour of environmental protection which causes to reduce the level of environmental degradation. Hence, there should be a negative

relationship between education and environmental degradation ($dE/dX_5 < 0$).

6. Participation index (X_6): Participation in economic activities reflects two views. First, it reflects economic prosperity in which people are earning handsome perks and living a luxurious life. Economic participation acts as a basis for social dignity and self respect for these people. Secondly, it reflects poverty in which male and female partners are engaged in short term activities earning just marginal money. In such a case, people depend upon the natural resources for their livelihood. So if the work participation is high, there should be a positive relationship between participation and environmental degradation ($dE/dX_6 > 0$).
7. Basic services index (X_7): The availability of basic facilities like water supply, tube well, electricity, sanitation, road lengths, road density, etc., within the region on the one hand would reduce dependency on natural resources and on the other hand, reduce out-migration and thus decreases degree of congestion and environmental pollution in the urban area. Thus, there should be a negative relationship between basic services and environmental degradation ($dE/dX_7 < 0$).

Further, to know the variations in deforestation rate (D), the following variables were selected:

1. Density of population (X_8): Population density refers to the number of persons at per square kilometre of area. So when the population of an area increases, the demand for land arises for fulfilling the basic needs of food and shelter. Forest area is the ultimate source for fulfilling these needs. Therefore, there should be a positive relation between population density and deforestation rate ($dD/dX_8 > 0$).
2. Decadal growth of population (X_9): If the rate of growth of population is high, the need of agricultural products and forest products is high. As a result, the land which is not suitable for cultivation is also cultivated. Besides, the pressure on forest also increases. So there should be a positive relationship between decadal growth of population and rate of deforestation ($dD/dX_9 > 0$).
3. Net sown area (X_{10}): For fulfilling the local demand of the population and also for the purpose of national and international trade, agricultural area is expanded which causes a decrease in forest area and pasture land. Hence, deforestation rate increases. There should be a positive relationship between net sown area and deforestation rate ($dD/dX_{10} > 0$).

4. Land man ratio (X_{11}): Land man ratio is measured as number of rural population per hectare of net sown area. A higher land man ratio means a more dependency on land and hence a decrease in marginal productivity and per capita income and hence a greater dependency on easily accessible natural resources. In essence higher land man ratio should imply a higher rate of deforestation ($dD/dX_{11} > 0$).
5. Cropping intensity (X_{12}): Cropping intensity reduces the expansion of forest land and hence the rate of deforestation. Hence it should have a negative relation with deforestation ($dD/dX_{12} < 0$).

Income index (X_3) and Square of income index (X_4) as discussed earlier are taken to test the Kuznets hypothesis that up to a certain level of income there is a positive relation between income and deforestation rate ($dD/dX_3 > 0$) and after that level of income, there is a negative relation between income and deforestation rate ($dD/dX_3 < 0$).

On the basis of above variables, the following two models were built:

1. $E = ß_0 + ß_1X_1 + ß_2X_2 + ß_3X_3 + ß_4X_4 + ß_5X_5 + ß_6X_6 + ß_7X_7$
2. $D = a_0 + ß_1X_8 + ß_2X_9 + ß_3X_{10} + ß_4X_{11} + ß_5X_{12} + ß_6X_{13} + ß_7X_{14}$

Position of Gujarat in Indian Economy

In Terms of Economic Development

The position of Gujarat in Indian economy is determined on the basis of 3-yearly averages of per capita NSDP. Table 1 shows that among the 15 major states, Gujarat has always remained at the 4th position after Punjab, Maharashtra and Haryana. Punjab and Maharashtra have interchanged their position during 2001–02 to 2003–04. From 2001–02 to 2003–04, Gujarat has contributed 142 per cent to the total NSDP while the contribution of Punjab, Maharashtra and Haryana is 148, 142 and 149 respectively. The rest of the states have shown fluctuations in their economic development during these periods.

In Terms of Environment

If we look at the quality of environment as in Table 2, it can be seen that the environment status is very poor in Gujarat. It is at the 11th position (i.e., fourth position from above in economic development and fourth position from below in quality of environment). Punjab and Haryana which are above Gujarat in terms of development are more poor in terms of environment as compared to Gujarat. Orissa, Bihar, Madhya Pradesh and Andhra Pradesh which are poor in terms of economic development,

Table 1

Per Capita NSDP (Rs) of Major Indian States

(3-yearly averages)

States	*Per capita $ NSDP 1980–81 to 1982–83*		*Per capita $ NSDP 1990–91 to 1992–93*		*Per capita $ NSDP 1998–99 to 2000–01*		*Per capita $ NSDP 2001–02 to 2003–04*	
	Amount (Rs)	*% of India*	*Amount (Rs)*	*% of India*	*Amount (Rs)*	*% of India*	*Amount (Rs)*	*% of India*
Punjab	2,818(1)	168	3,829(1)	169	14,881(1)	147	15,420(2)	148
Maharashtra	2,452(2)	146	3,573(2)	158	14,732(2)	145	15,567(1)	149
Haryana	2,419(3)	154	3,476(3)	153	13,681(3)	135	14,865(3)	142
Gujarat	2,011(4)	120	2,704(4)	119	13,153(4)	130	14,850(4)	142
W.Bengal	1,727(5)	103	2,236(6)	99	8,972(9)	157	10,981(8)	105
Karnataka	1,563(6)	93	2,193(7)	97	11,257(6)	111	12,563(6)	122
Tamil Nadu	1,555(7)	93	2,290(5)	101	12,315(5)	121	12,719(5)	120
Andhra Pradesh	1,504(8)	90	2,078(8)	92	9,534(8)	94	10,859(9)	109
Kerala	1,487(9)	89	1,958(9)	86	10,141(7)	100	11,402(7)	104
Assam	1,374(10)	82	1,559(13)	69	5,933(12)	58	6,269(12)	73
Madhya Pradesh	1,369(11)	82	1,617(12)	71	7,520(11)	74	7,666(11)	60
Uttar Pradesh	1,299(12)	78	1,631(11)	72	5,633(13)	56	5,600(14)	57
Orissa	1,265(13)	76	1,463(14)	64	5,206(14)	51	5,985(13)	79
Rajasthan	1,261(14)	75	1,891(10)	83	8,466(10)	83	8,250(10)	57
Bihar	933(15)	56	1,106(15)	49	3,294(15)	32	3,609(15)	35
All India NSDP	1,672		2,264		10,139		10,440	

$ At 1980–81prices, @ At 1993–94 prices

Table 2

Quality of Environment in India

States	*Quality of Environment*	*Rank*
Andhra Pradesh	23.2	4
Bihar	16.8	9
Gujarat	9.89	11
Haryana	3.78	14
Karnataka	20.14	6
Kerala	28.87	3
Madhya Pradesh	34.84	2
Maharashtra	20.75	5
Orissa	36.73	1
Punjab	5.76	13
Rajasthan	9.26	12
Tamil Nadu	17.4	8
Uttar Pradesh	17.55	7
West Bengal	13.38	10

Source: Gujarat Human Development Report, 2003.

are better in terms of quality of environment. It seems that development has taken place at the cost of environment.

Development Pattern in Gujarat

The development pattern in Gujarat is shown in Table 3. It is clear that the primary sector has undergone lot of fluctuations during the post reform period. The growth of the agriculture sector in Gujarat suffers from the erratic behaviour of south-west monsoon. Hence rainfall during the year 2003–04 has enhanced the prospects of agricultural sector in the state and resulted in production of all the important crops in the state. As per the human development report, 2004, Gujarat is the only major state reporting a negative growth rate in agriculture and allied sector in the 1990s.

Table 3

NSDP at Factor Cost by Economic Activity at Constant Prices (1993–94)

(Percentage change over the previous year)

Years	*Primary*	*Secondary*	*Tertiary*	*Total NSDP*	*Per Capita Income*
1994–95	39.08(31.13)	17.90(32.69)	9.06(36.18)	20.07	17.75
1995–96	-11.83(26.66)	9.33(34.70)	10.00(38.64)	2.99	0.99
1996–97	32.67(30.69)	11.96(33.72)	6.17(35.60)	15.24	13.37
1997–98	-8.44(28.10)	-6.28(31.60)	13.20(40.30)	-0.01	-1.43
1998–99	5.54(27.70)	7.76(31.81)	7.54(40.49)	7.05	5.51
1999–2000	-28.21(19.81)	11.82(35.44)	10.94(44.75)	0.37	-3.18
2000–01	-11.41(18.28)	-8.58(33.74)	2.97(47.98)	-3.97	-6.08
2001–02	27.35(21.47)	-0.16(31.07)	7.22(47.46)	8.41	5.95
2002–03	-11.94(17.00)	31.18(36.65)	8.63(46.35)	11.22	9.88
2003–04	66.12(24.03)	5.59(32.93)	9.12(43.04)	17.52	15.41

Figures in parentheses show the percentage distribution.

Source: Domestic Product of States of India 1960–61 to 2000–01, EPW Research Foundation, 2003, Gujarat Economic Review, 2005.

Gujarat has performed well mainly in terms of secondary and tertiary sector. Though the industrial sector is suffering from fluctuations, it has contributed about 33 per cent to the state domestic product in 2003–04. The tertiary sector has experienced an increasing growth trend and in 2003–04, its percentage in the state domestic product is 43.04 per cent. The percentage change in per capita income during 2002–03 and 2003–04 is 15.41 per cent.

On the whole, Gujarat has undergone significant structural transformation with the share of non-primary sector significantly increased. This cannot be considered satisfactory because the primary sector, particularly agriculture, has lagged far behind with almost stagnant long-term growth since the 1980s. Also agriculture in the state is highly unstable, which tends to leave the small farmers and farm labour in poverty. More than 50 per cent of the workforce is still engaged in this sector, contributing 15 per cent of the state NSDP (*Gujarat Economic Review*, 2005). It seems that there is no strong linkage between the primary and non-primary sector which may create problem for the sustainability of growth in future.

The indicators of development in Gujarat are shown in Table 4. In agricultural development, Surat has secured the first position followed by Junagadh, Valsad, Rajkot and Kheda, while Bharuch, Dang, Panchmahal, Surendranagar and Ahmedabad have lagged behind. For industrial development, Ahmedabad is at the top most position followed by Gandhinagar, Bhavnagar and Sabarkantha, while Vadodara is in the end preceded by Dangs, Valsad, Surendranagar and Mehsana. It makes somewhat clear that the districts which are at a good position in industrial development are at a poor position in agriculture. Now if we look at the other indicators, Gandhinagar is at the highest position in income index followed by Ahmedabad, Valsad, Rajkot and Jamnagar while Dang, Banaskantha, Panchmahal, Sabarkantha have very low income.

Similar is the situation with education, that Ahmedabad is at the top most position followed by Gandhinagar, Mehsana, Bharuch and Surat, while the lagging districts in education are Banaskantha, Dang, Panchmahal and Surendranagar. For health, Rajkot, Jamnagar, Vadodara and Bharuch have taken a lead while Banaskantha, Dang, Panchmahal and Surendranagar have lagged behind. Housing index is good in Ahmedabad, Surat, Rajkot, Gandhinagar and Vadodara while poor in Dang, Panchmahal, Banaskantha and Sabarkantha. Participation index is poor in Ahmedabad, Surat, Dang and Rajkot while good in Sabarkantha, Surendranagar, Mehsana and Kheda. Basic service index is better in Gandhinagar, Mehsana, Surat, Surendranagar and Ahmedabad while it is poor in Jamnagar, Vadodara, Bhavnagar and Dang. This implies that there is some sort of relationship between these indicators of development.

The districts are further ranked according to their level of development, quality of environment and rate of deforestation. The deforestation rate is determined by the percentage change in forest area during the decade 1991–2001 (Table 5). Ahmedabad is at the highest level of development as compared to other districts but has a poor quality of

Table 4

Indicators of Development in Gujarat

Districts	*Ag. Dev. Index*	*Ind. Dev. Index*	*Income Index*	*Education Index*	*Health Index*	*Housing Index*	*Partici. Index*	*Basic Servi. Index*
Ahmedabad	12.5 (14)	3(1)	0.217(2)	0.761(1)	0.738(6)	0.682(1)	0.416(18)	0.596(5)
Gandhinagar	9(10)	4(2.5)	0.298(1)	0.756(2)	0.674(11)	0.498(4)	0.442(13)	0.874(1)
Rajkot	6.75(4)	14(12)	0.131(4)	0.656(10)	0.829(1)	0.546(3)	0.429(15)	0.47(6)
Surat	3.25(1)	13.5(10.5)	0.116(7)	0.713(5)	0.724(7)	0.55(2)	0.426(17)	0.682(3)
Bharuch	16.75(18)	13.5(10.5)	0.066(9.5)	0.715(4)	0.763(4)	0.471(7)	0.472(6)	0.415(8)
Valsad	6.25 (3)	20.75(16)	0.202(3)	0.7(8)	0.742(5)	0.374(13)	0.468(7)	0.367(10)
Junagarh	5.5 (2)	11.5(8)	0.106(8)	0.685(9)	0.7(9)	0.484(6)	0.445(12)	0.419(7)
Jamnagar	8.75 (9)	11.5(8)	0.129(5)	0.61(14)	0.77(2.5)	0.447(8)	0.438(14)	0.172(18)
Vadodara	9.25 (11.5)	21(18)	0.02(14.5)	0.646(12)	50.77(2.5)	0.487(5)	0.454(10)	0.213(17)
Kheda	8 (5)	11.5(8)	0.118(6)	0.705(6)	0.625(12)	0.42(9)	0.481(4)	0.31(12)
Mehsana	8.25 (7)	18(14.5)	0.03 (11.5)	0.721(3)	0.621(13)	0.397(12)	0.496(3)	0.806(2)
Amreli	8.25 (7)	9(5.5)	0.0311.5)	0.646(12)	0.71(8)	0.414(10)	0.465(8)	0.26(13)
Bhavnagar	8.25 (7)	4(2.5)	0.06(9.5)	0.646(12)	0.676(10)	0.412(11)	0.446(11)	0.222(16)
Sabarkantha	9.25 (11.5)	5(4)	0.02(14.5)	0.702(7)	0.615(14)	0.291(15)	0.526(1)	0.407(9)
Surendra-nagar	12.75 (15)	18(14.5)	0.032(13)	0.615(15)	0.535(15)	0.357(14)	0.499(2)	0.643(4)
Panchmahal	15.75 (17)	17(13)	0.018(16)	0.582(16)	0.517(16)	0.15(17)	0.461(9)	0.247(14)
Banaskantha	11.25 (13)	9(5.5)	0.011(17)	0.484(18)	0.44(18)	0.169(16)	0.473(5)	0.334(11)
Dangs	14.5 (16)	22.75(17)	0.013(18)	0.561(17)	0.447(17)	0.05(18)	0.422(16)	0.238(15)

Source: Computed from Gujarat Human Development Report, 2004.

Table 5

Levels of Development, Environment and Deforestation in Gujarat

Districts	*Development*	*Environment*	*Forest*		*Deforestation*
			1991	*2001*	
Ahmedabad	0.63(1)	0.627(10)	13.21	1.31	-11.90
Gandhinagar	0.59(3.5)	0.940(1)	—	0.94	—
Rajkot	0.60(2)	0.435(13)	3.04	3.28	0.24
Surat	0.58(5)	0.739(9)	18.52	18.39	-0.13
Bharuch	0.53(8)	0.785(8)	16.04	3.76	-12.28
Valsad	0.54(7)	0.786(7)	23.82	39.14	15.32
Junagadh	0.50(9.5)	0.000(19)	18.79	20.42	1.63
Jamnagar	0.57(6)	0.340(14)	2.92	9.32	6.40
Vadodara	0.59(3.5)	0.803(6)	10.51	9.98	-0.53
Kheda	0.41(16)	0.823(4)	1.36	2.27	0.91
Mehsana	0.50(9.5)	0.841(3)	1.95	1.64	-0.31
Amreli	0.46(12.5)	0.820(5)	5.95	4.86	-1.09
Bhavnagar	0.48(11)	0.444(12)	2.80	2.68	-0.12
Sabarkantha	0.46(12.5)	0.333(15)	17.24	17.08	-0.16
Kachchh	0.35(18)	0.057(18)	6.26	—	—
Surendranagar	0.42(15)	0.173(17)	4.71	5.06	0.35
Panchmahal	0.36(17)	0.528(11)	25.30	23.25	-2.05
Banaskantha	0.32(19)	0.296(16)	11.76	10.29	-1.47
Dangs	0.43(14)	0.855(2)	96.20	59.79	-36.41

Source: Computed.

environment and has a comparatively high rate of deforestation. Rajkot is at the second position in development but it also has a poor level of environment. During the decade, Gandhinagar and Vadodara are at the third position in development and they are better in terms of environment. Dang has shown a poor level of development but has a high level of environment. Due to the lack of economic opportunities, people try to get their livelihood from the natural resources. Hence, it has the highest rate of deforestation.

To make the situation more clear, the districts are categorized in a two-way table (Table 6) according to their development level and quality of environment. Gandhinagar and Vadodara have high level of development and have also taken care of their environment. Ahmedabad and Surat have high level of development but they need to transfer their resources for improving the quality of environment. Rajkot and Jamnagar are high in terms of development, but they have not been able to diversify their resources for raising the environmental quality. Bharuch, Valsad and Bhavnagar have to take care of both development and environment. Kheda and Dang need more development without creating any harm to their environment. Kachchh, Surendranagar and Banaskantha are lagging in development as well as in environment.

Table 6

Relationship between Development and Environment in Gujarat (District Level)

		Environment		
	Levels → ↓	High	Medium	Low
Development	High	Gandhinagar, Vadodara	Ahmedabad, Surat	Rajkot, Jamnagar
	Medium	Mehsana, Amreli	Bharuch, Valsad, Bhavnagar	Junagadh, Sabarkantha
	Low	Kheda, Dangs	Panchmahals	Kachchh, Surendranagar, Banaskantha

Source: Computed.

In order to determine the impact of the indicators of development on environmental degradation, the regression results were obtained (Table 7(a)). It is found that the impact of agriculture on environmental degradation is positive but insignificant. The impact of industrial index on environmental degradation is positive and significant at 5 per cent level. This implies that as the industrial sector grows, the environmental degradation increases. Income index is found to have a positive and significant relationship with environmental degradation and the square of income index is having a negative and significant relationship. This satisfies the Kuznets hypothesis that the environmental quality deteriorates with low to middle levels of income and improves with middle to high level of income. In other words, the negative environment impact first increases with rising income and then decreases. Education has a negative and significant impact on environmental degradation. Economic participation and basic services are having a positive but insignificant impact on environmental degradation. R square shows that all the variables together explain about 56 per cent variation on environmental degradation.

Regression Results

Further, it is tried to determine the factors responsible for deforestation [Table 7(b)]. The regression results show that the density of population is having a positive but insignificant impact on rate of deforestation. This implies that the demand for the increasing population is fulfilled by importing things from other regions instead of growing food products in

Table 7(a)

Dependent Variable—Environmental Degradation

Variables	*ß's*	*t-value*
ß	1.0709	0.8345
X1	0.0038	0.1941
X2	-0.0195	1.8147*
X3	6.6622	1.9576*
X4	-21.4147	-1.9515*
X5	-3.6415	-3.0722*
X6	3.2777	1.3625
X7	0.3949	0.9923
Multiple R = 0.7493	R Square = 0.5615	Adjusted R Square = 0.2825

* represents 5% level of significance.

Source: Computed.

Table 7(b)

Dependent Variable = Deforestation Rate

Variables	*ß's*	*t-value*
ß	-18.1253	-1.3019
X8	0.0067	0.8209
X9	0.5384	3.4265*
X10	3.6705	1.9657*
X11	1.4533	2.3098*
X12	-0.0858	-0.6241
X3	118.35	2.3659*
X4	-687.50	-2.9021*
Multiple R = 0.8931	R Square = 0.7977	Adjusted R Square = 0.5279

* represents 5 per cent level of significance.

Source: Computed.

that particular region. The decadal growth of population is found to have a positive and significant impact on deforestation rate as the demand for fuel wood and shelter increases with the increase in the population in an area. Net sown area is positively and significantly influencing the rate of deforestation implying practicing of extensive cultivation by utilizing the forest land. Land man ratio is also having a positive and significant relationship with deforestation rate. Income is showing a positive and square of income is showing a negative and significant impact on the rate of deforestation. This shows that beyond a certain level of income, people become aware of the importance of forest.

Conclusion and Suggestions

The study shows that Gujarat is one of the developed states of the country but in terms of quality of environment, it is one of the deficit states. This is because of the lack of coordination between the developments of various sectors of the economy. A major section of population is engaged in primary sectors, still the state is not able to perform satisfactorily, while the secondary and tertiary sector have performed well in economic development of the state. For the sustainability of economic growth, both primary and non-primary sectors should receive proper concentration. It is also found that the districts which have taken a lead in economic development have lagged behind in terms of quality of environment. The rate of deforestation is high in these districts. It is concluded that in Gujarat, the economic development has taken place at the cost of environment. Besides, the districts which are very poor in development also have a very high deforestation rate. This shows that the forests are playing a major role in supporting their livelihood. Steps should be taken to create economic opportunities in these districts to save our forest resources.

Among the various indicators of development, it was found that industrial development has a positive impact on environmental degradation. Hence, eco-friendly approach should be adopted to raise productivity. Education is found to be an important factor for controlling the environmental degradation. There is need for generating more awareness about the importance of environment among people. Instead of density of population, decadal growth of population is the main cause of deforestation as the demand for food and shelter increases. Income and square of income were found to be supporting the Kuznet hypothesis. This shows that there is a need for improving the quality of life and to generate the demand for better quality of environment.

Select References

Arora, Balwinder (1998), "Participatory System in Controlling Environmental Degradation", *Contemporary Social Work*, Vol. XV, No. 2, October.

Awasthi, Dinesh N. (2000), "Recent Changes in Gujarat Industry: Issues and Evidence", *Economic and Political Weekly*, Vol. 35, Nos. 35–36.

Bagchi, A., Das, P. and Chattopadhyay, S.K. (2005), "Growth and Structural Change in the Economy of Gujarat, 1970–2000", *Economic and Political Weekly*, July 9, 2005.

Chauhan, J.S. and Chauhan, Arun (1998), *Environmental Degradation*, Rawat Publications, Jaipur.

"Domestic Product of State of India 1960–61 to 2000–01", *Economic and Political Weekly*, Research Foundation, 2003.

Gujarat Human Development Report (2004), Government of Gujarat.

Jana, M.M. (1991), *Environmental Degradation and Development Strategies in India*, Ashish Publishing House, New Delhi.

Jodha, N.S. (1986), "Common Property Resources and Rural Poor in Dry Regions of India", *Economic and Political Weekly*, Vol. 21, No. 2.

Kawadia, Ganesh and Jain, H. (2006), "Rural Poverty, Land Utilization and Deforestation in India", in Ganesh Kawadia and K. Ahuja (eds.) *Environmental Issues of Development*, The Associated Publishers, Ambala Cantt.

Mahajan, V.S. (ed.) (1993), *Environment Protection: Challenges and Issues*, Deep and Deep Publication, New Delhi.

Mathur, N. and Kashyap, S.P. (2000), "Agriculture in Gujarat: Problems and Prospects", *Economic and Political Weekly*, Vol. 35, No. 35–36.

Nigam, A.K. (1993), "Land Use: Trends and Perspectives", *Man and Development*, June, 1993.

Sehgal, J. and Abrol, I.P. (1994), *Soil Degradation in India: Status and Impact*, Oxford and IBH Publishing, New Delhi.

Steer, Andrew (1992), "The Environment for Development", *Finance and Development*, Vol. 29, No. 2.

Verma, S.S. (1989), *Urbanisation and Regional Development in India*, Chugh Publications, Allahabad.

Contributors

Ajit Kumar Singh, Professor and Director, Giri Institute of Development Studies, Lucknow. E-mail: aksingh101@rediffmail.com

Alok R. Chaurasia, Professor, Institute of Economic Growth, New Delhi. E-mail aranjan@iegindia.org

Amita Shah, Professor, Gujarat Institute of Development Research, Ahmedabad. E-mail: amitagidr@gmail.com

Basanta K. Sahu, Indian Institute of Foreign Trade (Deemed University) B-21, Qutab Institutional Area, New Delhi.
E-mail: basanta_sahu@yahoo.com

Binod Narayan, Faculty, Department of Sociology, Ranchi University, Ranchi. E-mail: bnsocioruster@ gmail.com

D.C. Sah, Professor and Director, Madhya Pradesh Institute of Social Science Research, Ujjain. E-mail: dc_sah @yahoo.co.uk

G. Palanithurai, Professor, Rajiv Gandhi Chair for Panchayati Raj Studies, Gandhigram Rural Institute, Deemed University, Gandhigram (Tamil Nadu). E-mail: gpgri_hung1@rediffmail.com

Ganesh Kawadia, Professor, School of Economics, Devi Ahilya University, Indore (Madhya Pradesh). E-mail: ganesh.kawadia@ gmail.com

Gunjan Malhotra, Senior Lecture, Institute of Management Technology, Ghaziabad. E-mail: mailforgunjan@ gmail.com

Hansa Jain, Associate Professor, Sardar Patel Institute of Economic and Social Research, Ahmedabad (Gujarat). E-mail: jainhansa123@yahoo.co.in

Jyotish Prakash Basu, Reader and Head, Department of Economics, Raja Peary Mohan College, Uttarpara, Hooghly, West Bengal. E-mail: bjyotish@yahoo.com

Madhusudan Ghosh, Professor, Department of Economics and Politics, Visva-Bharati, Santiniketan, Birbhum (West Bengal). E-mail: msghosh123@rediffmail.com

Rudra Narayan Mishra, Associate Faculty, Gujarat Institute of Development Research, Ahmedabad. E-mail: skpant@rediffmail.com

Seema Joshi, Sir Ratan Tata Senior Fellow, Institute of Economic Growth, Delhi. E-mail: seema.iipa @gmail.com

Shilp Shikha Singh, Research Scholar, Govind Ballabh Pant Social Science Institute, Allahabad. E-mail: shilpshikha@ rediffmail.com

William Joe, Research Scholar, Centre for Development Studies, Thiruvananthapuram. E-mail: william@cds.ac.in

Yatindra Singh Sisodia, Professor, Madhya Pradesh Institute of Social Science Research, Ujjain. E-mail: yatindra15@yahoo.com

Yogesh Bandhu Arya, Research Scholar, Giri Institute of Development Studies, Lucknow. E-mail: yogeshacadmic@yahoo.co.uk